SWINDON SPEEDWAY

THE DEFINITIVE HISTORY OF THE ROBINS

SWINDON SPEEDWAY

THE DEFINITIVE HISTORY OF THE ROBINS

ROBERT BAMFORD

TEMPUS

First published 2005

Tempus Publishing Limited
The Mill, Brimscombe Port,
Stroud, Gloucestershire, GL5 2QG
www.tempus-publishing.com

British Library Cataloguing in Publication Data.
A catalogue record for this book is available from the British Library.

ISBN 0 7524 3552 3

Typesetting and origination by Tempus Publishing Limited
Printed in Great Britain

CONTENTS

INTRODUCTION

Going through the years, one could be forgiven for perhaps thinking that the Robins have not enjoyed the best of fortunes. True, they have only been crowned League Champions on three occasions in fifty-six seasons of activity, the momentous years being 1956, 1957 and 1967. It's also correct to say that many seasons could be deemed as disastrous, as various sides either underachieved or were beset by injuries. The club's various promoters have always set out to construct a team capable of landing silverware, yet for one reason or another, success has been thin on the ground. However, to have completed fifty-six successive seasons to the end of 2004 is an achievement in itself and the Blunsdon raceway has produced many magical moments since the historic first meeting way back on Saturday 23 July 1949. Indeed, aside from the three title triumphs, there is a lot to savour, like the Pairs Championship victories in 1994 and 2004, the Knock-Out Cup and Young Shield double of 2000, plus the Four-Team Championship success in 2003. The Abbey Stadium has hosted numerous Test matches and big individual meetings too, and many of the sport's greatest riders have graced the super-fast racing strip; names like Jack Young, Ronnie Moore, Peter Craven, Ove Fundin, Barry Briggs, Ivan Mauger, Ole Olsen, Anders Michanek, Peter Collins, Michael Lee, Bruce Penhall, Erik Gundersen, Hans Nielsen, Per Jonsson, Sam Ermolenko and Tony Rickardsson – World Champions all. Then, there are those synonymous with the Robins, such as Bob Jones, who was present at every single Blunsdon meeting from the very first one right through to the end of the 1996 campaign. Mention must also be made of Martin Ashby, who holds all the club records in terms of meetings ridden and points scored; and one has to wonder if his statistics will ever be bettered. The aforementioned Barry Briggs was at the height of his powers during his time with the Robins, being so dominant and reeling off maximum after maximum. Bob Kilby is another name that trips off the tongue, not least for his electric starting technique, which left many opponents for dead during his time with the club. Durable Australian Phil Crump was another of Swindon's great servants and there were so many occasions when he seemed to take on the opposition almost single-handedly, yet his scoring always remained consistently high. Yes, the trophy cabinet might be a little on the empty side, but from the leg-trailing of Mick Mitchell in the early days to the armchair style of Leigh Adams in the modern era, there has been much to enthuse over.

Enjoy the read, but hold on to your hat; it's a bit of a roller-coaster ride!

Robert Bamford
June 2005

ACKNOWLEDGEMENTS

I am very grateful to a number of kind folk for their help with this publication, in particular Glynn Shailes, who attended the first meeting at Blunsdon in 1949 and still maintains such a wealth of knowledge on Swindon's history. Indeed, in terms of writing speedway books, I often think of Glynn as my mentor and I dread to think what my day job would have been without his valuable help and advice in recent years! I would also like to thank John Jarvis, who has always been willing to let me trawl through his substantial speedway collection in my quest for all-important snippets of information. Grateful thanks are also due to Matt Jackson for assisting with various riders' dates and places of birth. Geoff Parker too has been very helpful in lending me several of the photographs contained herein. That leads me on to the photographers themselves, and I would like to thank Mike Patrick (www.mike-patrick.com), Les Aubrey, Neil Ferguson, Ian Lewis, Terry Onslow, Alf Weedon and the late Mick Kilby for the fabulous images. Last, but not least, I would like to express my gratitude to *Speedway Star*, which has been a reliable and invaluable source of information over the years.

1949

Long after the demise of the Autodrome at Gorse Hill, which saw dirt-track racing in its original format of individual scratch races and handicap events from 1928 to 1930, Swindon was to have a new speedway venue at Blunsdon in 1949. This publication concentrates on the history of the Swindon Robins, the team that came about as a result of the combined ideas of two gentleman named Bert Hearse and Reg Witcomb. The former was a businessman in the building trade, while the latter was a man with much previous speedway experience, gained as general manager of the sport at Bristol. The two were joined by L.R. 'Nobby' Clark, whose background was also in building, as directors of the new Abbey Stadium venture.

Early in the year, work began on the construction of the stadium in Blunsdon, and a track measuring 410 yards was eventually constructed with a cinder surface. The nickname of the 'Robins' was chosen after that used by Swindon Town Football Club, although a 'Stallions' moniker had been suggested at one point, this being a reference to White Horse Hill, situated near Uffington. Trials were held and while most hopefuls did get a chance in the team, one who missed out was George Fisher, who had previously ridden for Hanley in 1947. The Bristol-born rider actually appeared in the very first squad photograph sporting a Swindon race-jacket, but in the event never turned a wheel for the club. He unfortunately suffered from poor health and drifted away from the sport.

Miss Barbara Willmott, an employee of the club and secretary to Reg Witcomb, started a supporters' club, with the aim being to attract 5,000 members in the first year. She played a full part in getting the fans organised into areas, not only in Swindon, but also in the surrounding towns and villages. Ted Morse, who was in business as a jeweller in Victoria Road, was the club's first chairman and he was to assist Swindon Speedway in various roles over many years, including serving on the board of directors. Swindon itself was divided into twenty-one regions, each with its own committee representative. The cost of joining the supporters' club was 3s 6d, for which folk received a membership card, plus a badge and year bar. Interestingly, in a close connection with the team, Mrs Olive Jones, mother of Bob, was the representative for the Oxford Road district. A war cry was quickly agreed upon, which went like this:

2-4-6-8
Who do we appreciate?
R-O-B-I-N-S
ROBINS!

It was on the warm summer evening of Saturday 23 July, at 6.30 p.m., that the Swindon Robins, who were to operate as a non-league club, first took to the track in a challenge match against Oxford, a side who raced in the Third Division of the National League. Reg Lambourne, formerly with Fleetwood, was Swindon's captain for the historic first meeting, with the rest of the side being Bill Downton, Ginger Nicholls, Harry Hughes, Bob Jones, Ivor Atkinson and the two reserves, Paul Best and Tom Wilson.

The attendance was recorded as some 8,000 people, although the stadium accountant at the time, Ted Nelson, always believed the crowd was nearer 10,000, many folk having probably sneaked in through the gaps in the hedge that surrounded the premises. Those present witnessed nineteen-year-old Patricia Dainton, the star of the Ivor Novello film *The Dancing Years*, cut the tape and declare the stadium open. Some two hours later, after fourteen heats of exciting racing, the Robins had lost by 45 points to 39. Ginger Nicholls was very much the main man of the show – having got married earlier that day in Poole, he dashed back to ride for the Robins and won the first ever race, established a track record of 82.8 seconds and top-scored with 11 points. Indeed, he only just missed out on a maximum when narrowly beaten by Jim Wright in the last heat.

Swindon supporters outside the post office in Regents Circus, awaiting the coach to Poole for not only the Robins' first-ever away match, but also the club's initial league fixture, on 5 September 1949.

RESULTS FROM THE FIRST SPEEDWAY MEETING AT THE ABBEY STADIUM

SWINDON 39					TOT	BON
Bill Downton	1	2	1	1	5	–
Ginger Nicholls	3	3	3	2	11	–
Reg Lambourne	2	2	1^1	2	7	1
Harry Hughes	1^1	1^1	1^1	3	6	3
Bob Jones	0	0	0	0	0	–
Ivor Atkinson	1	2	1	X	4	–
Paul Best	F	–	–	–	0	–
Tom Wilson	2	2	2^1	–	6	1

OXFORD 45					TOT	BON
Dennis Gray	R	F	3	3	6	–
Ernie Rawlins	2	3	2^1	1	8	1
Alf Viccary	R	1	3	0	4	–
Bert Croucher	3	3	3	2	11	–
Alf Elliott	3	0	0	0	3	–
Jim Wright	2^1	2	3	3	10	1
Oz Osborne	1	0	1	1	3	–

Note: Oxford had only seven riders, with Jim Wright moving up from number eight into the team to replace the absent Bill Kemp, while their other reserve Oz Osborne took four outings.

Left: *Ivor Atkinson.*

Opposite: *The Robins pictured at Blunsdon, prior to their historic first home league match v. Hastings on 17 September 1949. From left to right, back row: Alf Webster, Harry Hughes, Bill Downton, Reg Lambourne, Bob Jones, Tom Wilson. Front row: George Craig, club mascot, Mick Mitchell.*

RACE DETAILS

Heat one: Nicholls, Rawlins, Downton, Gray (ret), 82.8 secs (Track Record)
Heat two: Croucher, Lambourne, Hughes, Viccary (ret), 83.2 secs
Heat three: Elliott, Wright, Atkinson, Jones, 85.6 secs
Heat four: Croucher, Downton, Osborne, Best (fell), 83.4 secs
Heat five: Rawlins, Lambourne, Hughes, Gray (fell), 84.8 secs
Heat six: Croucher, Atkinson, Viccary, Jones, 84.8 secs
Heat seven: Nicholls, Wright, Downton, Elliott, 85.8 secs
Heat eight: Viccary, Wilson, Lambourne, Osborne, 87.0 secs
Heat nine: Gray, Rawlins, Atkinson, Jones, 87.4 secs
Heat ten: Nicholls, Croucher, Downton, Viccary, 84.0 secs
Heat eleven: Wright, Lambourne, Hughes, Elliott, 87.2 secs
Heat twelve: Gray, Wilson, Osborne, Jones, 85.8 secs
Heat thirteen: Hughes, Wilson, Osborne, Elliott, 85.2 secs
Heat fourteen: (Re-run) Wright, Nicholls, Rawlins, Atkinson (f, ex), 87.2 secs

Ginger Nicholls' track record didn't last long since, seven days later, Poole's Alan Chambers lowered it by 1.4 seconds when clocking 81.4 secs in the first heat of another challenge fixture. Ken Middleditch of Hastings subsequently equalled that best time in the third heat of a further challenge match on 20 August. Just one week after that the surface was changed from cinders to red shale and it certainly suited Bob Jones and his style of riding, for he immediately set a new track record of 77.4 seconds in the opening heat of an encounter with Plymouth. 'Joner', as he was affectionately known, was to go on and become a legend at Swindon and is widely regarded as 'Mr Swindon Speedway'. To give him his full name, Kenneth Robert Jones was born in Swindon in 1919 and was, in fact, the first rider to sign for the Robins. Indeed, having started his career with Bristol in 1947, it was said that he actually sat out most of the following season in order that he would be free to join his hometown track! Over the years, he served the club as a rider, mechanic, team manager and machine examiner.

After just two months of open licence meetings, Swindon received an unexpected boost when Third Division Hull were forced to close down, with the Robins invited to take over the remaining fixtures of the East Yorkshire side. Managing director Reg Witcomb was only too pleased to accept the offer on

behalf of Swindon. In order to strengthen the Robins' team, four of the defunct Hull side joined the Blunsdon set-up, those riders being Mick Mitchell, George Craig, Alf Webster and Derek Glover.

Cheered on by a coach-load of supporters, the Robins began their league campaign with an away fixture at Poole on 5 September. Unfortunately, they lost that first official match heavily, 53-31, with their line-up from the historic event recorded thus: 1. Mick Mitchell; 2. Bill Downton; 3. Derek Glover; 4. Allen Briggs; 5. Alf Webster; 6. Reg Lambourne; 7. George Craig; 8. Bob Jones. Swindon number one Mitchell topped his side's scoring with 10 points, but received very little backing against a powerful-looking Poole outfit for whom three riders scored double figures, namely Dennis 'Ticker' James (12), Cyril Quick (11) and Fred Pawson (10). The hefty defeat wasn't really a surprise; after all, it was the first time the chosen eight riders had ridden together, as Reg Witcomb explained to the travelling fans during the meeting.

A further four away defeats followed, at Hastings, Hanley, Plymouth and Leicester, before Swindon staged their first home league match. Hastings were the visitors to Blunsdon for the occasion on 17 September, but the Robins lost a thrilling meeting by just 2 points, 43-41. The following week, however, they did register a first league victory by defeating Oxford 42-41 in a thrilling derby encounter.

Prior to the aforementioned home match against Hastings, Reg Witcomb revealed that each club was only permitted to have twelve riders under contract, so aside from the four former Hull lads, the following eight speedsters were retained: Reg Lambourne, Bob Jones, Bill Downton, Harry Hughes, Tom Wilson, Arthur 'Bonny' Good, Paul Best and Norman Meek. The remainder, namely Mick Collett, Ginger Nicholls, Ivor Atkinson and Allen Briggs were given free transfers, with the biggest surprise being the failure of Nicholls to continue his good form of the opening meeting. Ginger, whose real name was actually Stan, had struggled badly and it was a major disappointment after his early success.

Swindon only completed thirteen league matches that year, as Hull had already ridden thirty-five of their scheduled fixtures at the time of their withdrawal. The combined record of the two tracks was enough for Swindon to finish in eleventh position in the thirteen-team league, with Mick Mitchell topping the Robins' averages on 7.13. George Craig was next in line (6.69), with Bob Jones (6.08) being the only other rider to achieve an average in excess of 6 points per match. One thing, however, was very clear; the fans of the Robins had shown their love of the sport in a very short time, with membership of the supporters' club topping the 5,000 mark, as targeted by Barbara Willmott.

Swindon v. Tamworth, 3 September 1949. Bill Downton leads from the visiting duo of Peter Orpwood and Cecil Hookham, with Norman Meek at the rear.

The track record at the end of the season stood at 76.8 seconds, established by Wembley skipper Bill Kitchen on 10 September. The Robins were actually riding an away league match at Hanley on the night, but to keep the Blunsdon regulars happy a challenge match was staged featuring a combined Swindon and Poole side *v.* Liverpool. Before the meeting there were two attempts to set a new best time, one by Poole's Cyril Quick and the other by Kitchen, with the Wembley speedster shaving six-tenths of a second off Bob Jones' previous record. It had originally been planned that Bill Longley, the New Cross captain, would make an attempt on the track record and meet Kitchen in a match race series, but injury prevented his attendance; hence he was replaced by Quick. The match itself resulted in a 43-40 victory for the home side, although the main points came from the three Poole lads in the team, namely Cyril Quick (11), Ticker James (10) and Dick Howard (10).

SWINDON ROBINS 1949

(Swindon's score shown first unless otherwise stated)

NATIONAL LEAGUE THIRD DIVISION

Opponents	Home	Away
Exeter	(L40-44)	(L36-48)
	W56-28	L26-58
Halifax	(L37-46)	(L26-57)
	(L39-45)	(L22-62)
Hanley	(L40-43)	(L20-63)
	(W47-37)	L19-64
Hastings	(W47-37)	(L39-45)
	L41-43	L30-54
Leicester	(W53-30)	(L35-49)
	L33-51	L27-57
Liverpool	(W53-31)	(L34-48)
	(W54-29)	(L36-48)
Oxford	(W60-24)	(W51-32)
	W42-41	(L29-54)

Plymouth	(W44-40)	(L25-59)
	L36-47	L34-50
Poole	(W54-30)	(L40-44)
	(W49-35)	L31-53
Rayleigh	(W62-22)	(L31-52)
	(W52-32)	L33-51
Tamworth	(W43-41)	(L30-53)
	(L37-46)	L17-67
Yarmouth	(D42-42)	(L18-66)
	(L35-49)	(L24-60)

Note: The results in parentheses refer to meetings ridden by Hull prior to their withdrawal from the league and Swindon taking over the remaining fixtures.

NATIONAL LEAGUE THIRD DIVISION TABLE

Team	Mts	Won	Drn	Lst	For	Agn.	Pts
Hanley	48	35	1	12	2,336	1,674	71
Yarmouth	48	35	1	12	2,330	1,676	71
Tamworth	48	33	0	15	2,294	1,722	66
Halifax	48	28	2	18	2,212	1,792	58
Plymouth	48	28	2	18	2,096	1,917	58
Poole	48	27	0	21	1,962.5	2,053.5	54
Exeter	48	24	0	24	2,038	1,973	48
Hastings	48	21	1	26	1,936	2,080	43
Liverpool	48	19	0	29	1,842	2,172	38
Leicester	48	17	1	30	1,878	2,140	35
Swindon*	48	15	1	32	1,809	2,207	31
Rayleigh	48	14	0	34	1,708	2,295	28
Oxford	48	11	1	36	1,637.5	2,377.5	23

The combination of Swindon and Hull results, with their separate records as shown below:

Hull	35	13	1	21	1,384	1,543	27
Swindon	13	2	0	11	425	664	4

LEAGUE AVERAGES

Rider	Mts	Rds	Pts	Bon.	Tot.	Avge	Maximums
Mick Mitchell	8	32	55	2	57	7.13	–
George Craig	13	52	85	2	87	6.69	1 full
Bob Jones	13	48	72	1	73	6.08	–
Alf Webster	11	40	52	5	57	5.70	–
Bill Downton	13	52	62	6	68	5.23	–
Derek Glover	7	24	25	4	29	4.83	–
Reg Lambourne	13	51	44	10	54	4.24	–
Paul Best	2	4	2	1	3	3.00	–
Harry Hughes	12	30	17	2	19	2.53	–
Tom Wilson	9	20	9	2	11	2.20	–
Allen Briggs	2	8	2	0	2	1.00	–
Bonny Good	1	3	0	0	0	0.00	–

CHALLENGE

Opponents	Home	Away
Exeter	W42-41	–
Hastings	L35-49	–
Leicester	L36-47	–
Liverpool	W43-40	–
Oxford	L39-45	L28-56
Plymouth	L20-63	–
Poole	L25-58	–
Tamworth	L29-54	–

Note: The side that rode in the home challenge match against Liverpool was billed as Swindon and Poole, being a composite side made up of riders from both teams.

1950

During the winter break floodlights were installed at Blunsdon and, for the opening meeting of the 1950 season before an estimated 10,000 crowd, the racing was illuminated under a blaze of bright light. The meeting, on 25 March, was a challenge match against Second Division Cradley Heath, but the Robins unfortunately went down to a 45-38 defeat. New signing Alex Gray, a Londoner who moved down from Liverpool (exchanged for Alf Webster and Derek Glover), rode well, as did Danny Malone, a Bristol lad who, legend has it, had originally been noticed practicing in a field by Reg Witcomb. The *Robins Monthly* magazine, which was published for members of the ever-expanding supporters' club, urged fans to refrain from showering the riders with gifts, as sweets, apples and pears regularly had to be cleared from the circuit!

Mick Mitchell had shaken the Swindon management when he asked for a transfer to St Austell during the close season, but the Control Board vetoed the move. Having been appointed captain of the Robins, Mitchell knuckled down to show brilliant form in the early part of the season, although in truth he is probably remembered more for a bizarre incident than his scoring ability. This happened in the home leg of a *Daily Mail* National Trophy tie *v.* Oxford on 22 April, when he found himself excluded from heat eight after his helmet had flown off during the race! In the very next heat of the same match, Bob Jones was on fire as he blitzed around the 410-yard Blunsdon circuit in 76.8 seconds to equal the track record, which had been established by Bill Kitchen at the back end of the previous season.

A home match against Tamworth on 6 May was memorable, not least because it was run in very wet conditions. Indeed, all the competitors came down in the first heat, which was eventually won by visiting rider Dick Tolley in a time of 90.6 seconds! Swindon actually trailed by 9 points at 25-16 after heat seven, but launched a tremendous fight-back to eventually win 42-41 in a last-heat decider.

A first ever individual meeting was held at Blunsdon on 3 June, when Tamworth's Brian Wilson was triumphant with 14 points in the Swindon Silver Trophy. Oxford's Frank Boyle (13) was second, while Harwood Pike (12) of Leicester was third in the thrill-packed event. Two weeks later, on 17 June, a qualifying round of the *Sunday Dispatch* World Championship was held at the Abbey, with Liverpool's Reg Duval emerging victorious on 14 points. Meanwhile, Bill Clifton of Cradley Heath and Sheffield's Jack Chignell tied for the runner-up spot on 13 points apiece.

Perhaps the most memorable night of Bob Jones' career occurred on 24 June, when the Robins entertained St Austell in a Third Division fixture. In heat five, 'Joner' clocked 76.4 seconds to break the track record, and then in heat nine, he went even faster, lowering his own best time to 76.2 seconds!

For some time Swindon topped the Third Division table, but injuries to Danny Malone and Ron Clark, who had been signed from defunct Hastings, put paid to their chances of success, although a final position of fourth in their first full season was a highly commendable achievement. The Robins' league record included away wins at Exeter, Leicester, Rayleigh and St Austell, although that was somewhat offset by three home defeats during the season. Regrettably, Swindon's involvement in the National Trophy didn't last long. Following a first round bye, they were knocked out by local rivals Oxford at the next hurdle, losing narrowly, 109-106, on aggregate.

Team changes during the campaign saw Frank Evans and Hugh Geddes join the club, while Bill Downton moved on to pastures new at Exeter. Mick Mitchell was finally allowed to leave and, after riding his last match for the Robins on 26 July, he subsequently joined Leicester, with his position as team skipper taken over by Alex Gray – a man with a beautiful 'armchair' style of riding. Second Division outfit Walthamstow visited Blunsdon on 23 September and, although it was only a challenge match, the gulf between the two leagues was quite apparent, Swindon suffering a 51-33 reverse, as Jimmy Grant (11 points), George Newton (10) and Jim Boyd (9) led the way for the free-scoring victors.

Swindon Robins, 1950. From left to right, back row: George Craig, Reg Lambourne, Alex Gray, Ron Clark, Reg Witcomb (Team Manager), Mick Mitchell. Front row: Danny Malone, Bill Downton, Bob Jones.

Alex Gray.

Swindon v. Oxford, 10 June 1950. Frank Evans and the leg-trailing Mick Mitchell race to a 5-1 heat success

By the end of the season the Blunsdon track record had been lowered to 75.2 seconds by Oxford's Pat Clarke, who established the time on 7 October. Reg Lambourne and Bob Jones remained ever-present throughout the year for the Robins, while three members of the team finished with 8-point league averages, namely Hugh Geddes (8.44), the departed Mick Mitchell (8.21) and Alex Gray (8.18). Both Gray and Geddes made it through to the Third Division Riders' Championship at Walthamstow on 23 October, but could only muster 6 and 3 points respectively in the big event.

SWINDON ROBINS 1950

(Swindon's score shown first unless otherwise stated)

NATIONAL LEAGUE THIRD DIVISION

Opponents	Home	Away
Aldershot	W49-35	D42-42
	W50-34	L34-50
Exeter	W54-30	L38-46
	W53-30	W48-36
Leicester	W50-34	W45-39
	W50-34	L26-58
Liverpool	W61-23	L32-51
	L37-47	L41-43
Oxford	L30-54	L41-43
	W44-37	L39-45
Poole	W62-21	L33-51
	W45-39	L30-54
Rayleigh	W53-31	W42-41
	L33-51	L34-50
St Austell	W48-34	W44-39
	W52-31	L16-68
Tamworth	W42-41	L37-47
	W46-38	L33-50

NATIONAL LEAGUE THIRD DIVISION TABLE

Team	Mts	Won	Drn	Lst	For	Agn.	Pts
Oxford	36	26	2	8	1,711.5	1,297.5	54
Poole	36	23	3	10	1,625.5	1,392.5	49
Leicester	36	21	0	15	1,637.5	1,372.5	42
Swindon	36	19	1	16	1,514	1,497	39
Aldershot	36	18	1	17	1,526.5	1,481.5	37
Tamworth	36	17	0	19	1,432	1,580	34
Exeter	36	16	1	19	1,533	1,481	33
Liverpool	36	14	1	21	1,383	1,626	29
Rayleigh	36	12	0	24	1,318	1,699	24
St Austell	36	9	1	26	1,380	1,634	19

LEAGUE AVERAGES

Rider	Mts	Rds	Pts	Bon.	Tot.	Avge	Maximums
Hugh Geddes	14	54	111	3	114	8.44	2 full
Mick Mitchell	21	75	144	10	154	8.21	1 full; 1 paid
Alex Gray	35	135	260	16	276	8.18	6 full; 1 paid
Bill Downton	8	25	37	6	43	6.88	–
Bob Jones	36	137	198	33	231	6.74	1 full; 1 paid
Frank Evans	25	97	141	14	155	6.39	–
Ron Clark	29	100	135	23	158	6.32	–
George Craig	35	140	201	18	219	6.26	1 full
Reg Lambourne	36	107	143	20	163	6.09	–
Danny Malone	30	103	121	33	154	5.98	1 paid
Harry Hughes	6	12	10	2	12	4.00	–
Norman Meek	8	16	10	3	13	3.25	–
Tom Wilson	3	5	2	1	3	2.40	–
Dudley Smith	1	2	1	0	1	2.00	–

DAILY MAIL NATIONAL TROPHY

Opponents	Home	Away	Aggregate
Bye (Round one)	–	–	–
Oxford (Round two)	W60-47	L46-62	L106-109

AUTUMN CUP

Opponents	Home	Away
Oxford	L32-51	L31-53
Poole	L41-43	L28-56

Note: The Autumn Cup was decided on aggregate points scored, with the final totals being Oxford 191, Poole 180, Swindon 132.

CHALLENGE

Opponents	Home	Away
Cradley Heath	L38-45	–
Long Eaton	–	(1) L32-52
Long Eaton	–	(2) L34-50
Midland Stars	W56-28	–
Sheffield	L39-45	–
Southampton/Plymouth	L31-53	–
Southern Stars	L39-45	–
Walthamstow	L33-51	–

FOUR-TEAM TOURNAMENT
(Staged at Aldershot)   Poole 30, Oxford 27, Swindon 22, Rayleigh 15.

THREE-TEAM TOURNAMENT
(Staged at Exeter)   Oxford 40, Aldershot 29, Swindon 25.

NATIONAL LEAGUE THIRD DIVISION RIDERS' CHAMPIONSHIP
(Staged at Walthamstow)   Alex Gray 6 points, Hugh Geddes 3 points.

1951

With Buster Brown adding to the team's strength, on loan from Wembley, the Robins had strong league title aspirations, but their hopes were to be dashed by a series of injuries. Firstly, Ron Clark fractured a leg in a *Daily Mail* National Trophy tie at Long Eaton on 29 March, which spelled the end of his speedway career. Following that Dennis Newton, a young novice who had shown brilliant form with 16+1 points against Cardiff in a Festival of Britain match at the Abbey on 14 April, unfortunately broke a thigh in the very next home match against Exeter in the National Trophy; the injury brought his season to a premature end.

That wasn't the end of Swindon's problems though, as Alex Gray suffered with poor health and Reg Lambourne missed several meetings with a damaged shoulder. Gray was particularly unlucky, since he got off to a bad start when he piled up during the pre-season practice. Then, in the very first meeting, a challenge against Oxford, he went up and over at the starting gate in the opening heat. From that point on, Swindon fans rarely saw him as dominant as he had been the previous year. Only occasionally did he show flashes of his old brilliance, as at Wolverhampton in a league encounter on 11 May, when he recorded a four-ride maximum. However, by June he had been relegated to a reserve berth, and a month later his health was such that he was forced into retirement from racing. Gray never rode again, although happily, in the final programme of the 1952 season, Robins' promoter Reg Witcomb reported that he had gradually regained his health and was in business in London. Fittingly, the Swindon boss stated: 'We shall never forget the many brilliant performances he put up for us.'

Under the captaincy of Bob Jones, the remaining Robins plugged away gamely to finish the season in fifth place, without any real top-end strength. This was a reasonable position though, considering the Robins had five riders with 7-point averages, the highest of which was Buster Brown on 7.84. The others were Alex Gray (7.69), Hugh Geddes (7.54), Danny Malone (7.35) and Frank Evans (7.13). The side also battled past both Long Eaton and Poole to reach the Third Division final of the National Trophy, before going down by an aggregate score of 124-92 to Exeter. Despite the injuries, support remained healthy and this was borne out by the fact that 1,500 Robins fans followed their favourites down to Poole for a league match!

The Abbey Stadium played host to two big individual meetings in 1951, with Hugh Geddes romping to success in a World Championship qualifying round on 2 June, courtesy of a 15-point maximum. Meanwhile, Bristol's Billy Hole won the Silver Trophy on 16 June, also with maximum points, plus a new track record of 74.6 seconds to boot! Two 'C' Test matches were staged at Blunsdon late on in the season, against New Zealand and America. On 1 September the Kiwis defeated England 57-51, and although Ken Middleditch plundered an 18-point maximum for the home nation, the rest of the homesters had no answer to New Zealand's three-pronged attack of Trevor Redmond (15+1), Bruce Abernethy (12+2) and Mick Holland (10+1).

England bounced back to beat the Americans 57-48 on 14 September, however, with Gerald Jackson scoring 14 points and Ken Middleditch netting a tally of 12+2. It was a much more solid England performance, although having said that, the visitors did boast three men in double figures, namely Ernie Roccio (13+1), Nick Nicolaides (12) and Don Hawley (12). Swindon riders Bob Jones, Buster Brown and Frank Evans proudly received caps during the Test series but, unluckily, Ray Ellis, an early-season signing from Harringay, missed out after he had suffered a fractured skull while riding for the Robins in a league match at Exeter on 20 August. The injured Ellis was subsequently replaced in the Swindon side by Berne Aldridge, a New Cross novice who lasted but one match. Then, for the remainder of the season, Mike Beddoe was drafted in after losing his team spot at Bristol.

There was one unwanted first at Blunsdon during the year and it occurred on 11 August, when the league match against Wolverhampton was rained off. Prior to that, the Abbey Stadium had successfully hosted sixty-five consecutive meetings since opening in 1949.

Swindon Robins, 1951. From left to right, back row: Reg Witcomb (Team Manager), Hugh Geddes, Danny Malone, Buster Brown, Bob Jones, Ray Ellis, Ken Wiggins, Frank Evans, Reg Lambourne. Front, on bike: Alex Gray.

By the end of the term, Trevor Redmond had the distinction of being the track record holder, having scorched around the Blunsdon bowl in 74.2 seconds while riding for Aldershot on 14 July. Chasing Redmond all the way in his record-breaking ride was Buster Brown and, in being timed at 74.8 seconds for second place, he became the fastest Swindon rider around the circuit.

Buster Brown was one of three Swindon representatives at the Cardiff-staged Third Division Riders' Championship on 23 October, but he only managed to score 6 points, while Danny Malone and meeting reserve Hugh Geddes recorded just a single point each.

SWINDON ROBINS 1951

(Swindon's score shown first unless otherwise stated)

NATIONAL LEAGUE THIRD DIVISION

Opponents	Home	Away
Aldershot	W53.5-30.5	L29-54
	W56-28	L31-52
Cardiff	W61-22	D42-42
	W46-38	D42-42
Exeter	L41-43	L38-45
	L38-46	L31-53
Long Eaton	W59-25	W45-39
	W49-35	L24-60
Plymouth	W52-32	W47-37
	W44-39	L37-47
Poole	L31-53	L36-48
	L38-46	L30-54
Rayleigh	L35-49	L34-50
	L41-43	L34-50
St Austell	W55-29	L34-50
	W45-39	L40-44
Wolverhampton	W61-23	W58-26
	W59-25	W44-38

Bob Jones.

NATIONAL LEAGUE THIRD DIVISION TABLE

Team	Mts	Won	Drn	Lst	For	Agn.	Pts
Poole	36	30	0	6	1,852.5	1,162.5	60
Exeter	36	28	0	8	1,736	1,275	56
Aldershot	36	21	1	14	1,640	1,370	43
Rayleigh	36	21	0	15	1,606.5	1,409.5	42
Swindon	36	16	2	18	1,540.5	1,476.5	34
Plymouth	36	16	1	19	1,520	1,498	33
Cardiff	36	13	3	20	1,439.5	1,567.5	29
St Austell	36	13	0	23	1,342	1,666	26
Long Eaton	36	13	0	23	1,291	1,722	26
Wolverhampton	36	5	1	30	1,093	1,914	11

LEAGUE AVERAGES

Rider	Mts	Rds	Pts	Bon.	Tot.	Avge	Maximums
Buster Brown	35	139	251.5	21	272.5	7.84	3 full; 2 paid
Alex Gray	7	26	45	5	50	7.69	1 full
Hugh Geddes	36	130	226	19	245	7.54	2 full; 4 paid
Danny Malone	34	136	226	24	250	7.35	2 full
Frank Evans	35	129	210	20	230	7.13	2 full; 2 paid
Bob Jones	36	138	214	24	238	6.90	1 full; 1 paid
Ray Ellis	26	97	148	17	165	6.80	1 full
Reg Lambourne	24	80	103	19	122	6.10	–
Mike Beddoe	9	27	32	4	36	5.33	–
Ken Wiggins	32	77	65	21	86	4.47	–
Dudley Smith	11	24	19	3	22	3.67	–
Berne Aldridge	1	2	1	0	1	2.00	–

DAILY MAIL NATIONAL TROPHY

Opponents	Home	Away	Aggregate
Long Eaton (Round one)	W71-37	W58-49	W129-86
Poole (Semi-final)	W66-41	L47-61	W113-102
Exeter (Final)	L47-61	L45-63	L92-124

Note: This was the qualifying competition of the National Trophy, with the winners, Exeter, going forward to the next eliminating stage.

FESTIVAL OF BRITAIN TROPHY

Opponents	Home	Away
Cardiff	D60-60	W61-59
Long Eaton	W86-34	W68-52
Rayleigh	L51-67	L43-77

FESTIVAL OF BRITAIN TROPHY (CENTRAL SECTION) TABLE

Team	Mts	Won	Drn	Lst	For	Agn.	Pts
Rayleigh	6	5	0	1	414	304	10
Swindon	6	3	1	2	369	349	7
Cardiff	6	2	1	3	375	344	5
Long Eaton	6	1	0	5	279	440	2

Note: Group winners, Rayleigh, progressed to the final.

CHALLENGE

Opponents	Home	Away
Bristol	L27-57	–
Dublin	–	D35.5-35.5
Exeter	–	L37-42
Ipswich	–	(1) W46-38
Ipswich	–	(2) W45-38
Oxford	L40-44	L26-58
Poole	W45-38	–

Note: The challenge match against Dublin was staged over twelve heats.

WESTERN AREA FOUR-TEAM TOURNAMENT

(Staged at Bristol)   Cardiff 39, Swindon 27, Poole 25, Exeter 25.

NATIONAL LEAGUE THIRD DIVISION RIDERS' CHAMPIONSHIP

(Staged at Cardiff)   Buster Brown 6 points; Danny Malone 1 point; Hugh Geddes 1 point.
Note: Hugh Geddes was one of the meeting reserves.

1952

The 1952 season was due to open at Blunsdon with a challenge match against Swedish side Kaparna on 29 March, but unfortunately the weather intervened and the meeting was never staged. The tapes went up on the campaign the following week (on 5 April) instead, with a match against Smederna, another Swedish team. Prior to the meeting, in something of a publicity stunt, promoter Reg Witcomb explained to the crowd that Dennis Newton's race-wear had been stolen. However, the leathers were returned just before the meeting was due to start and to everyone's amazement they had been freshly covered in eye-catching gold paint, with the Londoner promptly dubbed the 'Golden Boy'. Smederna were a powerful outfit in their homeland, so it was no real surprise that they walloped the Robins by 55 points to 29. Rune Sormander (11+1) and Bosse Andersson (9+3) both stormed to paid maximums for the tourists, while Olle Segerstrom chalked up 8+2 points and Lars-Erik Andersson collected 8+1. For the sorry homesters, the most points came from Buster Brown, and even he could only muster a tally of 7.

The Swindon management were caught in a difficult situation straight after the challenge against Smederna, since Buster Brown's parent club, Wembley, couldn't decide whether or not they wanted to extend his loan to the Robins. While the situation was ironed out he missed a couple of matches, before an agreement was reached for him to remain with Swindon. Although his future for the season was settled, the rider regrettably found it difficult to recapture the consistency he had shown in 1951.

The Third Division was renamed the Southern League, but after starting with eleven competing teams the number was reduced to ten when Long Eaton withdrew after twenty-one matches.

Swindon Robins, 1952. From left to right, back row: Bert McKechnie (Mechanic), Frank Evans, Bob Wells, Ian Williams, Danny Malone, Reg Witcomb (Team Manager). Front row: Reg Lambourne, Bob Jones, Buster Brown, Ray Ellis.

Changes in the Robins' nest saw Hugh Geddes leave for Cardiff to be replaced by Bob Wells, a veteran rider purchased from Wembley. However, perhaps the most significant signing was Ian Williams, younger brother of the Wembley riders Freddie and Eric. The Welshman made his debut against Long Eaton at Blunsdon on 12 April and scored 3+1 points. He was to develop into one of the finest riders ever to wear the Swindon colours and remained with the club all the way through until the end of 1963.

Following his nasty accident at Exeter the previous year, Ray Ellis returned to the Robins line-up at the start of the campaign, but he failed to find his best form, and only on a few occasions did the faithful fans see the Ellis of old. 'Golden Boy' Dennis Newton was another to find the going tough and after breaking a wrist bone he disappeared from the Swindon scene in April. Frank Evans, however, enjoyed a good season and two matches against Ipswich were particularly memorable for the Bristol-born speedster. The first was at Foxhall Heath on 19 September when, prior to the match, he received a telegram telling him of the birth of a son, who was subsequently named Robert. Obviously buoyed by the news, Frank celebrated by scoring 9 points and helping Swindon to a 44-40 success. Then, in the return match at Blunsdon on 27 September, Evans brilliantly compiled a 12-point full-house, as the Robins went on the rampage to win 57-27.

Individual success during the year at Swindon went to Cradley Heath's Harry Bastable, in a World Championship qualifying round on 31 May, and Dick Bradley of Bristol, who scooped the Silver Trophy on 19 July. A representative match was staged at Blunsdon on 6 September, when Young England lost 62-46 to Young Overseas. Former Robin Hugh Geddes appeared for the Overseas side, but failed to score from either of his rides. Following a fall in his first outing, Maurice Dunn (15) reeled off five straight wins to top-score for the victors, while England's best performers were Alan Smith (12) and George Wall (11).

The Robins finished sixth in the Southern League and, at the end of the season, Reg Witcomb, who had done so much to make speedway a success in the town, departed from the club for pastures new. Frank Evans remained ever-present throughout Swindon's thirty-six league matches and topped the averages on an 8.09 figure, with Danny Malone finishing on 7.37 and Bob Jones on 7.32. Joner, who also remained ever-present, plundered an impressive five full maximums during the campaign. In the *Daily Mail* National Trophy the story was much the same as the previous year, with the Robins having a first round bye before losing out to Cardiff, the Welsh side winning both legs for a convincing aggregate success.

After the end of the speedway season, a first midget car meeting was held at Blunsdon on 11 October, and greyhound racing was also introduced shortly afterwards on 1 November.

SWINDON ROBINS 1952

(Swindon's score shown first unless otherwise stated)

SOUTHERN LEAGUE

Opponents	Home	Away
Aldershot	W63-21	L38-46
	L41-43	L33-50
Cardiff	W44-40	L31.5-52.5
	L40-44	L30-53
Exeter	W48-36	L35-49
	W49-35	W45-39
Ipswich	W47-37	W45-39
	W57-27	W44-40
Long Eaton	W58-26	Not staged
	Not staged	Not staged
Plymouth	L41-43	L25-59
	W54-30	L39-44
Rayleigh	W50-34	L37-46
	L35-49	L24-60
St Austell	W62-22	L39-45
	W43-41	L37-47
Southampton	W65-19	W43-41
	W48.5-35.5	L38-46
Wolverhampton	W45.5-38.5	L39-45
	W55-29	L34-50

Note: *The results of meetings ridden by Long Eaton were expunged from the records, due to their withdrawal from the league after completing twenty-one matches.*

SOUTHERN LEAGUE TABLE

Team	Mts	Won	Drn	Lst	For	Agn.	Pts
Rayleigh	36	28	0	8	1,789	1,226	56
Cardiff	36	23	0	13	1,722.5	1,294.5	46
Plymouth	36	20	1	15	1,610	1,401	41
Wolverhampton	36	20	1	15	1,556.5	1,461.5	41
Exeter	36	20	1	15	1,491	1,523	41
Swindon	36	18	0	18	1,544.5	1,475.5	36
Aldershot	36	15	1	20	1,396	1,614	31
Ipswich	36	12	0	24	1,358	1,652	24
Southampton	36	11	0	25	1,311.5	1,695.5	22
St Austell	36	11	0	25	1,291	1,727	22

LEAGUE AVERAGES

Rider	Mts	Rds	Pts	Bon.	Tot.	Avge	Maximums
Frank Evans	36	139	265	16	281	8.09	2 full; 3 paid
Danny Malone	30	114	193	17	210	7.37	2 full; 1 paid
Bob Jones	36	136	226	23	249	7.32	5 full
Bob Wells	35	133	213	21	234	7.04	1 full; 2 paid
Buster Brown	35	126	192.5	23	215.5	6.84	2 paid
Reg Lambourne	35	101	138.5	21	159.5	6.32	–
Ian Williams	33	129	169	28	197	6.11	1 full; 1 paid
Ray Ellis	32	95	118	19	137	5.77	–
Ken Wiggins	14	29	25.5	4	29.5	4.07	–
George Bason	1	2	1	1	2	4.00	–
Dennis Newton	1	4	3	0	3	3.00	–

DAILY MAIL NATIONAL TROPHY

Opponents	Home	Away	Aggregate
Bye (Round one)	–	–	–
Cardiff (Round two)	L52-56	L32-74	L84-130

CHALLENGE

Opponents	Home	Away
Liverpool	W48-36	–
Oxford	W51-32	–
Poole	L32-52	–
Smederna	L29-55	–
Wigan	–	W49-35

1953

Following the departure of Reg Witcomb, it was strongly rumoured that Clem Mitchell, the former Edinburgh rider and manager, was to take over as Swindon promoter in 1953. In the end, however, it was Bill Dutton who was unveiled as the man in the hot seat, having previously held similar positions at both Exeter and Cardiff. Before the campaign got underway, Dutton and his colleague Don Weekes, the former Exeter mechanic, toured the various branches of the Swindon Supporters' Club, meeting many fans and answering questions. The public relations exercise was to pay off handsomely, as the club was happy to announce an increase in attendances at the end of the year.

Early in the season, on 11 April, Swedish side Filbyterna visited the Abbey Stadium and Swindon supporters had their first glimpse of Ove Fundin, who raced to a 12-point maximum. Fundin was well supported by Joel Jansson's 11-point haul, but Swindon battled hard and eventually lost by just 4 points, 44-40. During the year, a number of youngsters from New Zealand and Australia joined the club in the quest for fame and fortune, namely John Lee, John Lawrie, Les Saville and Bernard 'Bluey' McCoy. None of them stayed very long though, with McCoy being the most successful of the bunch.

Bob Wells got into a rich vein of scoring in the initial stages of the campaign, plundering maximums in successive home league matches against St Austell and Oxford on 18 April and 2 May respectively. In between, the Robins entertained Exeter in a *Daily Mail* National Trophy tie on 25 April, when the Hertfordshire man ripped to 16 points from six starts and equalled Trevor Redmond's track record of 74.2 seconds in the opening heat. Indeed, Wells seemed unstoppable at Swindon, but suddenly he seemed to lose his brilliance, and while he held down a regular team spot, he never again recaptured the same sparkle.

On 13 June, Blunsdon again held a Young England *v.* Young Overseas match, with the English going down to a 47-36 defeat. Three Swindon riders appeared for England, with Ian Williams recording 4+1 points and Danny Malone collecting a tally of 4, while Bob Jones failed to score. The previously mentioned Bluey McCoy rode for the Overseas outfit, but could only muster a single point. Johnny Chamberlain was by far the pick of the riders on show, scorching to a 12-point maximum for the victors.

Ian Williams continued to progress at a rate of knots, posting several double-figure scores, including being paid for the 'lot' (11+1) against Oxford at Blunsdon on 2 May, and also registering a full-house (12) against St Austell in another home match on 1 August. Following injury problems in the Robins' nest, Bill Grimes was signed during the season and this came as little surprise to the club's knowledgeable supporters, since the Londoner had greatly impressed while riding for Aldershot against Swindon the previous year. The stockily built rider was to do well until the Robins entertained Oxford in a Southern League meeting on 25 July, when he was involved in a terrible heat three crash. He was rushed away with multiple injuries and although he remained a patient at St Margaret's Hospital, Stratton for some time, the accident unluckily spelt the end of his speedway

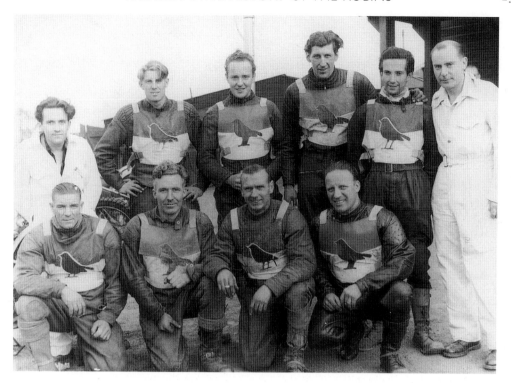

Swindon Robins, 1953. From left to right, back row: Don Weekes (Mechanic), Ian Williams, Bluey McCoy,
Bob Jones, Ron Swaine, Jack Cook (Mechanic). Front row: Bob Wells, Reg Lambourne, Frank Evans, Bill Grimes.

career. In his short time on board he had appeared in just nine league matches for the Robins, but had proved to be a game trier and a very good team man.

Reg Lambourne, Swindon's first ever captain, was in the twilight of his career, having turned forty-two years of age on 1 July. He only made eight league appearances that year and shortly after his birthday he brought the curtain down on his shale-shifting career following a league match at Southampton on 9 July. Gordon Leigh, another young Australian, joined the growing band of riders from Down Under who were trying to establish themselves in British racing. He first appeared for the Robins in July and his hectic style pleased many fans as he raced to 32 points in nine league matches. Frank Evans, top scorer in 1952, had a disappointing term; his form deserted him and he struggled to hold down a team place. He announced his retirement at the end of the season, although he was to later make a track return with his hometown side, Bristol.

In the National Trophy the Robins dispatched Exeter in the first round, but were beaten on aggregate by Motherwell at the next stage, losing the second leg heavily, 78-30, at the Scottish venue. Swindon and Oxford raced for the Supporters' Cup, and over the two legs the local rivalry was evident, as the boys in red and white clinched a narrow aggregate victory by 101 points to 90. The Robins finished fourth in the eight-team Southern League, with Ian Williams at the helm of the scoring in recording 220 points and a highly satisfactory 8.39 average. The stylish Welshman also ended the season as the Blunsdon track record holder, having twice bettered the best time shared by Trevor Redmond and Bob Wells in the same match against St Austell on 1 August. Firstly, in heat six, he was timed at 74.0 seconds, and then two races later he clocked 73.6. Meanwhile, Bristolian Danny Malone had a solid year, scoring 208 points for an 8.15 average. Ron Swaine, brought in from Harringay, developed into a most useful rider and Mick Holland, who was signed following the early closure of Cardiff, was an excellent scorer, although his appearances were restricted by injuries.

Ipswich v. Swindon, 21 May 1953. Bob Wells leads from home man Jim Blythe.

SWINDON ROBINS 1953

(Swindon's score shown first unless otherwise stated)

SOUTHERN LEAGUE

Opponents	Home	Away
Cardiff	L37-47	Not staged
	Not staged	Not staged
Exeter	L41-43	L26-58
	L41-43	L35-49
Ipswich	W43-40	L29-55
	W47-37	L32-52
Oxford	W46-36	D42-42
	W51-33	L35-49
Plymouth	W49-35	D42-42
	W46-38	W43-41
Rayleigh	W44-40	L24-59
	L39-45	L26-58
St Austell	W60-23	L37-47
	W62-22	L23-61
Southampton	W51-32	W49-35
	W43-41	L31-53

Note: The results of meetings ridden by Cardiff were expunged from the records due to their withdrawal from the league after completing just twelve matches.

SOUTHERN LEAGUE TABLE

Team	Mts	Won	Drn	Lst	For	Agn.	Pts
Rayleigh	26	21	1	4	1,259	919	43
Exeter	26	20	1	5	1,244	939	41
Ipswich	28	13	2	13	1,183	1,165	28
Swindon	28	13	2	13	1,137	1,209	28

Southampton	28	12	2	14	1,184	1,159	26
Oxford	28	9	1	18	1,118	1,228	19
St Austell	28	9	0	19	996	1,348	18
Plymouth	28	8	1	19	1,096	1,250	17

Note: Following separate protests by Rayleigh, two matches were deleted from the records: Rayleigh v. Exeter (first match) and Exeter v. Rayleigh (second match).

LEAGUE AVERAGES

Rider	Mts	Rds	Pts	Bon.	Tot.	Avge	Maximums
Ian Williams	28	112	220	15	235	8.39	1 full; 1 paid
Mick Holland	7	23	45	3	48	8.35	–
Danny Malone	27	107	208	10	218	8.15	3 full
Bob Wells	28	103	159	14	173	6.72	2 full
Ron Swaine	26	95	132	22	154	6.48	–
Reg Lambourne	8	24	30	7	37	6.17	–
Bob Jones	28	105	130	29	159	6.06	1 full; 1 paid
Mick Hard	10	32	33	10	43	5.38	–
Frank Evans	23	68	79	9	88	5.18	–
Roy Taylor	3	8	8	2	10	5.00	–
Gordon Leigh	9	33	32	7	39	4.73	–
Bill Grimes	9	28	29	3	32	4.57	–
Ken Wiggins	8	25	22	4	26	4.16	–
Les Saville	1	2	1	1	2	4.00	–
Lionel Pugh	3	6	3	1	4	2.67	–
Bluey McCoy	6	13	6	2	8	2.46	–

DAILY MAIL NATIONAL TROPHY

Opponents	Home	Away	Aggregate
Exeter (Round one)	W68-40	L48-60	W116-100
Motherwell (Round two)	W62-46	L30-78	L92-124

QUEEN'S CUP

Opponents	Home	Away
Cardiff (Round one)	W58-48	–
Ipswich (Round two)	–	L34-74

SUPPORTERS' CUP

Opponents	Home	Away	Aggregate
Oxford	W49-47	W52-43	W101-90

CHALLENGE

Opponents	Home	Away
Bristol	L28-53	–
Cardiff	–	L32-52
Filbyterna	L40-44	–
Poole	L26-56	–
Stoke	L35-48	–

1954

The mid-1950s were difficult times for speedway, with the introduction of television gripping the nation. Swindon continued to enjoy good support though, and 1954 saw the Second Division and the Southern League join forces to form a National League Second Division, consisting of fifteen teams. Unfortunately Glasgow and Wolverhampton closed prior to riding any league meetings, while Edinburgh and Plymouth closed after only racing in four and two matches respectively, thus reducing the league to just eleven sides.

Swindon Robins, 1954. From left to right, back row: Danny Malone, Ron Swaine, Ian Williams, Norman Parker (Team Manager), Bob Roger, Ray Harris, Mick Holland, George White. Front, on bike: Bob Jones.

At Swindon, an important signing was made when Norman Parker, the former Wimbledon rider and an international of note, joined the club as manager in place of Bill Dutton. Parker immediately began a team-building programme that saw Bob Roger (from Birmingham), Ray Harris (from Stoke) and George White (from New Cross) brought in to strengthen the side. Parker had been impressed by 'Chalky' White when he saw the diminutive rider winning an open meeting at Norwich the previous year, and his signing would prove to be a shrewd one. Bob Roger too was a marvellous rider to have on board, and he showed his paces when victorious in the Blunsdon-staged World Championship qualifying round on 10 July. Three weeks later Roger stormed to a five-ride maximum in the Jack Parker 100 Guineas Trophy, but he didn't carry off the title. This was because the top four scorers had to line up for a grand final in which Poole's Ken Middleditch raced to victory from Ken McKinlay of Leicester. Roger, meanwhile, came home in third place and the Swindon supporters made it clear that they didn't approve of the meeting's race formula.

Earlier, on 10 April, the season at Blunsdon had opened with a first ever visit from the legendary Belle Vue team. Somewhat surprisingly, the Robins sent their illustrious visitors packing, winning the challenge match 46-37. Ron Swaine (10+1) and Ian Williams (10) performed brilliantly for the super Swindon side, with the Aces' top men being Ken Sharples (9+1) and Harry Edwards (9). Meanwhile the 'Wizard of Balance', Peter Craven, only managed to score 6 points in what was a somewhat disappointing display by the Manchester side. Sharples did, however, have the satisfaction of lowering the track record to 72.8 seconds in the opening race. Following the meeting Johnnie Hoskins, Belle Vue's illustrious boss, made a substantial offer for the Swindon duo of Williams and Swaine, but understandably Norman Parker politely turned this down.

First Division Harringay visited Blunsdon for a challenge match on 28 August and with top man Bob Roger missing through injury, Swindon booked in Motherwell's Derek Close as a guest replacement.

Undaunted by their top-flight opponents, the Robins went to town and won convincingly by 78 points to 30, their scoring led by handsome returns from Ron Swaine (15+2), Mick Holland (14), George White (12+3) and Danny Malone (11+3). On top of that, in a remarkable performance, both guest Derek Close (9+2) and Ian Williams (8+2) were also paid for double figures.

Swindon finished the season in third position and used just nine riders during the campaign. Bob Roger was the leading rider, scoring 161 points for a brilliant 9.71 average. Ian Williams (8.26) and Kiwi Mick Holland (8.00) provided solid backing, while George White had a year of steady progress, scoring 109 points from his twenty league matches. In the *Daily Mail* National Trophy the Robins gained a 12-point aggregate success over Exeter in the first round, before facing Wolverhampton. As previously mentioned, the West Midlanders shut their doors to the sport, so did not stage their home leg scheduled for 21 May. Strangely, they did appear at Blunsdon the following evening though, when Swindon raced to a 69-39 success and were automatically given a walkover into round three. They were to progress no further, however, as their next opponents, Poole, won both legs to triumph 122-94 on aggregate.

The Robins boasted two riders on the rostrum at the Belle Vue-staged Second Division Riders' Championship on 16 October, with Ian Williams finishing as runner-up on 13 points and Bob Roger joint third on an 11-point tally. The Supporters' Cup probably meant as much as anything else to the fans of Swindon and Oxford and, to the delight of the Blunsdon faithful, it was the Robins who held on to the trophy with a brilliant 118-73 aggregate victory.

Swindon's track record was further lowered in 1954, with Bristol rider Dick Bradley being credited with a remarkable time of 71.0 seconds. Bradley's time was set on 8 May, a night when all the other heat times fluctuated between 75.4 and 78.8 seconds. To this day, many people still question the time given for his heat five ride. Some four years later, when nobody had got even remotely near to Bradley's time, it was decided that due to the introduction of a different type of tyre a new track record should be established. Finally for 1954, another sport was introduced to Blunsdon on 25 September, with a first stock car meeting being held at the stadium.

SWINDON ROBINS 1954

(Swindon's score shown first unless otherwise stated)

NATIONAL LEAGUE SECOND DIVISION

Opponents	Home	Away
Bristol	L39-45	L35-49
Coventry	W57-27	W48-35
Exeter	W49-35	L35-49
Ipswich	W62-22	L25-58
Leicester	L38-46	W45-39
Motherwell	W49-17	L35-49
Oxford	W45-39	L36-47
Poole	W54-30	L39-45
Rayleigh	W50-34	W43-41
Southampton	W48-36	L38-46

Note: The home match v. Motherwell was abandoned after heat eleven, with the result permitted to stand.

NATIONAL LEAGUE SECOND DIVISION TABLE

Team	Mts	Won	Drn	Lst	For	Agn.	Pts
Bristol	20	14	0	6	908.5	769.5	28
Poole	20	12	0	8	896.5	781.5	24
Swindon	20	11	0	9	870	789	22
Leicester	20	11	0	9	829	765	22
Ipswich	20	10	0	10	873	806	20
Exeter	20	10	0	10	851	827	20
Oxford	20	10	0	10	807	868	20
Coventry	20	10	0	10	807	869	20
Southampton	20	9	0	11	800	878	18
Motherwell	20	9	0	11	759	819	18
Rayleigh	20	4	0	16	725	954	8

LEAGUE AVERAGES

Rider	Mts	Rds	Pts	Bon.	Tot.	Avge	Maximums
Bob Roger	19	70	161	9	170	9.71	3 full
Ian Williams	20	78	151	10	161	8.26	1 full
Mick Holland	18	68	121	15	136	8.00	–
George White	20	76	109	20	129	6.79	1 paid
Ron Swaine	20	76	106	20	126	6.63	1 paid
Danny Malone	20	74	104	13	117	6.32	–
Bob Jones	15	35	38	10	48	5.49	–
Ray Harris	18	50	58	8	66	5.28	–
Gordon Leigh	10	27	22	6	28	4.15	–

DAILY MAIL NATIONAL TROPHY

Opponents	Home	Away	Aggregate
Exeter (Round one)	W65-43	L49-59	W114-102
Wolverhampton (Round two)	W69-39	Walkover	W69-39
Poole (Round three)	L53-55	L41-67	L94-122

Note: Wolverhampton closed down prior to their home leg of the National Trophy tie v. Swindon, but did appear in the second leg at Blunsdon the following evening, when the Robins won handsomely and were automatically given a walkover into the next round.

SOUTHERN SHIELD

Opponents	Home	Away
Bristol	L33-51	L30-53
Exeter	L31-53	L33-51
Oxford	W46-38	W46-37
Plymouth	W61-22	W53-31
Poole	W53-31	L29-55
Rayleigh	W48-36	L32-50
Southampton	W52-32	W44-40

Note: All results of meetings involving Plymouth were expunged from the records because the Devon outfit closed down prior to completion of their Southern Shield fixtures.

SOUTHERN SHIELD TABLE

Team	Mts	Won	Drn	Lst	For	Agn.	Pts
Bristol	12	9	0	3	563	440	18
Exeter	12	9	0	3	557	448	18
Poole	12	7	0	5	533	472	14
Swindon	12	6	0	6	477	527	12
Rayleigh	12	5	0	7	475	527	10
Oxford	12	4	0	8	478	526	8
Southampton	12	2	0	10	432	575	4

SUPPORTERS' CUP

Opponents	Home	Away	Aggregate
Oxford	W69-26	W49-47	W118-73

CHALLENGE

Opponents	Home	Away
Belle Vue	W46-37	–
Bristol	W49-34	–
Harringay	W78-30	–
Weymouth	–	L38-46
Wimbledon	W49-47	–

NATIONAL LEAGUE SECOND DIVISION RIDERS' CHAMPIONSHIP

(Staged at Belle Vue)   Ian Williams 13 points (2nd); Bob Roger 11 points (joint 3rd)

1955

In 1955 much was expected from an eleven-team Second Division, but things unfortunately went wrong. On the main speedway front, both Bristol and Weymouth closed down after completing less than half their scheduled fixtures. Meanwhile, Swindon were shocked when Mick Holland retired after just three league matches before returning home to his native New Zealand. As if that wasn't enough, Norman Parker resigned at the end of April due to the pressure of business. Therefore Vic Scales, who had joined the club purely to take care of the mechanical side of things, was left to reluctantly take over as team boss. To add insult to injury, soon after Parker's resignation, George White suffered a broken wrist in a Second Division fixture at Rayleigh on 30 May and was out of action for the rest of the year. Guest riders replaced him in the main, which was fine, except that the popular 'Chalky' was simply irreplaceable, since nobody was quite able to get the crowd on their toes like he was.

The tactical substitute rule had been introduced at the start of the season, but an odd interpretation of this was applied when Swindon entertained Bristol in a league fixture on 7 May, as visiting rider Dick Bradley actually took two such rides in the match! Having blown an engine in heat four, Bradley went home for another and while he was away, teammate Chris Boss took his programmed ride in heat seven. Bradley then replaced Geoff Pymar in heat eleven and the Bristol management's understanding of the rules was that their top-man could then also take one of Boss's rides, since Boss had previously covered one of his outings! ACU Steward C.H. King raised no objection and Bradley duly took his second tactical substitute ride of the meeting!

Upon Weymouth's closure, the Robins snapped up Ernie Lessiter after the Londoner had suitably impressed in a second-half trial at the Abbey on 28 May. The programme from the meeting revealed that West Ham's Howdy Byford had turned down the chance of joining Swindon. Thus, Lessiter made his debut as a Robin in a league match at Ipswich on 2 June, when he failed to score from three starts. At times it was frustrating as he tried to establish himself in the side thereafter for, despite his all-out efforts, his appearances were spasmodic to say the least.

Jimmy Gooch was another speedster to join the Robins, arriving on loan from Wembley to fill the gap left by Mick Holland. The Dagenham-born rider made a sound start too, first donning a Swindon race-jacket in a National Trophy tie v. Poole at Blunsdon on 4 June, when he netted 7+4 points from five rides. He was an instant hit with the regular patrons for, in his initial ride, he followed colleague Bob Jones across the line for a 5-1, before twice repeating the maximum dose alongside partners Ian Williams and Bob Roger in later heats. While referring to the National Trophy, the Wiltshire side had been handed a first round bye, prior to squeezing past Exeter. Then, in round three, despite winning 62-46 in the aforementioned match against Poole, they lost the return leg 68-40 at Wimborne Road to crash out on aggregate.

On 19 August Swindon raced a home league match against Coventry, with both teams tracking two guests. Alan Hunt and Eric Boothroyd (both Birmingham) rode for the Robins, while Bert Roger (West Ham) and Arthur Forrest (Odsal) represented the Bees. Although Coventry collected a 50-46 victory their promoter, Charles Ochiltree, was allegedly critical of the guest rider rule, as he believed it would ruin the sport.

Three big open meetings were staged at Blunsdon during the season, the first being a World Championship qualifying round on 9 July, which was won by Ian Williams with a brilliant 15-point maximum. Dick Bradley was triumphant in the Jack Parker 100 Guineas Trophy a month later on 6 August, while Exeter's Neil Street lifted the Sir Noel Arkell Trophy on 3 September after plundering a full 15-point tally.

Swindon's final home meeting of the season saw a first visit of the brilliant Wembley side to Blunsdon on 1 October, with the Lions recalling Jimmy Gooch for the occasion. To say the Robins were pulverised would be an understatement, as they crashed to a 67-29 defeat. Bob Roger and Danny Malone did their best to stem the tide with 11 points apiece, but they received very little in the way of backing. To be fair, Swindon were depleted through injuries and particularly missed Ian Williams; the Welshman's place was taken by Bob Jones who, along with teammate Ray Harris, plus guest riders Ronnie Genz and Alan Smith, all failed to open their account on the night. For the free-scoring visitors, Brian Crutcher bagged the 'lot' (15), while Eric French recorded a paid full-house (14+1) and Freddie Williams plundered 10+3.

In an indifferent sort of season, Swindon only just avoided the wooden spoon, which went instead to Exeter. Bob Roger, with 327 league points and Ian Williams (239) did their best to keep the flag flying, but with an endless string of guest riders and some mediocre performances the Robins didn't really deserve to finish any higher. Really, the only good news in a difficult season was an aggregate 125-91 victory over local rivals Oxford in the Supporters' Club Cup.

SWINDON ROBINS 1955

(Swindon's score shown first unless otherwise stated)

NATIONAL LEAGUE SECOND DIVISION

Opponents	Home	Away
Bristol	W57-39	Not staged
	Not staged	Not staged
Coventry	L46-50	L44-52
	L42-54	L22-74
Exeter	L47-49	W49-47
	W53-43	W50-46
Ipswich	W62-33	L32-64
	W49-47	L45-51
Leicester	W61-35	L41-55
	W55-41	L44-52
Oxford	W71-25	W49-47
	W60-36	L47-49
Poole	L47-49	L25-71
	W61-35	L44-52
Rayleigh	W60-36	L41-55
	L41-55	L34-62
Southampton	L47-49	W52-44
	W49-47	L45-51
Weymouth	Not staged	W60-36
	Not staged	Not staged

Note: The results of meetings ridden by Bristol and Weymouth were expunged from the records, due to their withdrawals from the league after completing fourteen and seven matches respectively.

NATIONAL LEAGUE SECOND DIVISION TABLE

Team	Mts	Won	Drn	Lst	For	Agn.	Pts
Poole	32	23	0	9	1,689	1,380	46
Coventry	32	19	0	13	1,534	1,535	38
Rayleigh	32	15	2	15	1,573	1,495	32
Oxford	32	15	1	16	1,424	1,644	31
Southampton	32	15	0	17	1,445	1,621	30
Ipswich	32	13	3	16	1,537	1,531	29
Leicester	32	14	0	18	1,539	1,529	28
Swindon	32	14	0	18	1,515	1,556	28
Exeter	32	13	0	19	1,553	1,518	26

LEAGUE AVERAGES

Rider	Mts	Rds	Pts	Bon.	Tot.	Avge	Maximums
Bert Roger	1	5	14	1	15	12.00	1 paid
Eric French	1	5	14	0	14	11.20	–
Trevor Redmond	1	5	11	2	13	10.40	–
Alan Smith	1	5	12	1	13	10.40	–

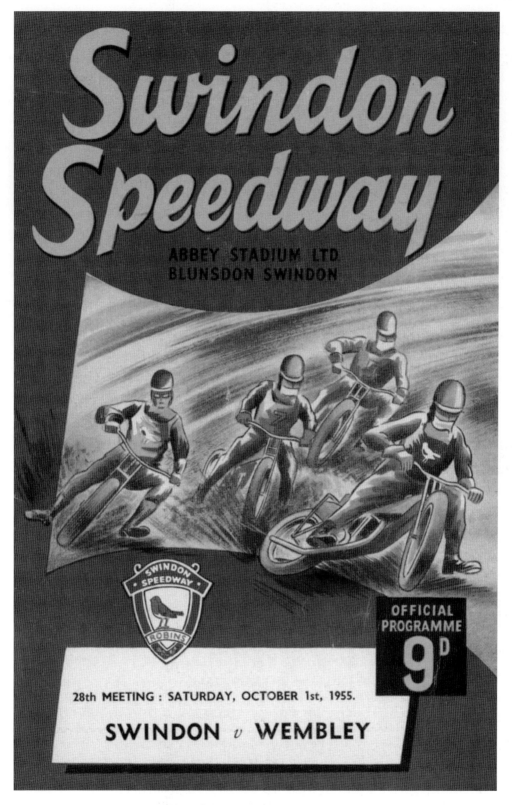

The programme from the first visit of the mighty Wembley side to the Abbey Stadium on 1 October 1955.

Eric Williams	1	5	12	1	13	10.40	–
Alan Hunt	2	10	22	2	24	9.60	–
Split Waterman	1	5	12	0	12	9.60	–
Gerry Hussey	1	6	13	1	14	9.33	–
Bob Roger	32	159	327	23	350	8.81	1 full; 3 paid
Ron Johnston	1	5	11	0	11	8.80	–
George White	9	46	91	8	99	8.61	1 full; 1 paid
Cyril Roger	3	15	28	3	31	8.27	–
Ian Williams	25	128	239	20	259	8.09	2 paid
Jack Biggs	1	6	11	0	11	7.33	–
Peter Moore	1	6	11	0	11	7.33	–
Harry Edwards	1	5	8	1	9	7.20	–
Jimmy Gooch	21	106	162	23	185	6.98	1 full; 2 paid
Mick Holland	3	15	21	2	23	6.13	–
Cyril Brine	1	6	9	0	9	6.00	–
Ron Swaine	32	144	175	29	204	5.67	2 paid
Eric Boothroyd	1	4	5	0	5	5.00	–
Danny Malone	32	138	142	28	170	4.93	–
Phil Clarke	1	5	5	1	6	4.80	–
Ray Harris	30	131	121	22	143	4.37	–
Bob Jones	12	34	24	5	29	3.41	–
Ernie Lessiter	8	21	14	3	17	3.24	–
Fred Brand	1	4	1	0	1	1.00	–

NATIONAL TROPHY

Opponents	Home	Away	Aggregate
Bye (Round one)	–	–	–
Exeter (Round two)	W66-42	L53-55	W119-97
Poole (Round three)	W62-46	L40-68	L102-114

SUPPORTERS' CLUB CUP

Opponents	Home	Away	Aggregate
Oxford	W69-39	W56-52	W125-91

CHALLENGE

Opponents	Home	Away
Birmingham	W63-32	–
Exeter	–	L46-50
Wembley	L29-67	–

FOUR-TEAM TOURNAMENT

(Staged at Swindon)   Swindon 'B' 35, Poole 31, Swindon 'A' 29, Southampton 25.

1956

In 1956 there were only seven teams in the Second Division of the National League, and the Robins boasted as fine a heat-leader trio as any club in Bob Roger, George White and Ian Williams. Team manager Vic Scales had moved on, and Swindon replaced him from within their own ranks by offering the post to Bob Jones, who had been an essential part of the club since the very first meeting. Thankfully, White's injury from the previous term had healed well, and the spectacular racer revealed good form in pre-season practice.

The opening meeting didn't bode well for the season ahead though, with the Robins losing 53-42 to Swedish touring side Monarkerna on 31 March. The visitors were superbly led by a full-house (15) from the legendary Ove Fundin, while Bernt Nilsson was paid for a maximum (14+1). Despite having plaster on a leg injury and hobbling around the pits with the aid of a stick, Olle Nygren also

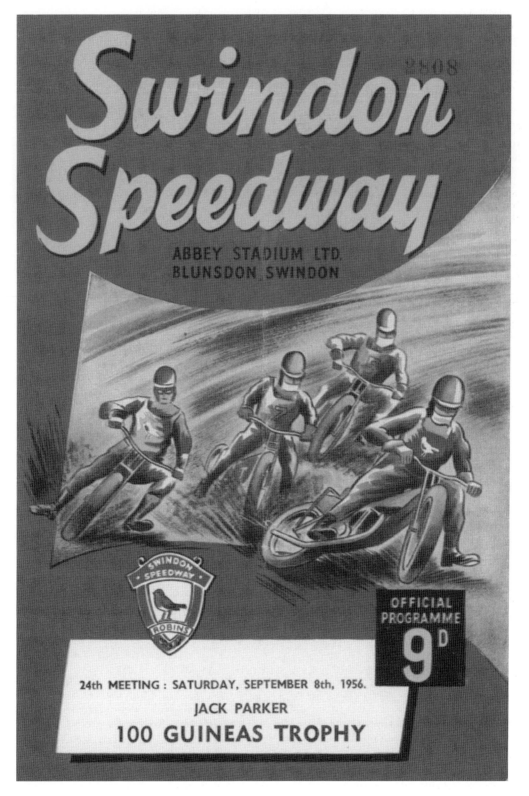

Programme illustration from the Jack Parker 100 Guineas Trophy at Blunsdon on 8 September 1956.

Ian Williams.

scored well for the Swedes, picking up 12 points after suffering an engine failure first time out. The Robins scored solidly throughout, but none of them reached double figures in a very disappointing start.

Things didn't go well in the RAC National Trophy either, with Swindon facing Leicester in the opening round. The first leg was staged at Blackbird Road on 20 April, when the Hunters gained a 65-43 success. The situation looked bleak for Swindon, but a superb performance in the return leg the following evening saw them win by the exact same scoreline to draw 108-108 on aggregate. However, in the replay, the Robins were thrashed 76-32 in the first leg at Leicester on 4 May, before slumping to a 56-51 reverse at Blunsdon just twenty-four hours later.

Once the league programme got into full swing, Swindon definitely looked the part around their own patch and they also collected away wins at Oxford, Ipswich (twice), Coventry and Leicester. Indeed, the Robins clocked up sixteen wins from their twenty-four league matches to pip Southampton by a point and win the Championship. A home defeat at the hands of Rayleigh on 23 June threatened to derail their title tilt, but the riders just about held their nerve in a nail-biting finish to the season. Fearless Bob Roger led Swindon's league averages with a massive 9.53 figure, which included seven full maximums along the way. There wasn't much to choose at the top end of the Robins' attack however, since ever-present Ian Williams finished with a 9.52 average, only fractionally behind Roger's figure. Completing a tremendous three-pronged spearhead, 'Chalky' White boasted a high 9.15 average, having yielded 262 points, also from a full quota of league matches.

Winning the league was a team effort though, and Ernie Lessiter, Ray Harris and Ron Swaine ably backed the 'big three' throughout the year. Others who made appearances as and when required were Al Sparrey, Roy Taylor and local boy Glyn Chandler, but the saddest event of the year was the retirement of stalwart Danny Malone. The Bristolian broke a wrist in a home league match against Oxford on 12 May and attempted to come back in an encounter with Southampton on 18 August, but after two scoreless outings he called it a day. Not satisfied with topping the averages, Bob Roger stormed to maximums as he took victory in both big meetings at Blunsdon during the year – the World Championship qualifying round on 25 July and the Jack Parker 100 Guineas Trophy on 8 September.

Earlier in the season, during May, there was transfer speculation when it was reported that First Division Norwich had made an offer for both George White and Bob Roger. Needless to say, the Swindon management weren't interested and issued a statement saying they wanted to hang on to all their best riders, as they hoped one day to compete at First Division level themselves. Little did they know then, but they wouldn't have long to wait! On the other side of the coin, the Robins made a bid to secure the services of Jimmy Gooch from Wembley, following his excellent showings in 1955, but the rider preferred to stay in the top division and eventually opted to link with Odsal.

In a welcome alternative to the cut and thrust of National League racing, the homeless Southern Rovers side used the Blunsdon circuit for one of their Southern Area League fixtures on 25 August, when they defeated California 42-41. Young Minety lad Mike Keen rode in the match for California, scoring 6 points, while Tommy Sweetman appeared in the Southern Rovers side and notched a tally of 8. Both would appear for Swindon in later years, with Keen going on to be a loyal clubman for more than a decade.

Once again, the Robins retained the Supporters' Club Cup with an aggregate 113-102 success over Oxford. Meanwhile, Wembley returned to Swindon for a challenge match on 1 September, and as a measure of the Robins' improvement since the famous Lions' visit the previous year, it was the homesters who ran out winners by 49 points to 47. Bob Roger blitzed the opposition with a full 15 points, while George White gleaned 12, and Ian Williams collected 10+1. For Wembley, Brian Crutcher (13+1) and Eric French (12) were the top scorers in a team that also included future Swindon star Mike Broadbanks, who mustered just 2 points.

Long after the dust had settled on the season's racing, Wimbledon staged a meeting on Boxing Day, namely the Christmas Vase, which was won in fine style by the Robins' exciting throttle merchant Bob Roger.

SWINDON ROBINS 1956

(Swindon's score shown first unless otherwise stated)

NATIONAL LEAGUE SECOND DIVISION

Opponents	Home	Away
Coventry	W53-41	W53-43
	W55-40	L45-51
Ipswich	W56-40	W49-47
	W65-31	W49-47
Leicester	W50-46	W51-45
	W61-34	L43-53
Oxford	W55-41	W49-47
	W56-39	L45-51
Rayleigh	W52-44	L32-64
	L46-49	L47-49
Southampton	W57-39	L37-59
	W51-45	L39-57

NATIONAL LEAGUE SECOND DIVISION TABLE

Team	Mts	Won	Drn	Lst	For	Agn.	Pts
Swindon	24	16	0	8	1,196	1,102	32
Southampton	24	15	1	8	1,223	1,081	31
Rayleigh	24	14	1	9	1,248	1,053	29
Ipswich	24	13	0	11	1,151	1,149	26
Coventry	24	12	0	12	1,150	1,149	24
Leicester	24	6	1	17	1,088	1,214	13
Oxford	24	6	1	17	996	1,304	13

LEAGUE AVERAGES

Rider	Mts	Rds	Pts	Bon.	Tot.	Avge	Maximums
Bob Roger	23	118	276	5	281	9.53	7 full
Ian Williams	24	124	286	9	295	9.52	3 full; 2 paid
George White	24	122	262	17	279	9.15	3 full; 1 paid
Ernie Lessiter	19	83	95	23	118	5.69	–
Ray Harris	24	116	115	23	138	4.76	–
Ron Swaine	23	94	83	14	97	4.13	–
Danny Malone	6	24	19	4	23	3.83	–
Al Sparrey	10	38	28	6	34	3.58	–
Roy Taylor	3	9	6	2	8	3.56	–
Glyn Chandler	12	39	26	4	30	3.08	–

RAC NATIONAL TROPHY

Opponents	Home	Away	Aggregate
Leicester (Round one)	W65-43	L43-65	D108-108
Leicester (Replay)	L51-56	L32-76	L83-132

INTER-DIVISION TOURNAMENT

Opponents	Home	Away
Poole	W51-45	–
Wimbledon	L33-63	–

INTER-DIVISION TOURNAMENT (GROUP TWO) TABLE

Team	Mts	Won	Drn	Lst	For	Agn.	Pts	Max.	%
Coventry	2	2	0	0	105	87	4	4	100
Wimbledon	2	1	0	1	109	83	3	6	50
Birmingham	2	1	0	1	98	93	3	6	50
Swindon	2	1	0	1	84	108	2	4	50
Belle Vue	2	0	0	2	87	105	0	6	0

Note: A rather strange tournament, which was split into three groups and made all the more confusing by the fact that despite racing against Poole and the result for Swindon being included in the Group Two table above, the result for the Pirates was included in the Group One table! The tournament was run on a scoring system of 2 points for a home win and 3 points for an away success. The positions in the table were decided on a percentage basis, according to how many points each team gained from the maximum they could possibly attain.

SUPPORTERS' CLUB CUP

Opponents	Home	Away	Aggregate
Oxford	W68-40	L45-62	W113-102

CHALLENGE

Opponents	Home	Away
Monarkerna	L42-53	–
Oxford	–	W50-46
Poole	–	31-53 (aban.)
Wembley	W49-47	–

Note: The scheduled eighteen-heat match at Poole was abandoned after heat fourteen.

1957

The year 1957 was an unhappy one for speedway in general, although an excellent one for the Robins. The First Division lost Wembley, Poole and Bradford, although the West Yorkshire outfit would later replace Birmingham in mid-season. The withdrawal of those teams had much to do with the remaining First and Second Division sides amalgamating to form the National League. So, with just a single eleven-strong league in operation, Swindon found themselves among the elite. In an

League Champions in 1957. From left to right, back row: Bob Roger, Ian Williams, Bob Jones (Team Manager), Neil Street, Ernie Lessiter. Front row, kneeling: Ken Middleditch, George White, Mike Broadbanks.

attempt to equalise team strengths the Robins were allocated ex-Wembley man Eric French, along with Ken Middleditch, formerly of Poole. French, however, didn't fancy the move and subsequently linked with Rayleigh. Swindon did sign Middleditch though, the rider having long been one of the most popular visitors to Blunsdon. Gerald Jackson was then allotted, but he wasn't keen on racing for a weekend track and eventually joined Wimbledon. Another Wimbledon rider, Cyril Maidment, was also allocated to Swindon, but he declined for the same reason as Jackson. Finally the Robins were to secure the services of Mike Broadbanks from Wembley for a fee of £50. This must rank as one of the best bargains of all-time, as 'Broady' went on to become a brilliant rider, not to mention a fine team skipper and a World Finalist during his time with the Robins.

The early season Britannia Shield matches showed Swindon as being a very competitive outfit, but they were missing a rider capable of consistently hitting 6 points or more per meeting. As if by magic, promoter Bert Hearse pulled a rabbit from the hat with the signing of Neil Street, who had stayed in his native Australia following the closure of Exeter at the end of 1955. Street arrived back in this country on 1 June, but due to baggage restrictions he brought with him just a frame and his hand luggage. However, for such a skilled man this represented little problem and he quickly built a machine ready for his club debut in a league match at Oxford on 6 June, when he netted 12+1 points as the Robins ran riot to win 59-37.

As far as Bert Hearse was concerned, Street was the final piece in his team-building jigsaw and the side certainly looked solid enough, with each man well capable of recording a double-figure score either at Blunsdon or on their travels. There can be no doubting that the shrewd Hearse knew what speedway was all about and his judgement proved to be spot on, since Swindon did not have a weak link. For the first time they completed their home league programme with a 100 per cent record, which included handing out several thrashings, most notably against Birmingham (77-19), Coventry (70-26), Leicester (64-32), Belle Vue (63-33) and Rayleigh (63-33). Away from the Abbey the Robins chalked up victories at Ipswich, Oxford, Rayleigh, Southampton and Wimbledon, while also securing a draw at Leicester. In a quite stunning campaign which went right down to the wire, it was Swindon who took the Championship, finishing just a single point ahead of second-placed Belle Vue.

Bob Roger had a great season, scoring 250 league points, and his team-riding with Ken Middleditch was a joy to behold. Ray Harris and Ron Swaine had moved out and the Robins used just nine riders during the campaign, plus a guest appearance from Dick Bradley at Coventry (where he scored a full 15-pointer). Ever-present Bob Roger's final average was a monumental 10.27, and his fantastic riding also yielded ten maximums (eight full and two paid). George White scored 195 points for an 8.61 average, while Ian Williams finished on an 8.17 figure. Super team-man Middleditch posted a 7.54 average over the course of the season, while Neil Street (6.70), Ernie Lessiter (6.44) and Mike Broadbanks (5.21) all played major roles. In the back-up department, Al Sparrey made two appearances, while Glyn Chandler partook in just a single match. What a wonderful season it was, with Bob Jones doing the team managing and taking care of any mechanical problems.

With a 121-71 aggregate victory over Oxford, the Robins yet again retained the Supporters' Club Cup – it being their fifth consecutive victory over their local rivals in the competition. A single individual meeting was held at Blunsdon during the year, with Ian Williams recording a 15-point maximum when winning a World Championship qualifying round on 13 July. Swindon subsequently boasted three World Finalists in Bob Roger, George White and Ian Williams; indeed, they were unlucky not to have four, as Ken Middleditch just missed out on qualifying by the skin of his teeth. The final at Wembley Stadium on 21 September saw Roger score 8 points, while White collected 4 and Williams claimed 3. The meeting, incidentally, was won by a man who would later become a real Robins legend, namely Barry Briggs, who beat Ove Fundin in a title run-off after both had finished level on 14 points apiece.

In a year to savour for Bob Roger, the Ashford-born speedster also challenged Peter Craven for the *Sunday Pictorial* British Match Race Championship. The first leg was held at the Abbey on 13 September and in brilliant style, the Swindon kingpin raced to a 2-0 success. He subsequently lost 2-0 to the man known widely as the 'Wizard of Balance' in the return leg at Belle Vue the following evening, with Craven taking the decider 2-1 at Norwich on 28 September.

Swindon v. Rayleigh, 29 June 1957. Ken Middleditch and Bob Roger lead from Les McGillivray and Eric French.

Above: *Swindon v. Wimbledon, 11 May 1957. Bob Roger and Ron How dice for the lead, with Ken Middleditch in the background.*

Right: *Bob Jones and Ian Williams.*

Ernie Lessiter.

Swindon v. Birmingham, 10 June 1957. George White and Neil Street lead Eric Boothroyd.

SWINDON ROBINS 1957
(Swindon's score shown first unless otherwise stated)

NATIONAL LEAGUE

Opponents	Home	Away
Belle Vue	W63-33	L41-55
Birmingham	W77-19	L30-66
Coventry	W70-26	L47-49
Ipswich	W61-35	W49-47
Leicester	W64-32	D48-48
Norwich	W51-45	L46-50
Oxford	W61-35	W59-37
Rayleigh	W63-33	W58-38
Southampton	W62-34	W49-47
Wimbledon	W55-41	W49-47

NATIONAL LEAGUE TABLE

Team	Mts	Won	Drn	Lst	For	Agn.	Pts
Swindon	20	15	1	4	1,103	817	31
Belle Vue	20	15	0	5	992	830	30
Wimbledon	20	12	0	8	997	919	24
Norwich	20	11	0	9	1,015	905	22
Leicester	20	10	1	9	938	977	21
Southampton	20	9	0	11	1,002	911	18
Bradford	20	9	0	11	884	939	18
Coventry	20	9	0	11	868	1,050	18
Oxford	20	7	1	12	880	1,036	15
Ipswich	20	6	0	14	885	1,032	12
Rayleigh	20	5	1	14	885	1,033	11

Note: Bradford took over the fixtures of Birmingham upon the Brummies' withdrawal from the league after completing just nine matches.

LEAGUE AVERAGES

Rider	Mts	Rds	Pts	Bon.	Tot.	Avge	Maximums
Dick Bradley	1	5	15	0	15	12.00	1 full
Bob Roger	20	102	250	12	262	10.27	8 full; 2 paid
George White	20	99	195	18	213	8.61	1 full; 2 paid
Ian Williams	19	93	183	7	190	8.17	2 full; 2 paid
Ken Middleditch	19	95	148	31	179	7.54	4 paid
Neil Street	18	89	134	15	149	6.70	–
Ernie Lessiter	20	54	70	17	87	6.44	–
Al Sparrey	2	5	7	1	8	6.40	–
Mike Broadbanks	20	96	100	25	125	5.21	1 paid
Glyn Chandler	1	2	1	0	1	2.00	–

BRITANNIA SHIELD

Opponents	Home	Away
Ipswich	W62-34	L45-51
Norwich	L45-51	L46-50
Rayleigh	W65-31	W50-46
Southampton	W52-44	L39-57
Wimbledon	L40-54	L29-67

BRITANNIA SHIELD (SOUTH SECTION) TABLE

Team	Mts	Won	Drn	Lst	For	Agn.	Pts
Norwich	10	8	0	2	552	406	16
Wimbledon	10	7	0	3	522	434	14
Southampton	10	5	1	4	487	470	11
Swindon	10	4	0	6	473	485	8
Ipswich	10	3	0	7	424	533	6
Rayleigh	10	2	1	7	414	544	5

Note: Group winners Norwich progressed to the final.

SUPPORTERS' CLUB CUP

Opponents	Home	Away	Aggregate
Oxford	W71-25	W50-46	W121-71

HANTS & WILTS TROPHY

Opponents	Home	Away
Southampton	–	L38-58

CHALLENGE

Opponents	Home	Away
East Anglia	–	L43-51
Exeter	–	W52-44
Norwich	L42-54	L33-62
Oxford	W53-43	(1) L40-55
Oxford	–	(2) L46-50
Poole	–	W61-35
The Rest	W51-45	–
Wimbledon	W51-44	W49-47

Note: The meeting against East Anglia was staged at Yarmouth.

1958

Everything seemed to go wrong for the Robins in 1958. Firstly, Ken Middleditch wanted to concentrate on his business interests; thankfully though, he wasn't lost to the sport as Swindon sportingly let him return to his former base at Poole. Having run with an open licence the previous season, the Wimborne Road venue had reopened under promoter Vic Gooden, who had moved his Rayleigh set-up lock, stock and barrel to the Dorset track. The second disaster of the year occurred on Easter Monday (7 April) and coincidentally again involved Poole. Unluckily, while guesting for the Pirates in a home challenge match against Southampton, the Robins' main man, Bob Roger, was involved in a very nasty heat eight crash with Split Waterman and Brian Crutcher which left him nursing a fractured skull. Regrettably, although Roger later attempted track returns in both 1961 and 1962, the accident effectively ended his speedway career.

Swindon welcomed Swedish tourists Monarkerna to the Abbey again on 12 April, but the visitors failed to provide any spark, with the Robins racing to a 63-30 victory. Birger Forsberg (8+1 points) and Olle Nygren (8) did their best for the Swedes, but received little support against the rampant homesters, for whom George White scorched to a paid maximum (13+2). Heat fourteen of the match was farcical though, as all the riders stopped at the end of the first lap after seeing the red lights switched on. However, this was apparently because Roy Moreton had been excluded for a tapes offence and eventually Mike Broadbanks continued on his way. Olle Nygren and Bengt Brannefors were not as quick to react and before they had got going again, Broady actually lapped them, prior to going on and taking victory in a winning time of 139.2 seconds – the slowest ever recorded at Blunsdon!

The Abbey Stadium played host to a couple of big individual meetings during the year, the first of which saw George White notch a 15-point maximum to win the Midland Riders' Championship qualifying round on 17 May. Then, on 19 July, a total of 14 points was sufficient for Wimbledon's Ron How to take the honours in a World Championship qualifier. On 11 June Blunsdon also staged the prestigious First Test of a five-meeting series between England and Australasia. The spectators were treated to a feast of speedway which saw the Australasians claim a hard-fought 57-51 victory. The great Barry Briggs headed the victors' scoring with a superb 18-point maximum, while Neil Street (12+2), Peter Moore (12+1) and Jack Young (11+1) weighed in with hefty contributions. England were led by 16 points from Peter Craven, but he received scant top-end support. Three Swindon

Swindon Robins, 1958. From left to right: Ernie Lessiter, Neil Street, Maurice Conway, Ian Williams, Bob Jones (Team Manager), Roy Moreton, Mike Broadbanks, George White.

riders appeared for the home nation, namely George White (8+1), Mike Broadbanks (7) and Ian Williams (4+3).

In August, it was decided that since a different type of tyre had been introduced to the sport, a new track record should be established at Blunsdon. Nobody had ever got near to the time Dick Bradley had set in 1954 and frankly this seemed like a good excuse to wipe the slate clean. Belle Vue's Peter Craven was quick to clock what was regarded as a new best time of 74.8 seconds on 23 August, albeit 3.8 seconds slower than Bradley's previous record!

The Robins had to rely on guest riders throughout the year, and with George White and Ian Williams slightly down on scoring power the side slumped to sixth position in a ten-team league. However, it wasn't all alarm at the Abbey, as Mike Broadbanks continued to make excellent progress, actually topping the league averages with an impressive 8.42 figure. Neil Street too was a model of consistency, scoring 166 points for a satisfactory average of exactly 8.00. Meanwhile Ernie Lessiter, such a brilliant reserve during the 1957 season, retired after completing ten league matches for a disappointing 3.89 average. Ron Swaine briefly came out of retirement to help the Robins during an injury crisis and the experienced Roy Moreton also made a comeback at Blunsdon.

Swindon made it through to the semi-final of the RAC National Trophy, but they were unable to contain Norwich and went down to a 129-111 aggregate defeat. The Robins did much better than they had done the previous season in the Britannia Shield though, finishing second in the Southern Group. However, only the top position was good enough for a passage through to the final and that honour went to Wimbledon. The whole club was given a great boost when Mike Broadbanks qualified for the World Final and he acquitted himself well, scoring 5 points in the Wembley showdown on 20 September. It was the first of five full World Finals for the popular speedster, who was not only one of speedway's real stylists, but also one of the most loyal riders to ever don the Robins' race bib in their long and distinguished history.

During the year, Swindon also entered a side in the Junior League, and although they ran two home matches none of the competing teams fulfilled their quota of fixtures and the competition ended in disarray.

SWINDON ROBINS 1958

(Swindon's score shown first unless otherwise stated)

NATIONAL LEAGUE

Opponents	Home	Away
Belle Vue	W56-40	W48-47
Coventry	L41-54	L35-61
Ipswich	W66-30	W50-46
Leicester	W57-39	L47-49
Norwich	W50-46	L37-59
Oxford	W56-40	W49-47
Poole	W66-30	L47-49
Southampton	W56-40	L41-55
Wimbledon	L42-54	L31-65

Note: The away match at Belle Vue originally ended in a 51-45 win to Swindon but, following an appeal, the result was later changed to a 48-47 victory for the Robins. On the night of the meeting, with weather conditions deteriorating, Swindon were unhappy to continue riding after heat six and asked the referee to inspect the track. However, the meeting official refused and put the riders for heat seven on two minutes. With neither Swindon representative (Mike Broadbanks and guest Ken McKinlay) making it to the start, Belle Vue rode untroubled to a 5-0 victory. The Robins then decided to contest the rest of the meeting, but asked that heat seven be rerun with its original line-up! The referee agreed and the race then ended as a 3-3, much to the disgust of the Aces, who then rode under protest. Therefore, the outcome of the appeal was that the ACU reinstated the original 5-0 result of heat seven, although it still meant an away success for Swindon.

NATIONAL LEAGUE TABLE

Team	Mts	Won	Drn	Lst	For	Agn.	Pts
Wimbledon	18	12	2	4	991	737	26
Norwich	18	12	0	6	945	782	24
Southampton	18	11	0	7	909	818	22
Leicester	18	11	0	7	869	858	22
Belle Vue	18	10	0	8	908	819	20
Swindon	18	10	0	8	875	851	20
Coventry	18	9	1	8	893	833	19
Oxford	18	5	2	11	783	943	12
Poole	18	6	0	12	754	973	12
Ipswich	18	1	1	16	707	1,020	3

LEAGUE AVERAGES

Rider	Mts	Rds	Pts	Bon.	Tot.	Avge	Maximums
Ronnie Moore	1	6	18	0	18	12.00	1 full
Ken McKinlay	2	9	18	3	21	9.33	–
Brian Hanham	2	10	18	4	22	8.80	–
Mike Broadbanks	17	86	174	7	181	8.42	2 full
George White	16	77	138	23	161	8.36	2 paid
Ian Williams	18	94	185	11	196	8.34	1 full; 1 paid
Neil Street	18	92	166	18	184	8.00	2 full
Dick Bradley	5	27	47	5	52	7.70	–
Jack Geran	1	5	5	3	8	6.40	–
Trevor Blokdyk	1	4	3	2	5	5.00	–
Al Sparrey	5	17	15	4	19	4.47	–
Maury McDermott	1	5	4	1	5	4.00	–
Ernie Lessiter	10	37	30	6	36	3.89	–
Gordon McGregor	1	5	3	1	4	3.20	–
Ivan Mauger	1	5	4	0	4	3.20	–
Arne Hendriksen	1	3	1	1	2	2.67	–
Chum Taylor	1	3	1	1	2	2.67	–
Roy Moreton	5	21	11	2	13	2.48	–
Ronnie Genz	1	5	3	0	3	2.40	–
Gerry Hussey	1	5	2	1	3	2.40	–
Maurice Conway	16	52	29	5	34	2.62	–
Ron Swaine	1	3	0	0	0	0.00	–
Roy Taylor	1	3	0	0	0	0.00	–

RAC NATIONAL TROPHY

Opponents	Home	Away	Aggregate
Bye (Round one)	–	–	–
Ipswich (Quarter-final)	W78-42	W77-42	W155-84
Norwich (Semi-final)	D60-60	L51-69	L111-129

BRITANNIA SHIELD

Opponents	Home	Away
Norwich	L47-49	W51-45
Poole	W52-44	W68-28
Southampton	W64-31	L39-57
Wimbledon	L42-54	L31-65

Note: Both league matches against Wimbledon also doubled-up as results in the Britannia Shield.

BRITANNIA SHIELD (SOUTH GROUP) TABLE

Team	Mts	Won	Drn	Lst	For	Agn.	Pts
Wimbledon	8	8	0	0	445	322	16
Swindon	8	4	0	4	394	373	8
Southampton	8	4	0	4	387	380	8
Norwich	8	3	0	5	376	390	6
Poole	8	1	0	7	315	452	2

Note: Wimbledon progressed to the final.

SUPPORTERS' TROPHY

Opponents	Home	Away
Oxford	–	L41-55

INTER-COUNTIES CHALLENGE CUP

Opponents	Home	Away
Coventry	L46-50	–

CHALLENGE

Opponents	Home	Away
Eastbourne	–	L20-52
Monarkerna	W63-30	–
Norwich	W65-31	–
St Austell	–	W54-42

Note: The challenge match at Eastbourne featured a Swindon Reserves side.

1959

The start of the 1959 season saw Swindon fans rocked when the 'Red Devil', Mike Broadbanks, asked for a transfer; a request he later withdrew in July. Meanwhile, an incoming rider was Australian Johnny Board, who made the 12,000-mile journey to this country after being recommended by Neil Street. In the Robins' opening meeting of the campaign on 27 March, Ray Harris made a return to the side, having last sported the red-and-white colours in 1956. The stocky Hereford-born rider duly netted 3+1 points in a 50-46 challenge match success against a battling Belle Vue outfit, for whom Peter Craven spectacularly carded 15 points from six starts.

A National Reserve League was formed to brighten the second half of meetings and Swindon's junior team went on to end the season in the cellar position, although the competition was never properly completed, with many fixtures left outstanding. Emphasising Swindon's weaknesses, the youngsters began their home fixtures with a challenge match against a strong Wimbledon quartet on 4 April and predictably went down to a 21-9 defeat. New arrival Johnny Board recorded only 1+1

Swindon Robins, 1959. From left to right, back row: Neil Street, Tommy Sweetman, Glyn Chandler, Tadeusz Teodorowicz, Bob Thomas, Ian Williams, Johnny Board, Bert Hearse (Promoter). Front row, kneeling: Mike Broadbanks, Ron Tuck, George White.

points in the five-heat match, although his all-out, fence-scraping style did at least provide plenty of excitement for the hordes on the terraces.

Always on the look-out for talent, promoter Bert Hearse made contact with Pole Tadeusz Teodorowicz, who, having applied for political asylum, had been living in Holland. 'Teo', as he was known, arrived in England on 15 April and made his Swindon debut just three days later when he took Ray Harris' position in the team for a Britannia Shield match against Norwich at Blunsdon. In a great start he tallied 6+3 points in a thrilling 45-45 draw and even led the redoubtable Ove Fundin for a time in one of his races! Teo was to settle in well, but on 15 June an international suspension was imposed on him by the Polish Motor Federation and upheld by the FIM. The Speedway Control Board could do nothing but enforce the suspension. However, Teo was so popular with his fellow riders that they threatened to strike and the FIM was forced to lift the suspension by early July.

Another signing was New Zealander Trevor Redmond but, although he had vast experience, the Kiwi failed to find his best form with the Robins. Gerry King was also recruited via Wimbledon and opportunities were given to promising Welshman Leo McAuliffe. Unfortunately, King was out of action almost as soon as he arrived. On his debut, he scored 4+1 points in a home league fixture against Belle Vue on 20 June, but a week later he was badly injured in the second half of a challenge match against Southampton. Although he did manage to recover from his injuries, it signalled the end of a promising racing career.

On the individual front, three top meetings were held at the Abbey Stadium during the season. Firstly, Leicester's Jack Geran was victorious in the Midland Riders' Championship qualifying round on 23 May, when he saw off strong challenges from Oxford's Gordon McGregor and the home duo of George White and Mike Broadbanks. Broady made sure of success in the next 'big one' at Blunsdon though, defeating Poole's Les McGillivray in a run-off to win a World Championship qualifying round on 11 July. Finally, the Jack Parker Trophy on 7 August saw a marvellous field of riders assembled, with the great Ove Fundin taking the plaudits after notching a magnificent 15-point maximum. Showing just how strong the line-up was, Peter Craven finished in second place, while Wimbledon's Ronnie Moore was equal third with Geoff Mardon of Southampton.

George White.

There was a general decline in some of the riders' performances, culminating in the Robins slipping to eighth place in the nine-team league. Mike Broadbanks, however, proved to be the top man for a second successive year, scoring 187 points for an impressive league average of 9.40. Second in the team figures was 'Chalky' White on a 7.78 average, with Ian Williams third on 7.22. Tadeusz Teodorowicz, meanwhile, did well to notch 111 points for a satisfactory 6.58 figure in his first season of British racing. White rode in the *Sunday Pictorial* World Final at Wembley on 19 September and scored 7 points, which was one of the few bright spots of a hugely disappointing season for the club as a whole. Local rivals Oxford finished one place above Swindon in the final league table and, having earlier knocked the Robins out of the RAC National Trophy in round one, the Cheetahs rubbed salt into the wound by also plundering the Supporters' Club Cup for the first time ever, courtesy of a 116-100 aggregate victory. There was no joy in the Britannia Shield either, as Swindon again failed to progress beyond the group stage, instead having to be satisfied with fourth position out of five teams.

The final meeting of the year at Blunsdon was a Test match between England and Australasia on 26 September. In a superb encounter it was England who scraped home by the narrowest of margins, 55-53, with Peter Craven topping the scorechart on 13+3 points. Mike Broadbanks and Ron How yielded 11+1 points apiece, while Ian Williams collected 8+1. A third Swindon rider, George White, had been due to represent England, but missed the meeting through injury, with Oxford's Gordon McGregor moving up from a reserve berth as his replacement. For the Australasians, the mighty Barry Briggs amassed 16+1 points and, just for good measure, reduced the track record to 72.0 seconds in the opening heat. Fellow Kiwi Ronnie Moore, who had become World Champion for a second time just a week earlier, was also a tall scorer in accruing a tally of 14+1.

Alterations to the Blunsdon circuit began in the winter of 1959, reducing the 410-yard racing strip to 395 yards in time for the opening meeting of the 1960 season.

SWINDON ROBINS 1959

(Swindon's score shown first unless otherwise stated)

NATIONAL LEAGUE

Opponents	Home	Away
Belle Vue	W51-39	W57-51
Coventry	L50-58	L39-51
Leicester	W59-31	L44-46
Norwich	W49-41	L42-48
Oxford	W45-44	L38-52
Poole	W63-27	L44-46
Southampton	L43-47	L36-54
Wimbledon	L39-68	L27-63

Note: A total of twenty-two National League matches had been completed over eighteen heats before the SCB decided that meetings should be run over fifteen heats; hence the disparity in the race points totals in Swindon's first three matches of the season v. Belle Vue (away), Wimbledon (home) and Coventry (home).

NATIONAL LEAGUE TABLE

Team	Mts	Won	Drn	Lst	For	Agn.	Pts
Wimbledon	16	13	0	3	893	635	26
Leicester	16	8	1	7	759	768	17
Coventry	16	8	1	7	750	797	17
Norwich	16	8	0	8	784	762	16
Southampton	16	8	0	8	769	758	16
Poole	16	8	0	8	716	813	16
Oxford	16	7	0	9	733	773	14
Swindon	16	6	0	10	726	766	12
Belle Vue	16	5	0	11	735	793	10

LEAGUE AVERAGES

Rider	Mts	Rds	Pts	Bon.	Tot.	Avge	Maximums
Mike Broadbanks	16	83	187	8	195	9.40	2 full
George White	15	72	126	14	140	7.78	–
Ian Williams	16	82	132	16	148	7.22	–
Tadeusz Teodorowicz	15	73	111	9	120	6.58	–
Neil Street	16	81	111	22	133	6.57	1 paid
Gerry King	1	5	4	1	5	4.00	–
Trevor Redmond	12	56	37	15	52	3.71	–
Johnny Board	3	10	7	2	9	3.60	–
Reg Luckhurst	1	4	2	1	3	3.00	–
Tommy Sweetman	2	5	2	1	3	2.40	–
Glyn Chandler	3	11	6	0	6	2.18	–
Bob Thomas	1	3	1	0	1	1.33	–
Leo McAuliffe	4	13	0	0	0	0.00	–

RAC NATIONAL TROPHY

Opponents	Home	Away	Aggregate
Oxford (Round one)	W55-52	L49-59	L111-104

BRITANNIA SHIELD

Opponents	Home	Away
Norwich	D45-45	L21-69
Poole	L42-48	W52-38
Southampton	W46-43	L40-50
Wimbledon	L44-46	L37-53

BRITANNIA SHIELD (SOUTHERN GROUP) TABLE

Team	Mts	Won	Drn	Lst	For	Agn.	Pts
Wimbledon	8	6	0	2	400	320	12
Southampton	8	5	0	3	365	354	10

Norwich	8	4	1	3	380	340	9
Swindon	8	2	1	5	327	392	5
Poole	8	2	0	6	327	393	4

Note: Wimbledon progressed to the final.

SUPPORTERS' CLUB CUP

Opponents	Home	Away	Aggregate
Oxford	L52-56	L48-60	L100-116

CHALLENGE

Opponents	Home	Away
Belle Vue	W50-46	–
Bristol	–	L40-49
Leicester	W57-51	–
Oxford	–	L44-46
Poland	L35-55	–
Southampton	W47-43	–
Wimbledon	W54-36	–

1960

Speedway in general was on the up-and-up in 1960 with the formation of the Provincial League which, like the National League, consisted of ten teams. However, it was not to be a very happy year for Swindon – they were wooden-spoon finishers for the first time, with a team that desperately needed some new faces. The Robins lost four home matches during the league campaign, as well as losing all nine of their away fixtures. That unfortunately left them languishing 4 points adrift at the foot of the table, behind Coventry.

Young Australian Johnny Board, who had joined the Swindon camp the previous year, returned for another go, while Ron Taylor, a very promising lad from the grass-track scene, was also signed. Promoter Bert Hearse brought in Brian Meredith too, the rider having enjoyed limited opportunities with Coventry, despite being a game trier.

The Robins entertained Wimbledon in a challenge match to open the Blunsdon season on 9 April, and Ronnie Moore wasted no time in setting a track record for the revamped 395-yard circuit, clocking 72.0 seconds in the first heat. This set the tone for the meeting as the Robins went down to a 56-34 hiding, with both Moore and teammate Ron How notching identical five-ride paid maximums (13+2 points) for the victorious Dons. The Kiwi's time actually equalled that of fellow countryman Barry Briggs, although Briggo's effort had been recorded on 26 September the previous year, when the track had been its original length of 410 yards. As the season wore on nobody could better Moore's record time, although it was equalled by both Ken McKinlay and Peter Craven.

The Robins had a very long tail, although things were significantly improved by the signing of Brian Brett from Southampton. Following a run of second-half outings, the Essex racer eventually got the opportunity to make his club debut in a challenge match at Oxford on 23 June, when he netted 3 points and helped his side to a 47-43 success.

When Swindon went to Norwich for a league match on 6 August, they had such a weakened side that Bob Jones was forced into making a return to the track. There was no George White and no Tadeusz Teodorowicz, so they rode with Brian Meredith at number one, Brian Brett at number four and Ron Taylor at number five, with Johnny Board and Bob Jones occupying the reserve berths. Unsurprisingly, the Robins crashed to a 56-34 loss, with Joner failing to score. He had created some record though, since not only had he ridden, but also filled his normal dual role of team manager/mechanic!

When the facts and figures were totted up at the close of the campaign, Mike Broadbanks was Swindon's leading league scorer with 161 points yielding an 8.33 average in what was a pretty mediocre side. George White finished the campaign with a 7.97 average, and while Ian Williams

Swindon Robins, 1960. From left to right, back row: Johnny Board, Ron Taylor, Brian Meredith, Tadeusz Teodorowicz, Mike Broadbanks, Neil Street, George White, Bob Jones (Team Manager). Front, on bike: Ian Williams.

(6.92), Neil Street (6.83) and Tadeusz Teodorowicz (6.74) all offered solid enough support, it was an out-and-out number one rider that the Robins desperately required. At the lower end of the side, Ron Taylor started the season reasonably well, but should have enjoyed more rides than he did in order to further his progress. Meanwhile, Brian Brett battled away and there was the promise of much more to come in the future.

Following a first round bye, Swindon defeated Southampton to reach the semi-final of the RAC National Trophy, but there was heartache as they went down to a crushing 131-84 defeat at the hands of Wimbledon, for whom the amazing Ronnie Moore plundered 16+1 points in the first leg at the Abbey on 16 July and followed it up by netting a paid maximum (16+2) in the return match nine days later. For a second successive year Swindon also lost the Supporters' Club Cup to chief rivals Oxford, going down 102-78 on aggregate. In the Britannia Shield the Robins won four of their group matches, but it was only enough to see them finish as runners-up to Wimbledon, so it was the Dons who progressed through to the final.

The Abbey Stadium played host to another three prestigious individual events during the year, the first of which saw Teo total 14 points to brilliantly win the Midland Riders' Championship qualifying round ahead of Mike Broadbanks (13) on 28 May. Then, Southampton's Chum Taylor produced a marvellous 15-point maximum to take victory in the World Championship qualifying round on 2 July, while fellow Saint Bjorn Knutsson plundered a full-house to lift the Jack Parker Trophy on 29 July. On 5 August Blunsdon staged a qualifying round in the inaugural World Team Cup competition. This saw Australia, New Zealand, England and a Challengers side battle it out to decide the qualifying place. England duly won the meeting with 33 points, from the Challengers (28), New Zealand (23) and Australia (12). Ian Williams rode for England as reserve, notching a single point, while Neil Street rode for Australia, but failed to score. Meanwhile, Mike Broadbanks appeared for the Challengers, netting 9 points.

Another event of note took place at Blunsdon late in the season, on Wednesday 21 September, being billed as a 'Grand Carnival of Speed'. The meeting was sponsored by the Rotary Club of Swindon and featured sidecars, speedcars and go-karts as well as a mini individual speedway tournament, which saw Oxford's Ronnie Genz take victory in the final. This was actually the second such composite event staged during the season, since a 'Cavalcade of Speed' had been held on 13 August, during which the Robins and the Challengers drew 15-15 in a five-heat match.

SWINDON ROBINS 1960

(Swindon's score shown first unless otherwise stated)

NATIONAL LEAGUE

Opponents	Home	Away
Belle Vue	W48-42	L39-51
Coventry	W54-36	L38-52
Ipswich	L43-47	L40-50
Leicester	W47-43	L38-52
New Cross	W47-43	L33-55
Norwich	W55-35	L34-56
Oxford	L44-46	L42-48
Southampton	L42-47	L30-60
Wimbledon	L44-46	L36-54

NATIONAL LEAGUE TABLE

Team	Mts	Won	Drn	Lst	For	Agn.	Pts
Wimbledon	17	13	0	4	838	691	26
Belle Vue	18	11	1	6	890	726	23
Oxford	18	11	0	7	816	797	22
Ipswich	18	10	0	8	751	863	20
Norwich	17	8	1	8	748.5	779.5	17
Leicester	18	7	2	9	793.5	825.5	16
Southampton	18	7	1	10	815	794	15
New Cross	18	7	1	10	770	840	15
Coventry	18	7	0	11	810	807	14
Swindon	18	5	0	13	754	863	10

Note: The Norwich v. Wimbledon match was not raced.

LEAGUE AVERAGES

Rider	Mts	Rds	Pts	Bon.	Tot.	Avge	Maximums
Mike Broadbanks	18	84	161	14	175	8.33	–
George White	12	59	108.5	9	117.5	7.97	–
Ian Williams	18	85	129	18	147	6.92	–
Neil Street	18	80	117.5	19	136.5	6.83	–
Tadeusz Teodorowicz	16	73	113	10	123	6.74	–
Johnny Board	16	41	41	7	48	4.68	–
Brian Meredith	16	43	39	6	45	4.19	–
Ron Taylor	17	40	29	7	36	3.60	–
Brian Brett	11	31	16	3	19	2.45	–
Bob Jones	1	2	0	0	0	0.00	–
Ernie Lessiter	1	2	0	0	0	0.00	–

RAC NATIONAL TROPHY

Opponents	Home	Away	Aggregate
Bye (Round one)	–	–	–
Southampton (Quarter-final)	W66-42	L52-55	W118-97
Wimbledon (Semi-final)	L48-60	L36-71	L84-131

BRITANNIA SHIELD

Opponents	Home	Away
New Cross	W62-28	W55-35

Norwich	W54-35	L42-47
Southampton	W53-37	L41-49
Wimbledon	L41-49	L34-56

BRITANNIA SHIELD (SOUTHERN GROUP) TABLE

Team	Mts	Won	Drn	Lst	For	Agn.	Pts
Wimbledon	8	7	0	1	427	289	14
Swindon	8	4	0	4	382	336	8
Norwich	8	4	0	4	369	349	8
Southampton	8	4	0	4	361	358	8
New Cross	8	1	0	7	255	462	2

Note: Wimbledon progressed to the final.

MIDLAND CUP

Opponents	Home	Away	Aggregate
Coventry (Semi-final)	W58-32	L31-58	L89-90

HUTCHINS TROPHY

Opponents	Home	Away	Aggregate
Oxford	W51-39	D45-45	W96-84

SUPPORTERS' CLUB CUP

Opponents	Home	Away	Aggregate
Oxford	L44-46	L34-56	L78-102

Note: The home league match against Oxford also doubled as the result of the Supporters' Club Cup.

CHALLENGE

Opponents	Home	Away
Ipswich	–	31-29 (aban.)
Oxford	–	W47-43
Poland	W50-40	–
Wimbledon	L34-56	–

Note: The match at Ipswich was abandoned after heat ten.

FOUR-TEAM TOURNAMENT

(Staged at Rye House)   Poole 31, Swindon 29, Rye House 29, Rayleigh 19.

1961

Following the 1960 season, the winter was a very worrying time for supporters of the Robins, as Mike Broadbanks spent much of it in hospital with a respiratory complaint. The run-up to the 1961 campaign soon came around though, and Swindon stepped up their search for a top rider. As such, the management turned their eyes to Sweden and signed youngster Arne Carlsson, who had finished seventh in the 1959 World Final. As it turned out, the Scandinavian was something of a disappointment and only completed seven league matches for a 6.00 average. Meanwhile Bob Roger, after two years of trying to convince the authorities that he was fully recovered from his injuries of 1958, tried a comeback, which ultimately wasn't successful and it saddened the Robins' faithful to see him struggle for points. Looking at the plus side, however, Brian Meredith and Brian Brett were good reserves in a Swindon side that had much more solidity about it than in the previous season.

    The boys in red and white moved up to fifth position in the ten-team National League, with Neil Street registering 127 league points to head the scoring and yield a 7.83 average. The diminutive George White was only just behind in the battle for top spot, his final average being 7.82. Meanwhile Mike Broadbanks, discharged from hospital in April, battled on gamely to achieve a 6.96 average from

The programme from the second leg of the RAC National Trophy final v. Southampton on 23 September 1961.

the dozen league matches he managed to complete. The biggest improvement in the camp came from Tadeusz Teodorowicz, who upped his average from 6.74 in 1960 to a solid 7.52 figure. This was a much better year for the Robins overall, although with a bit more consistency at Blunsdon it could have been even greater. A brace of home defeats at the hands of Southampton and Wimbledon cost the side dearly, but this was slightly offset by a solitary away victory at Oxford.

There were a couple of interesting happenings over the course of the league campaign, the first of which occurred on 20 May, when Leicester provided the opposition at Blunsdon. The Robins were fairly comfortable 44-34 winners, but of the visitors' total, Polish rider Pawel Waloszek netted a full five-ride maximum (15). Later, on 10 June, Swindon defeated Norwich 45-33 at the Abbey, with the brilliant Ove Fundin romping to an unbeaten 15-pointer for the Norfolk outfit. Curiously, the match also saw all seven riders in the Robins camp claim a bonus point apiece!

Swindon reached the RAC National Trophy final, having battled past both Leicester and Norwich, but there was huge disappointment for the fans when they lost out to Southampton in the big showdown, 98-70 on aggregate. There was some success though, as the Robins beat Oxford by a single point over two legs, 78-77, to retain the Hutchins Trophy, which they had scooped the year before. Then, in the Supporters' Club Cup, Swindon defeated the Cheetahs by a comfortable 98-58 aggregate scoreline.

The Abbey Stadium regulars were treated to no less than five individual events during the course of the season, the first of which saw Arne Pander win the Midland Riders' Championship qualifying round on 10 May, courtesy of a superb 15-point maximum. Next up was the prestigious Speedway Internationale on 17 June, and this saw Wimbledon's Ronnie Moore triumph with maximum points, ahead of Barry Briggs and Bob Andrews, who tied for second spot on 13 points apiece.

Blunsdon was lucky enough to be chosen to host the final of the Midland Riders' Championship on 21 June, when an all-star field produced a firecracker of a meeting and a dramatic finale. Having posted four straight wins, Oxford's Arne Pander looked in a class of his own. However, his engine dramatically blew to bits in his last ride, leaving him level on 12 points with Jack Geran of Leicester and thereby necessitating a run-off to decide the destiny of the title. Pander initially had no bike for the decider, but help was at hand in the shape of Geran's close pal Neil Street, who was quick to lend the Danish star his mount in an outstanding gesture of sportsmanship. Despite this, it was Geran who held his nerve to take the nail-biting run-off and with it the glory.

On 8 July, Swindon staged a World Championship qualifying round and this saw Wimbledon's Cyril Maidment scorch to an immaculate maximum and finish a point ahead of the popular Tadeusz Teodorowicz. The fifth and final big meeting on the Blunsdon calendar was the Jack Parker Trophy on 12 August, when a top-class line-up thrilled the packed terraces. Leicester's Ken McKinlay cleaned up with a 15-point haul, while there was a three-way tie for the runner-up spot between Barry Briggs, Ronnie Moore and the Robins' own Mike Broadbanks, each of whom netted a dozen points. Broady gamely qualified for the World Final in Malmo, Sweden on 15 September, but finished way down the field with just 2 points on the big night. Interestingly, the name of local youngster Martin Ashby began to feature in the second half of home meetings. Little did anyone know then, but Martin (or 'Crash', as he was somewhat unfairly dubbed) would go on to become the all-time number one at Swindon, making more appearances for the club than anyone else and, of course, scoring the most points as well.

SWINDON ROBINS 1961

(Swindon's score shown first unless otherwise stated)

NATIONAL LEAGUE

Opponents	Home	Away
Belle Vue	W45-33	L35-43
Coventry	W47-31	L24-54
Ipswich	W41-37	L36-42
Leicester	W44-34	L28-50
New Cross	W54-24	L33-44

Norwich	W45-33	L26-52
Oxford	W48-30	W46-32
Southampton	L37-41	L36-42
Wimbledon	L34-44	L24-53

NATIONAL LEAGUE TABLE

Team	Mts	Won	Drn	Lst	For	Agn.	Pts
Wimbledon	18	15	0	3	830	573	30
Southampton	18	13	2	3	788	613	28
Coventry	18	10	1	7	676	728	21
Belle Vue	18	10	0	8	761	642	20
Swindon	18	8	0	10	683	719	16
Ipswich	18	7	1	10	681.5	720.5	15
Norwich	18	7	0	11	691.5	700.5	14
New Cross	18	7	0	11	626	774	14
Oxford	18	6	1	11	665	727	13
Leicester	18	4	1	13	599	804	9

LEAGUE AVERAGES

Rider	Mts	Rds	Pts	Bon.	Tot.	Avge	Maximums
Neil Street	18	72	127	14	141	7.83	1 full; 2 paid
George White	17	68	118	15	133	7.82	1 full
Tadeusz Teodorowicz	17	66	116	8	124	7.52	1 full
Mike Broadbanks	12	46	73	7	80	6.96	1 full
Ian Williams	18	72	94	18	112	6.22	–
Arne Carlsson	7	30	40	5	45	6.00	–
Brian Meredith	17	46	45	17	62	5.39	–
Brian Brett	17	60	68	6	74	4.93	–
Bob Roger	3	8	2	0	2	1.00	–

RAC NATIONAL TROPHY

Opponents	Home	Away	Aggregate
Bye (Round one)	–	–	–
Leicester (Quarter-final)	W66-18	W45-38	W111-56
Norwich (Semi-final)	W56-28	L40-43	W96-71
Southampton (Final)	L41-43	L29-55	L70-98

KNOCK-OUT CUP

Opponents	Home	Away
Southampton (Round one)	L32-46	–

CENTRAL CHALLENGE SHIELD

Opponents	Home	Away
Coventry	W49-29	L30-48
Leicester	W48-30	L32-46
Oxford	W47-31	L31-47

CENTRAL CHALLENGE SHIELD TABLE

Team	Mts	Won	Drn	Lst	For	Agn.	Pts
Coventry	6	3	0	3	246	222	27
Swindon	6	3	0	3	237	231	25
Leicester	6	3	0	3	231	237	24
Oxford	6	3	0	3	222	246	20

Note: A unique points-scoring system was applied to the Central Shield as follows: up to 29 race points = nil; 30-32 race points = 1 point; 33-35 race points = 2 points; 36-38 race points = 3 points; 39 race points = 4 points; 40-42 race points = 5 points; 43-45 race points = 6 points; 46-48 race points = 7 points; 49 and over race points = 8 points.

HUTCHINS TROPHY

Opponents	Home	Away	Aggregate
Oxford	W46-31	L32-46	W78-77

SUPPORTERS' CLUB CUP

Opponents	Home	Away	Aggregate
Oxford	W59-19	D39-39	W98-58

CHALLENGE

Opponents	Home	Away
Belle Vue	–	L21-57
Exeter	–	(1) L38-39
Exeter	–	(2) W45-33
Oxford	–	D39-39
Poole	–	L42-54

Notes: The second challenge match at Exeter featured a Swindon Select team. The challenge match at Poole featured a Swindon 'B' side.

1962

The season of 1962 saw the Robins slip down the league table; also, handicap racing was introduced and George White retired. Meanwhile, former Bristol rider Roger Wise, a local man from Highworth, became team manager, leaving 'Mr Swindon Speedway' Bob Jones very ably to concentrate on the mechanical side of things. Ian Williams was reported to be joining Provincial League newcomers Neath, but the control board refused permission for him to drop down to the lower level of racing and the Welshman remained on board for his eleventh term in a Swindon race-jacket.

Bob Roger once again attempted a comeback, but after appearing in a couple of challenge matches and taking some second-half outings at Blunsdon, he called it a day and the career of one of the most colourful of all Robins unfortunately came to a premature close. His last meeting for the club was at Ipswich in a league encounter on 27 April, when he gleaned just 1+1 points. Some years after the failure of Roger to regain his golden touch, Ian Williams explained how he had tried to help his colleague. The two riders used to practice at Blunsdon and at Roger's request, Williams rode as hard as he could. After some of the sessions it looked as if the Ashford-born rider had regained his confidence, but regrettably he was unable to carry it into actual races. Puzzled by this, Williams asked him why he'd been so convincing in practice, to which Roger replied: 'But I know it's you, and I know you'd never do anything daft.'

There were seven teams in the National League and Swindon could only manage to finish in sixth position. As mentioned George White had retired, in order to concentrate on his business interests and to provide for his family, but Chalky was never really replaced and the Robins found life difficult as a result. Once again they were vulnerable at home, losing both league matches against Southampton, as well as being held to a draw on two occasions, by Belle Vue and Wimbledon. On their travels, they lost all but one of their twelve matches, the only success being a 40-37 victory at Oxford on 28 June.

The home league match against Wimbledon on 16 June was notable for several reasons. After getting stuck in heavy traffic, Cyril Brine was a non-arrival for the Dons, meaning they could only track one rider in heat four. With handicapped starts being the order of the day, heat times were not recorded, but that didn't prevent the Robins from streaking into a 22-8 lead after five races. Wimbledon fought a terrific rearguard action, however, and hauled themselves back into the match to eventually force a 39-39 draw. Before the meeting began, there was a 'vultures race' to determine who filled the reserve berth for Swindon. This featured team mechanic Bob Jones, along with a young novice by the name of Terry Keats, while completing the line-up was Buster Brown, a former Robin from the early 1950s. Having hardly ridden in eight years, amazingly it was Brown who took victory to claim a spot in the side!

Following a mid-season injury to Arne Carlsson, in an effort to strengthen the team Bert Hearse made a serious bid to bring Russian rider Igor Plechanov to Blunsdon, only for the authorities in

Swindon Robins, 1962. From left to right, back row: Brian Brett, Arne Carlsson, Tadeusz Teodorowicz, Mike Broadbanks, Neil Street, Martin Ashby. Front, on bike: Ian Williams.

the USSR to veto the idea. Swedish international Olle Nygren was therefore brought in for a couple of meetings, and when Ipswich prematurely closed down after completing fifteen league matches their Australian rider Peter Moore was allocated to the Robins' nest. Howard Cole (riding under the pseudonym Kid Bodie), Brian Leonard and Stuart Wallace were also used, as Swindon desperately tried to put together a winning combination. Mike Broadbanks was the number one rider, scoring 190 league points for an 8.21 average, but he received little top-end support, as reflected in the finishing averages of the main body of the side: Neil Street (6.81); Arne Carlsson (6.06); Ian Williams (6.00); Brian Brett (5.42); Tadeusz Teodorowicz (4.61); Martin Ashby (4.28).

For the second year running the Robins reached the RAC National Trophy final, after aggregate victories over Ipswich and Oxford. Unfortunately they again lost, this time to Wimbledon by an aggregate score of 94-74, but the highlight of the second leg at Blunsdon on 29 September was a quite brilliant 15-point maximum from young Martin Ashby, riding off scratch. Meanwhile, Swindon maintained the upper hand over Oxford, retaining the Hutchins Cup by an aggregate score of 86-69.

Ronnie Moore was triumphant in the Blunsdon-staged World Championship qualifying round on 30 June, romping to a full maximum to finish ahead of Les Owen and Bob Andrews, who finished joint second on 12-point tallies. Mike Broadbanks didn't compete in the Swindon round, but again made it through to the *Sunday Pictorial* World Final at Wembley on 8 September, where he repeated his 2-point tally of the previous year. One other big individual meeting was held at the Abbey Stadium in 1962, namely the Jack Parker Trophy on 10 August, and this saw the great Ove Fundin sweep to a majestic five-ride maximum and claim the first prize. Southampton star and future Robin Barry Briggs was runner-up on 14 points, while Peter Craven and Ronnie Moore shared third place with a dozen points apiece.

SWINDON ROBINS 1962

(Swindon's score shown first unless otherwise stated)

NATIONAL LEAGUE

Opponents	Home	Away
Belle Vue	W44-33	L35-43
	D39-39	L38-40
Coventry	W45-33	L30-48
	W40-37	L33-45
Ipswich	W57-21	L34-44
	Not staged	Not staged
Norwich	W44-34	L26-51
	W43-35	L28-50
Oxford	W40-38	W40-37
	W42-36	L37-41
Southampton	L36-41	L30-48
	L31-47	L35-42
Wimbledon	D39-39	L19-59
	W44-34	L31-47

Note: The results of meetings ridden by Ipswich were expunged from the records due to their withdrawal from the league after completing fifteen matches.

NATIONAL LEAGUE TABLE

Team	Mts	Won	Drn	Lst	For	Agn.	Pts
Southampton	24	18	0	6	1,084	785	36
Wimbledon	24	14	1	9	1,034	836	29
Coventry	24	13	0	11	992.5	875.5	26
Belle Vue	24	12	1	11	886	984	25
Norwich	24	12	0	12	909	962	24
Swindon	24	9	2	13	869	997	20
Oxford	24	4	0	20	767.5	1,102.5	8

LEAGUE AVERAGES

Rider	Mts	Rds	Pts	Bon.	Tot.	Avge	Maximums
Olle Nygren	2	8	19	1	20	10.00	–
Peter Moore	7	28	65	3	68	9.71	1 full
Mike Broadbanks	24	97	190	9	199	8.21	3 full; 2 paid
Brian Meredith	4	8	15	1	16	8.00	–
Neil Street	24	94	145	15	160	6.81	1 full; 1 paid
Arne Carlsson	17	66	90	10	100	6.06	–
Ian Williams	23	90	114	21	135	6.00	–
Brian Brett	24	96	113	17	130	5.42	–
Tadeusz Teodorowicz	9	33	33	5	38	4.61	–
Martin Ashby	24	86	82	10	92	4.28	–
Buster Brown	3	6	3	1	4	2.67	–
Kid Bodie	1	2	0	0	0	0.00	–
Brian Leonard	1	2	0	0	0	0.00	–
Norman Nevitt	1	2	0	0	0	0.00	–
Stuart Wallace	1	1	0	0	0	0.00	–

RAC NATIONAL TROPHY

Opponents	Home	Away	Aggregate
Ipswich (Quarter-final)	W51-33	L40-42	W91-75
Oxford (Semi-final)	W59-25	L39-45	W98-70
Wimbledon (Final)	W45-39	L29-55	L74-94

KNOCK-OUT CUP

Opponents	Home	Away
Wimbledon (Round one)	L31-47	–

CAPSTAN TROPHY

Opponents	Home	Away
Southampton	W41-37	–

HUTCHINS TROPHY

Opponents	Home	Away	Aggregate
Oxford	W43-34	W43-35	W86-69

CHALLENGE

Opponents	Home	Away
Oxford	–	L30-48
Plymouth	–	L34-43
Southampton	–	L34-44
Stoke	–	L36-42
Wolverhampton	–	D39-39

Note: The challenge matches at Plymouth, Stoke and Wolverhampton featured Swindon 'B' teams.

1963

1963 saw a virtually unchanged Swindon side in action and, although Arne Carlsson wasn't retained, the young Swede went on to surprise everyone, riding his way to Wembley for the *Sunday Mirror* World Final on 14 September! Meanwhile, great servant Bob Jones was back in his dual role of team manager and mechanic after Roger Wise had relinquished the post. The Robins kicked off in a league match at Coventry on 30 March, but went down to a 45-33 defeat, with speedy Scotsman Ken McKinlay blasting to a 12-point maximum for the Bees. Ever-loyal Port Talbot-born Ian Williams was once again in the Swindon line-up at what was the start of his twelfth and final year in the red-and-white colours.

Blunsdon opened for business on Good Friday 12 April, when Oxford were the opposition in the Hutchins Trophy. The match was a complete whitewash, with Swindon winning by a 58-26 scoreline. Young Martin Ashby scored 11+2 points, while Neil Street netted an unbeaten 10+2 tally, but the star of the evening was Tadeusz Teodorowicz, who posted a classic full 15-pointer. The Robins had already raced the first leg at Oxford in the afternoon, losing 46-38, but their huge home success ensured they retained the silverware on aggregate, 96-72.

Early-season problems with the weather saw Swindon's away league match at Norwich abandoned after eight heats on 13 April, while the following week's home meeting *v.* Southampton was called off without a wheel being turned. In what subsequently became only the second home meeting of the season on 27 April, Wimbledon's Ronnie Moore established a new track record of 71.8 seconds, bettering the previous best that had been set in 1960. Although the season went on through to the end of September, the Kiwi's time proved to be unbeatable and stood as the fastest recorded all year long.

There was an interesting occurrence in the home match against Wimbledon on 8 June, when Ivan Mauger recorded 11 points for the Dons. The Robins won the match 40-38, but it was subsequently decided to deduct Mauger's points as he had started from the wrong handicap. The man who would later go on to win the World Championship on six occasions rode the meeting from scratch, but should have actually ridden off a 10-yard handicap! The outcome had no bearing on the destiny of the two league points, however, with the result of the meeting amended to a 40-27 victory for the Wiltshire boys.

There were still just seven sides in the National League and Swindon finished in fifth spot. Once again it was home form that cost the side dearly, with three defeats and a draw witnessed by the Abbey Stadium faithful, although the Robins did win a couple of matches on the road, at Oxford and Southampton. Peter 'Piccolo' Moore, the fast-starting Aussie, became the club's number one rider, netting 207 league points to average 8.89. Ian Williams had handed over the team captaincy to Mike

Swindon Robins, 1963. From left to right, back row: Brian Brett, Jon Erskine, Bob Jones (Team Manager), Peter Moore, Tadeusz Teodorowicz. Front, kneeling: Mike Broadbanks, Neil Street, Martin Ashby.

Broadbanks, with the Hoddesdon-born racer subsequently finishing second in the statistical run-down on a solid 8.74 figure. There was quite a hefty drop to third-placed man Tadeusz Teodorowicz, whose end-of-term average was 6.57. However, there were a couple of bright spots in the team with Brian Brett moving his figure up to 6.44, while Martin Ashby showed steady improvement to finish on 5.80.

Following on from their Hutchins Trophy success over Oxford, the Robins also disposed of the Cheetahs in the quarter-final of the RAC National Trophy, only to then go down to a narrow 85-83 aggregate defeat against Norwich at the semi-final stage. On the individual front, Mike Broadbanks won a World Championship qualifying round at Blunsdon on 5 July. His winning total was 14.5 points, having dead-heated for first place with Ron How in a neck-and-neck heat seventeen. Broady also won his other qualifying round at Wimbledon on 1 July, but unfortunately didn't make the big night at Wembley after only finishing twelfth in the three-round British Final. Peter Moore did make it through though, and gave a good account to notch 6 points, while Tadeusz Teodorowicz proudly qualified as reserve, although he wasn't pressed into action.

The final meeting of the season at Blunsdon saw a top-class field compete for the W.D. and H.O. Wills-sponsored Bristol Tipped Trophy on 28 September. Despite riding with a plaster cast on his left leg, Oxford's Arne Pander eventually came out on top in the final, while Sverre Harrfeldt of Wimbledon was second and Mike Broadbanks third. Regrettably, Southampton closed down at the end of the season, leaving the National League with just six teams. Also at the end of the campaign, both Australians, Neil Street (after seven seasons) and Peter Moore (after a season-and-a-half), announced that they would not be returning to race in Britain in 1964.

SWINDON ROBINS 1963

(Swindon's score shown first unless otherwise stated)

NATIONAL LEAGUE

Opponents	Home	Away
Belle Vue	L37-41	L29-49
	L33-45	L31-47
Coventry	W47-31	L33-45
	W53-25	L34-44
Norwich	W48-30	L36-42
	D39-39	Not staged
Oxford	W43-35	W43-35
	W54-24	D39-39
Southampton	W49-29	L30-48
	L38-40	W40-38
Wimbledon	W44-34	L37-40
	W40-27	L30-48

Notes: The original result of the second home match v. Wimbledon was 40-38; however, the 11 points scored by Ivan Mauger for the visitors were later deducted as he had started from the wrong handicap. The original result of the first away match v. Wimbledon was 39-39; however, points recorded by the supplementary reserves in heat thirteen (Jim Tebby for the Dons and Swindon's Neil Street) were subsequently deducted as they were not eligible to ride.

NATIONAL LEAGUE TABLE

Team	Mts	Won	Drn	Lst	For	Agn.	Pts
Belle Vue	24	17	0	7	989	875	34
Norwich	24	13	2	9	911	879	28
Wimbledon	24	12	1	11	934	920	25
Coventry	24	11	2	11	912	957	24
Swindon	24	10	2	12	907	875	22
Southampton	24	11	0	13	933	936	22
Oxford	24	6	1	17	861	1,005	13

Note: The second Norwich v. Swindon match was not raced. Norwich were subsequently awarded the league points and this is therefore recorded as a win for the Stars and defeat for the Robins in the league table.

LEAGUE AVERAGES

Rider	Mts	Rds	Pts	Bon.	Tot.	Avge	Maximums
Peter Moore	23	99	207	13	220	8.89	1 full
Mike Broadbanks	23	92	185	16	201	8.74	1 full; 2 paid
Tadeusz Teodorowicz	23	84	127	11	138	6.57	1 paid
Brian Brett	22	77	106	18	124	6.44	1 paid
Neil Street	23	83	113	19	132	6.36	1 full
Martin Ashby	23	80	91	25	116	5.80	–
Ian Williams	22	79	78	21	99	5.01	–
Jon Erskine	1	2	0	0	0	0.00	–
Brian Meredith	1	1	0	0	0	0.00	–

RAC NATIONAL TROPHY

Opponents	Home	Away	Aggregate
Bye (Round one)	–	–	–
Oxford (Quarter-final)	W53-31	W45-39	W98-70
Norwich (Semi-final)	W48-36	L35-49	L83-85

KNOCK-OUT CUP

Opponents	Home	Away
Southampton (Round one)	–	L25-53

HUTCHINS TROPHY

Opponents	Home	Away	Aggregate
Oxford	W58-26	L38-46	W96-72

CHALLENGE

Opponents	Home	Away
PL Select	W41-37	W51-27
Southern Stars	–	36-17 (aban.)
Wimbledon	W41-37	–

Notes: The match against Southern Stars (a team actually billed as Silver's Southern Stars) was staged at Exeter, with the meeting abandoned after heat nine. The away match v. the Provincial League Select was also staged at Exeter.

MIDLAND FIVES THREE-TEAM TOURNAMENT

(Staged at Leicester)   Coventry 38, Oxford 32, Swindon 19.

1964

The National League as a whole combined to reopen West Ham in 1964, and also moved to promote Provincial League Champions Wolverhampton in a determined effort to strengthen up. In the end though, the side from the West Midlands turned down promotion and stayed in the successful Provincial League, which boasted twelve teams, while the National League struggled on with just seven sides. Regrettably, the two leagues just grew further and further apart, resulting in the Provincial League completing the season outside the jurisdiction of the Control Board.

The Robins remained in the National League and, as Southampton had closed at the end of the previous season, promoter Bert Hearse brought the Saints' superstar and former World Champion Barry Briggs to Swindon. The arrival of the New Zealander renewed interest in speedway in the town and the brilliant racer duly made his debut for the Robins at Oxford on 27 March in an Easter Cup match. Briggs was to provide plenty of top-end punch and, on 10 July, in an International Best Pairs event, which featured the first visit of Russian riders to Blunsdon, he captured the track record, reducing it to 71.0 seconds dead. Brian Brett had previously lowered the circuit's best time on 13 June in a league match against Norwich, but 'Briggo' made mincemeat of the Essex man's time of 71.6 seconds, shattering it by six-tenths of a second. Another newcomer to the Robins' nest was Colin Pratt, who arrived via Stoke, but he didn't stay long, never actually riding a league match for the club, and quickly returned to Provincial League racing with Hackney.

In mid-summer, Swindon had a shock when Barry Briggs threatened to retire unless the handicap system was abolished. This had hampered his scoring throughout the Britannia Shield competition, as well as in the early league matches. His views were supported by international referee Cecil Telling and, on 22 August, his protest was upheld and his retirement threat forgotten. The Robins had problems assembling a settled side for much of the campaign and quite a number of guests were used. In spite of this they had an interesting blend of youth and experience among their own asset base. Local boy Bob Kilby had his first rides and showed from the beginning that he had what it takes to make good in the sport. Martin Ashby was also progressing along the right lines, and with Brian Brett as well as the ever-reliable Mike Broadbanks, the future looked bright. Swindon also sprang a surprise by signing John Debbage from Norwich, where he had lost his team place. Meanwhile, the Robins gave a few rides to Kiwi Alan Stapleton, although he was only to appear in a single league match. Former Harringay stalwart Danny Dunton even had outings in the team's colours, as did both Roy Bowers and Leo Ramm.

The aforementioned International Best Pairs meeting on 10 July saw Mike Broadbanks and Martin Ashby ride to success, but all eyes were on the Russian pairing of Boris Samorodov and Anatoly Gruzintsev, who gleaned 12 points between them in spectacular fashion. Individually speaking, Brian Brett won a World Championship qualifying round at Swindon on 18 July by plundering a brilliant 15 points. In a tense meeting, no fewer than four riders finished on 12 points to tie for second place, these being Jimmy Gooch, Barry Briggs, Bob Andrews and Trevor Hedge. Less than two months later, at Gothenburg, Sweden, Briggo gave Swindon their first World Champion, scorching to the title with

Swindon Robins, 1964. From left to right, back row: Brian Brett, Barry Briggs, Tadeusz Teodorowicz, Bob Jones (Team Manager), Roy Bowers, Martin Ashby, Bob Kilby. Front, on bike: Mike Broadbanks.

a 15-point maximum. Mike Broadbanks also qualified for the big night on 11 September, and scored 6 points to occupy a middle-order position in the scorechart.

The wonderful successes of Barry Briggs, however, were overshadowed towards the end of the season by a terrible injury to Tadeusz Teodorowicz, sustained in the first leg of the National Trophy semi-final at West Ham on 1 September. A firm favourite with the fans, Teo had made excellent progress since joining the Robins in 1959. He had been so proud to be the British reserve in the 1963 World Final and, during 1964, had qualified for the British Final at Wembley. His chances of any further success ended when he took a nasty tumble in heat twelve of the match at Custom House Stadium, after he had appeared at first to simply over-slide. However, he was subsequently taken to hospital, having become unconscious in the ambulance. For over four months Teo fought for his life but tragically, on 22 January 1965, he was to lose the battle without ever regaining consciousness. He was just thirty-three years of age when he passed away. Fittingly, the inscription on his grave states: 'Too dearly loved to be forgotten.'

Fifth position in the seven-team National League was a disappointment, with the amazing Barry Briggs topping Swindon's scoring on 133 points and a monumental 10.51 average. With so few teams competing, each side completed just twelve fixtures and Briggo recorded six full maximums out of his dozen appearances! In terms of averages, the other mainstays of the Robins' finished as follows: Mike Broadbanks (9.80), Brian Brett (7.14), Tadeusz Teodorowicz (6.57), Martin Ashby (6.00), Bob Kilby (4.90) and Roy Bowers (2.88). As had become the norm, Swindon's home form was a let down, with four defeats suffered out of the six league matches held in front of their own fans. As least they reached the last four in the RAC National Trophy after defeating Wimbledon, but West Ham were much the stronger over the two legs and claimed a 92-76 success. The Britannia Shield had not been staged since 1960, but its return was to be for just the one season, with Swindon managing to win half of their twelve fixtures for a mid-table finishing position of fourth.

SWINDON ROBINS 1964

(Swindon's score shown first unless otherwise stated)

NATIONAL LEAGUE

Opponents	Home	Away
Belle Vue	W49-35	D42-42
Coventry	W44-40	L33-51
Norwich	L40-44	L41-43
Oxford	L40-43	L39-45
West Ham	W51-32	L41-43
Wimbledon	W48-35	L41-43

NATIONAL LEAGUE TABLE

Team	Mts	Won	Drn	Lst	For	Agn.	Pts
Oxford	12	9	0	3	545	461	18
Coventry	12	8	1	3	528.5	479.5	17
Norwich	12	6	0	6	490.5	517.5	12
Belle Vue	12	5	1	6	496	511	11
Swindon	12	4	1	7	509	496	9
Wimbledon	12	4	1	7	475	532	9
West Ham	12	4	0	8	479	526	8

LEAGUE AVERAGES

Rider	Mts	Rds	Pts	Bon.	Tot.	Avge	Maximums
Barry Briggs	12	51	133	1	134	10.51	6 full
Mike Broadbanks	12	49	115	5	120	9.80	2 full
Brian Brett	11	42	71	4	75	7.14	–
Tadeusz Teodorowicz	7	28	41	5	46	6.57	1 full
Martin Ashby	12	46	59	10	69	6.00	–
Leo McAuliffe	2	8	9	2	11	5.50	–
Bengt Jansson	1	4	4	1	5	5.00	–
Ron Mountford	1	4	5	0	5	5.00	–
Bob Kilby	12	31	30	8	38	4.90	–
Arne Pander	1	4	4	0	4	4.00	–
Alan Stapleton	1	2	1	1	2	4.00	–
John Debbage	9	26	17	2	19	2.92	–
Roy Bowers	11	32	19	4	23	2.88	–
Danny Dunton	1	2	1	0	1	2.00	–
Leo Ramm	1	2	0	0	0	0.00	–

RAC NATIONAL TROPHY

Opponents	Home	Away	Aggregate
Bye (Round one)	–	–	–
Wimbledon (Quarter-final)	W53-31	L38-46	W91-77
West Ham (Semi-final)	W43-41	L33-51	L76-92

BRITANNIA SHIELD

Opponents	Home	Away
Belle Vue	W50-34	L33-51
Coventry	L39-45	L33-51
Norwich	W47-37	L29-55
Oxford	W44-40	L31-53
West Ham	W46-38	L39-45
Wimbledon	W45-39	W43-41

BRITANNIA SHIELD TABLE

Team	Mts	Won	Drn	Lst	For	Agn.	Pts
Oxford	12	8	1	3	549	458	17
Coventry	12	8	0	4	541	465	16
Belle Vue	12	6	0	6	504	504	12

Swindon	12	6	0	6	479	529	12
Norwich	12	5	0	7	510	495	10
Wimbledon	12	5	0	7	479	527	10
West Ham	12	3	1	8	461	545	7

EASTER CHALLENGE CUP

Opponents	Home	Away
Oxford	L40-44	L24-60
West Ham	L38-46	L36-48

EASTER CHALLENGE CUP TABLE

Team	Mts	Won	Drn	Lst	For	Agn.	Pts
Norwich	4	3	1	0	180	156	7
Oxford	4	3	0	1	186	150	6
Coventry	4	3	0	1	175	161	6
West Ham	4	2	0	2	169	167	4
Belle Vue	4	1	1	2	170	165	3
Wimbledon	4	1	0	3	157	178	2
Swindon	4	0	0	4	138	198	0

Note: The Easter Challenge Cup was a rather ill-conceived idea involving seven teams who were not actually scheduled to meet each other home and away, like they would in a normal league programme.

CHALLENGE

Opponents	Home	Away
Oxford	–	L38-43

FOUR-TEAM TOURNAMENT

(Staged at Norwich)   Norwich 32, Swindon 31, Wimbledon 17, West Ham 16.

1965

An inquiry conducted by Lord Shawcross happily paved the way for speedway to move forward and get out of its self-made muddle. This resulted in the National and Provincial Leagues amalgamating in 1965 to form an eighteen-team British League, of which Swindon were founder members. Past feuds and disagreements were forgotten and the British Speedway Promoters' Association was formed. There was also a Rider Control Committee to watch over team strengths, and speedway was on the threshold of a new beginning.

Norman Parker was persuaded to return as team manager of the Robins, but things didn't look so great when the Rider Control Committee originally allocated Mike Broadbanks to Oxford, leaving the side with a top three of Barry Briggs, Brian Brett and Martin Ashby. However, Brett insisted he was retiring, so Broady stayed at Blunsdon, captained the side and enjoyed a terrific year, scoring freely wherever he rode. Completing the side were two local lads in Bob Kilby and Mike Keen, plus newcomers Peter Sampson and Alan Jackson. In the beginning Roy Bowers had another spell in the side, but he didn't last long and had lost his place by mid-May. Meanwhile, young Kiwi Frank Shuter had arrived and his fence-scraping antics provided much in the way of entertainment for the fans.

Swindon still struggled, despite having three of the best heat-leaders in the league, as they often received scant support from the back-up department of the side. This was very much a deciding factor in nine of the away matches, which were lost by just 4 points or less, and the Robins ended up occupying fifteenth place in the inaugural season of the British League, some nineteen points adrift of champions West Ham. Barry Briggs was magnificent throughout the year, scorching to a mammoth 378 points and a remarkable 21 maximums (20 full and 1 paid) from the league programme. While Briggo's final average was an amazing 10.91, the redoubtable Broady wasn't far

Swindon Robins, 1965. From left to right, back row: Alan Jackson, Bob Kilby, Roy Bowers, Norman Parker (Team Manager), Barry Briggs, Peter Sampson, Martin Ashby, Mike Keen. Front, on bike: Mike Broadbanks.

behind on a 10.54 figure. Meanwhile, Martin Ashby continued his improvement, raising his average to 8.75, but the remaining riders all finished around the 4-point mark or below, as follows: Roy Bowers (4.29), Bob Kilby (4.11), Mike Keen (3.89), Peter Sampson (3.17), Alan Jackson (2.00) and Frank Shuter (1.53).

The home league match against Wimbledon on 3 July was shrouded in controversy, with the Robins originally winning 41-37. However, the Dons protested about Swindon's use of Clive Hitch and the result was later amended to a 37-36 defeat! The problem arose because Hitch was, at the time, without a track to ride for and was therefore in the 'rider pool' awaiting allocation to another track by the Rider Control Committee. The Robins' use of Hitch was deemed illegal and the 6 points he recorded were expunged from the match result, with the other rider positions being upgraded accordingly. This, however, only affected Peter Sampson, whose points tally was increased from 2+1 to 3+1, to leave the final result of 37-36 in favour of the Dons. Hitch, incidentally, later found himself allocated to Long Eaton by the Rider Control Committee.

On 20 August, Swindon journeyed to Wolverhampton for a league match, but suffered an humiliating 54-24 thrashing. Mike Broadbanks was magnificent in defeat, however, notching a full 15-point maximum; his amazing haul amounting to no less than 62.5 per cent of the Robins' meagre total.

Looking at the Knock-Out Cup, Swindon had a bye in the first round, before digging deep to win 51-45 at Newcastle. Unfortunately, their run came to an end in round three when, despite a tremendous effort, they went down 49-46 at Glasgow on 13 August, with Charlie Monk hitting a marvellous 15-point maximum for the triumphant Tigers. There was some success though, as the lads in red and white recorded an aggregate 87-69 victory over old rivals Oxford in the Supporters' Club Cup.

A memorial meeting was staged at the Abbey for Tadeusz Teodorowicz on 22 May, when a star-studded field turned out to pay their respects to the popular Pole. Barry Briggs streaked to victory with 15 points, while West Ham's Sverre Harrfeldt took second place on 14. The ace New Zealander also scored a maximum when winning a World Championship qualifying round at Blunsdon on 12 June, and he followed that up with a further 15-pointer to take the W.D. & H.O. Wills-sponsored Woodbine

Trophy on 21 August. In the *Sunday Mirror* World Final at Wembley on 18 September Briggo finished fourth with 10 points, while Mike Broadbanks was a non-riding reserve. The brilliant Briggs also retained the Golden Helmet all season long, beating off the challenges of Charlie Monk, Ken McKinlay, George Hunter, Nigel Boocock, Sverre Harrfeldt and Olle Nygren. The icing on the cake for the Kiwi though was when he totalled 14 points to win the first staging of the British League Riders' Championship ahead of Jimmy Gooch (13) and Cyril Maidment (12) at Belle Vue on 16 October.

SWINDON ROBINS 1965

(Swindon's score shown first unless otherwise stated)

BRITISH LEAGUE

Opponents	Home	Away
Belle Vue	W41-37	L35-43
Coventry	W45-33	L30-48
Cradley Heath	L38-40	L38-40
Edinburgh	W49-29	L38-40
Exeter	W46-32	L30-48
Glasgow	W54-24	L38-40
Hackney	W46-32	L38-40
Halifax	L38-40	D39-39
Long Eaton	W44-34	L37-40
Newcastle	W43-35	L35-43
Newport	W48-30	L37-41
Oxford	L38-40	L37-41
Poole	D39-39	W40-37
Sheffield	W52-26	L38-40
West Ham	W45-33	L30-48
Wimbledon	L36-37	L37-41
Wolverhampton	W42-36	L24-54

Note: The home match v. Wimbledon originally ended as a 41-37 victory. However, the Dons protested about Swindon's use of Clive Hitch and the result was later amended to a 37-36 defeat. The problem arose because Hitch was, at the time, without a track to ride for and as such was in the 'rider pool' awaiting allocation to another track by the Rider Control Committee. Therefore, the Robins' use of Hitch was deemed illegal and the 6 points that he scored were expunged from the match result, with rider positions being upgraded accordingly. This, however, only affected Peter Sampson, with the result that instead of the 2+1 points he recorded on the night, his tally was increased by a single point to 3+1.

BRITISH LEAGUE TABLE

Team	Mts	Won	Drn	Lst	For	Agn.	Pts
West Ham	34	23	1	10	1,430	1,215	47
Wimbledon	34	22	2	10	1,396	1,245	46
Coventry	34	20	0	14	1,384	1,258	40
Oxford	34	19	2	13	1,308	1,340	40
Halifax	33	18	3	12	1,322	1,240	39
Newport	34	19	0	15	1,360	1,288	38
Wolverhampton	34	18	1	15	1,429	1,216	37
Hackney	34	18	1	15	1,327.5	1,319.5	37
Exeter	34	18	0	16	1,325.5	1,323.5	36
Poole	34	17	1	16	1,378	1,266	35
Sheffield	34	16	2	16	1,300	1,346	34
Newcastle	34	16	1	17	1,363	1,282	33
Glasgow	34	15	1	18	1,315	1,329	31
Belle Vue	34	15	0	19	1,328	1,312	30
Swindon	34	13	2	19	1,345	1,300	28
Cradley Heath	33	11	1	21	1,132	1,438	23
Edinburgh	34	11	0	23	1,173	1,471	22
Long Eaton	34	7	0	27	1,107	1,534	14

Note: Cradley Heath v. Halifax was not raced.

LEAGUE AVERAGES

Rider	Mts	Rds	Pts	Bon.	Tot.	Avge	Maximums
Barry Briggs	32	139	378	1	379	10.91	20 full; 1 paid
Mike Broadbanks	34	140	358	11	369	10.54	9 full; 6 paid
Martin Ashby	33	139	283	21	304	8.75	6 full; 2 paid
Doug Dearden	1	3	4	0	4	5.33	–
Roy Bowers	7	28	29	1	30	4.29	–
Bob Kilby	30	109	91	21	112	4.11	–
Mike Keen	30	108	89	16	105	3.89	–
Peter Sampson	30	101	73	7	80	3.17	–
Tony Eadon	1	4	2	1	3	3.00	–
Alan Stapleton	2	6	4	0	4	2.67	–
Ray Harris	1	2	1	0	1	2.00	–
Alan Jackson	17	48	19	5	24	2.00	–
Frank Shuter	18	47	14	4	18	1.53	–
Trevor Chamberlain	1	2	0	0	0	0.00	–

KNOCK-OUT CUP

Opponents	Home	Away
Bye (Round one)	–	–
Newcastle (Round two)	–	W51-45
Glasgow (Round three)	–	L46-49

SUPPORTERS' CLUB CUP

Opponents	Home	Away	Aggregate
Oxford	W47-31	W40-38	W87-69

CHALLENGE

Opponents	Home	Away
Hackney	–	L33-45
Oxford	–	W41-36

FOUR-TEAM TOURNAMENT

(Staged at Wolverhampton) Wolverhampton 38, Cradley Heath 21, Sheffield 20, Swindon 17.

BRITISH LEAGUE RIDERS' CHAMPIONSHIP

(Staged at Belle Vue)   Barry Briggs 14 points (1st).

1966

In 1966 things really improved at Blunsdon, with the Robins eventually finishing third in the British League after, at one stage, mounting a real challenge for the Championship. Happily, Clive Hitch joined the club legally, following his controversial appearance the previous year. Pete Munday also arrived, allocated from Poole, while Bob Kilby and Mike Keen came on in leaps and bounds. Six of the team scored at least one full or paid maximum as the Robins went unbeaten at home all season for only the second time in their history. They also won five matches on their travels, these successes being at Glasgow, King's Lynn, Long Eaton, Poole and Wimbledon. During the year, Clive Hitch became the thrill-maker in chief; indeed, his so-called 'Hitchy' dives on the third and fourth bends really had the Swindon faithful cheering.

The season at Blunsdon opened on 8 April, when Cradley Heath were the opponents for a British League encounter. The Heathens used Long Eaton's Ray Wilson as a guest replacement for the absent Clive Featherby, but this didn't prevent the Robins from going on the rampage to win 54-24. Both Barry Briggs and Mike Broadbanks hit four-ride maximums, while Martin Ashby weighed in with a

Swindon Robins, 1966. From left to right, back row: Bob Kilby, Frank Shuter, Barry Briggs, Norman Parker (Team Manager), Clive Hitch, Bill Chandler (Speedway Administrator), Martin Ashby, Mike Keen. Front, on bike: Mike Broadbanks.

haul of 10+1 points. Meanwhile, Clive Hitch gave an indication of what was in store for the faithful fans, with his all-action style netting a tally of 5+2 points.

A home league match *v.* Newcastle on 14 May was memorable, not least because a number of riders suffered engine failures when well placed, culminating in an odd-looking 42-33 scoreline in favour of the Robins. The fun and games began as early as the opening heat, when Clive Hitch ended up doing four laps on his own in a twice re-run race. This was after both visiting riders, Peter Kelly and Mike Watkin, had been excluded for falling, while Barry Briggs also missed out due to not being under power at the time of the second stoppage. Later, both Bob Kilby and Broady were also beset by mechanical gremlins in heats five and twelve respectively, and the meeting was to close in dramatic fashion. Kiwi greats Ivan Mauger and Barry Briggs were expected to give the crowd a grand finale. However, both were plagued by machine troubles. Mauger unfortunately dropped out of the race, but Briggs managed to steer his malfunctioning steed home for third place, taking his tally for the night to an unusually low 7+1 points. At the other end of the spectrum was former Swindon rider Brian Brett, who headed the Newcastle scorechart on 14 points; his only defeat ironically suffered at the hands of Briggs in an exciting heat eleven!

Barry Briggs' dominance at Blunsdon continued unabated, as he roared to victory in both of the big meetings staged during the year, namely the Midland Riders' Championship qualifying round on 18 May and a World Championship qualifying round ten days later. Briggo went on to win the World Championship courtesy of a full 15-point tally at the Ullevi Stadium in Gothenburg, Sweden on 23 September and his teammate Mike Broadbanks also rode, scoring 4 points. Then, at the end of the season, on 22 October, Briggs raced to his second British League Riders' Championship success at Belle Vue with another 15-point full-house. The immaculate Kiwi again topped Swindon's averages with an 11.08 figure and, continuing his catalogue of success, he rattled up a quite staggering eighteen full maximums during the course of his thirty-one league matches! As in 1965, he also retained the Golden Helmet for the entire season, defeating Nigel Boocock, Gote Nordin, Arne Pander, Mike Broadbanks, Ivan Mauger and Sverre Harrfeldt along the way. Regrettably though, Briggo never got the chance to extend his winning streak in the Golden Helmet, since the competition was suspended at the end of the 1966 season and did not resume until 1970.

Mike Broadbanks.

Meanwhile Martin Ashby had a great year and, like Ginger Nicholls in 1949, was married in the morning before making the dash to ride at Swindon, where he plundered an unbeaten 12 points in a comfortable 52-25 victory over Newport on 10 September. 'Crash', as he was affectionately known, recorded 271 league points over the course of the season to finish with a 9.01 average. In a much more solid Robins outfit, Mike Broadbanks averaged 9.70, with Clive Hitch on 5.91 and Bob Kilby on 5.76. Mike Keen progressed well, moving his average up to 5.39, while Frank Shuter also headed in the right direction, finishing with a 4.46 figure.

While Swindon's league form was pretty good, they didn't fare too well in other competitions. For instance, in the Knock-Out Cup, following an earlier bye, they were beaten 50-46 at Wimbledon in the second round. Turning to the Midland Cup, despite home victories against both Wolverhampton and Cradley Heath, the Robins failed to progress to the final, as the qualifying stage was run on a league basis and away defeats in the return matches left them sitting in second position.

It's impossible to cover the 1966 season without mentioning a really special meeting that was held at the Abbey Stadium on 9 July. This was when a West of England team took on the tourists from the USSR in an international challenge match. The meeting resulted in a 59-49 win for the West of Englanders, their success including a sparkling 18-point maximum from the mighty Barry Briggs, as well as 16 points from Mike Broadbanks. A third Robin also appeared in the English side, with Martin Ashby collecting a useful tally of 6+3 points. The spectacular Russians proved to be extraordinary entertainers, with four of their septet finishing on double figures, namely Boris Samorodov (13), Igor Plechanov (12+1), Viktor Trofimov (12) and Yuri Chekranov (10+3). The meeting gave Plechanov the ideal platform to show what he could have done had Swindon been allowed to sign him a few years previously, and when he wasn't in the thick of the action on the track, the fan-friendly racer was busy signing autographs and exchanging badges!

SWINDON ROBINS 1966

(Swindon's score shown first unless otherwise stated)

BRITISH LEAGUE

Opponents	Home	Away
Belle Vue	W53-25	L35-43
Coventry	W45-33	L24-54
Cradley Heath	W54-24	L38-39
Edinburgh	W52-26	L33-45
Exeter	W52-26	L30-48
Glasgow	W53-25	W40-38
Hackney	W46-32	L37-41
Halifax	W49-29	L36-42
King's Lynn	W53-25	W45-33
Long Eaton	W44-34	W39-38

Newcastle	W42-33	L38-40
Newport	W52-25	L34-44
Oxford	W60-18	L38-40
Poole	W45-33	W40-38
Sheffield	W45-33	L38-40
West Ham	W45-33	L37-41
Wimbledon	W43-35	W42-36
Wolverhampton	W58-20	L38-39

BRITISH LEAGUE TABLE

Team	Mts	Won	Drn	Lst	For	Agn.	Pts
Halifax	36	27	0	9	1,574	1,229	54
Coventry	36	25	1	10	1,548	1,255	51
Swindon	36	23	0	13	1,553	1,248	46
Wimbledon	36	22	0	14	1,485	1,314	44
Newcastle	36	20	0	16	1,491.5	1,304.5	40
Poole	36	19	2	15	1,443	1,356	40
West Ham	36	19	1	16	1,499.5	1,304.5	39
Glasgow	36	18	0	18	1,395	1,394	36
Wolverhampton	36	17	2	17	1,340.5	1,461.5	36
Exeter	36	17	1	18	1,392.5	1,403.5	35
Sheffield	36	17	0	19	1,410	1,394	34
Edinburgh	35	17	0	18	1,310.5	1,413.5	34
Belle Vue	36	16	0	20	1,362	1,443	32
Hackney	36	15	1	20	1,347.5	1,456.5	31
Oxford	36	14	2	20	1,291	1,510	30
King's Lynn	36	15	0	21	1,275	1,524	30
Newport	36	12	1	23	1,319	1,486	25
Long Eaton	36	12	1	23	1,286	1,516	25
Cradley Heath	35	10	0	25	1,196	1,506	20

Note: Cradley Heath v. Edinburgh was not raced.

LEAGUE AVERAGES

Rider	Mts	Rds	Pts	Bon.	Tot.	Avge	Maximums
Barry Briggs	31	131	360	3	363	11.08	18 full
Ivan Mauger	1	4	9	1	10	10.00	–
Gote Nordin	1	6	15	0	15	10.00	–
Mike Broadbanks	35	146	342	12	354	9.70	8 full; 2 paid
Martin Ashby	32	131	271	24	295	9.01	3 full
John Ellis	1	2	2	1	3	6.00	–
Clive Hitch	34	130	160	32	192	5.91	3 paid
Bob Kilby	36	136	169	27	196	5.76	2 full; 1 paid
Mike Keen	23	89	98	22	120	5.39	1 paid
Frank Shuter	32	105	97	20	117	4.46	–
Dai Evans	1	4	4	0	4	4.00	–
Pete Munday	18	41	21	5	26	2.54	–
Alan Stapleton	4	9	4	1	5	2.22	–
Brian Black	1	2	1	0	1	2.00	–

KNOCK-OUT CUP

Opponents	Home	Away
Bye (Round one)	–	–
Wimbledon (Round two)	–	L46-50

MIDLAND CUP

Opponents	Home	Away
Wolverhampton	W52-26	L35-43
Cradley Heath	W61-17	L38-40

MIDLAND CUP (WESTERN SECTION) TABLE

Team	Mts	Won	Drn	Lst	For	Agn.	Pts
Wolverhampton	4	3	0	1	154	158	6
Swindon	4	2	0	2	186	126	4
Cradley Heath	4	1	0	3	128	184	2

Note: Wolverhampton progressed to the final.

CHALLENGE

Opponents	Home	Away
Coventry	–	L37-41
Newport	–	L35-43

FOUR-TEAM TOURNAMENT

(Staged at Exeter)   Swindon 44, Exeter 'A' 30, Exeter 'B' 25, Poole 15.

BRITISH LEAGUE RIDERS' CHAMPIONSHIP

(Staged at Belle Vue)   Barry Briggs 15 points (1st).

1967

Swindon became Champions of the British League in 1967. Prior to the season and to the disappointment of the supporters, the Rider Control Board posted the spectacular Clive Hitch to Coventry, but nevertheless the side still boasted four heat-leaders in Mike Broadbanks, Barry Briggs, Martin Ashby and Bob Kilby. The race for the league title was a cliffhanger, since the Championship wasn't won until the very last match against King's Lynn, at the Norfolk club's circuit. Earlier in the year, on 16 June, the Robins had lost their league match at Saddlebow Road by 46 points to 32, but a protest over the homesters' use of Howard Cole earned them a reprieve. Cole had been allocated to the Stars as a replacement for the soon-to-be-leaving former Swindon rider Peter Moore, but there was also an additional proviso that he was allowed to ride if either Terry Betts or David Crane were unfit. However, all four riders (Cole, Moore, Betts and Crane) were not permitted to appear at the same time, as they actually did in the meeting. The match was subsequently declared void and ordered to be restaged. The first attempt to rerun the fixture (on 14 October) was foiled by the weather, but the following week on 20 October, the Robins raced to a 44-34 win and the Championship was on its way to Blunsdon. Little did anyone know then but, aside from a Pairs Championship success in 1994, it would be another thirty-three years before Swindon would lift any further major silverware!

The rampant Robins again won all their home matches, while also gaining valuable away wins at Coventry, Glasgow, Newcastle, Newport and Wimbledon, as well as the aforementioned vital victory at King's Lynn. Barry Briggs had a final league average of 11.05 points per match, and Martin Ashby (8.79), Mike Broadbanks (8.48) and Bob Kilby (8.46) provided the necessary firepower to support the legendary Kiwi all the way. Backing the four-pronged attack were Frank Shuter (4.52), Mike Keen (4.40) and Pete Munday (4.37). The only other rider that Swindon used during a glorious year was Peter Jackson, who had been allocated from Wimbledon at the start of the season, but his opportunities were restricted to just four league matches, from which he averaged 3.43. Peter, incidentally, was the elder brother of Alan, who had also enjoyed outings for the Robins in 1965. In the Knock-Out Cup, Swindon had a bye in the opening round, before defeating Exeter at Blunsdon. They were dumped out of the competition in the next round though, when they lost 51-45 at West Ham on 1 August. An 88-68 aggregate win over Coventry in the Midland Cup final, however, brought another trophy to Wiltshire in what was undoubtedly one of the best years in the Robins' long history.

The season served up its usual share of super racing and incident, with the Blunsdon faithful witnessing one of the most horrific crashes ever seen at the venue when Poole visited for a league

Swindon's Championship-winning squad of 1967, pictured when they returned to Blunsdon for a special meeting twenty-one years later, on 8 October 1988. From left to right, back row: Barry Briggs, Martin Ashby, Mike Keen, Norman Parker (Team Manager), Pete Munday. Front row: Bob Kilby, Mike Broadbanks, Frank Shuter, Peter Jackson.

match on 17 June. Briggo was unfortunately absent for the meeting, but with the Pirates' top man Gote Nordin also missing, both managements used common sense by promoting their number eight riders into their respective sides, namely Peter Jackson (Swindon) and Tony Lewis (Poole). In a thrilling scrap, the Robins claimed a 42-35 success, with both Mike Broadbanks and Bob Kilby bagging 12-point maximums. For the Pirates, Tony Lewis posted two superb race wins, before he was brought into heat ten for an extra outing as a replacement for Norman Strachan. That was when the alarming accident occurred, with the Bournemouth-born rider losing control on the exit of the second bend and going straight over the safety fence, narrowly missing a lamp standard in the process. Thankfully there was an audible sigh of relief a few minutes later when Lewis was able to walk away, albeit gingerly, although quite understandably he didn't ride again on the night.

Three prestigious meetings were held at Blunsdon during the year, the first being a World Championship qualifying round on 13 May, which saw Glasgow's main man Charlie Monk take victory after defeating Martin Ashby in a run-off, both men having tallied 14 points. Wolverhampton's Jim Airey recorded a maximum when winning a Midland Riders' Championship qualifying round on 10 June, while Ray Wilson's 14 points were enough for him to emerge victorious in the Tadeusz Teodorowicz Memorial Trophy on 13 September. Turning to the *Sunday Mirror* World Final, which was held just three days later at Wembley Stadium on 16 September, Barry Briggs had to settle for fifth place after scoring 11 points, while Mike Broadbanks qualified as a reserve, but unfortunately didn't get a ride on the night. Briggo, however, did have the satisfaction of completing a hat-trick of successes in the Belle Vue-staged British League Riders' Championship on 21 October, his five-ride full-house giving him a single-point victory from Coventry's Nigel Boocock.

During the winter months Mike Broadbanks held a very successful training school at Blunsdon, with Mick Bell (who would later become team manager of Swindon in 1997) and local boy Barry Duke showing great potential. Both Broady and Bob Kilby also toured the Soviet Union with the Belle Vue team, and the experience was particularly beneficial to the young 'Kilb'.

SWINDON ROBINS 1967

(Swindon's score shown first unless otherwise stated)

BRITISH LEAGUE

Opponents	Home	Away
Belle Vue	W51-27	L35-43
Coventry	W47-31	W41-37
Cradley Heath	W44-33	L31-46
Edinburgh	W46-32	L28-50
Exeter	W56-22	L30-48
Glasgow	W52-26	W43-35
Hackney	W55-23	L33-45
Halifax	W52-26	L36-42
King's Lynn	W44-34	W44-34
Long Eaton	W47-31	L37-41
Newcastle	W53-24	W46-32
Newport	W52-26	W40-38
Oxford	W53-25	L32-46
Poole	W42-35	L30-48
Sheffield	W51-27	L35-43
West Ham	W50-28	L34-44
Wimbledon	W47-31	W39-38
Wolverhampton	W45-33	L35-42

Note: The Robins had originally ridden and lost 46-32 at King's Lynn on 16 June. However, a Swindon protest that the home side had illegally used both new signing Howard Cole and the rider he was to replace, Peter Moore, was upheld and the meeting declared void. The rescheduled fixture turned out to be the Robins' last league match of the season (on 20 October) and thus had a crucial bearing on the outcome of the title. As things turned out, Swindon made no mistake, racing to a 44-34 victory and becoming League Champions.

BRITISH LEAGUE TABLE

Team	Mts	Won	Drn	Lst	For	Agn.	Pts
Swindon	36	24	0	12	1,536	1,266	48
Coventry	36	22	2	12	1,524	1,275	46
West Ham	36	21	3	12	1,514	1,288	45
Edinburgh	36	20	2	14	1,485	1,318	42
Hackney	36	20	1	15	1,402	1,400	41
Poole	36	17	3	16	1,462	1,339	37
Halifax	36	18	1	17	1,456	1,349	37
Wolverhampton	36	18	1	17	1,423	1,376	37
Sheffield	36	18	1	17	1,333.5	1,470.5	37
Newcastle	36	18	0	18	1,386	1,417	36
Wimbledon	36	16	3	17	1,392	1,409	35
Newport	36	17	1	18	1,387	1,413	35
Glasgow	36	16	2	18	1,343	1,457	34
Oxford	36	16	1	19	1,368.5	1,432.5	33
Exeter	36	16	0	20	1,384.5	1,418.5	32
Belle Vue	36	16	0	20	1,333.5	1,463.5	32
Long Eaton	36	14	3	19	1,322	1,481	31
Cradley Heath	36	12	0	24	1,262	1,533	24
King's Lynn	36	11	0	25	1,297	1,505	22

LEAGUE AVERAGES

Rider	Mts	Rds	Pts	Bon.	Tot.	Avge	Maximums
Barry Briggs	31	126	347	1	348	11.05	17 full; 1 paid
Martin Ashby	36	152	308	26	334	8.79	1 full; 5 paid
Mike Broadbanks	36	141	264	35	299	8.48	4 full; 4 paid
Bob Kilby	36	147	284	27	311	8.46	6 full; 3 paid
Frank Shuter	36	122	105	33	138	4.52	–
Mike Keen	36	120	109	23	132	4.40	–
Pete Munday	35	120	114	17	131	4.37	–
Peter Jackson	4	7	5	1	6	3.43	–

KNOCK-OUT CUP

Opponents	Home	Away
Bye (Round one)	–	–
Exeter (Round two)	W61-35	–
West Ham (Round three)	–	L45-51

MIDLAND CUP

Opponents	Home	Away	Aggregate
Oxford (Semi-final)	W48-30	W40-38	W88-68
Coventry (Final)	W51-27	L37-41	W88-68

CHALLENGE

Opponents	Home	Away
Coventry	W58-50	L26-52
Long Eaton	–	L34-44
Newport	–	L28-50
Oxford	–	L37-41
Wolverhampton	–	W40-38

BRITISH LEAGUE RIDERS' CHAMPIONSHIP

(Staged at Belle Vue)	Barry Briggs 15 points (1st).

1968

Swindon's 'reward' for winning the League Championship was losing Martin Ashby in 1968, allocated to Exeter by the Rider Control Committee. Crash certainly didn't want to leave the Robins' camp, but there is little doubt he matured as a rider as a result of the move. Indeed, he went on to make a World Final appearance at Gothenburg, Sweden on 6 September, when he posted a 5-point tally in a meeting won by Ivan Mauger (15), while Barry Briggs (12) finished as runner-up.

On the administrative front, Norman Parker retired as team manager, with his place being taken by Dick Bradley, a local man from Netheravon and a former rider with both Bristol and Southampton. Happily, Clive Hitch was back after a year at Coventry and while he didn't miss a match for Swindon, it was unreasonable to expect him to be a ready-made replacement for the departed Martin Ashby.

Meanwhile, Bob Kilby missed several meetings through injury after he lost the top of an index finger in a frightful crash at Oxford on 20 June. This, plus the loss of Ashby and the burden of being without Barry Briggs for much of the season due to injuries and international calls, finally took its toll. Operating the rider-replacement facility for the great New Zealander, the Robins lost a proud home record, which had stretched back for over two-and-a-half years. This occurred when Newcastle visited the Abbey Stadium for a league match on 29 June and won a controversial encounter by the narrowest of margins, 39-38. Prior to that, the last time Swindon had lost at the Abbey had actually been on 1 October 1965, when Halifax gained a 40-38 success from a British League encounter. Thus, the defeat against the Diamonds brought to an end an impressive run of fifty-four consecutive victories, which comprised forty-seven league matches, two in the Knock-Out Cup, four in the Midland Cup and a single challenge match. Regrettably, the rot set in at Blunsdon afterwards and further home defeats followed against Cradley Heath, Hackney and West Ham.

Away from home, it was a sorry tale of fourteen defeats, although the Robins did manage to win at Oxford, Poole and West Ham, as well as forcing a 39-39 draw at Cradley Heath. In the final analysis, the side slumped to eleventh position in the nineteen-team British League First Division. Of the thirty-six league fixtures, Briggo rode only in twenty, but he still achieved a brilliant 10.88 average and recorded eleven maximums (10 full and 1 paid). Mike Broadbanks meanwhile remained ever-present throughout a difficult season, and topped the Swindon scoring with 304 points for an

Swindon Robins, 1968. From left to right, back row: Frank Shuter, Clive Hitch, Barry Briggs, Pete Munday. Front, kneeling: Mike Keen, Bob Kilby. On bike: Mike Broadbanks.

8.49 average. Bob Kilby averaged 8.28, with Clive Hitch (6.27), Mike Keen (6.23) and Frank Shuter (5.44) proving solid middle-order men. Meanwhile, Pete Munday wrote his name in the Swindon history books at Blunsdon on 4 May when, riding at reserve in a league match against his old club Poole, he raced to a four-ride maximum (12) in wet and miserable conditions. Points-wise, Munday had a steady season overall, with his spectacular style yielding a 4.89 average. Rounding up the regular riders, Peter Jackson was called into action on sixteen occasions, raising his league average from 3.43 to 4.24.

Swindon had hoped for some luck in the Knock-Out Cup, having seen off the challenges of Oxford and Poole (after a replay) in the second round and quarter-final respectively. However, in the semi-final they unfortunately crashed to an almighty 80-28 defeat at Wimbledon on 12 September. There was some success for the Robins though, when they gained a slender 78-77 aggregate victory over Leicester in the final of the Midland Cup. Having surprisingly failed to win a single big meeting at Blunsdon the previous season, Barry Briggs was back to form in recording a scintillating 15-point maximum to win a World Championship qualifying round at the circuit on 1 June. There was one other individual meeting at the Abbey during the year and this saw Wolverhampton's Jim Airey plunder a full-house to win a Midland Riders' Championship qualifying round on 10 August. As previously mentioned, Briggo may have finished second in the Gothenburg-staged World Final but, yet again, he won the British League Riders' Championship at Belle Vue on 19 October, edging out Eric Boocock of Halifax in a run-off for the title, after both had tied on 14 points.

During the year, on 20 July to be precise, the Abbey Stadium hosted a Test match between Great Britain and Sweden, which featured many of the world's big stars. The British boys came out on top with a 62-46 victory, and leading the way with 15+2 points was former Robin Martin Ashby. Meanwhile, Mike Broadbanks gleaned 14+1 points for the victorious side, while Nigel Boocock chipped in with a tally of 11+2. For the Swedes, Bengt Jansson headed the scoring on 15 points, with Anders Michanek netting 14 and Soren Sjosten grabbing 10+1. Once again, during the winter months, both Mike Broadbanks and Bob Kilby went on tour, this time to Australia with the British Lions. The highlights of the trip for Kilb were 8-point returns at Brisbane and Melbourne, while Broady's best performance was 10 points at Brisbane.

SWINDON ROBINS 1968

(Swindon's score shown first unless otherwise stated)

BRITISH LEAGUE FIRST DIVISION

Opponents	Home	Away
Belle Vue	W56-22	L23-55
Coatbridge	W57-20	L35-43
Coventry	W43-34	L35-43
Cradley Heath	L36-42	D39-39
Exeter	W50-28	L29-49
Glasgow	W61-17	L35-43
Hackney	L36-42	L31-47
Halifax	W48-30	L33-45
King's Lynn	W51-27	L36-42
Leicester	W43-35	L33-45
Newcastle	L38-39	L32-46
Newport	W54-24	L31-47
Oxford	W45-33	W40-38
Poole	W53-24	W40-38
Sheffield	W47-31	L28-50
West Ham	L36-42	W40-37
Wimbledon	W39-38	L34-43
Wolverhampton	W46-32	L35-43

BRITISH LEAGUE FIRST DIVISION TABLE

Team	Mts	Won	Drn	Lst	For	Agn.	Pts
Coventry	36	22	0	14	1,436	1,369	44
Hackney	36	21	2	13	1,421	1,383	44
Exeter	36	20	1	15	1,556.5	1,248.5	41
Sheffield	36	20	1	15	1,463.5	1,337.5	41
Newcastle	36	20	0	16	1,454	1,350	40
West Ham	36	19	1	16	1,454	1,348	39
Halifax	36	19	1	16	1,424	1,379	39
Coatbridge	36	18	1	17	1,404	1,397	37
Wimbledon	36	18	0	18	1,411	1,384	36
Belle Vue	36	18	0	18	1,387	1,417	36
Swindon	36	17	1	18	1,448	1,353	35
Leicester	36	17	1	18	1,373	1,430	35
Newport	36	17	1	18	1,348	1,457	35
Cradley Heath	36	15	4	17	1,373	1,430	34
Oxford	36	17	0	19	1,319	1,487	34
Wolverhampton	36	16	0	20	1,388	1,413	32
Poole	36	13	2	21	1,327	1,478	28
King's Lynn	36	13	1	22	1,330	1,473	27
Glasgow	36	13	1	22	1,312	1,495	27

LEAGUE AVERAGES

Rider	Mts	Rds	Pts	Bon.	Tot.	Avge	Maximums
Barry Briggs	20	86	232	2	234	10.88	10 full; 1 paid
Neil Street	1	4	6	4	10	10.00	–
Mike Broadbanks	36	156	304	27	331	8.49	3 paid
Bob Kilby	31	115	225	13	238	8.28	4 full
Ronnie Genz	1	4	8	0	8	8.00	–
Bill Andrew	1	6	10	1	11	7.33	–
Roy Trigg	1	5	7	2	9	7.20	–
Clive Hitch	36	141	182	39	221	6.27	1 paid
Mike Keen	36	133	165	42	207	6.23	2 paid
Geoff Mudge	1	4	5	1	6	6.00	–
Frank Shuter	34	117	146	13	159	5.44	–
Pete Munday	36	130	132	27	159	4.89	1 full
Peter Jackson	16	34	26	10	36	4.24	–

KNOCK-OUT CUP

Opponents	Home	Away
Bye (Round one)	–	–
Oxford (Round two)	W58-50	–
Poole (Quarter-final)	–	D54-54
Poole (Replay)	W60-47	–
Wimbledon (Semi-final)	–	L28-80

MIDLAND CUP

Opponents	Home	Away	Aggregate
Oxford (Semi-final)	W46-32	W39-38	W85-70
Leicester (Final)	W42-35	L36-42	W78-77

CHALLENGE

Opponents	Home	Away
Coventry	W43-35	W39-38
Oxford	–	W41-37

BRITISH LEAGUE FIRST DIVISION RIDERS' CHAMPIONSHIP

(Staged at Belle Vue)   Barry Briggs 14 points (1st).

1969

On the team front in 1969, the Rider Control Committee moved Frank Shuter to Poole, while Peter Jackson linked with Wolverhampton. As had happened with the posting of Martin Ashby to Exeter the previous year, neither rider wanted to leave the Robins' nest. Both Malcolm 'Mac' Woolford and Barry Duke were given opportunities in the Swindon side and, at the latter end of the season, Norwegian Jon Odegaard (who was to become European Long-track Champion in 1970) rode in a couple of league matches. Meanwhile, Des Lukehurst rode in a single match for the Robins and young Australian Bob Tabet also had a couple of outings.

Early on in the season, on 19 April, Barry Briggs knocked a fifth of a second off his own track record, which had stood since 1964. His new best time of 70.8 seconds was set in the opening heat of a First Division match against Poole. Prior to that, Swindon had begun the season with a creditable 39-39 draw in the Shires Challenge Cup at Coventry on 22 March, when Martin Ashby guested in place of Barry Briggs and raced to a fabulous 12-point maximum. The home programme opened the following Saturday, 29 March, with the Robins facing Halifax in a league encounter. The meeting had an unusual 3.15 p.m. start time, which had been agreed due to a key match for Swindon Town FC at the County Ground later in the evening. Briggs returned to the line-up for the match and although his steeds seemed to be lacking in power, he still netted 8+2 points in a 43-34 success. Clive Hitch also carded 8+2, but it was the diminutive Mike Keen who headed the scorechart on 9 points. One of the loudest cheers occurred in heat two, however, when the inexperienced Barry Duke took the flag in an impressive 73.8 seconds. Following the main match, the Blunsdon faithful couldn't quite believe their eyes when visiting number one Eric Boocock sped away to defeat Briggs in the Silver Sash Match Race.

A terrific buzz reverberated around the Abbey Stadium on 3 May, when Belle Vue visited for a First Division fixture. The start of the meeting was delayed in order to allow all the patrons a chance to find a vantage point before the heat one battle between Kiwi giants Barry Briggs and Ivan Mauger. In the event, they were to witness Briggs suffer an exclusion after Norman Nevitt had tumbled down. The majority in the huge crowd felt the decision harsh and voiced their feelings in no uncertain terms. There was no wavering from referee Cecil Telling though, with Mauger and Nevitt duly collecting an untroubled 5-0 in the rerun after Pete Munday had fallen. Mauger went on to record a four-ride full-house, but it was the Robins who came out on top in a hard-fought encounter, winning 40-36.

Swindon Robins, 1969. From left to right, back row: Bob Kilby, Barry Duke, Barry Briggs, Mac Woolford, Pete Munday, Clive Hitch, Dick Bradley (Team Manager), Mike Keen. On bike: Mike Broadbanks.

One of two special events staged during the season was the Twenty-First Anniversary Challenge on 19 July, when Wimbledon (including Ronnie Moore) were the visitors. The night was a memorable one, for not only did Swindon win 44-34, but also many former Robins riders returned to Blunsdon and a highlight was their parade around the track, throwing sticks of rock to the children. The second noteworthy event of the year was the England *v.* New Zealand Test match on 6 August, when Martin Ashby returned to Blunsdon to ride for the Lions and netted 12 points. Bob Kilby was also capped at reserve, but failed to record any points. Meanwhile, Barry Briggs captained and top scored for the Kiwis with an unbeaten 17+1 points from six starts, his efforts helping the New Zealanders to a crushing 65-43 victory. During the year, the Abbey Stadium also played host to two important individual meetings, with Wolverhampton's Norman Hunter recording 14 points to win a Midland Riders' Championship qualifying round on 14 May, while the remarkable Barry Briggs plundered a five-ride maximum to emerge triumphant from a World Championship qualifying round on 11 June. In a repeat of the previous year, Briggo was to go on and finish as runner-up to Ivan Mauger in the *Sunday Mirror* World Final at Wembley on 13 September, after defeating Soren Sjosten in a run-off.

It wasn't the best of seasons for Swindon, who finished tenth in a nineteen-team British League First Division. Home form was again the side's Achilles heel as three matches ended in defeat, against Coatbridge, Glasgow and Poole. Having said that, away victories were gained at Coventry, Exeter and Hackney, but in winning exactly half of their allotted fixtures, the Robins finished 17 points adrift of the Champions, Poole, in the final standings. In the Knock-Out Cup Swindon lost out to Cradley Heath in the quarter-final, while defeat in the Midland Cup came at the semi-final stage to a determined Leicester outfit who won both legs. Barry Briggs once again topped the league averages with an 11.09 figure, scoring 425 points and recording 17 full maximums. Amazingly, for the fifth season in a row, Briggo again travelled up to Belle Vue to win the prestigious British League Riders' Championship, which was run on 18 October and jointly sponsored by local companies B. French of Salford and Relite from Oldham. The tall-scoring Kiwi lacked real support at Swindon, however, with Bob Kilby next in the averages on 7.80, followed by Mike Keen on 6.80. Regrettably, the outstanding career of Mike Broadbanks was temporarily halted in a home league match against Hackney on 26 July, when the Robins' skipper crashed heavily and was taken to hospital with a broken thigh. The injury was a serious one and was to keep Broady out of action for well over a year.

SWINDON ROBINS 1969

(Swindon's score shown first unless otherwise stated)

BRITISH LEAGUE FIRST DIVISION

Opponents	Home	Away
Belle Vue	W40-36	L31-47
Coatbridge	L38-40	L38-40
Coventry	W40-38	W39-38
Cradley Heath	W42-35	L33-45
Exeter	W46-32	W39-38
Glasgow	L35-43	L36-42
Hackney	W40-38	W42-36
Halifax	W43-34	L28-50
King's Lynn	W41-37	L34-44
Leicester	W40-38	L30-48
Newcastle	W45-32	L34-44
Newport	W54-24	L37-41
Oxford	W49-29	L33-45
Poole	L37-41	L29-48
Sheffield	W40-38	L32-46
West Ham	W57-20	L38-40
Wimbledon	W40-37	L32-46
Wolverhampton	W43-35	L35-43

BRITISH LEAGUE FIRST DIVISION TABLE

Team	Mts	Won	Drn	Lst	For	Agn.	Pts
Poole	36	26	1	9	1,518.5	1,284.5	53
Belle Vue	36	23	1	12	1,533	1,268	47
Wimbledon	36	22	2	12	1,555.5	1,248.5	46
Halifax	36	22	2	12	1,483	1,244	46
Leicester	36	21	2	13	1,493	1,312	44
Sheffield	36	19	1	16	1,467.5	1,336.5	39
Cradley Heath	36	18	2	16	1,376	1,426	38
Glasgow	36	17	3	16	1,423	1,380	37
King's Lynn	36	18	0	18	1,413	1,390	36
Swindon	36	18	0	18	1,390	1,408	36
Coatbridge	36	17	1	18	1,390	1,418	35
Exeter	36	16	0	20	1,378	1,425	32
Newcastle	36	15	2	19	1,348	1,450	32
Coventry	36	14	3	19	1,419.5	1,383.5	31
Oxford	36	15	1	20	1,290	1,436	31
Wolverhampton	36	13	1	22	1,311	1,494	27
Newport	36	13	1	22	1,256	1,546	27
West Ham	36	11	3	22	1,276	1,527	25
Hackney	36	10	2	24	1,229	1,573	22

LEAGUE AVERAGES

Rider	Mts	Rds	Pts	Bon.	Tot.	Avge	Maximums
Martin Ashby	1	5	15	0	15	12.00	1 full
Barry Briggs	33	154	425	2	427	11.09	17 full
Bob Kilby	31	123	223	17	240	7.80	3 full
Mike Keen	29	107	165	17	182	6.80	1 full
Mike Broadbanks	22	85	114	16	130	6.12	–
Pete Bradshaw	1	2	3	0	3	6.00	–
Des Lukehurst	1	4	6	0	6	6.00	–
Clive Hitch	36	150	167	35	202	5.39	–
Pete Munday	35	137	141	24	165	4.82	1 paid
Barry Duke	32	107	102	22	124	4.64	–

Jon Odegaard	2	8	9	0	9	4.50	–
Mac Woolford	19	49	20	5	25	2.04	–
Bob Tabet	2	4	0	0	0	0.00	–

KNOCK-OUT CUP

Opponents	Home	Away
Bye (Round one)	–	–
Leicester (Round two)	W47-31	–
Cradley Heath (Quarter-final)	–	L37-41

MIDLAND CUP

Opponents	Home	Away	Aggregate
Leicester (Semi-final)	L38-40	L33.5-44.5	L71.5-84.5

SHIRES CHALLENGE CUP

Opponents	Home	Away	Aggregate
Coventry	W49-29	D39-39	W88-68

TWENTY-FIRST-ANNIVERSARY CHALLENGE

Opponents	Home	Away
Wimbledon	W44-34	–

CHALLENGE

Opponents	Home	Away
Newport	–	W43-35
Oxford	–	L32-46

B. FRENCH/RELITE BRITISH LEAGUE FIRST DIVISION RIDERS' CHAMPIONSHIP

(Staged at Belle Vue)   Barry Briggs 14 points (1st).

1970

In 1970, Swindon found themselves at the lower end of the league table; in sixteenth position to be exact, but the standard of racing was terrific and the home meetings against Sheffield and Halifax left the fans quite breathless. In both matches the Robins came from 10 points behind, forcing a 39-39 draw v. Sheffield on 22 August, before clinching a 41-37 victory against Halifax seven days afterwards. As had become commonplace though, Swindon dropped several league points at home, losing to Belle Vue, Cradley Heath, Poole and Wimbledon, while drawing against Sheffield in the previously mentioned match.

John Bishop joined the club from Oxford, but it was a season of struggle as he could only muster 66 points from his thirty-one league matches, and a 3.40 average told its own story. Barry Duke was ever-present in league matches and impressed greatly with a tally of 155 points yielding a 5.37 average. At the top end, Bob Kilby (359 points) outscored Barry Briggs (351) during the season, but to be fair, Briggo rode in five fewer matches. Kilby had really established himself as an international rider and his final league average was a high 9.64, with 10 full maximums and a paid one to boot. As ever though, Briggs topped the statistical run-down, finishing with a massive 10.51 figure and a dozen full maximums to his name.

Swindon went straight into the league campaign, opening with a home match against Coventry on 27 March, when Bob Kilby plundered an unbeaten 11+1 points in a 42-36 success. The second event of the year at Blunsdon brought an Ove Fundin-led Wembley to town on further league business. The sparks really flew when 'Kilb' met the brilliant Swede in heat three, but in a race that was twice

Swindon Robins, 1970. From left to right, back row: Barry Duke, Bob Jones (Mechanic), Bob Kilby, Pete Munday, Clive Hitch, Dick Bradley (Team Manager), Mike Keen, John Bishop. Front, on bike: Barry Briggs.

rerun, the fast-starting Robin showed his mettle to take victory and, as an added bonus, teammate Pete Munday relegated Fundin to third place! Both Kilby and Barry Briggs went on to record four-ride full-houses in an excellent Swindon win by 48 points to 29.

The Robins battled past Wolverhampton and Leicester on their way to the Knock-Out Cup semi-final, where they regrettably went down to a 44-34 defeat at Wimbledon on 24 September. Meanwhile, for the second year running, Leicester knocked Swindon out of the Midland Cup at the semi-final stage, with the victorious Lions again winning both legs.

The Blunsdon track record was broken in successive weeks, firstly when Bob Kilby brought the time down to 70.6 seconds in the Midland Riders' Championship qualifying round on 1 August. Seven days later, the great Barry Briggs scorched around in 70.2 seconds against Hackney in a First Division fixture and, needless to say, nobody else got near the new best time during the remainder of the season.

Barry Briggs was again triumphant on the individual front, winning two more events at Blunsdon. The first was a World Championship qualifying round on 2 May, when he compiled a faultless 15-point total to triumph ahead of fellow Robin Bob Kilby (14). Then, in the aforementioned Midland Riders' Championship qualifying round, he carded another five-ride maximum to again finish a single point in front of Kilby. The amazing New Zealander wasn't so fortunate in the World Final at the Olympic Stadium, Wroclaw in Poland on 6 September, however, when he could only muster 7 points. He bounced back in typical fashion though, beating Anders Michanek and Eric Boocock in a title run-off to notch his sixth straight victory in the British League Riders' Championship at Belle Vue on 17 October!

Having been rained off on 19 August, the Junior Championship of the British Isles subsequently went ahead at the Abbey Stadium on 2 September. Unluckily, Barry Duke's chances of success were dashed when he suffered a broken collarbone in his very first outing. Instead, Barry Thomas eventually won the meeting after defeating Dave Jessup in a dramatic title run-off, but the line-up also featured several other riders who would go on and grace the British racing scene for many years, including the third-placed Mick Bell, plus the likes of Bobby Beaton, Ian Turner and Gordon Kennett. While on the subject of youth, Swindon sent a Young Robins side on the road for three challenge matches

Clive Hitch.

during the summer. The fledglings were beaten at both Plymouth and Sheffield, but emerged from Shelbourne Park in Dublin with a 39-38 victory under their belts. While recovering from his injuries of the previous year, Mike Broadbanks spent much time helping the juniors and indeed it was he who took the so-called Swindon 'B' side to Shelbourne for their match on 5 July. While the meeting certainly provided plenty of thrills for the spectators, it created nightmares for the statistically minded since, although the points for each rider were recorded, the heat details still remain a mystery to this day!

Late in the season there was great joy in the home league match against Cradley Heath on 5 September, when Mike Broadbanks returned to active racing, scoring 7 points. Unfortunately, Broady rode in just one more league fixture and a Midland Cup match before ending his comeback for the year.

SWINDON ROBINS 1970

(Swindon's score shown first unless otherwise stated)

BRITISH LEAGUE FIRST DIVISION

Opponents	Home	Away
Belle Vue	L38-40	L35-43
Coventry	W42-36	L32-46
Cradley Heath	L33-45	L27-51
Exeter	W57-21	L32-46
Glasgow	W40-38	D39-39
Hackney	W41-37	L36-42
Halifax	W41-37	L28-49
King's Lynn	W40-37	L36-42
Leicester	W43-35	L38-40
Newcastle	W51-27	L36-42
Newport	W56-22	L34-44
Oxford	W43-34	L29-49
Poole	L37-41	L30-48
Sheffield	D39-39	L32-46

Wembley	W48-29	L37-41
West Ham	W43-35	W41-37
Wimbledon	L38-40	L34-44
Wolverhampton	W48-30	L32-46

BRITISH LEAGUE FIRST DIVISION TABLE

Team	Mts	Won	Drn	Lst	For	Agn.	Pts
Belle Vue	36	27	2	7	1,595.5	1,205.5	56
Wimbledon	36	22	2	12	1,506	1,297	46
Coventry	36	22	1	13	1,517.5	1,287.5	45
Leicester	36	21	0	15	1,423	1,381	42
Poole	36	20	0	16	1,392	1,409	40
Halifax	36	19	1	16	1,492.5	1,313.5	39
Sheffield	36	18	3	15	1,414.5	1,391.5	39
Glasgow	36	18	1	17	1,438	1,367	37
Wolverhampton	36	16	2	18	1,371	1,433	34
Exeter	36	16	1	19	1,369.5	1,434.5	33
Hackney	36	15	2	19	1,369.5	1,435.5	32
King's Lynn	36	16	0	20	1,359	1,443	32
Oxford	36	16	0	20	1,360.5	1,445.5	32
Wembley	36	15	2	19	1,327.5	1,474.5	32
Cradley Heath	36	15	1	20	1,351.5	1,445.5	31
Swindon	36	14	2	20	1,386	1,418	30
Newcastle	36	15	0	21	1,364	1,444	30
West Ham	36	14	2	20	1,341.5	1,463.5	30
Newport	36	12	0	24	1,258	1,548	24

LEAGUE AVERAGES

Rider	Mts	Rds	Pts	Bon.	Tot.	Avge	Maximums
Barry Briggs	31	134	351	1	352	10.51	12 full
Bob Kilby	36	151	359	5	364	9.64	10 full; 1 paid
Tony Clarke	2	9	16	2	18	8.00	–
John Boulger	1	5	8	0	8	6.40	–
Mike Broadbanks	2	7	9	1	10	5.71	–
Clive Hitch	36	139	163	27	190	5.47	1 paid
Barry Duke	36	140	155	33	188	5.37	1 paid
Pete Munday	36	138	140	22	162	4.70	–
Mike Keen	35	117	108	17	125	4.27	–
Pat Johnson	1	1	1	0	1	4.00	–
John Bishop	31	93	66	13	79	3.40	–
Mac Woolford	4	11	9	0	9	3.27	–
Pete Smith	1	3	1	0	1	1.33	–

KNOCK-OUT CUP

Opponents	Home	Away
Bye (Round one)	–	–
Wolverhampton (Round two)	W44-34	–
Leicester (Quarter-final)	W46-32	–
Wimbledon (Semi-final)	–	L34-44

MIDLAND CUP

Opponents	Home	Away	Aggregate
Oxford (Quarter-final)	W46-32	W41-37	W87-69
Leicester (Semi-final)	L36-41	L33-45	L69-86

50 GUINEAS CHALLENGE

Opponents	Home	Away	Aggregate
Poole	W41-37	L36-41	L77-78

CHALLENGE

Opponents	Home	Away
Plymouth	–	L32-46
Sheffield 'B'	–	L16-62
Shelbourne	–	W39-38

Note: In all three challenge matches, the Swindon side was billed as 'Young Robins'.

BRITISH LEAGUE FIRST DIVISION RIDERS' CHAMPIONSHIP

(Staged at Belle Vue)   Barry Briggs 13 points (1st).

1971

There was good and bad news for the Swindon supporters before the 1971 season got underway. On the positive front, Martin Ashby was welcomed back to Blunsdon after three years at Exeter. However, the downside of having Ashby back was that the Rider Control Committee posted Bob Kilby to the Falcons as his replacement! This was tempered somewhat by a full-time return from Mike Broadbanks, who was able to resume having finally overcome the effects of a serious leg injury suffered in a home league match *v.* Hackney on 26 July 1969.

The Robins first took to the track on 27 March, when West Ham provided the opposition for a league match at Blunsdon. The boys in red and white were eager to get going and this was evident as they swamped the Hammers, winning 47-31. Both Barry Briggs and Martin Ashby powered to faultless 12-point maximums, while Mike Keen revealed sparkling form to score a paid full-house (11+1). The second heat produced the loudest cheer of the evening when Mike Broadbanks raced to victory and, making it extra special, young teammate Clark Facey followed him home for a 5-1.

Local rivals Reading then visited Swindon on 3 April and found the Robins too hot to handle. Led by another undefeated total from Martin Ashby (12), the homesters ran out 45-33 victors, with Mike Keen (10+1) again scoring well. Meanwhile, Barry Briggs netted 9+1 points, being beaten by Reading guest Norman Hunter in the opening race, before later running a third place behind the second Racers stand-in, Ray Wilson, and the other Swindon representative in the heat, Clive Hitch. Such was his standing in the world of speedway that it was a real talking point if the Kiwi failed to finish outside the first two positions in any race!

With the Briggs/Ashby spearhead the Robins looked a powerful outfit, but often on away trips the scoring was left solely to the dynamic duo. Mike Keen looked very good at times, but a series of niggling injuries countered his 'try-all-the-time' efforts. The returned Mike Broadbanks, along with Clive Hitch and Pete Munday all struggled to find their best form, while a young Scot, Jimmy Gallacher, appeared on the scene, and James Bond also arrived via Wolverhampton.

The Abbey Stadium regulars were treated to several mouth-watering meetings during the year, the first of which saw Barry Briggs net a full 15 points to again win a World Championship qualifying round on 17 April. Fellow Robin Martin Ashby filled second position a point behind, while Glasgow's George Hunter occupied third place with a tally of 13. Then Great Britain annihilated Poland by 80 points to 28 in a particularly one-sided Test match on 22 May, with both Ronnie Moore (14+1) and Trevor Hedge (12+3) posting paid maximums, while Jim Airey (13+1), Ray Wilson (12), Jim McMillan (11+3) and Bruce Cribb (10+1) also hit double figures. For the beleaguered Poles, Andrzej Wygleda (8) and future World Champion Jerzy Szczakiel (7+1) were the best of a disappointing bunch.

On 14 July, Blunsdon again played host to the Junior Championship of the British Isles, which was won in emphatic style by Ian 'Tiddler' Turner of King's Lynn with a faultless 15-point maximum. The runner-up from the previous year, Dave Jessup, had to be satisfied with the same position again, while other competitors included Tony Davey, Gordon Kennett, Peter Collins and future Robin Geoff Bouchard. The fourth and final 'biggie' of the year at Swindon was the Midland Riders'

Programme illustration from the Junior Championship of the British Isles, which was staged at Blunsdon on 14 July 1971.

Championship qualifying round on 16 July, which was won by Barry Briggs with a full 15-point score. Martin Ashby (14) again finished second to the Kiwi great, while Leicester's John Boulger (12) completed the podium positions.

Home form once more cost Swindon dearly, with defeats against Belle Vue, Exeter, King's Lynn and Leicester being difficult for the Blunsdon faithful to swallow. However, thanks to an impressive list of away triumphs at Cradley Heath, Hackney, Oxford, West Ham and Wolverhampton, the Robins managed to finish fifth in the league standings. A 41-37 defeat at Exeter on 6 September also turned into a victory, following an appeal. This after the Falcons had tracked all three of their heat-leaders and used rider replacement as well! Swindon's protest was subsequently upheld and the 8 points realised by rider-replacement were expunged, with the race positions upgraded accordingly to give Swindon a 42-36 victory.

The Robins didn't remain in any other competitions for too long, losing at home to Hackney in round two of the *Speedway Star*-sponsored Knock-Out Cup, having overcome Wimbledon at the first hurdle. Meanwhile, in the Midland Cup they suffered an opening-round loss at the hands of Wolverhampton, being beaten by a handful of points in both legs for an aggregate reverse of 82-71.

Barry Briggs was again top of the averages on a mighty 10.64 figure, but for the first time he failed to retain the British League Riders' Championship, run at Belle Vue on 16 October. With 14 points, it was compatriot Ivan Mauger who took the title, while Briggo eventually finished second after defeating Glasgow's Jim McMillan in a run-off, both speedsters having tallied a dozen points. Regrettably, Briggs created another unwanted record when he missed out on a World Final place for the very first time in eighteen years. The returning Martin Ashby plundered 361 points during the league campaign for an average of 9.70, which proved what a tremendous rider he had developed into during his time at Exeter. The popular Crash also set a new track record at Blunsdon, storming around the 395-yard raceway in 70.0 seconds dead in heat five of a First Division match against Belle Vue on 1 May. Ever-present Mike Keen averaged 6.70 but, after that, the other Robins' figures dropped away steeply. Although Mike Broadbanks only missed a single league match, he was unfortunately a pale shadow of his former self, scoring just 121 points for a 4.94 average. Both Clive Hitch and Pete Munday struggled too, averaging 4.79 and 3.84 respectively, while the new boys also fared poorly, with Jimmy Gallacher finishing on 3.93, and James Bond on 3.43.

SWINDON ROBINS 1971

(Swindon's score shown first unless otherwise stated)

BRITISH LEAGUE FIRST DIVISION

Opponents	Home	Away
Belle Vue	L36-41	L23-55
Coventry	W48-30	L29-49
Cradley Heath	W42-36	W42-36
Exeter	L37-41	W42-36
Glasgow	W43-35	L28-50
Hackney	D39-39	W45-33
Halifax	W42-36	L38-40
King's Lynn	L35-43	L34-44
Leicester	L38-40	L31-47
Newport	W47-31	L31-47
Oxford	W49-29	W41-36
Poole	W42-36	L38-40
Reading	W45-33	D39-39
Sheffield	W41-37	L31-47
Wembley	W43-34	L35-43
West Ham	W47-31	W41-37
Wimbledon	W50-28	D39-39
Wolverhampton	W42-36	W40-38

Note: The away match at Exeter originally ended in a 41-37 defeat; however, after successfully appealing, the result was amended to a 42-36 victory for Swindon. Despite having all three of their heat leaders in action on the night, Exeter also used rider replacement as well. The Robins' protest was upheld and the 8 points recorded from rider replacement outings were expunged, with the race positions being upgraded accordingly.

BRITISH LEAGUE FIRST DIVISION TABLE

Team	Mts	Won	Drn	Lst	For	Agn.	Pts
Belle Vue	36	25	1	10	1,583	1,217	51
Leicester	36	22	3	11	1,490	1,309	47
Coventry	36	23	0	13	1,495	1,310	46
Sheffield	36	21	1	14	1,450	1,357	43
Swindon	36	19	3	14	1,413	1,392	41
Reading	36	18	4	14	1,438	1,361	40
Hackney	36	17	4	15	1,410	1,393	38
Newport	36	19	0	17	1,390	1,416	38
Wembley	36	17	3	16	1,433	1,372	37
Wimbledon	36	18	1	17	1,389	1,415	37
Poole	36	17	2	17	1,407	1,399	36
Wolverhampton	36	17	1	18	1,382	1,412	35
King's Lynn	36	16	2	18	1,396.5	1,406.5	34
Halifax	36	16	2	18	1,374	1,430	34
Exeter	36	16	0	20	1,379	1,424	32
Glasgow	36	15	1	20	1,403	1,401	31
Oxford	36	12	1	23	1,263.5	1,537.5	25
Cradley Heath	36	8	4	24	1,298	1,507	20
West Ham	36	9	1	26	1,236	1,571	19

LEAGUE AVERAGES

Rider	Mts	Rds	Pts	Bon.	Tot.	Avge	Maximums
Terry Betts	1	4	10	1	11	11.00	–
Barry Briggs	33	144	382	1	383	10.64	12 full
Olle Nygren	1	4	9	1	10	10.00	–
Martin Ashby	35	153	361	10	371	9.70	8 full
Trevor Hedge	1	4	7	0	7	7.00	–
Mike Keen	36	135	209	17	226	6.70	1 paid
Mike Broadbanks	35	124	121	32	153	4.94	–
Clive Hitch	30	111	115	18	133	4.79	–
Jimmy Gallacher	16	54	49	4	53	3.93	–
Pete Munday	34	127	106	16	122	3.84	1 paid
James Bond	17	49	33	9	42	3.43	–
Barry Duke	3	10	5	1	6	2.40	–
Clark Facey	5	13	5	2	7	2.15	–
Ralph Waller	1	2	1	0	1	2.00	–
George Beaton	1	2	0	0	0	0.00	–
Bob Coles	1	2	0	0	0	0.00	–
Brian Murray	1	2	0	0	0	0.00	–
Paul Tyrer	1	2	0	0	0	0.00	–

SPEEDWAY STAR KNOCK-OUT CUP

Opponents	Home	Away
Wimbledon (Round one)	W43-35	–
Hackney (Round two)	L36-42	–

MIDLAND CUP

Opponents	Home	Away	Aggregate
Wolverhampton (Round one)	L35-41	L36-41	L71-82

CHALLENGE

Opponents	Home	Away
Reading	W42-36	–

FOUR COUNTIES FOUR-TEAM TOURNAMENT

(Staged at Newport)   Newport 32, Swindon 26, Poole 25, Exeter 12.

FOUR-TEAM TOURNAMENT

(Staged at Swindon)   Swindon 29, Coventry 28, Exeter 25, Wimbledon 14.
(Staged at Newport)   Newport 36, Swindon 21, Exeter 21, Coventry 18.

BRITISH LEAGUE FIRST DIVISION RIDERS' CHAMPIONSHIP

(Staged at Belle Vue)   Barry Briggs 12 points (2nd).

1972

There were many changes and disappointments during the 1972 campaign as far as Swindon were concerned. Barry Briggs and Martin Ashby again formed the attack, while Brian Leonard joined the Robins' nest from Wembley as a replacement for the retired Pete Munday. After coming on board via Wolverhampton the previous summer, James Bond was in the starting line-up for the season but, having attained a league average of only 3.76 from twelve matches, he was 'rested' by general manager Ted Nelson. Swindon had hoped to purchase Garry Flood from Crewe but, in the end, the Kings' boss Maury Littlechild understandably decided not to part with the up-and-coming Aussie. A move that did go through occurred in late July, when Norman Hunter got his wish and joined the Robins following a disagreement with Wolverhampton. Unsurprisingly, Briggs and Ashby both finished the campaign with averages in excess of 10 points per match. However Briggo, following a run of machine problems and a disappointing display in the Wills Internationale at Wimbledon on 29 May, took a two-week break from speedway in sunny Spain. Having come on board, 'Storming' Norman Hunter bolstered up the middle order, finishing with a 6.08 figure, while Mike Broadbanks (5.01) and Clive Hitch (4.25) enjoyed only mediocre seasons. David Ashby, the younger brother of Martin, looked very promising and rode in nine league matches. Later, in order to further his learning curve, he was loaned to Second Division Peterborough. Meanwhile, Mike Keen's scoring took a dive and he ended the season with just 83 league points and an average of 3.96.

It wasn't surprising then that the Robins could only manage fifteenth position in the final league table. Very much as usual, many points were dropped at home, with losses suffered at the hands of Belle Vue, Hackney, Reading and Sheffield, while the match against Leicester was drawn. The theory has long since been that the brilliant Blunsdon raceway is too fair and gives all teams a chance of success when visiting its wide-open spaces. The campaign was marred by the death of Svein Kaasa when Swindon visited Glasgow on 29 September. The twenty-five-year-old had started the season at Oxford, prior to linking with the Scottish outfit after losing his place in the Cheetahs side to Preben Rosenkilde. Unfortunately, in heat eleven of the match against the Robins the Norwegian inadvertently clipped Martin Ashby's rear wheel while trying to overtake on the outside, and was thrown head-first into the safety fence. Tragically, after falling unconscious, the popular youngster lost his life on the Hampden Park track.

An interesting youngster appeared on the scene in the second half of meetings at Blunsdon, going by the name of Bobo Valentine. His real first name was actually David and he hailed from Auckland, New Zealand. Of all the juniors, he was one of the most impressive and he even enjoyed a couple of senior league outings towards the end of the season.

Losing to Exeter in the first round of the *Speedway Star* Knock-Out Cup did nothing to lift morale, while bogey side Leicester again dumped the Robins out of the Midland Cup at the semi-final stage. This was after a controversial quarter-final replay at the home of old rivals Oxford, which had originally ended in a 41-36 defeat. However, after successfully appealing, the result was amended to a 40-38 victory. The bone of contention occurred in heat eleven, which had ended as a 4-2 to the Robins' pairing of Barry Briggs and Clive Hitch. Inexplicably, the referee deemed that there had been a starting gate infringement prior to the race and ordered a rerun! The two Swindon lads refused to come to the line for the restart and were excluded, with the Oxford duo of Rick Timmo and Colin Gooddy subsequently riding to an untroubled 5-0. The Speedway Control Board was quick to act and upheld the Robins' appeal, reinstating the original result of the heat.

The programme from the first staging of the Silver Plume at the Abbey Stadium on 14 June 1972.

Blunsdon staged an Inter-Nations Championship match between Sweden and New Zealand on 15 July and, in a one-sided affair, it was the Swedes who ran out convincing winners by 50 points to 28. The Scandinavians were led to victory by unbeaten tallies from Christer Lofqvist (12) and Hasse Holmqvist (9+3), with Anders Michanek netting 11 points. Meanwhile, the Kiwis' top men were Ronnie Moore (9) and Bob Andrews (8). The Abbey Stadium also played host to three individual meetings during the year, with Leicester's Ray Wilson taking the honours in the Midland Riders' Championship qualifying round on 17 May, prior to claiming a further success shortly afterwards in the first ever staging of the prestigious Silver Plume on 14 June. The latter event featured many world-class stars such as Ole Olsen, Ronnie Moore, Anders Michanek and Ivan Mauger. On a night of superb racing, Wilson went about the business of compiling a quite beautiful full-house (15) to take victory from home man Barry Briggs (14) and Exeter's Bob Kilby (12).

Staged in-between, on 27 May, the other big event of the season was a World Championship qualifying round, which was won in great style by maximum man Barry Briggs (15), ahead of club colleague Martin Ashby (14) and Crewe's Phil Crump (12). The season would be remembered for the *Sunday Mirror* World Final at Wembley on 16 September when, after beating Ivan Mauger in his opening outing, Briggs was involved in a crash with Bernt Persson and Valeri Gordeev which forced him to withdraw from the meeting due to serious hand injuries. Unfortunately, later on in hospital, the index finger on his left hand was amputated. With the great Kiwi out of action, Martin Ashby was the Swindon representative in the British League Riders' Championship at Belle Vue on 21 October, when a brilliant performance saw him register 14 points and finish as runner-up to the undefeated Ole Olsen of Wolverhampton.

SWINDON ROBINS 1972

(Swindon's score shown first unless otherwise stated)

BRITISH LEAGUE FIRST DIVISION

Opponents	Home	Away
Belle Vue	L36-42	L33-45
Coventry	W47-30	L33-45
Cradley Heath	W42-36	L37-41
Exeter	W48-30	L32-46
Glasgow	W45-33	L35-43
Hackney	L38-40	L38-40
Halifax	W54-24	L34-44
Ipswich	W41-37	L29-49
King's Lynn	W44-34	L27-51
Leicester	D39-39	L33-45
Newport	W46-32	L36-42
Oxford	W43-35	L35-43
Poole	W50-28	L33-45
Reading	L34-44	L34-44
Sheffield	L38-40	L33-45
Wimbledon	W45-33	L38-40
Wolverhampton	W46-32	L38-40

BRITISH LEAGUE FIRST DIVISION TABLE

Team	Mts	Won	Drn	Lst	For	Agn.	Pts
Belle Vue	34	31	1	2	1,592.5	1,051.5	63
Reading	34	25	1	8	1,454	1,194	51
King's Lynn	34	24	3	7	1,432	1,219	51
Sheffield	34	23	3	8	1,488	1,163	49
Leicester	34	17	5	12	1,365	1,287	39
Ipswich	34	17	1	16	1,332	1,313	35
Poole	34	15	2	17	1,307	1,342	32
Hackney	34	16	0	18	1,306	1,341	32
Wolverhampton	34	16	0	18	1,302	1,348	32
Coventry	34	14	2	18	1,327	1,317	30
Exeter	34	13	2	19	1,291.5	1,357.5	28

Halifax	34	13	2	19	1,261	1,388	28
Wimbledon	34	14	0	20	1,225	1,421	28
Glasgow	34	12	2	20	1,263	1,385	26
Swindon	34	12	1	21	1,314	1,337	25
Cradley Heath	34	11	3	20	1,234.5	1,416.5	25
Oxford	34	10	0	24	1,200.5	1,443.5	20
Newport	34	9	0	25	1,139	1,510	18

LEAGUE AVERAGES

Rider	Mts	Rds	Pts	Bon.	Tot.	Avge	Maximums
Terry Betts	1	5	15	0	15	12.00	1 full
Bob Kilby	2	9	24	1	25	11.11	1 full
Ronnie Moore	1	4	11	0	11	11.00	–
Ray Wilson	2	9	23	1	24	10.67	1 full
Dave Jessup	1	5	12	1	13	10.40	–
Barry Briggs	23	104	268	2	270	10.38	7 full
Martin Ashby	33	149	368	8	376	10.09	5 full
Reidar Eide	1	5	12	0	12	9.60	–
Dag Lovaas	1	5	12	0	12	9.60	–
Edgar Stangeland	1	5	12	0	12	9.60	–
Garry Middleton	1	4	7	2	9	9.00	–
Norman Hunter	13	50	69	7	76	6.08	–
Mike Broadbanks	32	115	122	22	144	5.01	–
Brian Leonard	33	132	129	27	156	4.73	–
Clive Hitch	33	128	112	24	136	4.25	–
Billy Wall	1	3	2	1	3	4.00	–
Mike Keen	32	98	83	14	97	3.96	–
James Bond	12	34	24	8	32	3.76	–
David Ashby	9	18	7	2	9	2.00	–
Garry Flood	2	4	1	0	1	1.00	–
Bobo Valentine	2	6	1	0	1	0.67	–

SPEEDWAY STAR KNOCK-OUT CUP

Opponents	Home	Away
Exeter (Round one)	–	L30-48

MIDLAND CUP

Opponents	Home	Away	Aggregate
Oxford (Quarter-final)	W44-34	L34-44	D78-78
Oxford (Replay)	D39-39	W40-38	W79-77
Leicester (Semi-final)	W42-36	L30-48	L72-84

Note: The original result of the Midland Cup replay at Oxford was a 41-36 defeat. However, after successfully appealing, the result was amended to a 40-38 victory. On the night of the meeting, controversy surrounded heat eleven, which originally ended as a 4-2 to the Swindon pairing of Barry Briggs and Clive Hitch. Inexplicably, the referee deemed that there had been a starting gate infringement prior to the race and ordered a restart! With both Robins excluded after refusing to compete, Oxford won the rerun 5-0 and went on to record a 41-36 victory on the night. However, the SCB acted quickly to uphold Swindon's appeal and reinstate the original result of heat eleven.

CHALLENGE

Opponents	Home	Away
Reading	W49-29	L32-46

FOUR-TEAM TOURNAMENT

(Staged at Oxford)   Reading 32, Swindon 27, Oxford 21, Young Rebels 16.

FIVE-TEAM TOURNAMENT

(Staged at Coventry)   Coventry 'B' 23, Leicester 22, Swindon 17, Coventry 'A' 16, Cradley Heath 12.

BRITISH LEAGUE FIRST DIVISION RIDERS' CHAMPIONSHIP

(Staged at Belle Vue)   Martin Ashby 14 points (2nd).

1973

It was the end of an era in 1973 when Barry Briggs announced his retirement prior to the season, although he later returned to the domestic scene, riding for both Wimbledon (1974-75) and Hull (1976). During the year, the brilliant Kiwi was deservedly awarded an MBE for services to sport and he is arguably the greatest sportsman ever to represent the town of Swindon. Replacing Briggo was a rider who had long expressed a desire to ride for the Robins, namely Norwegian Edgar Stangeland, who was brought in via Exeter. Meanwhile, a newcomer who arrived with a fine reputation was American Sumner McKnight, recommended to the club by none other than Barry Briggs himself. Another new rider to appear on the scene was Geoff Bouchard, who rode for Second Division Long Eaton, but also made seven league appearances in Swindon's colours when the side was short-handed. The Leicester-born speedster very much impressed the supporters with his never-say-die style, and would eventually go on to become a full-time Robin in 1975. Norman Hunter had a good year and a 7.02 average put him second in the club's end-of-term statistics to the immaculate Martin Ashby, who took over as top man from the departed Briggs and rode brilliantly, scoring 390 league points for a 10.11 average. A First Division fixture at Hackney on 24 August emphasised Ashby's immense value to the team, since Swindon lost the match 48-30, with the Marlborough-born racer netting a magnificent 15-point maximum and with it half his side's total!

Martin Hitch, son of Clive, joined the camp but only rode in a single *Speedway Star* Knock-Out Cup match. The meeting in question took place at Hackney on 27 April and history was made, since it remains the only time Swindon have tracked a father and son combination in the same team line-up! Mick Handley was another newcomer with bags of ability, but regrettably he struggled due to poor equipment. Sad to say, Sumner McKnight found the pace of British League racing far too hot and left after riding in seven league matches for just 4 points.

There was another interesting occurrence when Swindon entertained Halifax for a league meeting on 20 April, as Mike Keen rode brilliantly to bag a full 15-pointer, while visitor Eric Boocock was paid for the 'lot' (16+2) from six outings. It's not very often that a rider from each team goes through the card unbeaten, but such was the race format that neither rider met throughout the thirteen-heat match.

The Robins were again at the wrong end of the final league table, ending up in thirteenth place. Away wins were gained at Coatbridge, Poole and Wolverhampton, but this was more than offset by the usual poor home form, which saw four losses, versus Hackney, King's Lynn, Leicester and Reading, plus three draws, against Cradley United, Exeter and Poole. Black Country outfit Wolverhampton proved to be a thorn in the side, as they ousted the Robins from the Knock-Out Cup at the quarter-final stage. Then, having reached the semi-final of the Midland Cup, where the Wolves were to have provided the opposition, Swindon were forced to withdraw due to a congested fixture list!

Blunsdon played host to a further three high-profile individual meetings during the season, the first of which was the Midland Riders' Championship qualifying round on 9 May. The event proved fruitful for track specialist Ray Wilson, who stormed to victory courtesy of a 15-point full-house, with Cradley United's Bernt Persson (13) filling the runner-up slot. Just ten days later a World Championship qualifying round was run at the Abbey Stadium and this resulted in an emphatic success for Jim McMillan of Coatbridge by virtue of a five-ride maximum. Completing the trio of big solo events was the second staging of the Silver Plume, which eventually went ahead on 12 September, having earlier been rained off on 20 June. Those competing served up quite a spectacle and, after twenty heats of pulsating action, Martin Ashby and Hackney's Bengt Jansson had tied for top spot on 13 points apiece. That necessitated a run-off for the first prize and it was Jansson who sped to victory from the home favourite.

One other major meeting took place at Blunsdon on 30 June, when New Zealand faced Sweden in the *Daily Mirror* International Tournament. In a highly charged meeting, the Swedes emerged

Swindon Robins, 1973. From left to right, back row: Sumner McKnight, Clive Hitch, Brian Leonard, Mike Keen. Front row: Norman Hunter, Martin Ashby, Alun Rossiter (Club Mascot), Edgar Stangeland.

victorious by a 42-35 scoreline, led by paid maximum man Christer Lofqvist (11+1), with solid support from Anders Michanek (9+1). For New Zealand, Ivan Mauger recorded 10+2 points, while in a rare 1973 appearance, ex-Robin Barry Briggs netted a tally of 8. In the opening heat, Lofqvist zoomed around the Blunsdon circuit in a new track-record time of 69.8 seconds, becoming the first ever rider to circumnavigate four laps of the 395-yard track in less than 70 seconds. There was further excitement for the large attendance in the second half, when Anders Michanek equalled the time set by Lofqvist in the Rider of the Night contest.

During the season, Martin Ashby took the Golden Helmet from Chris Pusey at Belle Vue on 9 June, but lost it six days later to Barry Thomas at Hackney. The Robins' leading rider again represented the club in the Player's No. 10-sponsored British League Riders' Championship at Belle Vue, where he scored 10 points to occupy sixth position in a quality field. In a late finish to the season the meeting was actually held on 3 November, having previously been postponed on 20 October. Prior to that, Swindon had aimed to finish their home fixtures with a four-team tournament on 6 October, which would have featured a one-meeting comeback by former stalwart George White. Unfortunately, the meeting fell victim to inclement weather and Chalky remained in retirement, although he did eventually make a return to the track some years later in the inaugural Golden Greats meeting at Coventry on 14 August 1988!

SWINDON ROBINS 1973

(Swindon's score shown first unless otherwise stated)

BRITISH LEAGUE FIRST DIVISION

Opponents	Home	Away
Belle Vue	W42-35	L32-46
Coatbridge	W43-35	W41-37
Coventry	W44-34	L37-41
Cradley United	D39-39	L30-48
Exeter	D39-39	L28-50
Hackney	L37-41	L30-48
Halifax	W42-36	L33-45
Ipswich	W40-38	L31-47
King's Lynn	L33-45	L37-41
Leicester	L35-43	L36-42
Newport	W40-38	L30-48
Oxford	W40-38	L34-44
Poole	D39-39	W40-38
Reading	L35-43	L31-47
Sheffield	W44-34	L27-51
Wimbledon	W42-36	L32-46
Wolverhampton	W41-37	W40-38

BRITISH LEAGUE FIRST DIVISION TABLE

Team	Mts	Won	Drn	Lst	For	Agn.	Pts
Reading	34	25	1	8	1,494	1,156	51
Sheffield	34	22	3	9	1,489	1,157	47
King's Lynn	34	20	3	11	1,395	1,253	43
Leicester	34	21	0	13	1,394	1,254	42
Ipswich	34	19	3	12	1,393	1,255	41
Belle Vue	34	19	1	14	1,451	1,188	39
Wolverhampton	34	18	1	15	1,319	1,331	37
Exeter	34	16	3	15	1,344.5	1,303.5	35
Halifax	34	16	2	16	1,255	1,394	34
Newport	34	16	0	18	1,350.5	1,295.5	32
Oxford	34	14	2	18	1,267	1,381	30
Wimbledon	34	14	1	19	1,263	1,383	29
Swindon	34	13	3	18	1,244	1,407	29
Poole	34	13	2	19	1,300	1,351	28
Coventry	34	13	0	21	1,233	1,415	26
Hackney	34	11	4	19	1,227	1,421	26
Coatbridge	34	12	1	21	1,219	1,421	25
Cradley United	34	7	4	23	1,187	1,459	18

LEAGUE AVERAGES

Rider	Mts	Rds	Pts	Bon.	Tot.	Avge	Maximums
Tony Davey	1	4	11	1	12	12.00	1 paid
Martin Ashby	34	159	390	12	402	10.11	8 full; 1 paid
Barry Thomas	1	4	8	0	8	8.00	–
Norman Hunter	34	143	240	11	251	7.02	1 full
Edgar Stangeland	32	145	221	31	252	6.95	2 full
Mike Keen	17	67	97	13	110	6.57	1 full
Arthur Browning	1	3	3	1	4	5.33	–
Paul Gachet	1	3	3	1	4	5.33	–
Geoff Bouchard	7	24	27	3	30	5.00	–
Carl Glover	1	5	6	0	6	4.80	–
Brian Leonard	33	120	102	23	125	4.17	–
Clive Hitch	21	71	54	14	68	3.83	–
George Barclay	1	3	3	0	3	4.00	–
Russell Osborne	1	2	1	1	2	4.00	–
Mick Handley	14	51	45	5	50	3.92	–
Doug Underwood	1	3	2	0	2	2.67	–

David Ashby	16	48	25	5	30	2.50	–
Roger Johns	1	2	1	0	1	2.00	–
Sumner McKnight	7	15	4	0	4	1.07	–
Billy Wall	7	14	1	1	2	0.57	–
Peter Murray	1	3	0	0	0	0.00	–

SPEEDWAY STAR KNOCK-OUT CUP

Opponents	Home	Away	Aggregate
Bye (Round one)	–	–	–
Hackney (Round two)	W43-35	L35-43	D78-78
Hackney (Replay)	W52-25	L35-43	W87-68
Wolverhampton (Quarter-final)	D39-39	L35-43	L74-82

MIDLAND CUP

Opponents	Home	Away	Aggregate
Oxford (Quarter-final)	W51-27	L38-40	W89-67
Wolverhampton (Semi-final)	Withdrew	Withdrew	L-Walkover

Note: Swindon withdrew from the Midland Cup due to a congested fixture list and Wolverhampton were given a walkover to the final.

CHALLENGE

Opponents	Home	Away
Oxford	–	L37-40
Reading	L32-46	–

FOUR-TEAM TOURNAMENT

(Staged at Exeter)   Exeter 31, Reading 29, Devon 24, Swindon 12.

PLAYER'S No. 10 BRITISH LEAGUE FIRST DIVISION RIDERS' CHAMPIONSHIP

(Staged at Belle Vue)   Martin Ashby 10 points (6th).

1974

The 1974 season saw the Robins celebrate twenty-five consecutive years of speedway at Blunsdon, with the club firmly established as one of the premier circuits in Britain. Swindon marked the landmark with the publication of a smashing little handbook, priced at just twenty-five pence! With Reading closing for the season while their new stadium was constructed at Smallmead the Robins utilised the services of Bernie Leigh, and he proved to be an excellent addition to their riding squad, appearing in all thirty-two matches of the First Division programme and averaging 5.26. Ever-loyal Mike Keen lined-up for his tenth year in the Swindon colours, although the likeable lad from nearby Minety saw his average dip to 4.18. Regrettably, the spectacular Clive Hitch retired in order to concentrate on his plastering business, although he did subsequently ride in a few Second Division matches for Rye House, who were based just a stone's throw from his home.

Martin Ashby proved to be an inspiring leader – he was ever-present, posted a league average of 10.10 and recorded ten maximums (9 full and 1 paid) during the campaign. As an example of his immeasurable worth to the club, the Robins lost 55-23 in a league match at Sheffield on 6 June and Ashby's contribution was 12 points – some 52.17 per cent of the team's total! Again, at Halifax on 12 October, he hit over half the side's score, when constructing a beautiful 15-point full-house in a 49-29 defeat.

Edgar Stangeland was next in the Robins' averages and his 7.87 figure emphasised the fact that the team needed more strength at the top end. Norman Hunter had a steady if unspectacular year, averaging 6.49, while David Ashby achieved a highly creditable 4.51 figure from his fifteen league

Programme illustration from the Twenty-Fifth Anniversary meeting v. Oxford at Blunsdon on 13 July 1974.

matches. Meanwhile Mick Bell, a man who was to feature strongly with the club many years later in an off-track role, made a tremendous guest appearance in a double-header against Belle Vue and Hackney at Blunsdon on 14 September, scoring a total of 21 points from just eight starts.

The action had begun at Blunsdon on 23 March, with the first leg of the Champagne Stakes against Poole, both sides having clubbed together to purchase a case or two of 'bubbly', with the aggregate victors taking all! The immaculate Martin Ashby duly opened up with a polished maximum (12), as the Robins raced to a 44-34 success and their supporters hoped the 10-point cushion would be sufficient for overall glory. This did indeed prove so, since the Swindon boys secured a 39-39 draw in the second leg at Wimborne Road four days later, thereby winning on aggregate by 83 points to 73.

The Robins went on to end the league campaign in twelfth position out of the seventeen competing teams. As had happened so many times in the past, they would have doubtless finished far higher in the standings but for some poor results at Blunsdon, where two matches were drawn and another three were lost. The *Speedway Star* Knock-Out Cup saw a first round exit at the hands of Newport, although this was slightly offset by an aggregate victory over the Welsh side in the Severn Bridge Trophy. The Robins reached the semi-final of the Midland Cup, only to crash out courtesy of home and away defeats to Leicester. The twenty-fifth anniversary was celebrated on 13 July when a challenge match pitched Swindon against an Oxford side led by ex-Robin Bob Kilby. It was a grand occasion, as the two sides that first faced each other in the Blunsdon opener in 1949 once again drew swords on the track. However, despite 11 points from Edgar Stangeland and 10 from Martin Ashby, Swindon lost the match 42-36.

The regular Blunsdon patrons enjoyed several prestigious meetings during the season. One of the undoubted highlights was when the Russians came for a Test match on 27 July, with Martin Ashby skippering England to a 66-41 victory and top-scoring with a massive 17 points. Tony Davey and Dave Jessup lent Ashby great support, both mustering 16 points, while the Russians' best were Vladimir Gordeev (13), Grigori Khlinovsky (11) and Anatoli Kuzmin (10+1). On the individual front, Ipswich's John Louis totalled 14 points to win a World Championship qualifying round on 15 May, with Martin Ashby finishing as runner-up just one point behind. Victory in the next 'biggie' went to Wolverhampton's George Hunter, who tallied 14 points in a Midland Riders' Championship qualifying round on 28 August, with second spot filled by Cradley United's Arthur Price (13).

Another tremendous field assembled at the Abbey Stadium on 18 September, when Martin Ashby produced a flawless performance to accrue an unbeaten 15 points and take the spoils of victory ahead of John Louis (13) and Eric Boocock (12) in the Silver Plume. That capped a tremendous year for Ashby, which had also seen him establish a new track-record time of 69.6 seconds at the Blunsdon raceway in the opening heat of the First Division fixture against Wolverhampton on 17 August. The Marlborough-born rider was again Swindon's representative at Belle Vue for the British League Riders' Championship on 19 October, when he scored 8 points to occupy seventh position.

SWINDON ROBINS 1974

(Swindon's score shown first unless otherwise stated)

BRITISH LEAGUE FIRST DIVISION

Opponents	Home	Away
Belle Vue	L38-40	L25-53
Coventry	W45-33	L36-42
Cradley United	W49-29	L33-44
Exeter	L38-40	L32-46
Hackney	W41-37	L29-49
Halifax	D39-39	L29-49
Hull	W49-29	L30-48
Ipswich	W40-38	L38-40
King's Lynn	W41-37	L34-44
Leicester	W44-34	L25-53
Newport	D39-39	L36-42
Oxford	L32-46	W42-36
Poole	W46-32	L35-43

Sheffield	W44-34	L23-55
Wimbledon	W45-33	L23-55
Wolverhampton	W44-34	L35-43

BRITISH LEAGUE FIRST DIVISION TABLE

Team	Mts	Won	Drn	Lst	For	Agn.	Pts
Exeter	32	25	1	6	1,375	1,117	51
Belle Vue	32	23	0	9	1,380	1,106	46
Ipswich	32	22	1	9	1,364	1,128	45
Sheffield	32	21	0	11	1,426	1,067	42
King's Lynn	32	20	1	11	1,281	1,210	41
Newport	32	17	3	12	1,299	1,197	37
Halifax	32	14	3	15	1,209	1,286	31
Wimbledon	32	14	1	17	1,200	1,287	29
Hackney	32	13	2	17	1,218	1,273	28
Leicester	32	13	1	18	1,210	1,282	27
Wolverhampton	32	13	1	18	1,157.5	1,332.5	27
Swindon	32	12	2	18	1,179	1,316	26
Cradley United	32	12	1	19	1,171	1,322	25
Poole	32	12	1	19	1,147	1,344	25
Coventry	32	12	0	20	1,147	1,342	24
Hull	32	10	0	22	1,212	1,269	20
Oxford	32	10	0	22	1,196.5	1,293.5	20

LEAGUE AVERAGES

Rider	Mts	Rds	Pts	Bon.	Tot.	Avge	Maximums
Mick Bell	2	8	21	0	21	10.50	–
Martin Ashby	32	141	351	5	356	10.10	9 full; 1 paid
Phil Herne	1	5	11	1	12	9.60	–
Edgar Stangeland	28	122	231	9	240	7.87	1 full
Norman Hunter	30	122	183	15	198	6.49	–
Bernie Leigh	32	124	129	34	163	5.26	–
David Ashby	15	47	43	10	53	4.51	–
Mike Keen	27	87	75	16	91	4.18	–
Gordon Kennett	1	4	3	1	4	4.00	–
Mick Handley	19	62	57	2	59	3.81	–
Brian Leonard	24	79	57	15	72	3.65	–
Geoff Bouchard	9	32	17	3	20	2.50	–
Alan Sorensen	1	2	1	0	1	2.00	–

SPEEDWAY STAR KNOCK-OUT CUP

Opponents	Home	Away	Aggregate
Newport (Round one)	W40-38	L36-42	L76-80

MIDLAND CUP

Opponents	Home	Away	Aggregate
Oxford (Quarter-final)	W44-34	L37-41	W81-75
Leicester (Semi-final)	L37-41	L37-41	L74-82

CHAMPAGNE STAKES

Opponents	Home	Away	Aggregate
Poole	W44-34	D39-39	W83-73

SEVERN BRIDGE TROPHY

Opponents	Home	Away	Aggregate
Newport	W46-32	L33-45	W79-77

TWENTY-FIFTH ANNIVERSARY CHALLENGE

Opponents	Home	Away
Oxford	L36-42	–

CHALLENGE

Opponents	Home	Away
Oxford	–	L28-50

WESSEX FOUR-TEAM TOURNAMENT

(Staged at Newport)	Newport 41, Swindon 22, Oxford 22, Exeter 11.
(Staged at Swindon)	Oxford 33, Newport 31, Swindon 18, Exeter 14.
(Staged at Oxford)	Oxford 34, Newport 31, Swindon 18, Exeter 13.
(Staged at Exeter)	Exeter 17, Newport 17, Swindon 15, Oxford 11.
Aggregate result:	Newport 120, Oxford 100, Swindon 73, Exeter 55.

Note: The fourth leg at Exeter was abandoned after heat ten, with the result permitted to stand.

FOUR-TEAM TOURNAMENT

(Staged at Swindon)	Leicester 31, Swindon 'A' 25, Swindon 'B' 24, Wimbledon 16.

BRITISH LEAGUE FIRST DIVISION RIDERS' CHAMPIONSHIP

(Staged at Belle Vue)	Martin Ashby 8 points (7th).

1975

Bob Kilby was welcomed back for the 1975 campaign but, with Reading reopening, it was goodbye to Bernie Leigh. However, with Kilby's teammates including Martin Ashby, Edgar Stangeland, Norman Hunter and Geoff Bouchard, Swindon looked to have a very solid squad. Things looked even better when promoter Ted Nelson dipped into the coffers to purchase Bobby McNeil from Second Division Eastbourne, but by the time Leicester came to Blunsdon for a league match on 12 April Stangeland was already wanting away, citing lucrative weekend long-track bookings as his reason. Regrettably, the Norwegian duly left the Robins' nest, although he was later to appear in the colours of Wimbledon, where he rode alongside former Swindon legend Barry Briggs. Robins' boss Ted Nelson again looked to the transfer market but, having no luck, cast his eyes abroad and came up with an outstanding young prospect in Jan Andersson. The talented Swede made his club debut on 26 April in a Gulf Oil British League match against Sheffield and won his first ever race at the Abbey, before going on to total 4+1 points in a 45-33 defeat. Later on, Alan Grahame was also signed on loan from National League Birmingham.

The season had opened in a positive manner at Poole on 19 March, when the Robins raced to a 41-37 success in the first leg of the Champagne Stakes. Unfortunately that proved to be a false dawn, since three days later the side crashed to a huge 47-31 loss in the return match at Blunsdon. Bob Kilby showed great form to top score with 13 points, but with Martin Ashby, Mike Keen and Bobby McNeil all hampered by machine troubles the Pirates took full advantage to win with plenty of room to spare. The Robins began their home league programme against Wolverhampton on 5 April, when Martin Ashby was back at his brilliant best. Indeed, the skipper needed to be too, as his 15-point maximum helped the side to a narrow 40-38 victory over a determined Wolves outfit.

Despite having a useful squad on paper a series of injuries, particularly to Mike Keen, and indifferent form saw Swindon slide to the bottom of the league table and collect the wooden spoon. They lost every one of their seventeen away matches, as well as suffering a quite staggering nine home losses, to Coventry, Cradley United, Exeter, Halifax, Ipswich, King's Lynn, Newport, Oxford and Sheffield. The top two of Martin Ashby and Bob Kilby did their best to stem the tidal wave, but there was very little in the way of support. Ashby stood out like a beacon though, and one match that gave another indication of his value to club occurred in the home league fixture against Halifax on 9 July. This saw the Robins suffer an embarrassing 46-32 reverse, but while things were falling apart around him, Ashby coolly and efficiently compiled a wonderful five-ride maximum (15). In total, the club's number one

The programme from the Artdeans Mobylette Trophy, held at the Abbey Stadium on 28 June 1975.

speedster scored 385 league points to yield an average of 10.13, while Kilb plundered 286 points to average 8.31. Briefly, while Edgar Stangeland was around, he averaged 6.36 from five matches, but the figures then dropped sharply, as follows: Norman Hunter (5.24), Alan Grahame (4.95), Bobby McNeil (4.23), Jan Andersson (4.20), Geoff Bouchard (4.12), Mike Keen (3.38) and David Ashby (2.89).

Aside from the league, Swindon also fared poorly in other competitions as well, suffering a second round defeat to Leicester in the *Speedway Star* Knock-Out Cup and, after a replay, a first round exit to Oxford in the Midland Cup. The Robins overcame a potential banana skin in the Inter-League Knock-Out Cup, winning 39-38 at National League Workington. They were then drawn at home to Boston in the next round. However, due to fixture congestion Swindon applied to have the meeting raced at the New Hammond Beck Road home of the Lincolnshire club, but the idea was vetoed by the powers-that-be and Boston were handed a walkover into the next round.

The Blunsdon track record was again broken in 1975, with Martin Ashby lowering his own best time to 69.2 seconds against Wolverhampton on 5 April. That wasn't the season's fastest though, for Bob Kilby screamed around in 68.8 seconds in the opening heat of the league encounter with Cradley United on 20 September, his time being eight-tenths of a second faster than the record that had stood at the beginning of the season.

Four prestigious individual meetings were held at the Abbey Stadium during the year, the first of which saw Bob Kilby total 14 points to take victory in the Midland Riders' Championship qualifying round on 14 May. Later that month, on 31 May, the ultra-professional Ivan Mauger recorded a brilliant five-ride full-house to win a World Championship qualifying round, finishing just a single point ahead of home favourite Martin Ashby. On 28 June future Swindon superstar Phil Crump, then of Newport fame, produced a dazzling display, tallying 14 points to win the Artdeans Mobylette Trophy, with Bob Kilby (13) and the redoubtable Ashby (12) finishing second and third respectively. The final open event of the year took place on 6 August and saw Belle Vue's racer supreme Peter Collins storm to a full maximum and win the highly coveted Silver Plume ahead of Martin Ashby (14) and Leicester's Ray Wilson (13).

Stepping up a level, Martin Ashby qualified as a reserve for the *Sunday Mirror* World Final at Wembley Stadium on 6 September, but unfortunately didn't get a ride on the night. There was some consolation for the Swindon stylist though when he carded 11 points and then defeated John Louis in a run-off for third place in the Skol-sponsored British League Riders' Championship at Belle Vue on 18 October. Ashby also ended the season as Golden Helmet holder after relieving John Louis of the title over three dramatic legs, held on successive nights. Louis gained a 2-0 win at Belle Vue on 15 October, only for Ashby to hit back with a 2-1 victory at Ipswich the following evening, thereby setting up a decider at Hackney, where the Robins' representative made no mistake to triumph 2-0.

SWINDON ROBINS 1975

(Swindon's score shown first unless otherwise stated)

GULF OIL BRITISH LEAGUE

Opponents	Home	Away
Belle Vue	W40-38	L30-48
Coventry	L37-41	L34-44
Cradley United	L33-45	L35-43
Exeter	L36-41	L31-47
Hackney	W46-31	L29-49
Halifax	L32-46	L36-42
Hull	W42-36	L35-43
Ipswich	L36-42	L31-47
King's Lynn	L36-42	L37-41
Leicester	W42-36	L32-46
Newport	L29-49	L31-47
Oxford	L37-41	L34-44
Poole	W44-34	L33-45
Reading	W48-30	L28-50

Sheffield	L33-45	L27-51
Wimbledon	W41-37	L35-42
Wolverhampton	W40-38	L32-46

GULF OIL BRITISH LEAGUE TABLE

Team	Mts	Won	Drn	Lst	For	Agn.	Pts
Ipswich	34	26	1	7	1,458	1,192	53
Belle Vue	34	25	2	7	1,488	1,164	52
Newport	34	24	1	9	1,538	1,112	49
Exeter	34	20	3	11	1,410	1,240	43
Sheffield	34	21	0	13	1,368	1,281	42
Reading	34	21	0	13	1,342	1,308	42
Oxford	34	18	0	16	1,370	1,274	36
Leicester	34	16	4	14	1,348	1,303	36
Wimbledon	34	16	2	16	1,317	1,331	34
Halifax	34	15	3	16	1,289	1,362	33
Cradley United	34	15	2	17	1,288	1,356	32
King's Lynn	34	14	3	17	1,295	1,355	31
Wolverhampton	34	13	1	20	1,237	1,414	27
Hull	34	10	4	20	1,258	1,393	24
Poole	34	10	3	21	1,240	1,411	23
Coventry	34	9	2	23	1,176.5	1,473.5	20
Hackney	34	9	1	24	1,221.5	1,429.5	19
Swindon	34	8	0	26	1,202	1,447	16

LEAGUE AVERAGES

Rider	Mts	Rds	Pts	Bon.	Tot.	Avge	Maximums
Martin Ashby	33	156	385	10	395	10.13	4 full; 1 paid
Bob Kilby	31	143	286	11	297	8.31	2 full
Chris Morton	1	5	9	0	9	7.20	–
Edgar Stangeland	5	22	34	1	35	6.36	–
Norman Hunter	29	100	110	21	131	5.24	–
Alan Grahame	11	42	44	8	52	4.95	–
Tony Davey	1	5	6	0	6	4.80	–
Bobby McNeil	29	105	92	19	111	4.23	–
Jan Andersson	15	59	54	8	62	4.20	–
Geoff Bouchard	34	136	118	22	140	4.12	–
Pete Wigley	1	4	4	0	4	4.00	–
Steve Wilcock	1	3	2	1	3	4.00	–
Mike Keen	12	32	23	4	27	3.38	–
David Ashby	17	54	30	9	39	2.89	–
Mick Handley	1	3	1	0	1	1.33	–
Geoff Pusey	1	3	1	0	1	1.33	–
Barry Duke	6	10	3	0	3	1.20	–
Graham Crook	1	3	0	0	0	0.00	–
Ron Henderson	1	2	0	0	0	0.00	–
Ted Hubbard	1	2	0	0	0	0.00	–
Wayne Hughes	1	2	0	0	0	0.00	–
Ken Matthews	1	2	0	0	0	0.00	–
Dave Patten	1	2	0	0	0	0.00	–
Colin Richardson	1	3	0	0	0	0.00	–

SPEEDWAY STAR KNOCK-OUT CUP

Opponents	Home	Away	Aggregate
Hull (Round one)	W47-31	L32-46	W79-77
Leicester (Round two)	L35-43	L36-42	L71-85

INTER-LEAGUE KNOCK-OUT CUP

Opponents	Home	Away
Workington (Round one)	–	W39-38
Boston (Round two)	L-walkover	–

Note: Swindon were drawn at home to Boston in the second round of the Inter-League Knock-Out Cup. However, due to fixture congestion, the Robins' management applied to have the meeting raced at their opponents' venue. This idea was subsequently vetoed by the powers-that-be and the Barracudas gained a walkover into the next round.

MIDLAND CUP

Opponents	Home	Away	Aggregate
Oxford (Round one)	D39-39	D39-39	D78-78
Oxford (Replay)	W44-33	L25-53	L69-86

CHAMPAGNE STAKES

Opponents	Home	Away	Aggregate
Poole	L31-47	W41-37	L72-84

SEVERN BRIDGE TROPHY

Opponents	Home	Away	Aggregate
Newport	W45-33	D39-39	W84-72

FOUR-TEAM TOURNAMENT

(Staged at Birmingham)   Newport 35, Ipswich 25, Birmingham 22, Swindon 13.
(Staged at Swindon)   Swindon 'B' 35, Newport 23, Swindon 'A' 19, Oxford 18.

GWENT TRIANGULAR TOURNAMENT

(Staged at Newport)   Overseas 26, Newport 25, Swindon 21.

SKOL BRITISH LEAGUE RIDERS' CHAMPIONSHIP

(Staged at Belle Vue)   Martin Ashby 11 points (3rd).

1976

In 1976 Swedish rider Soren Karlsson, who had previously ridden for Sheffield, was allocated to the Robins by the Rider Control Committee, but his compatriot Jan Andersson was missing at first due to the effects of a nasty collarbone injury and the call of national service. The season got underway at Blunsdon on 20 March, when Swindon faced Poole in the Champagne Stakes. Prior to the match, Martin Ashby defeated Malcolm Simmons 2-0 in the Golden Helmet Match Race Championship, having relieved John Louis of the trophy at the back-end of 1975. The Robins then got the campaign off to a rousing start by walloping the Pirates 51-27, with both Ashby (12) and teammate Geoff Bouchard (11+1) going through the card unbeaten. Four days later, at Poole, Ashby completed the job in the Golden Helmet, again beating Simmons 2-0, before Swindon swept to a 42-35 victory for an aggregate success in the Champagne Stakes. Ashby was to lose his grip on the Golden Helmet the following month to Wimbledon's Swedish ace Tommy Jansson. Tragically, the brilliant Jansson was killed shortly afterwards while riding in a World Championship qualifying round in his home country on 20 May.

The wonderfully loyal Mike Keen was granted a benefit meeting on 19 June and, typical of 'Keener's' luck, in what was a generally fine and particularly hot summer it rained on his big day. Despite the elements, a Swindon Select beat a Mike Keen Seven by 47 points to 31. Bob Kilby topped the Robins' scoring with 9 points, while their opponents were superbly spearheaded by a quite marvellous 15-point maximum from Dag Lovaas of White City.

The previous week had seen the Russian riders back at Blunsdon, this time riding against Swindon in a challenge match. The homesters won an excellent contest 47-31, with Bob Kilby scorching to an unbeaten total of 12 points from his four starts. Meanwhile, for the Soviet visitors, Grigori Khlinovsky was the pick of the bunch in netting a tally of 8.

Swindon's top two of Kilby and Martin Ashby kept up their private battle to see who was the quickest around Blunsdon during the season, with 'Killer' lowering the track record to 68.6 seconds in the Midland Riders' Championship qualifying round on 23 June. His record didn't last long

Swindon Robins, 1976. From left to right, back row: Soren Karlsson, Norman Hunter, Dick Bradley (Team Manager), Bob Jones (Mechanic), Bobby McNeil, Geoff Bouchard. On bikes: David Ashby, Martin Ashby, Bob Kilby. Kneeling: Alun Rossiter (Club Mascot).

though, as Ashby blitzed around the circuit to establish a faster time of 68.0 seconds dead in the *Daily Mirror* Grand Prix qualifying round on 10 July.

On the Gulf Oil British League front Swindon rose to fifth place in the final table so, all in all, it was an excellent year of progress at Blunsdon, despite Norman Hunter retiring in August in order to concentrate on his motorcycle business. The key to the Robins' rise was an improved home record, which saw three draws (against Coventry, Exeter and Ipswich) but, perhaps more significantly, no defeats! On the road, Swindon also fared much better, chalking up four successes – at Hull, Leicester, White City and Wimbledon, as well as forcing a draw at King's Lynn.

At the top of the Robins' scoring, having posted averages in excess of 9, were Messrs Ashby and Kilby – Martin on a 9.89 figure, with Bob on 9.15. As far as Ashby was concerned, one league match really stood out, when the team travelled to Wolverhampton on 3 September. With Kilby missing through injury and rider replacement in operation, Ashby registered a mammoth 21 points from eight starts, as Swindon narrowly lost 41-37; his tally being 56.76 per cent of the team's total!

Bobby McNeil had a very good year, raising his average from 4.23 to 7.55, while Jan Andersson made rapid progress, achieving a solid 6.84 figure. Soren Karlsson missed many meetings due to overseas commitments and injury, but when around he more often than not bolstered up the middle order, scoring 117 points to yield a 6.38 average. Meanwhile, in statistical terms, the remaining regulars finished thus: Geoff Bouchard (5.96), Norman Hunter (5.51) and David Ashby (4.12).

Looking briefly at the other leading competitions, after beating Poole in the first round of the *Speedway Star* Knock-Out Cup, Swindon lost narrowly on aggregate to Ipswich, 79-77, in the second round. Meanwhile, in the Midland Cup, it was the familiar story of defeat at the semi-final stage, this time to Wolverhampton.

Once again, Blunsdon played host to no less than four first-class individual meetings during the course of the season. The first was a World Championship qualifying round on 24 April and this resulted in victory for Cradley United's Dave Perks, who swept all before him to accumulate a fine 15-point maximum. Fellow Heathen and future Robin Steve Bastable (12) ended the night as runner-up, while Newcastle's Tom Owen (11) finished in third position. Next up was the Marlboro-sponsored Midland

Riders' Championship qualifying round on 23 June, which saw a Swindon one-two of Bob Kilby (15) and Martin Ashby (14), with Cradley's John Boulger (13) in third place. As previously touched upon, a qualifying round for the *Daily Mirror* Grand Prix was held the following month, with victory going to Poole's Malcolm Simmons (15) ahead of Bob Kilby (13). Having begun in 1972, the fifth running of the Silver Plume was held on 11 August, when, aside from the coveted trophy, a first prize of £100 was up for grabs. Showing a penchant for the Blunsdon raceway, visiting riders Dave Jessup (Reading) and Peter Collins (Belle Vue) raced to 14 points apiece, before 'PC' claimed the accolades in a tense title run-off. Finally in 1976, Martin Ashby again did well at Belle Vue in the Leyland Cars British League Riders' Championship on 16 October, finishing in fourth position with a well-taken 12 points.

SWINDON ROBINS 1976

(Swindon's score shown first unless otherwise stated)

GULF OIL BRITISH LEAGUE

Opponents	Home	Away
Belle Vue	W40-38	L31-47
Birmingham	W52-26	L36-42
Coventry	D39-39	L24-54
Cradley United	W45-33	L38-40
Exeter	D39-39	L38-40
Hackney	W42-35	L37-41
Halifax	W51-27	L31-47
Hull	W45-33	W40-38
Ipswich	D39-39	L25-53
King's Lynn	W45-33	D39-39
Leicester	W44-34	W43-35
Newport	W54-24	L32-45
Poole	W48-30	L36-42
Reading	W41-37	L31-47
Sheffield	W53-25	L33-45
White City	W47-31	W43-35
Wimbledon	W52-25	W40-38
Wolverhampton	W52-26	L37-41

GULF OIL BRITISH LEAGUE TABLE

Team	Mts	Won	Drn	Lst	For	Agn.	Pts
Ipswich	36	27	1	8	1,555	1,252	55
Belle Vue	36	23	2	11	1,515	1,289	48
Exeter	36	23	2	11	1,460	1,338	48
Coventry	36	21	2	13	1,446	1,358	44
Swindon	36	19	4	13	1,462	1,343	42
Reading	36	19	3	14	1,477	1,325	41
Hackney	36	20	0	16	1,392	1,404	40
Newport	36	19	1	16	1,436.5	1,366.5	39
Cradley United	36	19	1	16	1,397	1,408	39
Poole	36	18	1	17	1,391	1,412	37
Wolverhampton	36	18	1	17	1,347	1,456	37
Hull	36	18	0	18	1,469.5	1,331.5	36
White City	36	16	3	17	1,437.5	1,367.5	35
King's Lynn	36	16	3	17	1,426	1,375	35
Halifax	36	14	1	21	1,304.5	1,500.5	29
Wimbledon	36	12	3	21	1,360.5	1,443.5	27
Sheffield	36	13	1	22	1,321	1,483	27
Birmingham	36	7	0	29	1,196.5	1,603.5	14
Leicester	36	5	1	30	1,233	1,571	11

LEAGUE AVERAGES

Rider	Mts	Rds	Pts	Bon.	Tot.	Avge	Maximums
Martin Ashby	36	159	374	19	393	9.89	5 full
Bob Kilby	34	146	318	16	334	9.15	3 full; 1 paid

Doug Underwood	1	3	4	2	6	8.00	–
Bobby McNeil	29	107	175	27	202	7.55	1 full
Jan Andersson	19	76	115	15	130	6.84	–
Craig Pendlebury	1	5	7	1	8	6.40	–
Soren Karlsson	22	84	117	17	134	6.38	–
Bob Humphreys	1	4	5	1	6	6.00	–
Chris Robins	1	2	2	1	3	6.00	–
Geoff Bouchard	35	149	185	37	222	5.96	–
Norman Hunter	22	77	85	21	106	5.51	–
David Ashby	23	65	54	13	67	4.12	–
Ian Clark	1	4	3	1	4	4.00	–
Colin Richardson	1	4	4	0	4	4.00	–
Pete Reading	1	3	2	0	2	2.67	–
Danny Kennedy	1	2	1	0	1	2.00	–
Cliff Anderson	9	21	8	1	9	1.71	–
Kevin Pope	4	12	2	1	3	1.00	–
John Titman	1	4	1	0	1	1.00	–
Phil Bass	1	2	0	0	0	0.00	–
Karl Fiala	1	3	0	0	0	0.00	–
Brian Leonard	1	2	0	0	0	0.00	–
Kelvin Mullarkey	1	3	0	0	0	0.00	–

SPEEDWAY STAR KNOCK-OUT CUP

Opponents	Home	Away	Aggregate
Poole (Round one)	W54-24	L36-42	W90-66
Ipswich (Round two)	W44-34	L33-45	L77-79

MIDLAND CUP

Opponents	Home	Away	Aggregate
Leicester (Quarter-final)	W49-29	W44-34	W93-63
Wolverhampton (Semi-final)	W42-36	L34-44	L76-80

CHAMPAGNE STAKES

Opponents	Home	Away	Aggregate
Poole	W51-27	W42-35	W93-62

SEVERN BRIDGE TROPHY

Opponents	Home	Away	Aggregate
Newport	W49-29	L33-45	W82-74

CHALLENGE

Opponents	Home	Away
Mike Keen Select	W47-31	–
Exeter	–	L32-46
Soviet Union	W47-31	–
Wimbledon	–	L36-42

FOUR-TEAM TOURNAMENT

(Staged at Oxford)	White City 38, Coventry 25, Swindon 21, Oxford 12.
(Staged at Reading)	Reading 35, Swindon 27, Hackney 19, Wimbledon 15.

GAULOISES BRITISH LEAGUE PAIRS CHAMPIONSHIP

Semi-Final (Staged at Hackney)	Ipswich 24, Belle Vue 24, Poole 21, Hackney 19, Swindon 13, White City 13, Exeter 11.

LEYLAND CARS BRITISH LEAGUE RIDERS' CHAMPIONSHIP

(Staged at Belle Vue)	Martin Ashby 12 points (4th).

1977

It was very much 'as you were' on the team front at Blunsdon in 1977, although a number of very promising junior riders began to show encouraging signs. Among the hopefuls were Kevin Pope, Kevin Young, Malcolm Holloway and Richard Evans. To gain further experience, Holloway was loaned to Oxford, where Young was already establishing himself, while Evans linked with Weymouth.

Swindon were pretty formidable on their own circuit, with only Reading winning at Blunsdon, although Exeter forced a last-heat draw on 17 September when, with top man Martin Ashby missing through injury, the Robins operated rider replacement and Bob Kilby rode out of his skin to score 16 points. Both Jan Andersson and Ashby were unfortunate to suffer collarbone fractures during the year, with the latter's season ending abruptly as a result of a frightening crash in heat eighteen of the Gauloises-sponsored British League Pairs Championship semi-final at Sheffield on 15 September. The accident also involved Bristol's Phil Crump, who suffered a broken leg, and occurred amid deteriorating conditions caused by persistent rain. Up to that point Ashby had enjoyed another high-scoring year, which yielded a league average of 9.80. He was sorely missed, no more so than in a Midland Cup semi-final tie against Coventry on 22 September. Swindon were putting up sturdy resistance and after nine heats there wasn't a lot to choose between the sides as the Bees narrowly led 28-25. However, it was then that Ole Olsen and his boys hit the unfortunate Robins with 5-1 successes in the last four races of the match to convincingly win 48-29.

Bob Kilby plundered 338 points in the Gulf Oil British League, with his average dropping slightly to 8.68, but this was hardly surprising given all the extra rides he had to take in the second half of the season. It must be said, though, that Kilb put together several remarkable performances during the campaign, especially in the league match at Coventry on 23 July. Martin Ashby had been ruled out of the meeting after clashing with Ole Olsen in the opening heat, leaving Kilby to carry the side. This he did admirably, netting 19 points from seven rides as the Robins went down 43-35; the quick-gating Swindonian's efforts equating to 54.29 per cent of the team's total. Later, at Ipswich on 20 October, in the very last match of the season Swindon lost 47-31 and in scoring 17 points Kilby slightly increased his contribution to 54.84 per cent.

When fit, Jan Andersson continued to progress, pushing his average up to 7.77. Aside from landing two paid maximums, the Swede particularly starred alongside Bob Kilby in the away match at Birmingham on 10 October. Swindon lost the match 41-37, Kilby notching 17 points and Andersson 16+2, as between them they scored all but 4 points for the side. Looking at the other regular riders, Bobby McNeil's average dropped by a point to 6.56 and Soren Karlsson also had a dip in form, achieving only a 5.74 average. Meanwhile Geoff Bouchard was an ever-present, finishing with a useful 5.56 average and his battling qualities certainly endeared him to the Blunsdon faithful.

The Robins ended up occupying eleventh place in the league, which was a backward step from the previous season and probably due mainly to the injuries sustained by Jan Andersson and Martin Ashby. In the *Speedway Star* Knock-Out Cup it was Exeter who put paid to any hopes Swindon had of progressing, with the Falcons claiming an aggregate victory by 85 points to 71 in their first round clash. Meanwhile, Coventry ended the Robins' aspirations in the Midland Cup following the aforementioned thumping they handed out at Blunsdon in the second leg of their semi-final tie.

Prior to his injury, Martin Ashby further lowered the track record at Blunsdon, screaming around the circuit in 67.6 seconds on his way to victory in the Wadworth Jubilee Trophy on 20 August. The meeting featured a top-class line-up, but Ashby simply blew the opposition away to register a 15-point maximum and claim the first prize of £100. With a hard-earned dozen points to his name, Geoff Bouchard was a popular runner-up, while Exeter's John Titman finished third (11).

The Wadworth Jubilee Trophy was actually the second of three individual meetings held at the Abbey Stadium during the year, with the first being a qualifying round for the Midland Riders' Championship on 21 July. The meeting had originally been scheduled for 28 April, but inclement

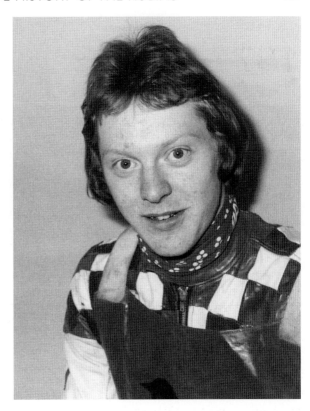

Kevin Young, who made ten league appearances for the Robins in 1977.

weather meant another date had to be found. At the second attempt, a terrific meeting ended in a three-man run-off after Jim McMillan, Mitch Shirra and Steve Bastable had totalled 12 points apiece. Victory in the end went the way of McMillan, who held his nerve to take the chequered flag from Shirra, while Bastable had to settle for third spot. It wasn't the best of nights for the Swindon riders, however, for although Jan Andersson bagged 11 points and Martin Ashby scored 10, both missed out on rostrum positions. Added to that, Bob Kilby retired with engine trouble after his second ride, while Geoff Bouchard recorded 8 points and Soren Karlsson could only muster a tally of 5.

The third big event of the season at Blunsdon was a Volkswagen Grand Prix qualifying round on 3 September, when former Robin Edgar Stangeland, then of Bristol, was a non-arrival. Regrettably that meant three riders only competing in the Norwegian's programmed heats, although the remaining fifteen riders more than made up for his absence. Poole's Malcolm Simmons was simply majestic in compiling a 15-point full-house to win on the night ahead of Reading's John Davis (14), while Barry Thomas (11) of Hackney completed the podium 1-2-3. With Martin Ashby injured, Swindon were represented by Bob Kilby in the Leyland Cars British League Riders' Championship at Belle Vue on 15 October, and he didn't disgrace himself against the cream of the domestic scene, netting 7 points.

SWINDON ROBINS 1977

(Swindon's score shown first unless otherwise stated)

GULF OIL BRITISH LEAGUE

Opponents	Home	Away
Belle Vue	W50-28	L32-46
Birmingham	W47-31	L37-41
Bristol	W51-27	L36-42
Coventry	W44.5-33.5	L35-43

Cradley Heath	W41-37	W42-36
Exeter	D39-39	L22-56
Hackney	W51-27	L28-50
Halifax	W62-15	L28-49
Hull	W46-32	L37-41
Ipswich	W41-37	L31-47
King's Lynn	W40-38	L31-47
Leicester	W43-35	L37-41
Poole	W47-31	L36-42
Reading	L32-46	L34-44
Sheffield	W52-26	L23-54
White City	W46-32	L26-52
Wimbledon	W50-27	L38-39
Wolverhampton	W50-28	L38-40

GULF OIL BRITISH LEAGUE TABLE

Team	Mts	Won	Drn	Lst	For	Agn.	Pts
White City	36	27	1	8	1,543	1,258	55
Exeter	36	25	3	8	1,625	1,178	53
Reading	36	25	3	8	1,482	1,323	53
Ipswich	36	25	1	10	1,507	1,293	51
Belle Vue	36	19	3	14	1,473.5	1,330.5	41
King's Lynn	36	19	2	15	1,448	1,350	40
Cradley Heath	36	20	0	16	1,437.5	1,357.5	40
Coventry	36	19	1	16	1,454.5	1,340.5	39
Wimbledon	36	17	2	17	1,413	1,387	36
Poole	36	17	2	17	1,382	1,416	36
Swindon	36	17	1	18	1,423.5	1,379.5	35
Bristol	36	17	0	19	1,381	1,417	34
Sheffield	36	16	2	18	1,374.5	1,430.5	34
Hull	36	15	0	21	1,349.5	1,454.5	30
Wolverhampton	36	14	0	22	1,334	1,468	28
Hackney	36	13	1	22	1,256.5	1,537.5	27
Halifax	36	12	0	24	1,288	1,504	24
Birmingham	36	8	0	28	1,220	1,581	16
Leicester	36	6	0	30	1,206.5	1,593.5	12

LEAGUE AVERAGES

Rider	Mts	Rds	Pts	Bon.	Tot.	Avge	Maximums
Martin Ashby	27	112	266.5	8	274.5	9.80	7 full; 1 paid
Bruce Cribb	1	4	9	0	9	9.00	–
Ian Cartwright	1	5	11	0	11	8.80	–
Bob Kilby	35	160	338	9	347	8.68	2 full; 1 paid
Arnold Haley	1	6	12	1	13	8.67	–
Bernie Leigh	1	3	5	1	6	8.00	–
Jan Andersson	23	106	183	23	206	7.77	2 paid
Bobby McNeil	29	111	146	36	182	6.56	1 paid
Doug Underwood	1	4	5	1	6	6.00	–
Steve Weatherley	1	4	6	0	6	6.00	–
Soren Karlsson	27	92	107	25	132	5.74	1 paid
Geoff Bouchard	36	167	192	40	232	5.56	–
David Ashby	29	92	98	17	115	5.00	–
Barry Thomas	1	4	4	1	5	5.00	–
Bob Spelta	1	7	8	0	8	4.57	–
Kevin Young	10	25	17	2	19	3.04	–
Richard Evans	6	16	10	2	12	3.00	–
Kevin Pope	3	4	2	1	3	3.00	–
Malcolm Holloway	7	18	4	1	5	1.11	–

SPEEDWAY STAR KNOCK-OUT CUP

Opponents	Home	Away	Aggregate
Exeter (Round one)	W43-35	L28-50	L71-85

MIDLAND CUP

Opponents	Home	Away	Aggregate
Birmingham (Quarter-final)	W52-26	W42-36	W94-62
Coventry (Semi-final)	L29-48	L24-54	L53-102

CHAMPAGNE CHALLENGE

Opponents	Home	Away	Aggregate
Poole	D48-48	D48-48	D96-96

INTER-COUNTY CHALLENGE

Opponents	Home	Away	Aggregate
Reading	W43-35	L37-41	W80-76

CHALLENGE

Opponents	Home	Away
Bristol	W48-30	–

FOUR-TEAM TOURNAMENT

(Staged at Oxford)   Cradley Heath 38, Swindon 25, Bristol 22, Oxford 11.
(Staged at Reading)   Reading 39, Bristol 23, Swindon 19, Poole 15.

GAULOISES BRITISH LEAGUE PAIRS CHAMPIONSHIP

Semi-Final (Staged at Sheffield) Sheffield 23, Wolverhampton 22, Belle Vue 21, King's Lynn 20, Bristol 16, Swindon 13, Exeter 8.

LEYLAND CARS BRITISH LEAGUE RIDERS' CHAMPIONSHIP

(Staged at Belle Vue)   Bob Kilby 7 points.

1978

Polish riders Leonard Raba and Jerzy Trzeszkowski were introduced to the Swindon side in 1978, but neither was a success. This was after it appeared that Alan Grahame was close to signing from Birmingham, with the rider eventually relocating to Cradley Heath instead. It had been hoped to sign the Midlander as a replacement for Bobby McNeil, who had departed the Robins' nest for Hackney. Going back to the Polish duo, Raba disappeared after a point-less performance at home to Leicester on 8 April and although Trzeszkowski lasted a little longer, he too was gone after the Robins had entertained Coventry on 6 May. Richard Evans, the son of 1950s rider Frank, initially replaced Raba, with Malcolm Holloway subsequently coming into the side at the expense of Trzeszkowski. National League boy Robert Henry of Mildenhall then came on board, closely followed by the return of Soren Karlsson. All found points hard to obtain though and surprisingly Trzeszkowski returned in time for a match against Sheffield at Blunsdon on 24 June. That match ended in a 39-39 draw and the next ten meetings on the bounce were all lost; six in the league, two in the Knock-Out Cup and two in the Midland Cup. During that dismal spell, Trzeszkowski again departed, along with Karlsson, who had completely lost his touch.

The Swindon management looked elsewhere and firstly unearthed Norwegian Rolf Gramstad, with Dane Steen Mastrup also joining as the team embarked on another losing streak that saw seven league defeats on the trot, five of them occurring on the road. Of the two signings Gramstad was the most impressive, but both did enough to warrant invitations to return in 1979. In mid-August, out of the blue, Leonard Raba returned for a further two scoreless league meetings, but he was gone again almost as quickly as he had reappeared!

Martin Ashby unfortunately spent the season struggling with injury and illness and it was left to Jan Andersson and Bob Kilby to head the Robins' scoring. Indeed, Andersson came on a bundle and showed his undoubted class by reaching the *Sunday Mirror* World Final at Wembley on 2 September, when he scored 3 points. Meanwhile, Geoff Bouchard, with his all-action riding, became the darling of the Blunsdon terraces, and scored his first ever maximum in top-level league racing with a 15-pointer against Leicester at Blunsdon on 8 April.

In a season to forget, Swindon slipped further down the final table to sixteenth place in the Gulf Oil British League, losing all but two of their away fixtures, the exceptions being a 42-36 win at Wolverhampton and a 39-39 draw at Reading. At home there were five defeats, against Belle Vue, Coventry, Exeter, Hull and White City, while two matches were drawn, against Halifax and Sheffield. The worst of those home performances saw the Robins embarrassingly crushed 52-26 when Coventry were in town on 6 May. Swindon guest Malcolm Simmons, in for the absent Jan Andersson, was the only home rider to perform on the night, notching 9+1 points, while club doyens Martin Ashby and Bob Kilby could only manage 5 and 3 points respectively. In the final analysis, Andersson topped the league averages on 8.18, slightly ahead of Kilby on 8.15, with the other regulars finishing as follows: Martin Ashby (7.69), Geoff Bouchard (6.52), David Ashby (4.57), Rolf Gramstad (4.22), Robert Henry (3.52), Malcolm Holloway (2.29) and Steen Mastrup (1.88).

In the *Speedway Star* Knock-Out Cup the Robins had a first round bye, but at the next hurdle against Poole both sides lost their home leg by the exact same score, 42-36, to draw on aggregate. In the replay, Swindon again lost their home leg before being soundly thrashed at Wimborne Road, going out on aggregate by a 90-66 scoreline. Much earlier in the year, the Robins had raced against local rivals Reading in the County Challenge Cup but, after winning 39-38 in the home leg, the lads in red and white refused to ride in the return match at Smallmead due to poor track conditions caused by heavy rainfall. Referee Reg Trott awarded Reading the match by default, with the Racers' management then staging an impromptu Best Pairs meeting in order to keep faith with the 4,000 spectators in attendance. The Swindon riders subsequently received SCB fines totalling £95 each for failing to partake in the meeting.

On the individual front at the Abbey Stadium, Belle Vue's Peter Collins took the spoils of victory in the *Sunday Mirror* World Championship/Volkswagen Grand Prix qualifying round on 18 May, when he romped to an unbeaten 15 points to take first place from home man Jan Andersson (14) and Cradley Heath's Dave Perks (12). Having not been run in 1977, the Arkells-sponsored Silver Plume returned to the Blunsdon calendar on 29 June, when a three-man run-off was required to determine the rostrum positions after Bob Kilby had tied on 13 points with Wolverhampton's Jim McMillan and Exeter's Norwegian thrill-merchant Reidar Eide. The extra race saw McMillan claim the top prize of £100, although Kilby snapped at his heels all the way, despite breaking a footrest in his ultimately unsuccessful chase. The remaining big meeting of the season at Blunsdon saw Wolverhampton's Dave Morton net 14 points to take victory in the Artdeans Trophy on 26 August. Fellow Wolves representative Hans Nielsen filled the runner-up spot after defeating Leicester's John Boulger in a run-off after both had finished on 13 points. Regrettably, for the first time, Swindon had no representative in the BL Cars British League Riders' Championship at Belle Vue on 21 October; the meeting won by Ole Olsen, who had secured his third World title at Wembley just seven weeks previously.

The final meeting of the season at the Abbey pitched the Robins in a challenge match, somewhat ironically as things were to turn out, against Bristol. Little did the fans know when they streamed from the stadium, following a morale-boosting 54-24 victory on 14 October, that it was to be the end of an era. Indeed, it was to prove the last meeting under the old system, which had seen speedway promoted by the company that owned and ran the stadium. In the winter conference of the British Speedway Promoters' Association, Ted Nelson, the long-time Swindon boss, reached agreement with Wally Mawdsley for his company to take over the running of the sport at Blunsdon. Mr Mawdsley had been promoting to huge crowds at Eastville Stadium in Bristol, but an injunction on noise and nuisance grounds meant that the venue saw only two seasons of racing in 1977 and 1978. The multi-track promoter therefore turned his attentions to Swindon and successfully negotiated a five-year lease with Mr Nelson.

Swindon Robins, 1978. From left to right, back row: Geoff Bouchard, Jan Andersson, Dick Bradley (Team Manager), Jerzy Trzeszkowski, David Ashby, Kevin Pope, Leonard Raba, Bob Kilby. Front row: Alun Rossiter (Club Mascot), Richard Evans, Malcolm Holloway. On bike: Martin Ashby.

With the change at the top the Robins had to say goodbye to Dick Bradley as team manager, as he was no longer required by the new promotion. The former Bristol, Southampton and Newport rider had done sterling work for the club, having held the position ever since succeeding Norman Parker in 1968. On the plus side, the Bristol riders, including Phil Crump, were without a club and rumours quickly did the rounds suggesting that 'Crumpie' would be happy to ride for the Robins. The tough Australian had always shown a liking for the Blunsdon circuit and this had again been evident when, riding for Bristol in a league match on 29 July, he equalled Martin Ashby's track record of 67.6 seconds in the opening heat. The thought that he might be seen sporting a Robins race-jacket was certainly a mouth-watering one for the Swindon supporters.

SWINDON ROBINS 1978

(Swindon's score shown first unless otherwise stated)

GULF OIL BRITISH LEAGUE

Opponents	Home	Away
Belle Vue	L37-41	L31-47
Birmingham	W44-34	L31-47
Bristol	W41-36	L31-47
Coventry	L26-52	L25-53
Cradley Heath	W40-37	L26-52
Exeter	L35-43	L25-53
Hackney	W42-36	L27-51
Halifax	D39-39	L28-50
Hull	L34-44	L29-49
Ipswich	W42-36	L28-50
King's Lynn	W47-31	L31-47

Leicester	W48-30	L32-46
Poole	W42-36	L35-43
Reading	W40-38	D39-39
Sheffield	D39-39	L24-54
White City	L36-42	L29-42
Wimbledon	W41-37	L28-50
Wolverhampton	W41-37	W42-36

GULF OIL BRITISH LEAGUE TABLE

Team	Mts	Won	Drn	Lst	For	Agn.	Pts
Coventry	36	27	0	9	1,542	1,257	54
Belle Vue	36	26	0	10	1,491.5	1,315.5	52
Hull	36	22	2	12	1,477	1,325	46
Wimbledon	36	22	1	13	1,502	1,300	45
Cradley Heath	36	21	1	14	1,477	1,322	43
Ipswich	36	21	1	14	1,471	1,330	43
Exeter	36	20	1	15	1,532	1,269	41
Sheffield	36	19	2	15	1,366.5	1,439.5	40
Bristol	36	19	0	17	1,432	1,367	38
Poole	36	17	3	16	1,426	1,379	37
Leicester	36	17	0	19	1,368	1,434	34
Halifax	36	14	3	19	1,371.5	1,431.5	31
King's Lynn	36	14	2	20	1,391	1,412	30
Reading	36	13	3	20	1,338	1,462	29
White City	36	12	3	21	1,319.5	1,474.5	27
Swindon	36	12	3	21	1,255	1,544	27
Wolverhampton	36	11	1	24	1,312	1,491	23
Birmingham	36	11	1	24	1,280	1,525	23
Hackney	36	10	1	25	1,264	1,538	21

LEAGUE AVERAGES

Rider	Mts	Rds	Pts	Bon.	Tot.	Avge	Maximums
Dave Morton	1	4	10	1	11	11.00	–
Finn Thomsen	1	4	10	0	10	10.00	–
Keith White	1	5	10	1	11	8.80	–
Jan Andersson	29	135	266	10	276	8.18	2 full
Bob Kilby	33	136	268	9	277	8.15	3 full; 1 paid
Chris Bevan	1	1	1	1	2	8.00	–
Phil Crump	1	5	8	2	10	8.00	–
Malcolm Simmons	1	5	9	1	10	8.00	–
Martin Ashby	27	117	209	16	225	7.69	1 full
Geoff Bouchard	36	159	227	32	259	6.52	1 full
David Ashby	31	120	116	21	137	4.57	–
Rolf Gramstad	10	37	29	10	39	4.22	–
Phil Herne	1	2	1	1	2	4.00	–
Robert Henry	14	50	36	8	44	3.52	–
Jerzy Trzeszkowski	11	33	17	3	20	2.42	–
Malcolm Holloway	15	42	20	4	24	2.29	–
Tim Nunan	1	2	1	0	1	2.00	–
Steen Mastrup	13	34	12	4	16	1.88	–
Richard Evans	6	12	3	2	5	1.67	–
Bobby McNeil	1	3	1	0	1	1.33	–
Soren Karlsson	4	14	1	1	2	0.57	–
Richard Greer	1	3	0	0	0	0.00	–
Bob Humphreys	1	2	0	0	0	0.00	–
Leonard Raba	5	11	0	0	0	0.00	–
Derek Richardson	1	2	0	0	0	0.00	–

SPEEDWAY STAR KNOCK-OUT CUP

Opponents	Home	Away	Aggregate
Bye (Round one)	–	–	–
Poole (Round two)	L36-42	W42-36	D78-78
Poole (Replay)	L37-41	L29-49	L66-90

MIDLAND CUP

Opponents	Home	Away	Aggregate
Leicester (Round one)	L16-26	L27-51	L43-77

Note: The home match against Leicester was abandoned after heat eight, with the result standing.

COUNTY CHALLENGE CUP

Opponents	Home	Away
Reading	W39-38	Lost

Note: With regard to what was scheduled to be the second leg of the County Challenge Cup at Reading, the Swindon riders felt the Smallmead circuit was unfit to race on and refused to compete on the night. The referee, however, awarded Reading the match by default, with the Racers' management then staging an impromptu Best Pairs meeting in order to keep faith with the attending supporters.

CHALLENGE

Opponents	Home	Away	Aggregate
Bristol	(1) W42-36	L34-43	L76-79
Bristol	(2) W54-24	–	–
Reading	L37-41	–	–

BL CARS BRITISH LEAGUE RIDERS' CHAMPIONSHIP

Swindon had no representative.

1979

The arrival of Wally Mawdsley as Swindon promoter brought with it some much-needed strength to the team. With Bristol forced to close down, the Robins acquired the services of Australian international Phil Crump and American Steve Gresham. Departures from Blunsdon saw the promising and highly competent Jan Andersson move to Reading, while David Ashby went on loan to Milton Keynes in the National League. With the change of promotion there also came a new-look body colour, with the traditional design replaced by a robin constructed around a large capital 'R'.

The new era for Swindon Speedway was due to begin on Friday 16 March, with a quality field put together to contest the Mirrorsport Trophy. Unfortunately for all the supporters and the new management, a carpet of snow had covered the Blunsdon raceway and the meeting had to be postponed. It was hastily rescheduled for 22 March, when the weather was much kinder. There was a strange atmosphere, however, with all the behind-the-scenes staff going about their various duties, for although Ted Nelson was, as always present, it did seem odd to not have him directing operations. Reigning World Champion Ole Olsen gave a sizzling display to win the event with a full five-ride maximum, while a run-off was required to determine second place after Phil Crump and Bob Kilby had tied on 13 points apiece. As a contest, the extra race didn't last long, since Kilby fell on the second bend, leaving the Aussie an unchallenged passage to the runner-up spot on the podium.

Although Swindon had an excellent squad, regrettably they were to achieve nothing of note from the season. Martin Ashby, in a year when he was granted a Testimonial, struggled to find his best form and found himself at reserve for many matches. Every so often there were flashes of the Ashby of old, but it was a disappointing year for him generally. To offset this, new Robin Phil Crump was quite brilliant, piling up a total of 340 points in league meetings for an average of 10.36. Meanwhile Bob Kilby, despite a period when little went right with his machinery, picked himself up and finished the year with a 7.57 average.

Rolf Gramstad's season began very well, but he seemed to lose his way as the year progressed. He did however have one memorable meeting, away at Eastbourne on 29 June, when he scorched to 13+1 points. The Robins suffered a cruel blow in a Midland Cup encounter at Leicester on 28 August when the hugely popular Geoff Bouchard crashed and was badly hurt, suffering fractured ribs and a

Swindon Robins, 1979. From left to right, back row: Bob Kilby, Phil Crump, Wally Mawdsley (Promoter), Steen Mastrup, Steve Gresham, Henry Hitch (Team Manager), Geoff Bouchard, Rolf Gramstad. Front, on bike: Martin Ashby.

punctured lung. Unfortunately he never rode competitively again, but he will always have a special place in the hearts of the Blunsdon faithful for his on-track battling qualities. Swindon initially looked to Czech racer Petr Ondrasik as a replacement, but it was fellow countryman Milan Spinka who came on board in October, and did reasonably well in the five league matches in which he rode.

This was an incredible season for fixtures at the Abbey, with a total of thirty-seven home meetings staged! This was more than had ever been held in a single year, with the previous highest total being thirty-one in 1951. The fewest staged was fourteen in the initial, short 1949 season, although only nineteen meetings were held during the course of a full 1963 campaign. The quite staggering total of meetings for 1979 included no fewer than seven individual events. Also included, on 27 July, was a Test match between England and Australasia, which the home nation won by 67 points to 41. Leading the way for the victorious English side were Michael Lee (16+1), Dave Jessup (15+1) and Chris Morton (11+4), while the Australasians' scoring was headed by Ivan Mauger (12), Phil Crump (10+2) and Billy Sanders (10). The meeting also saw Crump become the 'King of Blunsdon', as he sliced six-tenths of a second off the previous best time in establishing 67 seconds dead as the new all-time track record. Then, amazingly, on 22 September, 'Crumpie' blitzed around the circuit in 66.5 seconds in heat one of his Golden Helmet challenge with Peter Collins, which took place immediately prior to the league match with Belle Vue. Five days later though, Collins himself zoomed around the Blunsdon bowl in 66.5 seconds on his way to victory in the *Daily Mirror* Silver Plume.

Martin Ashby's Testimonial went ahead on 23 September, when a star-studded individual meeting took place. The line-up read like a 'Speedway Who's Who', with Michael Lee coming out on top thanks to a 15-point maximum. Other participants in the special meeting included England internationals Doug Wyer, Peter Collins, Malcolm Simmons, John Davis, Terry Betts and Dave Jessup, which was a measure of the high regard in which Crash was held.

Aside from Ole Olsen's victory in the Mirrorsport Trophy and Peter Collins' success in the Silver Plume, other individual triumphs went as follows: Phil Crump (*Sunday Mirror*/Berger Grand Prix World Championship qualifying round), John Davis (Artdeans Knock-Out Trophy), Barry Allaway (Master of

Phil Crump.

Junior Speedway), Dave Jessup (Duplex Litho Press Trophy) and Michael Lee, as previously mentioned in the Martin Ashby Testimonial. Briefly going back to the Golden Helmet, Peter Collins had held the title all through the season until Phil Crump relieved him of the coveted trophy. Regrettably though, 'Crumpie' didn't keep it for long, losing out to Bruce Penhall in his first defence.

The Robins ended their Gulf Oil British League campaign in eighth position, with the usual indifferent home form prevailing, which saw four defeats and a draw. On the road the side notched wins at Birmingham, Eastbourne and Hackney, while also forcing draws at both Belle Vue and Poole. In the *Speedway Star* Knock-Out Cup Exeter put paid to Swindon's hopes in the third round, while Leicester dumped the Robins out of the Midland Cup at the semi-final stage. Meanwhile, the Wiltshire side eclipsed Stoke in the first round of the Inter-League Knock-Out Cup, but they were beaten 44-34 by Hackney at the next stage, when Steve Gresham was barred from riding due to an illegal silencer.

On 20 October, Phil Crump represented the side at Belle Vue in the Gauntlet British League Riders' Championship, scoring 9 points in a meeting won by John Louis of Ipswich. Following that and due to the congested fixture list, Blunsdon had its latest-ever finish to a speedway season, with the Robins facing Exeter in a British League match on a freezing cold 1 November.

With the encouragement of youth firmly in mind, the year also saw the formation of the Swindon Sprockets side, which entered the twelve-team Trackstar Anglia Junior League. The new team did reasonably well too, occupying sixth place in the final standings, with enthusiastic Swindon-born teenager Martin Hewlett posting an impressive 9.05 average as the top man. Other regulars were Alan Leaver, Neil Farnish and Terry Freeman, while Neville Moore and Kevin Brown appeared in one match apiece. It was Leaver who represented the Sprockets in the Anglia Junior League Riders' Championship at Mildenhall on 29 August. He did well, scoring 10 points for third spot on the rostrum, behind winner Nigel Sparshott (14) and runner-up Mark Baldwin (13).

SWINDON ROBINS 1979

(Swindon's score shown first unless otherwise stated)

GULF OIL BRITISH LEAGUE

Opponents	Home	Away
Belle Vue	W41-37	D39-39
Birmingham	W49-29	W40-38
Coventry	L37-41	L35-43
Cradley Heath	W40-38	L28-50
Eastbourne	W48-30	W47-31
Exeter	L38-39	L34-44
Hackney	W46-31	W49-29
Halifax	W40-38	L33-45
Hull	D39-39	L23-55
Ipswich	W46-32	L35-43
King's Lynn	L38-40	L34-44
Leicester	W59-19	L37-41
Poole	L36-42	D39-39
Reading	W45-33	L35-43
Sheffield	W50-27	L32-46
Wimbledon	W40-38	L34-44
Wolverhampton	W46-32	L38-40

GULF OIL BRITISH LEAGUE TABLE

Team	Mts	Won	Drn	Lst	For	Agn.	Pts
Coventry	34	26	0	8	1,418	1,231	52
Hull	34	24	2	8	1,546	1,099	50
Cradley Heath	34	24	0	10	1,500	1,146	48
King's Lynn	34	22	1	11	1,396	1,256	45
Exeter	34	21	0	13	1,413	1,230	42
Halifax	34	18	0	16	1,336.5	1,311.5	36
Reading	34	17	0	17	1,345	1,305	34
Swindon	34	15	3	16	1,350	1,299	33
Wimbledon	34	16	1	17	1,327	1,320	33
Belle Vue	34	14	4	16	1,323	1,326	32
Wolverhampton	34	15	1	18	1,306	1,342	31
Poole	34	14	3	17	1,297	1,352	31
Sheffield	34	14	2	18	1,228	1,420	30
Birmingham	34	13	2	19	1,257	1,392	28
Ipswich	34	12	2	20	1,264	1,381	26
Eastbourne	34	10	2	22	1,242	1,406	22
Leicester	34	10	0	24	1,150.5	1,497.5	20
Hackney	34	9	1	24	1,130	1,515	19

LEAGUE AVERAGES

Rider	Mts	Rds	Pts	Bon.	Tot.	Avge	Maximums
Phil Crump	31	134	340	7	347	10.36	11 full; 1 paid
Vaclav Verner	1	4	8	1	9	9.00	–
Bob Kilby	33	129	231	13	244	7.57	3 full
Steve Gresham	29	110	181	13	194	7.05	–
Geoff Bouchard	25	98	125	32	157	6.41	1 full
Steen Mastrup	25	86	107	24	131	6.09	–
Martin Ashby	34	135	167	32	199	5.90	1 paid
Milan Spinka	5	20	24	3	27	5.40	–
Rolf Gramstad	33	113	126	12	138	4.88	–
Emil Sova	1	5	4	1	5	4.00	–
Malcolm Holloway	11	41	29	6	35	3.41	–
David Ashby	3	9	6	0	6	2.67	–
Martin Hewlett	1	3	2	0	2	2.67	–
Louis Carr	1	4	0	0	0	0.00	–

SPEEDWAY STAR KNOCK-OUT CUP

Opponents	Home	Away	Aggregate
Bye (Round one)	–	–	–
Birmingham (Round two)	W62-46	L49-59	W111-105
Exeter (Quarter-final)	L46-62	L52-56	L98-118

MIDLAND CUP

Opponents	Home	Away	Aggregate
Birmingham (Quarter-final)	W47-31	W46-32	W93-63
Leicester (Semi-final)	W40-38	L33.5-44.5	L73.5-82.5

INTER-LEAGUE KNOCK-OUT CUP

Opponents	Home	Away
Stoke (Round one)	–	W46-32
Hackney (Round two)	–	L34-44

SARJENTS SILVER SPANNER TROPHY

Opponents	Home	Away	Aggregate
Reading	D39-39	L34-43	L73-82

CHALLENGE

Opponents	Home	Away
Exeter	–	L48-60
Poole	(1) W50-28	(1) L35-43
Poole	(2) W49-29	(2) 29-37 (aban.)
Reading	W52-26	L35-43

Note: The second challenge match at Poole was abandoned after heat eleven.

BRITISH LEAGUE FOUR-TEAM CHAMPIONSHIP

Qualifying group:	
(First leg at Poole)	Exeter 38, Poole 31, Swindon 20, Oxford 7.
(Second leg at Exeter)	Exeter 35, Poole 26, Swindon 23, Oxford 12.
(Third leg at Oxford)	Poole 32, Exeter 26, Swindon 19, Oxford 19.
(Fourth leg at Swindon)	Swindon 38, Exeter 31, Poole 22, Oxford 4.
Aggregate result:	Exeter 130, Poole 111, Swindon 100, Oxford 42.

SOUTHERN CHALLENGE FOUR-TEAM TOURNAMENT

(Staged at Oxford)	Swindon 33, Poole 29, Reading 24, Oxford 10.

GAUNTLET BRITISH LEAGUE RIDERS' CHAMPIONSHIP

(Staged at Belle Vue)	Phil Crump 9 points.

SWINDON SPROCKETS

TRACKSTAR ANGLIA JUNIOR LEAGUE TABLE

Team	Mts	Won	Drn	Lst	For	Agn.	Pts
Mildenhall	22	18	0	4	236	156	36
King's Lynn	22	15	2	5	237	153	32
Crayford	22	14	1	7	216	165	29
Peterborough	22	13	0	9	209	176	26
Wimbledon	22	12	1	9	193	184	25
Swindon	22	11	1	10	205	169	23
Rye House	22	11	0	11	170	191	22
Reading	22	10	1	11	184	200	21
Ipswich	22	8	4	10	190	197	20
Cradley Heath	22	7	1	14	154	209	15
Oxford	22	6	0	16	156	227	12
Nottingham	22	1	1	20	129	252	3

1980

In 1980 it was Bob Kilby's turn to celebrate a Testimonial year, and the Swindon rider, elected as captain, was in excellent form until a crash at Poole caused him to miss a chunk of the season through injury. There were, as to be expected, a number of comings and goings as promoter Wally Mawdsley sought a winning combination. To the disappointment of many, the Robins' all-time record points man, Martin Ashby, was released, and he went off up the M4 to join Reading. His contribution had been immense over the years and in league matches alone he had made 452 appearances in the famous Robins race jacket, scoring 3,980.5 points, plus 236 bonus. In the programme from the Blunsdon opener, ironically against Reading in the Sarjents Tools Challenge Trophy on 22 March, Swindon boss Mawdsley explained that to have kept Ashby on board within the 50-point rule, it would have meant losing both Steve Gresham and Steen Mastrup. Meanwhile, popular Norwegian Rolf Gramstad was another to depart from Blunsdon, and he subsequently linked up with Leicester.

Two riders were signed from Exeter – Scott Autrey, the American international, and Australian Steve Koppe. Autrey finished the season as top man, scoring 329 points for an average of 9.97, but Koppe failed to find form and was gone before the end of April. Unfortunately, the high-scoring Phil Crump didn't appear until June, having been given leave of absence by Mawdsley to remain at home in Australia in order to set up and establish a motorcycle business. Milan Spinka was missing more times than he was actually around and John Barker, another new arrival, found the pace of British League racing far too hot. Youngster Robert Craven was also signed at the beginning of the season, but the son of former double World Champion Peter suffered with a shoulder injury and never turned a wheel for the Robins, instead making just two appearances for National League Scunthorpe before quitting. To assist Swindon, veterans Reidar Eide and Nigel Boocock made fleeting appearances, but the most promising name on the horizon was Zimbabwean Mike Ferreira, who was really setting the National League on fire at Canterbury. Another bright spot was the improved form of Steve Gresham, who ceased to be a villain and became the hero of the Robins' fans. In a season that saw the services of many riders utilized, Australian Bob Humphreys also came on board, combining his duties with National League Milton Keynes. Right at the end of the season, in October, there was another signing in the shape of Czech racer Jan Verner, who appeared in the side's last three league fixtures.

Swindon were a real Jekyll and Hyde team, managing to win no less than five league matches away from home, but to offset that they lost three and drew two meetings at Blunsdon! Once Crumpie had returned he backed Scott Autrey all way, averaging 9.41, but the Robins lacked a third heat-leader as the final averages of the other most-used team members proved: Steve Gresham (7.40), Bob Kilby (7.23), Milan Spinka (6.46), Steen Mastrup (5.49) and Malcolm Holloway (4.93). Swindon actually ended the season without three of their regulars – Messrs Kilby, Crump and Gresham. All three were missing for various reasons, Kilby on medical advice some two months after injuring his back in a nasty crash at Poole on 11 June. Meanwhile, having started the season late, Crumpie only rode until the end of September before returning home to his business interests. As for Gresham, the last but not least of the trio, like Kilby he ended up on the injured list, having suffered broken bones in his ankle.

The Robins could only manage eighth position in the league again, and Wally Mawdsley expressed concern at a fall in crowd figures. Although fewer fixtures were staged than the previous season, Blunsdon still hosted a remarkable thirty-four meetings throughout the year. Just two full-blown individual events were held in 1980 – as opposed to the seven such meetings in 1979 – with Wimbledon's Larry Ross tasting glory in the Artdeans Knock-Out Trophy on 14 June, prior to Michael Lee of King's Lynn scooping the *Daily Mirror*-sponsored Silver Plume on 3 October. The Master of Junior Speedway was also held, but only as the second half of an Anglia League representative match against the Scottish Junior League on 4 October, when future Robin David Blackburn emerged as the victor ahead of Ipswich-born novice Steve Bryenton.

'American Express' Scott Autrey, who recorded 329 league points for a 9.97 average in 1980.

Scott Autrey.

In the *Speedway Star* Knock-Out Cup, Swindon battled past Eastbourne and Ipswich to reach the semi-final, but despite a terrific effort the Robins went down to a narrow aggregate defeat, 111-105, at the hands of Belle Vue. In the Midland Cup it was the same story, with defeat at the semi-final hurdle to Coventry, by 79 points to 77 on aggregate. They did fare better in the Inter-League Knock-Out Cup, however, overcoming Peterborough in the first round, Eastbourne in the quarter-final and Leicester in the semi-final. However, on a bitterly cold 25 September at the Abbey, Swindon flattered to deceive, going down to a 41-37 defeat in the first leg of the final against King's Lynn. Although they battled hard in the second leg at Saddlebow Road on 29 October, the Robins lost 42-36, with the aggregate result unfortunately being an 83-73 defeat.

Blunsdon proudly staged a Test match between England and the USA on 24 May, with the Americans claiming a well-earned 59-49 success to take overall victory in the five-match series. Scott Autrey (15+1) and Dennis Sigalos (15) led the Americans to success, while future double World Champion Bruce Penhall gained 14 points. Meanwhile, for England, the top dogs were Dave Jessup (12+1), Michael Lee (12) and John Louis (10). A four-team tournament was staged as Bob Kilby's Testimonial meeting on 31 August, when a Vikings team scored 34 points to win, with the Yankees in second place (30), ahead of the Union Jacks (19) and the Global Stars (13). Among the riders paying their respects to Kilb in his special meeting were Hans Nielsen, Bo Petersen, Erik Gundersen, Bruce Penhall, Bobby Schwartz, Dave Jessup and Malcolm Simmons. In the big domestic meeting of 1980 – the Gauntlet British League Riders' Championship at Belle Vue on 18 October – Scott Autrey represented the Robins and scored 8 points; the prestigious event was won by Leicester's Les Collins.

Swindon's junior side, the Sprockets, contested the Anglia Junior League and finished sixth out of the nine competing sides, with both Chris Hunt and Martin Satchell remaining ever-present throughout the sixteen-match programme. Looking a little further into the team, Neville Moore made nine appearances, while Martin Hewlett (who successfully spent the season on loan at National League Exeter), Alan Leaver, Terry Broadbank and Marcus Williams also enjoyed outings.

SWINDON ROBINS 1980

(Swindon's score shown first unless otherwise stated)

BRITISH LEAGUE

Opponents	Home	Away
Belle Vue	D39-39	L25-52
Birmingham	W52-26	W43-35
Coventry	W43-35	L34-44
Cradley Heath	L35-43	L32-46
Eastbourne	W43-35	W48-30
Hackney	L32-46	L35-43
Halifax	W44-34	L36-42
Hull	W46-32	L36-42
Ipswich	D39-39	L30-48
King's Lynn	W40-38	L34-44
Leicester	W45-33	W40-38
Poole	W49-29	L34-44
Reading	L33-45	W40-38
Sheffield	W59-19	L33-45
Wimbledon	W41-37	L35-43
Wolverhampton	W46-32	W43-35

BRITISH LEAGUE TABLE

Team	Mts	Won	Drn	Lst	For	Agn.	Pts
Reading	32	24	1	7	1,434	1,062	49
Hackney	32	23	0	9	1,300	1,188	46
Belle Vue	32	21	1	10	1,298	1,193	43
Coventry	32	20	2	10	1,326	1,170	42
Cradley Heath	32	20	0	12	1,302	1,189	40
King's Lynn	32	17	0	15	1,353	1,141	34
Ipswich	32	16	2	14	1,298	1,194	34
Swindon	32	16	2	14	1,264	1,231	34
Poole	32	15	2	15	1,254	1,237	32
Halifax	32	15	1	16	1,219	1,271	31
Leicester	32	14	0	18	1,253	1,241	28
Hull	32	11	5	16	1,207	1,286	27
Wimbledon	32	12	2	18	1,195	1,294	26
Birmingham	32	11	1	20	1,158	1,338	23
Wolverhampton	32	9	2	21	1,192	1,297	20
Eastbourne	32	9	1	22	1,093	1,399	19
Sheffield	32	8	0	24	1,039	1,454	16

LEAGUE AVERAGES

Rider	Mts	Rds	Pts	Bon.	Tot.	Avge	Maximums
Ron Preston	1	1	3	0	3	12.00	–
Scott Autrey	30	136	329	10	339	9.97	6 full
Phil Crump	16	71	157	10	167	9.41	1 full; 3 paid
Martin Hewlett	1	3	4	2	6	8.00	–
Phil White	2	8	11	4	15	7.50	–
Steve Gresham	30	120	204	18	222	7.40	1 paid
Bob Kilby	17	62	104	8	112	7.23	1 full
John Davis	1	4	7	0	7	7.00	–
Milan Spinka	15	52	66	18	84	6.46	–
Jan Verner	3	11	15	2	17	6.18	–
Martin Yeates	2	8	12	0	12	6.00	–
Reidar Eide	5	21	27	4	31	5.90	–
Steen Mastrup	26	94	105	24	129	5.49	–
Bob Humphreys	9	38	42	10	52	5.47	–
Nicky Allott	1	3	4	0	4	5.33	–
Mike Spink	1	3	3	1	4	5.33	–
Mike Ferreira	6	22	26	3	29	5.27	–
Malcolm Holloway	30	107	111	21	132	4.93	–
Nigel Flatman	3	10	9	2	11	4.40	–

John Barker	7	19	11	1	12	2.53	–
Steve Koppe	2	8	5	0	5	2.50	–
Nigel Boocock	8	22	7	1	8	1.45	–
Rolf Gramstad	1	3	1	0	1	1.33	–
Sean Willmott	1	3	1	0	1	1.33	–
Louis Carr	1	3	0	0	0	0.00	–

SPEEDWAY STAR KNOCK-OUT CUP

Opponents	Home	Away	Aggregate
Bye (Round one)	–	–	–
Eastbourne (Round two)	W62-46	W55.5-52.5	W117.5-98.5
Ipswich (Quarter-final)	W63-45	L53-55	W116-100
Belle Vue (Semi-final)	W56-52	L49-59	L105-111

INTER-LEAGUE KNOCK-OUT CUP

Opponents	Home	Away	Aggregate
Peterborough (Round one)	–	W47-31	–
Eastbourne (Quarter-final)	W42-36	–	–
Leicester (Semi-final)	–	W40-38	–
King's Lynn (Final)	L37-41	L36-42	L73-83

MIDLAND CUP

Opponents	Home	Away	Aggregate
Wolverhampton (Quarter-final)	W43-35	D39-39	W82-74
Coventry (Semi-final)	W41-37	L36-42	L77-79

GAUNTLET GOLD CUP

Opponents	Home	Away
Eastbourne	W44-34	L28-50
Poole	L37-40	L35-43
Wimbledon	W42-36	W40-38

GAUNTLET GOLD CUP (WESTERN SECTOR) TABLE

Team	Mts	Won	Drn	Lst	For	Agn.	Pts
Poole	6	4	0	2	243	224	8
Eastbourne	6	3	0	3	242	226	6
Swindon	6	3	0	3	226	241	6
Wimbledon	6	2	0	4	224	244	4

DUPLEX LITHO PRESS TROPHY

Opponents	Home	Away	Aggregate
Reading	L38-40	L27-51	L65-91

SARJENTS TOOLS SILVER SPANNER TROPHY

Opponents	Home	Away	Aggregate
Reading	D39-39	W41-37	W80-76

CHALLENGE

Opponents	Home	Away
Cradley Heath	W42-36	–
Leicester	W44-34	–
Poole	–	L38-40
Wimbledon	–	L36-42

FOUR-TEAM TOURNAMENT

| (Staged at Rye House) | Hackney 41, Rye House 25, Swindon 22, Wimbledon 7. |
| (Staged at Weymouth) | Poole 32, Reading 23, Weymouth 21, Swindon 20. |

GAUNTLET BRITISH LEAGUE RIDERS' CHAMPIONSHIP

(Staged at Belle Vue)   Scott Autrey 8 points.

SWINDON SPROCKETS

ANGLIA JUNIOR LEAGUE TABLE

Team	Mts	Won	Drn	Lst	For	Agn.	Pts
Ipswich	16	13	1	2	176	106	27
Mildenhall	16	11	1	4	169	114	23
Leicester	16	7	2	7	133	136	16
Rye House	16	7	1	8	135	132	15
Peterborough	16	7	0	9	130	152	14
Swindon	16	6	2	8	118	152	14
Crayford	16	6	1	9	133	143	13
Milton Keynes	16	5	2	9	125	160	12
Cradley Heath	16	3	4	9	122	146	10

1981

Off-track movements at the Abbey in 1981 saw head man Wally Mawdsley make a number of changes, with Bob Radford taking up the position of press officer while future club promoter Ron Byford became pit marshal. Meanwhile, Bert Harrison took over from Graham Hambly as announcer, with Paul Johnson moving in from Ipswich as promotions executive. On the team front, Scott Autrey relocated to Poole after seriously contemplating missing out on the British scene altogether due to a hankering to ride on the rodeo circuit in his American homeland. Coming in to sport the number one race-jacket, Steve Bastable arrived via Birmingham and was also made skipper of the side, in place of Bob Kilby. The long-serving Kilb was still getting over a back injury sustained at Poole the previous season and, in the end, didn't ride at all. Young Swede Bjorn Andersson, the brother of Jan, also arrived at Blunsdon and, together with the immaculate Phil Crump, plus Steve Gresham, Malcolm Holloway and Steen Mastrup, it gave Swindon a very useful top six that virtually picked itself.

Mike Ferreira, still at National League Canterbury, was a tremendous number eight rider, but it was the second reserve spot in the team that was up for grabs, with many riders being tried throughout the year. Young Finn Veijo Tuoriniemi, who had been with Eastbourne during 1980, was given an opportunity, but failed miserably. A number of raw but promising novices were also given a run-out and these included Terry Broadbank (the son of Mike, who preferred the correct spelling of his surname, without the addition of an 's' on the end), Steve Bishop, Kevin Smart and Martin Satchell, but like young Australian Darryl Simpson, they were out of their depth in the British League. Dane Henry Nielsen (brother of Hans) and Swede Lennart Bengtsson were also given opportunities. Nielsen, who rode during his holiday period, looked as though he could be the final piece of the Swindon jigsaw, but unfortunately he wasn't keen on a full-time speedway career in Britain.

The Blunsdon season had been due to kick-off with the Arkells Brewery Super Pairs on 21 March, but inclement weather put paid to the meeting. The Robins therefore made their season's bow at Wimbledon in the newly launched League Cup five days later, when Phil Crump scorched to an 18-point maximum and helped his side to a 49-46 victory. A week later than planned, the Swindon doors opened for the first time on 28 March, when Steve Bastable raced to a paid maximum (13+2), as his new side overwhelmed Hackney 62-34 in a League Cup encounter.

As the season went on the problem reserve slot became increasingly noticeable, but despite this Swindon rose to a final position of third in the sixteen-team British League, thanks in the main to the marvellous Phil Crump. Indeed, Crumpie was back to his very best and bagged another mountain of points (313 to be precise) to finish with a 10.39 average. He was well backed by Steve Bastable, who also won the British Final, courtesy of a wonderful display at Coventry on 3 June, when he defeated Kenny Carter and John Louis in a three-man run-off for the title. 'Stevie B' attained an 8.75 average for the Robins, while there was a great deal of solidity about the rest of the team, as borne out by the final averages of the other regular riders: Steve Gresham (7.18), Steen Mastrup (6.85), Malcolm Holloway (6.83) and Bjorn Andersson (5.01). Meanwhile, Mike Ferreira did very well, yielding 68 points from eleven league matches for a highly creditable 6.73 average. The Robins' shift up the league table saw a marked improvement in home form, with two losses (against Hackney and Wimbledon) and a single draw (against Ipswich) to report. Away from the Abbey, the side remarkably tasted victory on seven occasions – at Belle Vue, Coventry, Eastbourne, Hackney, King's Lynn, Leicester and Reading – while draws were attained at Hull and Ipswich.

In the *Speedway Star* Knock-Out Cup, Swindon met Edinburgh from the National League, and a train carrying the team, management and supporters was organised by Malcolm Holloway and aptly dubbed as the 'Mad Wellie Express' after the rider's nickname. The Supporters' Club also deserved much praise for the success of the project, since they put down the deposit required by British Rail and stood guarantor for the finance. The journey to the Scottish capital for the second leg of the tie took place on 12 June and, in what was a thrilling match, the Robins won by just 2 points, 49-47, thanks largely to a wonderful 18-point maximum from the amazing Phil Crump. Swindon went on to beat Leicester in the next round, before losing both legs of the semi-final at the hands of Ipswich. Earlier, in the League Cup, the Wiltshire boys didn't fare too well, finishing fifth in the eight-team Section B table. A couple of home defeats (against Ipswich and King's Lynn) out of seven matches gave them little chance of progressing in the competition, and so it proved.

Test match speedway was again held at Blunsdon, with England facing the USA on 2 May and this saw the Lions avenge their defeat of the previous year, running out victors by 64 points to 43. Michael Lee topped the England scoring with 16 points, while Steve Bastable and Dave Jessup each bagged 13+1. For the Americans, Bruce Penhall scored 11, with Steve Gresham notching 10. The local Swindon newspaper began their sponsorship of a big individual meeting in 1981, with Hackney's

Swindon Robins, 1981. From left to right, back row: Martin Hewlett, Steve Bastable, Steen Mastrup, Bjorn Andersson, Malcolm Holloway. Kneeling: Mike Ferreira, Denzil Kent. On bike: Phil Crump.

Bo Petersen becoming the first *Evening Advertiser* Superstar on 4 July. The only other big individual meeting at the Abbey was the Godden–Newton 16-Lap Super on 12 September, when Phil Crump showed his immense stamina to emerge victorious. Crumpie also later represented Swindon in the Belle Vue-staged *Daily Mirror* British League Riders' Championship on 17 October, recording 10 points for fourth place, in a meeting won by Kenny Carter of Halifax.

The Sprockets took a year out in 1981 and only a handful of junior challenge matches were held at Blunsdon with the side running under the name of 'Young Swindon'. Among the hopefuls who represented the team and appeared in second-half racing throughout the season were Steve Bishop, Terry Broadbank, Brian Butterfield, Gary Hale, Chris Hunt, Kevin Smart and Martin Satchell. Another youngster who started racing in post-match practice was one-time mascot Alun Rossiter, who would go on to skipper his hometown club and later become promoter.

SWINDON ROBINS 1981

(Swindon's score shown first unless otherwise stated)

BRITISH LEAGUE

Opponents	Home	Away
Belle Vue	W41-37	W40-38
Birmingham	W46-32	L36-42
Coventry	W42-36	W41-37
Cradley Heath	W42-36	L35-43
Eastbourne	W51-27	W39-38
Hackney	L38-40	W40-38
Halifax	W42-36	L35-42
Hull	W40-14	D39-39
Ipswich	D39-39	D39-39
King's Lynn	W43-35	W44-34
Leicester	W49-29	W40-38
Poole	W42-36	L35-42
Reading	W41-36	W44-34
Sheffield	W47-30	L37-41
Wimbledon	L38-40	L37-41

Note: The home meeting v. Hull was abandoned after heat nine, with the result permitted to stand.

BRITISH LEAGUE TABLE

Team	Mts	Won	Drn	Lst	For	Agn.	Pts
Cradley Heath	30	26	1	3	1,339	983	53
Ipswich	30	21	4	5	1,250	1,085	46
Swindon	30	19	3	8	1,222	1,089	41
Belle Vue	30	19	1	10	1,239	1,086	39
Coventry	30	18	0	12	1,232	1,103	36
Birmingham	30	13	1	16	1,163	1,174	27
Halifax	30	13	1	16	1,149	1,188	27
Hackney	30	12	2	16	1,182	1,157	26
Poole	30	12	2	16	1,128.5	1,208.5	26
Sheffield	30	13	0	17	1,120	1,214	26
Reading	30	9	7	14	1,129	1,208	25
Hull	30	10	4	16	1,068	1,245	24
Eastbourne	30	10	3	17	1,094	1,244	23
King's Lynn	30	10	2	18	1,182	1,158	22
Leicester	30	11	0	19	1,117.5	1,221.5	22
Wimbledon	30	7	3	20	1,042	1,293	17

LEAGUE AVERAGES

Rider	Mts	Rds	Pts	Bon.	Tot.	Avge	Maximums
Phil Crump	29	124	313	9	322	10.39	3 full; 1 paid
Steve Bastable	26	106	221	11	232	8.75	1 full
Steve Gresham	24	97	147	27	174	7.18	–
Steen Mastrup	27	94	134	27	161	6.85	1 paid
Malcolm Holloway	29	116	177	21	198	6.83	–

Mike Ferreira	11	44	68	6	74	6.73	–
Steve Bishop	1	2	2	1	3	6.00	–
Steve Lawson	1	4	4	2	6	6.00	–
Martin Yeates	9	34	37	8	45	5.29	–
Bjorn Andersson	20	71	81	8	89	5.01	–
Hans Nielsen	1	4	4	1	5	5.00	–
Bob Humphreys	1	3	2	1	3	4.00	–
Henry Nielsen	5	17	9	5	14	3.29	–
Lennart Bengtsson	5	16	9	4	13	3.25	–
Martin Hewlett	4	7	3	2	5	2.86	–
Denzil Kent	3	9	6	0	6	2.67	–
Martin Satchell	6	13	5	2	7	2.15	–
Terry Broadbank	1	2	0	0	0	0.00	–
Veijo Tuoriniemi	2	4	0	0	0	0.00	–

SPEEDWAY STAR KNOCK-OUT CUP

Opponents	Home	Away	Aggregate
Bye (Round one)	–	–	–
Edinburgh (Round two)	W69-27	W49-47	W118-74
Leicester (Quarter-final)	W74-22	W51-45	W125-67
Ipswich (Semi-final)	L46-50	L39-57	L85-107

LEAGUE CUP

Opponents	Home	Away
Eastbourne	W57-39	L46-50
Hackney	W62-34	W55-41
Ipswich	L42-54	L37-59
King's Lynn	L47-49	L40-55
Poole	W51-44	L42-54
Reading	W50-46	L32-64
Wimbledon	W52-44	W49-46

LEAGUE CUP (SECTION B) TABLE

Team	Mts	Won	Drn	Lst	For	Agn.	Pts
King's Lynn	14	10	1	3	708	633	21
Reading	14	10	0	4	740.5	600.5	20
Ipswich	14	9	0	5	745	595	18
Poole	14	7	0	7	685.5	654.5	14
Swindon	14	7	0	7	662	679	14
Hackney	14	5	1	8	621.5	718.5	11
Eastbourne	14	5	0	9	636	704	10
Wimbledon	14	2	0	12	563.5	777.5	4

Note: King's Lynn and Reading progressed to the semi-finals.

MIDLAND CUP

Opponents	Home	Away	Aggregate
Birmingham (Quarter-final)	W41-37	D39-39	W80-76
Cradley Heath (Semi-final)	W44-33	L32-46	L76-79

CHALLENGE

Opponents	Home	Away
Halifax	–	L33-45
Poole	–	L52-56
Wimbledon	W60-48	–

FOUR-TEAM TOURNAMENT

(Staged at Milton Keynes)   Swindon 35, Birmingham 27, Hackney 25, Milton Keynes 9.
(Staged at Oxford)   Oxford 33, Swindon 26, Eastbourne 23, Reading 14.

DAILY MIRROR BRITISH LEAGUE RIDERS' CHAMPIONSHIP

(Staged at Belle Vue)   Phil Crump 10 points (4th).

1982

The year 1982 brought changes to the speedway scene at Blunsdon. Steve Gresham, the often-controversial American, was posted to Reading, while Mike Ferreira became a fully fledged Robin after doing such a great job as the club's number eight. Regrettably, the rider from Zimbabwe failed to settle at the Abbey Stadium raceway and was, in fact, far better for the side on their travels. The highly promising Martin Hewlett also became a full-time Robin, following his loan spell at National League Exeter. Czech rider Jan Verner was also introduced to the team, but he struggled badly and was released after completing five league matches. That said, a broken wrist sustained in a League Cup match at Reading on 12 April didn't help his cause.

Augmenting the newcomers, most of the old guard were back, including the brilliant Phil Crump, along with Steve Bastable, Steen Mastrup and Malcolm Holloway, who was named as the new team skipper. Meanwhile, Bjorn Andersson was a late arrival on the scene, thanks to a stint in the Swedish Army and a battle with the Department of Employment in order to secure a work permit. Promoter Wally Mawdsley's efforts with the DOE proved to be successful and, after arriving in June, the rider fully justified his boss's faith by upping his average by almost one-and-a-half points per match.

The season began with the League Cup but, having started well by gaining home and away wins against Poole, everything went pear-shaped for Swindon, as they finished bottom of their group after winning only one further match! The Robins fared no better in the *Speedway Star* Knock-Out Cup, with a quick-fire first round exit against Eastbourne, courtesy of defeats in both legs. They did reach the semi-final of the Midland Cup however, only to be crushed by a powerful Cradley Heath side. After losing the first leg 49-29 at Dudley Wood on 28 August, Swindon went down to an embarrassing 54-24 reverse at the Abbey in the return match two days later. In the British League, the team just couldn't put it together consistently, but considering that, a final position of eighth wasn't too bad. A total of four defeats at home didn't help, but at least they enjoyed a similar number of away victories, at Halifax, King's Lynn, Leicester and Poole. Phil Crump led the scoring as usual, and when Bjorn Andersson arrived he played his part, but Steve Bastable's contribution was down and with Mike Ferreira failing to master the Blunsdon circuit, it was hardly surprising that the Robins lacked any consistency. Malcolm Holloway tried hard and had a reasonable year, his personal highlight being a one and only appearance in the British Final at Coventry on 2 June, when he scored 3 points.

The year also saw the Sprockets return to the track after the formation of the Swindon Speedway Junior Club during the winter. The club's primary aim was to finance the Sprockets' participation in the newly formed six-team Central Junior League and the team swept all before them to win the Championship, losing just one fixture along the way. Terry Broadbank remained ever-present throughout the ten-match programme, while his various teammates were Steve Bishop, Brian Butterfield, Gary Chessell, Alun Rossiter and Kevin Smart. There was joy on the individual front as well, with both Bishop and Smart occupying podium positions in the Central Junior League Riders' Championship at Long Eaton on 6 October. In a thrilling meeting, the two Sprockets ended level with Birmingham's Steve Mildoon on the 12-point mark, necessitating a title run-off. Dramatically, Smart was excluded after a fall in the first attempt to stage the deciding race, meaning he had to settle for third position. There was good news from the re-run, however, for despite not making the best of starts, a determined Bishop daringly came from behind in mid-race to scoop the first prize. The only black spot of the year for the juniors was a serious accident that saw David Smart break both legs at Blunsdon on 22 May, after dicing for position with his brother, Kevin, during the second half.

Reverting back to the senior side, Phil Crump piled up 272 points in the league, averaging 9.44, but he was very much a one-man band, with Steve Bastable next in the statistical run-down on 7.71. Meanwhile, Bjorn Andersson obtained a useful 6.47 average and Malcolm 'Mad Wellie' Holloway

The all-conquering Swindon Sprockets of 1982. From left to right, back row: John Tremblin (Team Manager),
Gary Chessell, David Main, Kevin Smart, David Smart, Brian Butterfield. Front row: Steve Bishop, Alun Rossiter,
Terry Broadbank.

could not be faulted for finishing with a 6.13 figure. However, the expected performances from Mike Ferreira and Steen Mastrup never materialised, as their respective final averages of 5.27 and 4.62 reveal. There was a lot of public sympathy for Mastrup though, since the fan-friendly Dane sustained serious pelvic and vertebrae injuries at Leicester on 1 June which kept him out of action until mid-August.

Crumpie made it to Los Angeles for the World Final on 28 August and in a controversial meeting that will forever be remembered for Bruce Penhall's clash with Kenny Carter the durable Aussie could only register 4 points, which was clearly not a true reflection of his ability. On 16 October Steve Bastable appeared at Belle Vue in the British League Riders' Championship, and while the aforementioned Carter was racing to the title, the Robins' representative accumulated 7 points. Stevie B appeared in the meeting instead of Phil Crump, who had returned to his homeland after requiring surgery on an injured wrist. The Australian had actually broken his scaphoid in August, yet bravely rode on for a month, giving his best for the club as ever.

Tragedy struck on Saturday 11 September when, after scoring 8+1 points in a home British League match against Birmingham, twenty-year-old Martin Hewlett collapsed and sadly died the following Wednesday, due to the effects of a massive brain haemorrhage. It was a terrible shock for all concerned and a trust fund was quickly set up to help the dependants in the young rider's family. Hewlett had come through the junior ranks at the club and was on his way up the speedway ladder. The youngster had impressed with his on-track battling and had done well to average 4.62 in a team that had often struggled. On a night of great emotion, a benefit meeting was held at Exeter on 18 October, resulting in a 54-42 success for the Falcons over Swindon. A second benefit meeting was staged at Blunsdon on

30 October and this saw the Robins defeat Reading 43-35, prior to a bolstered Sprockets side beating Exeter by the same score in the second part of the special double-header. Former Swindon favourites Martin Ashby, Barry Briggs, Bob Kilby, Edgar Stangeland, David Ashby, Geoff Bouchard and Norman Hunter also took to the track in order to help raise funds to help the youngster's dependants.

In spite of the Robins' indifferent performances, Wally Mawdsley could not be faulted for giving the public plenty of speedway action, as he staged thirty-six meetings throughout the season. That total included the *Evening Advertiser* Superstar event on 6 August, which was won emphatically with a 15-point maximum by Phil Crump, and the Newton Oils/*Daily Mirror* Marathon on 15 October, which resulted in victory for Cradley Heath's Alan Grahame. As a prelude to the first of those individual meetings, the mega-popular Crump raced to a 2-1 success over holder Shawn Moran in the first leg of the Golden Helmet. However, Moran hit back to take the second leg by the same score at Sheffield on 2 September but, due to Crump's wrist problems, there was no decider and the spectacular American retained the title by default.

Among other prestigious meetings held at Blunsdon was a Test match between England and the USA on 2 May, which the Americans won by 60 points to 47. Bruce Penhall (12+2), Shawn Moran (12), Scott Autrey (11+2) and Dennis Sigalos (10) provided a powerful spearhead for the victorious Americans, while England's best were Dave Jessup (12+1), Kenny Carter (11) and Chris Morton (10+1).

The National League held their Pairs Championship at the Abbey on 28 August, when supporters from all over the country converged on Blunsdon for a real feast of speedway. Eventual winners of the event were Weymouth, who were represented by Martin Yeates and Simon Wigg, while the runners-up were the Long Eaton duo of Alan Molyneux and Dave Perks. The famous Czech team Red Star of Prague visited the Abbey Stadium for a challenge match on 9 October, when Swindon ran out winners by 45 points to 33. The visitors' side included former Robins Jan Verner and Milan Spinka among its ranks, with the rest of the team made up of Jiri Stancl, Jiri Hnidak, Petr Ondrasik, Ladislav Hradecky and Stanislaw Kubicek.

Swindon Robins, 1982. From left to right, back row: Phil Crump, Steen Mastrup, Steve Bastable, Henry Hitch (Team Manager), Martin Hewlett, Jan Verner, Mike Ferreira. Front, on bike: Malcolm Holloway.

SWINDON ROBINS 1982

(Swindon's score shown first unless otherwise stated)

BRITISH LEAGUE

Opponents	Home	Away
Belle Vue	L36-42	L21-56
Birmingham	W41-37	L35-43
Coventry	W42-36	L37-41
Cradley Heath	L33-45	L29-49
Eastbourne	L30-48	L34-44
Hackney	W41-37	L31-47
Halifax	W41-37	W41-36
Ipswich	W41-37	L24-54
King's Lynn	W44-34	W41-37
Leicester	W42-36	W40-38
Poole	W46-32	W43-35
Reading	D39-39	L38-40
Sheffield	W44-34	L37-41
Wimbledon	L36-42	L35-43

BRITISH LEAGUE TABLE

Team	Mts	Won	Drn	Lst	For	Agn.	Pts
Belle Vue	28	23	0	5	1,224	957	46
Cradley Heath	28	20	0	8	1,208	972	40
Ipswich	28	16	2	10	1,159.5	1,022.5	34
Coventry	28	16	2	10	1,120	1,061	34
Sheffield	28	14	3	11	1,124	1,059	31
Birmingham	28	13	1	14	1,096	1,084	27
Hackney	28	12	3	13	1,058.5	1,121.5	27
Swindon	28	13	1	14	1,042	1,140	27
Reading	28	12	2	14	1,078	1,103	26
Leicester	28	13	0	15	1,061	1,122	26
Wimbledon	28	12	2	14	1,010.5	1,171.5	26
Eastbourne	28	11	3	14	1,099	1,082	25
Halifax	28	10	1	17	1,076	1,104	21
King's Lynn	28	9	3	16	1,025	1,156	21
Poole	28	3	3	22	978.5	1,204.5	9

LEAGUE AVERAGES

Rider	Mts	Rds	Pts	Bon.	Tot.	Avge	Maximums
Phil Crump	27	117	272	4	276	9.44	5 full
Gary Guglielmi	1	4	9	0	9	9.00	–
Steve Bastable	27	112	205	11	216	7.71	–
Bjorn Andersson	20	86	127	12	139	6.47	–
Jan Andersson	1	5	7	1	8	6.40	–
Malcolm Holloway	24	94	120	24	144	6.13	1 full
Ari Koponen	1	6	8	1	9	6.00	–
Keith Millard	2	5	6	1	7	5.60	–
Tim Hunt	1	6	7	1	8	5.33	–
Mike Ferreira	24	91	103	17	120	5.27	–
Martin Hewlett	23	77	73	16	89	4.62	–
Steen Mastrup	15	45	43	9	52	4.62	–
Martin Yeates	12	38	32	9	41	4.32	–
Steve Gresham	1	4	4	0	4	4.00	–
Steve Schofield	1	2	1	1	2	4.00	–
Jan Verner	5	14	14	0	14	4.00	–
Eric Broadbelt	4	12	9	2	11	3.67	–
Kevin Smart	3	7	2	2	4	2.29	–
Steve Bishop	1	2	0	0	0	0.00	–

SPEEDWAY STAR KNOCK-OUT CUP

Opponents	Home	Away	Aggregate
Eastbourne (Round one)	L38-40	L32-46	L70-86

LEAGUE CUP

Opponents	Home	Away
Eastbourne	D39-39	L29-49
Hackney	L37-41	L30-48
Ipswich	L35-43	L32-46
King's Lynn	L38-40	L36-42
Poole	W46-32	W41-37
Reading	W39-38	L38-40
Wimbledon	L36-42	L32-46

LEAGUE CUP (SOUTHERN SECTION) TABLE

Team	Mts	Won	Drn	Lst	For	Agn.	Pts
Ipswich	14	12	0	2	602	486	24
Eastbourne	14	8	2	4	555	535	18
Wimbledon	14	8	1	5	560	531	17
Poole	14	6	0	8	542	549	12
Hackney	14	6	0	8	541	549	12
Reading	14	6	0	8	533	558	12
King's Lynn	14	5	0	9	521	571	10
Swindon	14	3	1	10	508	583	7

Note: Ipswich and Eastbourne progressed to the semi-finals.

MIDLAND CUP

Opponents	Home	Away	Aggregate
Birmingham (Quarter-final)	W44-34	W41-37	W85-71
Cradley Heath (Semi-final)	L24-54	L29-49	L53-103

MARTIN HEWLETT TRUST FUND

Opponents	Home	Away
Reading	W43-35	–
Exeter	W45-33	L42-54

Note: For the home meeting against Exeter in aid of the Martin Hewlett Trust Fund, the Swindon team was billed as the 'Sprockets'.

PRIDE OF THE SOUTH TROPHY

Opponents	Home	Away	Aggregate
Poole	W43-35	W41-37	W84-72

SARJENTS TOOLS TROPHY

Opponents	Home	Away	Aggregate
Reading	L30.5-47.5	W41-37	L71.5-84.5

CHALLENGE

Opponents	Home	Away
Malcolm Simmons Select	L34-43	–
Red Star, Prague	W45-33	–
Weymouth	–	L34-44

BRITISH LEAGUE RIDERS' CHAMPIONSHIP

(Staged at Belle Vue)	Steve Bastable 7 points

SWINDON SPROCKETS

CENTRAL JUNIOR LEAGUE TABLE

Team	Mts	Won	Drn	Lst	For	Agn.	Pts
Swindon	10	8	1	1	113	65	17
Stoke	10	5	1	4	97	81	11
Birmingham	10	5	1	4	84	93	11
Long Eaton	10	5	0	5	83	94	10
Leicester	10	3	1	6	88	91	7
Coventry	10	2	0	8	69	110	4

1983

In 1983, following a fraught close season, the team, taken over by Wally Mawdsley's partner-cum-accountant Richard Vowles, was woefully weak. Despite having much sympathy for their new promoter, the situation was a tad confusing for supporters, as the Swindon programme indicated that the club was being run by M.V. Enterprises (R.A. Vowles & W. Mawdsley). One bright spot was that Phil Crump remained a Robin, for the Aussie, who was due a Testimonial, had allegedly refused to carry on riding for Wally Mawdsley. Well-liked Scandinavians Steen Mastrup and Bjorn Andersson stayed on board as well, and team skipper Malcolm Holloway, who had also apparently been at loggerheads with Mawdsley, remained at Blunsdon too. Somewhat surprisingly, American Steve Gresham returned from M4 rivals Reading, despite something of an indifferent year with the Racers in 1982. Meanwhile, Steve Bastable moved on to Coventry as part of a three-way deal, which saw Danish rider Alf Busk head in the opposite direction to the Robins' nest, while Mitch Shirra left Brandon to link with Reading. Off track there were also a couple of changes, with John Tremblin replacing Henry Hitch as team manager, while Dave Eaton took over as press officer, a post he was to hold for two seasons.

In the early weeks of the season, it was a case of the superb Phil Crump almost single-handedly taking on the opposition. To be fair though, teammate Bjorn Andersson started well in the League Cup, but then suffered an ankle injury in his native land in May. During his purple patch, Andersson's finest hour occurred at the Abbey on 9 April, when he raced to a four-ride 12-point maximum against Eastbourne. The Swede was to miss many matches before finally returning in a British League fixture against Reading at Blunsdon on 20 August. Understandably, the early season spark had gone, although he did manage to garner a few good scores towards the end of the campaign. Adding to Richard Vowles' problems, Steve Gresham didn't show anything like the form he was capable of and things reached a head in heat eleven of the first leg of the *Speedway Star* Knock-Out Cup encounter with Wimbledon at Blunsdon on 25 June, when referee Frank Ebdon fined him for not making a bona-fide attempt to race. Then, following a single-point return from the second leg at Plough Lane five days later, Gresham returned to America to sort out what he described as 'personal problems.' His appearance at Wimbledon was to prove the last that British speedway saw of one of its most colourful characters.

Looking further into the side, Martin Yeates was something of an enigma, since before he left to continue his career with National League Weymouth he had shown that he did have what it takes at Swindon by beating some of the leading British League heat-leaders, yet, on the other side of the coin, he would mysteriously lose points to lesser riders. Having got back to his best with the Wildcats, he later returned to the Robins' line-up in the number eight position towards the end of the season.

German speedster Bernd Odermatt and Swede Stefan Karlsson were both announced as joining the club at one time or another during the campaign, although neither actually turned a wheel for the side. However, Australian Phil Herne did sign from Leicester in June and showed a reasonable turn of pace, while young Dane Per Sorensen also came along later in the month, but he was not the heat-leader

Aussie Phil Herne, who arrived from Leicester to bolster the Robins in June 1983.

that Vowles sought. Alf Busk took time to find any sort of rhythm, and Bob Kilby tried a brief but unsuccessful comeback, having not ridden since sustaining a back injury in 1980. Not only had Steve Gresham gone by the end of June, but Steen Mastrup had departed too. The Dane was released to join Leicester and, while he was popular at Blunsdon, like Gresham he had lost form and was struggling. Czech Milan Spinka reappeared for a spell, but he was off the pace, and was gone after just eleven league matches. Small wonder then that the Wiltshire side ended up in the cellar position in the British League, although promoter Vowles clearly learned a great deal. The Robins won just six home league matches and enjoyed a solitary away success at Leicester. Phil Crump, alias Mr Consistent, carried the side all season long and finished head and shoulders above his colleagues with an average of 9.85, a figure all the more remarkable given Swindon's plight. The mighty Aussie also represented the Robins in the British League Riders' Championship at Belle Vue on 15 October, scoring 8 points.

Many guest riders, together with the likes of Steve Bishop, Alun Rossiter, David Smart and Tim Hunt (the latter joining from Reading for a late-season stint) were used throughout the campaign, but to no avail, and the support for Crumpie was minimal. Behind him in the final analysis were Bjorn Andersson (6.27), Martin Yeates (5.74), Malcolm Holloway (5.39), Phil Herne (5.38), Alf Busk (5.03) and Per Sorensen (3.09). In what was quite simply a disastrous season, Swindon also finished rock bottom of their League Cup group for the second year running, and suffered a first round Knock-Out Cup exit in the previously mentioned clash with Wimbledon.

The Abbey Stadium again played host to Test match speedway during the year, with England facing the USA in front of a large audience on 24 April. It was the Lions' turn to win by 57 points to 51, with Chris Morton (16), Dave Jessup (12+1) and Simon Wigg (10) topping the scoring. Meanwhile, Bobby Schwartz (11+1), Dennis Sigalos (11+1), Lance King (10+1) and Kelly Moran (10+1) headed the American scorechart.

Michael Lee enjoyed himself in the wide-open spaces of Blunsdon in 1983, for on 1 July he lapped the circuit in 66.5 seconds to equal the four-year-old track record. The meeting in which the former World Champion equalled the circuit's best time was the *Evening Advertiser* Superstar event, and it was fitting that he should go on and take the prestigious title. Phil Crump enjoyed a very successful and much-deserved Testimonial year and his meeting (a three-team tournament) was staged on 2 October, with many of the world's leading riders taking part. The result was a win for the Michael Lee Select, who tallied 43 points, while Ole Olsen's Vikings scored 42 and the Pacific Stars recorded 22. Among those who turned out to honour Crump on the day were Erik Gundersen, Hans Nielsen, Billy Sanders, Simon Wigg and Jan Andersson.

Briefly turning to the Sprockets, the young brigade did well to occupy third spot in the eight-team Central Junior League, finishing 5 points behind Championship-winning Leicester. Under the management of Brian Carter, the regulars in the side were Brian Butterfield, Mark Chessell and David Main, along with David Smart, who thankfully showed no ill effects of the serious leg injuries he had suffered in 1982. Meanwhile, other second-half lads looking to make strides included Barry Byford, Mark Gibbs, Steve Goodwin and Phil Harris. On 4 October the Central Junior League Riders' Championship was held at Leicester and, in an action-packed meeting, David Smart finished joint-top of the pile on 13 points with Robert Price of Leicester. In the title run-off, Smart emulated the achievement of Steve Bishop the previous year, brilliantly swooping from behind for another Sprockets success.

SWINDON ROBINS 1983

(Swindon's score shown first unless otherwise stated)

BRITISH LEAGUE

Opponents	Home	Away
Belle Vue	L34-44	L31-47
Birmingham	L30-47	L35-43
Coventry	L28-50	L25-53
Cradley Heath	L29-49	L25-53
Eastbourne	W46-32	L38-40

Hackney	L38-40	L29-49
Halifax	W45-33	L35-43
Ipswich	L37-41	L37-41
King's Lynn	W44-34	L29-49
Leicester	W40-38	W40-38
Poole	W43-35	L37-41
Reading	L34-44	L30-48
Sheffield	W40-38	L30-47
Wimbledon	L35-43	L30-48

BRITISH LEAGUE TABLE

Team	Mts	Won	Drn	Lst	For	Agn.	Pts
Cradley Heath	28	26	0	2	1,389	795	52
Ipswich	28	22	1	5	1,177	1,007	45
Coventry	28	19	0	9	1,189	992	38
Reading	28	17	0	11	1,137	1,044	34
Belle Vue	28	15	3	10	1,092	1,089	33
Wimbledon	28	15	1	12	1,122	1,059	31
Hackney	28	14	0	14	1,072	1,106	28
King's Lynn	28	12	1	15	1,088	1,095	25
Birmingham	28	12	0	16	1,114	1,066	24
Sheffield	28	10	2	16	986	1,197	22
Halifax	28	10	1	17	1,033	1,150	21
Leicester	28	9	2	17	1,040	1,142	20
Poole	28	9	0	19	1,017	1,164	18
Eastbourne	28	7	1	20	933	1,249	15
Swindon	28	7	0	21	974	1,208	14

LEAGUE AVERAGES

Rider	Mts	Rds	Pts	Bon.	Tot.	Avge	Maximums
Richard Hellsen	1	5	14	0	14	11.20	–
Phil Collins	1	4	10	0	10	10.00	–
Phil Crump	28	134	324	6	330	9.85	4 full; 1 paid
John Davis	1	4	9	0	9	9.00	–
Kelvin Tatum	1	4	8	1	9	9.00	–
Andy Grahame	2	9	15	1	16	7.11	–
Alan Grahame	1	4	7	0	7	7.00	–
Finn Thomsen	1	4	7	0	7	7.00	–
Kevin Jolly	1	5	8	0	8	6.40	–
Ari Koponen	1	5	7	1	8	6.40	–
Sean Willmott	2	7	10	1	11	6.29	–
Bjorn Andersson	10	44	64	5	69	6.27	–
Martin Yeates	10	39	53	3	56	5.74	–
Malcolm Holloway	18	69	86	7	93	5.39	–
Phil Herne	22	78	88	17	105	5.38	–
Alf Busk	27	105	116	16	132	5.03	–
Steve Bastable	1	4	5	0	5	5.00	–
Preben Eriksen	1	4	4	1	5	5.00	–
Steve Gresham	5	19	19	2	21	4.42	–
Tim Hunt	5	19	18	3	21	4.42	–
Neil Evitts	1	4	4	0	4	4.00	–
Bob Kilby	1	3	3	0	3	4.00	–
Kevin Smith	1	5	5	0	5	4.00	–
John Titman	1	4	3	1	4	4.00	–
Steen Mastrup	8	23	19	2	21	3.65	–
Steve Bishop	2	5	2	2	4	3.20	–
Lance King	1	5	4	0	4	3.20	–
Per Sorensen	21	70	43	11	54	3.09	–
Alun Rossiter	3	6	4	0	4	2.67	–
Milan Spinka	11	27	13	0	13	1.93	–
Paul Bosley	3	7	2	1	3	1.71	–
Peter Glanz	1	2	0	0	0	0.00	–
David Smart	1	2	0	0	0	0.00	–

SPEEDWAY STAR KNOCK-OUT CUP

Opponents	Home	Away	Aggregate
Wimbledon (Round one)	L34-44	L32-46	L66-90

LEAGUE CUP

Opponents	Home	Away
Eastbourne	W43-35	L35-43
Hackney	W43-35	L28-50
Ipswich	L34-44	L36-42
King's Lynn	L31-47	35-37 (aban.)
Poole	L36-42	L36-42
Reading	L32-46	L36-42
Wimbledon	L37-41	L34-44

Note: The away match at King's Lynn was abandoned after heat twelve and as the score was inconclusive, it was not included in the League Cup table.

LEAGUE CUP (SOUTHERN SECTION) TABLE

Team	Mts	Won	Drn	Lst	For	Agn.	Pts
Wimbledon	14	11	0	3	582	510	22
Ipswich	14	9	0	5	558	532	18
Reading	14	8	0	6	573	519	16
Poole	14	8	0	6	564	527	16
Hackney	14	8	0	6	544	546	16
King's Lynn	13	6	1	6	526	487	13
Eastbourne	14	2	1	11	479	613	5
Swindon	13	2	0	11	461	553	4

Note: Wimbledon and Ipswich progressed to the semi-finals.

MIDLAND CUP

Opponents	Home	Away	Aggregate
Leicester (Quarter-final)	W46-32	W40-38	W86-70
Cradley Heath (Semi-final)	L38-40	L18-60	L56-100

CHALLENGE

Opponents	Home	Away
Bo Petersen Select	W47-37	–
Exeter	–	W55-23
Hackney	W65-55	–
Leicester	–	L32-46
Oxford	–	W73-22
Poole	–	W40-38
Reading	L37-41	L34-42

BRITISH LEAGUE RIDERS' CHAMPIONSHIP

(Staged at Belle Vue)   Phil Crump 8 points.

SWINDON SPROCKETS

CENTRAL JUNIOR LEAGUE TABLE

Team	Mts	Won	Drn	Lst	For	Agn.	Pts
Leicester	14	10	2	2	157	95	22
Sheffield	13	9	1	3	133	101	19
Swindon	14	7	3	4	139	110	17
Stoke	14	5	2	7	119	131	12
Long Eaton	14	5	2	7	113	136	12
Birmingham	13	4	3	6	112	120	11
Peterborough	12	4	1	7	100	115	9
Halifax	12	2	0	10	74	139	4

Note: Three matches, Birmingham v. Sheffield, Halifax v. Peterborough and Peterborough v. Halifax were not raced.

1984

Before 'tapes-up' in 1984, extensive improvements were made to the Blunsdon circuit, thanks in the main to the Oxford track maintenance duo of John White and Barry Strange, plus Swindon's diligent clerk of the course Ray Morse and his willing band of helpers. That was just part of promoter Richard Vowles' determination to ensure things would be better than the previous year, and in order to establish Swindon Speedway on a sound basis he attempted to form a limited company. Nothing came of this, however, and it was rumoured that the failure to set up the company was due to it being contrary to the agreement the Robins' boss had with the stadium owners. In spite of this, Vowles showed that he wasn't afraid to spend money, splashing out a hefty fee to Hackney for Danish international and known Blunsdon track specialist Bo Petersen. Other changes on the rider front saw Malcolm Holloway move up the road to Reading, while Martin Yeates returned to the fold after deciding to give British League racing another shot. Finn Ari Koponen joined the Robins at the start of the season, and late in May flamboyant American Shawn McConnell arrived on board, but one move that didn't come off was that of another racer from the USA, namely Mike Faria. The hard-working Swindon promoter had actually signed the effervescent rider after he had represented his country in Test match action at the Abbey Stadium the previous year, but in the event the American was to miss out on domestic British racing until linking with Belle Vue in 1988. Another thing that Vowles did was to reintroduce the traditional race-jacket, depicting a much more normal-looking robin. This move was certainly welcomed by most, if not all on the Abbey Stadium terracing.

One rider who literally jumped at the chance of some outings in the side was Alun Rossiter, who had developed through the junior ranks, having initially been involved with the Robins as the club mascot when just four years of age. 'Rosco' gleefully moved up into a first-team slot as a useful number eight, while also assisting Weymouth in the National League. On the down side, injuries regrettably forced the early retirement of the very talented Bjorn Andersson. The Swede's form had been a little patchy at the beginning of the season, but the ability was still there, as indicated by a paid maximum (11+1) against Eastbourne at Blunsdon in the League Cup on 28 April. His commuting meant missing several matches and a kidney problem was clearly a hindrance he could have done without. It was during one of his trips away that Andersson also picked up a complex knee injury, which eventually required an operation. The Robins utilised the rider-replacement facility in his absence until the end of September, by which time it had become obvious that a return to track action was out of the question. What turned out to be Andersson's Swindon swansong occurred on 30 June, when he fell in his opening ride against Ipswich in a *Speedway Star* Knock-Out Cup tie at Blunsdon.

A day to forget occurred on 28 May, when Swindon were due to face M4 rivals Reading in home and away League Cup fixtures. The afternoon match at Smallmead was postponed due to inclement weather, but in the evening the Racers ran riot to triumph 49-29 at the Abbey. With 13 points to his name, only Phil Crump came out of the meeting with any credit. Richard Vowles reacted by asking John Tremblin to stand down as team manager, although he was at pains to point out that he didn't blame the outgoing man for the 'shambles' against Reading, commenting: 'Once the riders are on the track, it is up to them to deliver the goods.' For a few weeks, Vowles took on the team manager's job 'to try and find out first hand if there was a problem', he stated. By August, the vastly experienced Maurice Morley had been appointed team manager and he was to stay in position until the season's end.

In the final analysis, Swindon fared a little better in their League Cup section, finishing one off the bottom and handing over the wooden spoon to Exeter! They also moved up the British League table to ninth place, their home form being much more consistent, with just two defeats, against Cradley Heath and Ipswich, and a couple of draws, against Belle Vue and Eastbourne, to report. Away from the

Swindon Robins, 1984. From left to right, back row: Per Sorensen, Shawn McConnell, Bo Petersen, Bjorn Andersson, Ari Koponen, Alf Busk. Front, on bike: Phil Crump.

Abbey, however, there was just a single success (at Coventry), while in spite of three attempts to race the league fixture at Belle Vue, bad weather intervened and the match was never held. In the Knock-Out Cup, Ipswich won both legs of the first-round tie to dump Swindon out of the competition in unceremonious fashion, but in the Midland Cup the Robins became embroiled in an epic semi-final battle with Coventry. At the first time of asking, both sides won their home leg by the exact same score, 45-33, thereby drawing 78-78 on aggregate. Unbelievably, both teams again won their home leg by the same score, 46-32, in the replay, to again finish level on aggregate. With the match going to a second replay, Swindon dug deep, narrowly losing the first leg, 40-38, at Brandon, before finishing the job off at Blunsdon with a 43-34 success. Unfortunately there was no fairytale ending though, with Cradley Heath subsequently defeating the Robins in both legs of the final.

It was felt by many that promoter Richard Vowles deserved better luck, as he had shown that he wasn't afraid to use the cheque book to strengthen his side. He seemingly paid the price for predominantly tracking overseas riders since, aside from Bjorn Andersson's problems, often someone else was missing through international duty. Although irritating, there was precious little that Vowles could have done about it. There can be no doubting that had he been able to track his strongest septet in every match, and that the riders in turn had ridden to their best form, the Robins would have finished a good deal higher in the league standings.

Phil Crump again headed the team's averages on a 9.94 figure, and although Bo Petersen never quite hit the expected highs he did notch 239 points for an 8.06 average. After the top two the figures tapered off dramatically, thus: Ari Koponen (6.23), Shawn McConnell (5.54), Per Sorensen (4.91) and Alf Busk (4.84). Near the season's end, Kevin Smith arrived on loan from Poole, riding in three league fixtures and totalling 9 points. Meanwhile, Martin Yeates' decision to return to the top flight didn't really work out for either the rider or the club. He only managed to attain a 3.73 average from nine League Cup matches and, after completing two league meetings, he again went back to Weymouth. The Salisbury-born racer subsequently emphasised his ability when defeating both Dave Jessup and Kenny Carter on his way to 10 points and fifth place in the British Final at Coventry on 20 June. In so doing, he became the first rider from the lower league to qualify for the Overseas Final. Regrettably, in the big meeting at Belle Vue on 15 July he could only score 2 points and finished last, but at least he had got there.

Although McConnell finished below a 6-point average he was deserving of high praise, as he was real 'box office' and could produce the most amazing feats on a speedway bike. Indeed, he would perform fabulous wheelies, not as a celebration after a race but during the heat of the battle. He could dash through gaps where there didn't appear to be any and he would make space to manoeuvre through the tightest of situations, seemingly at any given point on all circuits.

For the fifth successive year, England faced the USA in a Test match at the Blunsdon bowl, with the Americans taking a 58-50 victory on 14 April. In carding a magnificent 17-point haul Dennis Sigalos led them to success, with great backing from John Cook (12+1) and Shawn Moran (12), while England's best were Chris Morton (13), Dave Jessup (12+1) and Kenny Carter (10+1). On the individual front, Bo Petersen qualified for the World Final on 1 September, held in Gothenburg, Sweden, where he did very well, notching 9 points. Meanwhile, Phil Crump represented Swindon in the British League Riders' Championship at Belle Vue on 20 October, but unfortunately could only total 5 points in a meeting won by home rider Chris Morton after a title run-off. However, Crump did win the only open event at Blunsdon in 1984, becoming the *Evening Advertiser* Superstar on 6 July by romping to a full 15-point maximum against class opposition, which included Hans Nielsen, Mitch Shirra, John Davis and Bobby Schwartz among others.

Brian Carter's junior side, the Sprockets, spent the year participating in both the Anglia Junior League and the British Junior League, finishing sixth in each. Keen to encourage the younger element as ever, several riders made appearances for the side, including Nick Bates, Barry Byford, Gary Chessell, Mark Gibbs, Steve Goodwin, Brian Hussey, David Main and Allen Theobald. On the individual front, the British Junior League Riders' Championship was held at King's Lynn on 10 October and Gary Chessell performed well, scoring 11 points to finish in third place behind Lawrie Bloomfield (13) and Michael Keepe (12).

Swindon Sprockets, 1984. From left to right, back row: David Main, Barry Byford, Steve Goodwin, Mark Gibbs, Allen Theobald. Front, on bike: Mark Chessell.

SWINDON ROBINS 1984

(Swindon's score shown first unless otherwise stated)

BRITISH LEAGUE

Opponents	Home	Away
Belle Vue	D39-39	Not staged
Coventry	W47-31	W40-38
Cradley Heath	L32-46	L27-51
Eastbourne	D39-39	L38-40
Exeter	W53-25	L34-44
Halifax	W49-29	L36-42
Ipswich	L32-46	L38-40
King's Lynn	W48-30	L33-45
Newcastle	W51.5-26.5	L32-46
Oxford	W40-38	L37-41
Poole	W44-34	L37-41
Reading	W41-37	L32-46
Sheffield	W40-38	L37-41
Wimbledon	W46-32	L38-40
Wolverhampton	W45-33	L37-41

BRITISH LEAGUE TABLE

Team	Mts	Won	Drn	Lst	For	Agn.	Pts
Ipswich	30	25	2	3	1,343	994	52
Belle Vue	29	23	3	3	1,322	938	49
Cradley Heath	30	21	2	7	1,308	1,031	44
Reading	30	17	1	12	1,202.5	1,126.5	35
Sheffield	30	15	0	15	1,191	1,148	30
King's Lynn	30	15	0	15	1,143	1,196	30
Wimbledon	30	15	0	15	1,139	1,198	30
Oxford	30	14	1	15	1,174	1,166	29
Swindon	29	12	2	15	1,142.5	1,119.5	26
Wolverhampton	30	13	0	17	1,141.5	1,193.5	26
Eastbourne	30	12	1	17	1,157	1,178	25
Coventry	30	11	2	17	1,169	1,168	24
Poole	30	10	1	19	1,075	1,258	21
Halifax	30	9	3	18	1,029	1,311	21
Exeter	30	8	2	20	1,045	1,293	18
Newcastle	30	9	0	21	1,036.5	1,299.5	18

Note: Belle Vue v. Swindon was not raced.

LEAGUE AVERAGES

Rider	Mts	Rds	Pts	Bon.	Tot.	Avge	Maximums
Per Jonsson	1	5	15	0	15	12.00	1 full
Phil Crump	28	138	335	8	343	9.94	2 full
John Cook	1	4	8	1	9	9.00	–
Dave Jessup	1	5	11	0	11	8.80	–
Bo Petersen	26	125	239	13	252	8.06	1 full; 3 paid
Ari Koponen	26	106	152	13	165	6.23	1 full
Colin Richardson	1	2	2	1	3	6.00	–
Shawn McConnell	27	109	125	26	151	5.54	–
Bjorn Andersson	1	4	4	1	5	5.00	–
Per Sorensen	26	101	113	11	124	4.91	–
Alf Busk	27	88	90.5	16	106.5	4.84	–
Alun Rossiter	19	46	29	17	46	4.00	–
Martin Yeates	2	6	4	2	6	4.00	–
Kevin Smith	3	11	9	1	10	3.64	–
Colin Cook	2	8	6	0	6	3.00	–
David Smart	1	2	0	0	0	0.00	–

SPEEDWAY STAR KNOCK-OUT CUP

Opponents	Home	Away	Aggregate
Ipswich (Round one)	L36-42	L33-45	L69-87

LEAGUE CUP

Opponents	Home	Away
Eastbourne	W44-34	L38-40
Exeter	W55-23	W50-28
Ipswich	D39-39	L31-47
King's Lynn	W40-38	L37-41
Oxford	W41-37	L35-43
Poole	L37-41	L38-40
Reading	L29-49	L31-47
Wimbledon	1 36-42	L36-42

LEAGUE CUP (SOUTHERN SECTION) TABLE

Team	Mts	Won	Drn	Lst	For	Agn.	Pts
Reading	16	11	0	5	676	570	22
Wimbledon	16	11	0	5	664	584	22
Ipswich	16	10	1	5	679	568	21
Eastbourne	16	9	1	6	633.5	613.5	19
Oxford	16	9	0	7	648	599	18
Poole	16	8	0	8	592.5	652.5	16
King's Lynn	16	7	0	9	619	627	14
Swindon	16	5	1	10	617	631	11
Exeter	16	0	1	15	481	765	1

Note: Reading and Wimbledon progressed to the semi-finals.

MIDLAND CUP

Opponents	Home	Away	Aggregate
Coventry (Semi-final)	W45-33	L33-45	D78-78
Coventry (Replay)	W46-32	L32-46	D78-78
Coventry (Second replay)	W43-34	L38-40	W81-74
Cradley Heath (Final)	L37-40	L35-43	L72-83

CHALLENGE

Opponents	Home	Away
Oxford	–	L38-40
Reading	–	L33-45
Wimbledon	–	L37-41

FOUR-TEAM TOURNAMENT

(Staged at Weymouth)   Exeter 0, Oxford 0, Swindon 0, Weymouth 0.
Note: The four-team tournament was abandoned following two unsuccessful attempts to run heat one.

EASTER TRIANGLE THREE-TEAM TOURNAMENT

(First leg at Oxford)	Reading 41, Oxford 35, Swindon 31.
(Second leg at Swindon)	Oxford 38, Reading 36, Swindon 34.
(Third leg at Reading)	Reading 42, Swindon 37, Oxford 29.
Aggregate result:	Reading 119, Swindon 102, Oxford 102.

BRITISH OPEN PAIRS CHAMPIONSHIP

(Staged at Wolverhampton) Group D: Wimbledon 16, Sheffield 16, Wolverhampton 14, Swindon 8.

BRITISH LEAGUE RIDERS' CHAMPIONSHIP

(Staged at Belle Vue)   Phil Crump 5 points.

SWINDON SPROCKETS

BRITISH JUNIOR LEAGUE TABLE

Team	Mts	Won	Drn	Lst	For	Agn.	Pts
Ipswich	13	11	1	1	345	198	23
King's Lynn	14	9	0	5	312	268	18
Coventry	14	7	0	7	314	269	14
Wimbledon	14	7	0	7	294	291	14
Sheffield	12	7	0	5	278	221	14
Swindon	14	5	1	8	267	317	11
Reading	14	4	0	10	242	340	8
Cradley Heath	13	3	0	10	196	344	6

Note: Two matches, Ipswich v. Sheffield and Sheffield v. Cradley Heath, were not raced.

ANGLIA JUNIOR LEAGUE TABLE

Team	Mts	Won	Drn	Lst	For	Agn.	Pts
Long Eaton	16	13	2	1	219	162	28
Ipswich	16	10	0	6	225.5	155.5	20
Milton Keynes	16	9	2	5	208	170	20
King's Lynn	16	8	1	7	205	175	17
Rye House	16	6	3	7	179	196	15
Swindon	16	7	0	9	166	213	14
Hackney	16	5	2	9	181.5	200.5	12
Stoke	15	4	2	9	146	211	10
Mildenhall	15	3	0	12	150	197	6

Note: The Mildenhall v. Stoke match was abandoned after heat two and never restaged.

1985

In 1985 the team became known as the Adver Robins, having received valuable sponsorship from the local *Evening Advertiser* newspaper, the deal brokered by hard-working commercial manager Dave Prowse, who was to enjoy three spells with the club (1984-94, 1997 and 1999-2005). With Wimbledon opting for National League racing, England international Malcolm Simmons came to Blunsdon, giving the Robins a third heat-leader alongside Bo Petersen and Phil Crump. When Swede Jimmy Nilsen finally arrived, promoter Richard Vowles, after much effort on his part, at last had the basis of a good side. The signing of Nilsen was a feather in the Swindon promoter's cap, since the Department of Employment had refused, at first, to grant the young rider a work permit. Dave Prowse, on behalf of the club, approached and enlisted the help of Simon Coombs, the local MP, and together he and Vowles fought the decision tooth and nail and were finally successful. Nilsen proved his worth with 91 points from sixteen league matches, for an impressive first-season average of 6.54. The Swede's arrival spelt the end of the road for Alf Busk, who had missed many matches after fracturing a scaphoid in a League Cup match at Halifax on 6 May. The Dane unluckily received another knock to the wrist at Ipswich on 18 July in what turned out to be his only league match of the year in the Robins' colours, prior to linking with Sheffield on loan in August.

With Vowles also filling the role of team manager again, Swindon made a fast exit from the *Speedway Star* Knock-Out Cup, losing both legs of their first round clash with Ipswich. In the League Cup, the Robins had to be satisfied with mid-table mediocrity in a competition they had never been successful in. There was to be no chance of glory in the Midland Cup either, with the Wiltshire side losing to old rivals Oxford at the semi-final stage. The Robins finished eighth in a diminished British League, which boasted just eleven tracks. Home form again proved the Achilles heel, with losses suffered at the hands of Coventry, Oxford and Sheffield, while Reading stole away with a draw.

Late in the campaign, the Robins actually rode in two away league matches on the same day! This rare occurrence came about because of prior rain-offs and happened on 13 October, when they raced at Halifax in the afternoon, losing 44-34. Then, in the evening, they appeared at Belle Vue, where a hefty 50-28 defeat was suffered.

Swindon Robins, 1985. From left to right, back row: Alun Rossiter, Jimmy Nilsen, Bo Petersen, Malcolm Simmons, David Smart, Per Sorensen. Front, on bike: Phil Crump.

The Blunsdon track record took a battering in 1985. Firstly, Shawn Moran reduced the best-ever time to 66.4 seconds on 27 April, when Sheffield were the visitors in a League Cup encounter. Four months later, on 26 August, Erik Gundersen ran riot, slicing an incredible seven-tenths of a second off the record when clocking 65.7 seconds in heat four of the Robins' British League match against Cradley Heath. Remarkably, two heats later in the same match, Gundersen blitzed around the Abbey circuit in 65.2 seconds – a full 1.2 seconds faster than Moran's record which had stood at the start of the meeting!

The evening of Thursday 19 September will be remembered for all the wrong reasons, as the Robins attempted to stage a home league match against King's Lynn. Referee George Thomas called a halt to the meeting after a three-man pile-up in the very first heat, declaring the track 'unfit and impossible to be improved sufficiently to enable racing to continue'. Arguments raged and, following the abandonment, which was effectively due to serious over-watering in the afternoon, Richard Vowles sensationally quit as promoter – a decision that left doubts about the future of the sport in Swindon. Happily, peace was soon restored, with Vowles taking on Bryan Talbot and former Robins' rider Neil Street as joint-team managers in order to relieve some of the pressure. However, Vowles was a disillusioned man and, although he stayed on, he never really forgot the events of that fateful night. Indeed, his programme notes for the following home match against Halifax on 28 September spelt out exactly how he felt. He stated: 'My reaction to what happened is simple. I am both shattered and heartbroken after all I have tried to do for Swindon Speedway. It seems my efforts have been in vain and have been destroyed in one evening.'

At the end of the season, Bo Petersen stated he was retiring, while Malcolm Simmons hankered after National League racing at Hackney. The Robins would miss Petersen, who enjoyed a much more productive campaign than in 1984 and actually outscored Phil Crump to finish on top of the averages with a 9.33 figure. However, Crumpie was hampered by a reoccurrence of his old wrist injury and missed all of the October fixtures, his final league average being 8.53. Typical of the man, despite his obvious discomfort he signed off at Blunsdon with a paid maximum (11+1) in a league fixture against Halifax on 28 September. Turning to the remaining team members, 'Simmo', after going like a steam-train in the earlier part of the season, suffered an alarming dip in form to finish with a 6.72 league average; meanwhile Per Sorensen showed some real flashes of brilliance and upped his 'vital statistic' to 6.59. Finn Ari Koponen found points hard to come by, but still averaged 6.46, while Alun Rossiter slightly increased his figure to 4.13. Former World Final runner-up Gordon Kennett had dropped into the National League with Eastbourne, but came into the Robins' line-up when required and did an excellent job to average 6.93 from four league matches. There were also outings for David Smart and Martin Yeates, both of whom were also National League regulars, with Arena-Essex and Poole respectively.

Home favourite Bo Petersen won the prestigious Blunsdon-staged *Evening Advertiser* Superstar event on 14 June, and also represented the Robins at Belle Vue in the TNT Sameday British League Riders' Championship on 20 October, scoring 5 points in a meeting won by World Champion Erik Gundersen.

The Abbey once again hosted an England *v.* USA Test match on 8 September, when the Americans thundered to a 66-42 victory. Lance King topped the victors' scoring with 17 points, receiving great support from Shawn Moran (13+1) and Bobby Schwartz (10+1). Meanwhile, for England, Kelvin Tatum (12) was the only rider to reach double figures.

Swindon's other team, the Sprockets, who were sponsored by Belchers Breakers, spent the year competing in the British Junior League, but they endured a difficult time of it, winning only five matches and finishing ninth out of the eleven competing sides. Prior to that, Brian Carter's boys had fared a tad better in the British Junior League Cup, occupying seventh place in the final table. Extrovert crowd-pleaser Mike Fitzpatrick topped the league averages on a 7.91 figure, with Brian Hussey (7.48) and Phil Harris (6.49) next in line. Other regulars were Steve Goodwin and Steve Brennan, while Nick Bates, Mark Gibbs and Allen Theobald also made appearances. Gary Chessell enjoyed outings with the Sprockets too, making seven appearances in the League Cup for an average of 9.71.

SWINDON ADVER ROBINS 1985

(Swindon's score shown first unless otherwise stated)

BRITISH LEAGUE

Opponents	Home	Away	Aggregate
Belle Vue	W61-16	L28-50	W89-66
Coventry	L35-43	L38-39	L73-82
Cradley Heath	W45-33	L38-40	W83-73
Halifax	W47-31	L34-44	W81-75
Ipswich	W49-29	L35-43	W84-72
King's Lynn	W46-32	W42-36	W88-68
Oxford	L38-40	L33-45	L71-85
Reading	D39-39	L32-46	L71-85
Sheffield	L37-41	L30-48	L67-89
Wolverhampton	W49-29	W40-38	W89-67

BRITISH LEAGUE TABLE

Team	Mts	Won	Drn	Lst	For	Agn.	Pts	Bon.	Tot.
Oxford	20	16	1	3	849	708	33	10	43
Sheffield	20	13	1	6	816	741	27	6	33
Coventry	20	11	2	7	817	740	24	7	31
Halifax	20	9	1	10	783	774	19	5	24

Ipswich	20	9	2	9	781	778	20	4	24
Belle Vue	20	10	0	10	778	777	20	4	24
Cradley Heath	19	10	0	9	740	740	20	4	24
Swindon	20	8	1	11	796	762	17	6	23
Reading	19	6	4	9	734	743	16	6	22
Wolverhampton	20	5	2	13	715	843	12	2	14
King's Lynn	20	5	0	15	677	880	10	0	10

Note: Reading v. Cradley Heath was not raced.

LEAGUE AVERAGES

Rider	Mts	Rds	Pts	Bon.	Tot.	Avge	Maximums
Per Jonsson	1	4	11	1	12	12.00	1 paid
Phil Collins	1	4	9	1	10	10.00	–
Richard Knight	1	4	9	1	10	10.00	–
Simon Wigg	1	5	12	0	12	9.60	–
Bo Petersen	19	81	177	12	189	9.33	2 full; 1 paid
Peter Collins	1	5	10	1	11	8.80	–
Phil Crump	11	45	91	5	96	8.53	2 paid
Neil Evitts	1	4	6	1	7	7.00	–
Gordon Kennett	4	15	21	5	26	6.93	–
Malcolm Simmons	20	81	121	15	136	6.72	1 full
Per Sorensen	19	71	91	26	117	6.59	1 paid
Jimmy Nilsen	16	63	91	12	103	6.54	1 paid
Ari Koponen	19	65	94	11	105	6.46	–
Alun Rossiter	20	64	48	18	66	4.13	–
Preben Eriksen	1	4	4	0	4	4.00	–
David Smart	2	6	1	0	1	0.67	–
Alf Busk	1	1	0	0	0	0.00	–
Martin Yeates	1	3	0	0	0	0.00	–

SPEEDWAY STAR KNOCK-OUT CUP

Opponents	Home	Away	Aggregate
Ipswich (Round one)	L36-42	L33-45	L69-87

LEAGUE CUP

Opponents	Home	Away	Aggregate
Belle Vue	W43-35	L27-51	L70-86
Coventry	W47-31	L36-42	W83-73
Cradley Heath	L35-43	L31-47	L66-90
Halifax	W42-36	L34-44	L76-80
Ipswich	W48-30	W42-36	W90-66
King's Lynn	W50-28	W40-38	W90-66
Oxford	L37-41	W40-38	L77-79
Reading	W43-35	W41-37	W84-72
Sheffield	W41-37	L26-52	L67-89
Wolverhampton	L33-45	L31-47	L64-92

LEAGUE CUP TABLE

Team	Mts	Won	Drn	Lst	For	Agn.	Pts	Bon.	Tot.
Cradley Heath	20	13	1	6	822	737	27	7	34
Oxford	20	11	2	7	820	738	24	8	32
Ipswich	20	12	1	7	808	752	25	7	32
Coventry	20	10	3	7	797	762	23	7	30
Wolverhampton	20	10	1	9	805	754	21	6	27
Swindon	20	11	0	9	767	793	22	4	26
Belle Vue	20	9	2	9	777	783	20	4	24
Reading	20	8	2	10	770	789	18	3	21
Halifax	20	8	0	12	740	819	16	4	20
Sheffield	20	7	1	12	767	793	15	4	19
King's Lynn	20	4	1	15	703	856	9	1	10

Note: Cradley Heath, Oxford, Ipswich and Coventry progressed to the semi-finals.

MIDLAND CUP

Opponents	Home	Away	Aggregate
Oxford (Semi-final)	D39-39	L36-42	L75-81

DOUBLE-DECKER TROPHY

Opponents	Home	Away
Wolverhampton	W73-47	–

CHALLENGE

Opponents	Home	Away
Exeter	–	W80-40
Ipswich	L44-46	–
Oxford	D45-45	–
Poole	–	W40-38

FOUR-TEAM TOURNAMENT

(Staged at Poole) Swindon 30, Cradley Heath 25, Poole 23, Oxford 18.

EASTER TRIANGLE THREE-TEAM TOURNAMENT

(First leg at Oxford)	Reading 38, Swindon 36, Oxford 33.
(Second leg at Swindon)	Swindon 19, Reading 18, Oxford 17.
(Third leg at Reading)	Swindon 40, Reading 39, Oxford 29.
Aggregate result:	Swindon 95, Reading 95, Oxford 63 (Trophy shared by Swindon and Reading).

Note: The second leg was abandoned after heat nine, with the result permitted to stand.

BRITISH OPEN PAIRS CHAMPIONSHIP

(Staged at Wolverhampton) Oxford 35, Reading 34, Cradley Heath 33, Sheffield 26, Belle Vue 23, Coventry 17, Swindon 15.

TNT SAMEDAY BRITISH LEAGUE RIDERS' CHAMPIONSHIP

(Staged at Belle Vue) Bo Petersen 5 points.

SWINDON BELCHERS BREAKERS SPROCKETS

BRITISH JUNIOR LEAGUE TABLE

Team	Mts	Won	Drn	Lst	For	Agn.	Pts
King's Lynn	20	16	1	3	502	335	33
Cradley Heath	19	14	1	4	449	347	29
Belle Vue	20	12	2	6	478	355	26
Coventry	20	11	1	8	441	395	23
Sheffield	20	10	2	8	439	397	22
Halifax	20	10	1	9	431	407	21
Oxford	20	9	0	11	394	439	18
Ipswich	20	5	2	13	384	452	12
Swindon	20	5	2	13	367	469	12
Wolverhampton	20	5	2	13	355	476	12
Reading	19	4	2	13	313	481	10

Note: One match, Reading v. Cradley Heath, was not raced.

1986

In 1986, Richard Vowles tried yet again to make the Swindon Adver Robins successful. He signed Finnish star Kai Niemi from Ipswich, and Alan Grahame also came on loan from Cradley Heath. Danish international Finn Thomsen, whose previous tracks included Wolverhampton, Hackney and Poole, was also signed, but unluckily broke an ankle in the second pre-season practice session, so Swede Richard Hellsen was quickly drafted in from King's Lynn to plug the gap. With each side having to track a junior, Rob Fortune was also brought in at the bottom end. The ever-reliable Phil Crump was back for another term, as was Jimmy Nilsen, so things looked pretty good on the team front. When Finn Thomsen was fit again, Per Sorensen, who'd struggled somewhat to find form, was released and subsequently joined Oxford. This move proved to be the making of Sorensen, since he linked up with compatriot Hans Nielsen at Cowley and learned much from the man known throughout the speedway world as the 'Main Dane'.

All was not well behind the scenes at Blunsdon during the year and, following a League Cup fixture at home to Sheffield on 31 May, Richard Vowles began to express his concern at crowd levels. Again, in his programme notes for a League Cup meeting against Reading on 21 June, he brought up the subject, stating: 'The last two meetings at Swindon (a pairs event and a challenge match) have certainly provided good racing, but I have kept wondering if it is worth all the time and effort putting on such meetings when on each occasion, less than one thousand people have attended. That is nowhere near the break-even figure and I am left questioning the sense in running every week.' The Robins' promoter continued to bring up the matter in subsequent programmes and was also critical of the local press, commenting that 'sensationalism' seemed to be the hallmark, rather than fact. Vowles soon realised that he couldn't possibly carry on and his last meeting in charge proved to be a challenge match against a British League Select on 2 August. In the race day magazine, he said: 'Tonight, for me, has to be a sad occasion, because it is the last meeting I shall be promoting here at Swindon. It was not a decision I wanted to make, but in the end I unfortunately had to make that decision for financial reasons.'

Following the departure of Richard Vowles, the team went back to the stadium owners BCA (British Car Auctions). Kai Niemi returned to Ipswich and, for a brief but worrying week, Swindon Speedway effectively closed down while the ownership of the licence was sorted out. Ultimately though, with BCA at the helm, it meant that Ted Nelson and Bill Chandler were left in charge of speedway matters. With the takeover, Neil Street left and Bryan Talbot became team manager in his own right, having previously shared the job with Street. To replace Niemi, a very promising Danish boy called Brian Karger was eventually signed in mid-September.

On 20 September, Blunsdon staged its 1,000th speedway meeting, when Cradley Heath were the visitors for a league match. A presentation was made to Bob Jones for his ever-loyal service to the club. Joner was still working at the track as machine examiner and had served Swindon superbly over many years. Remarkably in fact, he had never missed a meeting in one capacity or another, since the circuit first opened way back in 1949.

Veteran Richard Hellsen proved to be a very shrewd signing, finishing the season with a 5.95 average. Meanwhile, at the top end of the side, the majestic Phil Crump, with an average of 9.17, again led Swindon's scoring. Looking at the other team members, Jimmy Nilsen, despite missing a number of meetings because of compulsory army service, still finished the year with a creditable 7.90 figure. Alan Grahame was a real hero; indeed, having suffered from Hodgkin's Disease throughout much of the season and therefore often riding in considerable discomfort, the Birmingham-born rider kept going as best he could, averaging 5.50. He even bounced back after spending a couple of months on the sidelines with a broken right ankle suffered in a League Cup match at Wolverhampton on 19 May.

Of the Danish connection, Finn Thomsen was something of a disappointment, scoring just 84 league points for a 5.37 average, but Brian Karger looked to be a real prospect and got better with every one of his fourteen matches to average 4.89. Rob Fortune tried hard, but was out of his depth

Swindon Robins, 1986. From left to right, back row: Jimmy Nilsen, Finn Thomsen, Per Sorensen, Rob Fortune. Front, on bikes: Kai Niemi, Phil Crump, Alan Grahame.

in the cut-and-thrust of the British League, and a final average of 3.40 gave a fair indication of a season of struggle for the youngster.

A bitter pill for the faithful Blunsdon fans to swallow occurred in a league match against Oxford on 11 October, when Swindon's oldest rivals ran riot to win 56-21. Remarkably, no fewer than four riders hit paid maximums for the triumphant Cheetahs, namely Hans Nielsen (11+1), Marvyn Cox (11+1), Simon Wigg (10+2) and former Robin Per Sorensen (10+2). Swindon finished the league campaign in eighth place and, as had happened in 1984, the away match at Belle Vue was never staged due to inclement weather. The team did at least keep their travelling fans happy with away victories at Coventry, Ipswich and King's Lynn, but the beleaguered home supporters certainly didn't welcome four defeats at the Abbey. The opinion had long since been echoed that the Blunsdon circuit was too fair and all visiting riders were capable of turning up and doing well, irrespective of whether they had previously ridden on the track or not. This theory could certainly be borne out by a closer look at Swindon's home results over the years!

After overcoming Ipswich at the first hurdle in the *Speedway Star* Knock-Out Cup, the Robins came unstuck against the old enemy Oxford, losing both legs of their quarter-final encounter. Swindon did enjoy their best-ever League Cup campaign, however, ending up fifth in the final standings and only missing out on a semi-final place by one position. The gritty Alan Grahame represented the side in the TNT Sameday British League Riders' Championship at Belle Vue on 12 October, scoring 6 points in a meeting won emphatically by Hans Nielsen. 'Big Al', as he was affectionately known, also won the only individual meeting held at Blunsdon in 1986, namely the World Championship qualifying round, which was run early in the season on 11 May. Moving on to the last stage of the competition, Jimmy Nilsen, often referred to as the 'Jewel in the Crown' by certain sections at Blunsdon, qualified for his first World Final in Katowice, Poland on 30 August and rode brilliantly to finish fourth on 11 points.

The Sprockets, who were sponsored by Finebush (a retail supplier of aquarium needs), fared even worse than their senior counterparts, winning only four matches to finish tenth out of the eleven teams in the British Junior League. The side, again managed by Brian Carter, actually only avoided the basement position by virtue of having a slightly better race points difference than Belle Vue. Prior to that, they had done marginally better in the League Cup, occupying ninth spot in the final table. In the Knock-Out Cup the Sprockets fell at the first hurdle and heavily too, losing both legs by the same score of 31-11 to a potent Ipswich side. A figure of 9.96 put Rob Fortune way out on top of the league averages, the youngster from Kidderminster having accrued 125 points from seventeen matches. Nick Bates was next in line with an average of 6.62, while other regulars were Matthew Cross (6.44), Steve Goodwin (4.22), Brian Hussey (3.81) and Mark Cochrane (3.38). Several others also had the odd outing, including Darren Knapman, Sean Burton, Andy Jeffries and Francis Dale.

SWINDON ADVER ROBINS 1986

(Swindon's score shown first unless otherwise stated)

BRITISH LEAGUE

Opponents	Home	Away	Aggregate
Belle Vue	W44-34	Not staged	–
Bradford	W42-35	L32-46	L74-81
Coventry	W42-36	W44-34	W86-70
Cradley Heath	D39-39	L36-42	L75-81
Ipswich	W41-37	W46-32	W87-69
King's Lynn	L36-42	W42-36	D78-78
Oxford	L21-56	L20-58	L41-114
Reading	W49-28	L35-43	W84-71
Sheffield	L36-41	L23-55	L59-96
Wolverhampton	L36-41	L29-49	L65-90

Note: Following the away match at King's Lynn, guest Sam Nikolajsen defeated Bobby Schwartz in a run-off to win the bonus point for the Robins.

BRITISH LEAGUE TABLE

Team	Mts	Won	Drn	Lst	For	Agn.	Pts	Bon.	Tot.
Oxford	18	18	0	0	863	540	36	8	44
Cradley Heath	20	13	3	4	854	706	29	9	38
Wolverhampton	19	13	0	6	771	710	26	6	32
Sheffield	19	10	2	7	783	697	22	6	28
Coventry	20	10	1	9	829	731	21	6	27
Bradford	20	8	1	11	758	799	17	4	21
Reading	20	7	3	10	757	801	17	4	21
Swindon	19	8	1	10	693	784	17	4	21
Ipswich	20	7	1	12	729	831	15	3	18
Belle Vue	19	5	0	14	675	805	10	2	12
King's Lynn	20	2	0	18	626	934	4	0	4

Note: Three matches were not raced: Belle Vue v. Swindon; Oxford v. Sheffield; Oxford v. Wolverhampton.

LEAGUE AVERAGES

Rider	Mts	Rds	Pts	Bon.	Tot.	Avge	Maximums
Mitch Shirra	1	5	14	0	14	11.20	–
Marvyn Cox	3	13	33	0	33	10.15	1 full
Phil Crump	15	65	145	4	149	9.17	–
Sam Nikolajsen	1	4	9	0	9	9.00	–
Carl Blackbird	1	4	6	2	8	8.00	–
Andy Grahame	2	8	15	1	16	8.00	–
Lance King	1	4	6	2	8	8.00	–
Jimmy Nilsen	10	42	75	8	83	7.90	–
Kai Niemi	3	12	22	1	23	7.67	–
Peter Carr	2	8	13	1	14	7.00	–
Richard Hellsen	19	74	95	15	110	5.95	–
Alan Grahame	13	48	55	11	66	5.50	–
Finn Thomsen	19	70	84	10	94	5.37	–
Dave Jessup	2	9	11	1	12	5.33	–
Kevin Jolly	1	3	4	0	4	5.33	–

Peter Glanz	1	4	5	0	5	5.00	–
Kevin Smith	1	4	5	0	5	5.00	–
Brian Karger	14	45	51	4	55	4.89	–
Phil Collins	1	5	4	1	5	4.00	–
Rob Fortune	19	60	39	12	51	3.40	–
Alun Rossiter	1	4	2	0	2	2.00	–
Steve Bishop	1	3	0	0	0	0.00	–
Preben Eriksen	1	1	0	0	0	0.00	–

SPEEDWAY STAR KNOCK-OUT CUP

Opponents	Home	Away	Aggregate
Ipswich (Round one)	W47-31	W40-38	W87-69
Oxford (Quarter-final)	L37-41	L30-48	L67-89

LEAGUE CUP

Opponents	Home	Away	Aggregate
Belle Vue	W52-26	D39-39	W91-65
Bradford	W53-25	L31-47	W84-72
Coventry	W45-33	L32-46	L77-79
Cradley Heath	W41-37	L36-42	L77-79
Ipswich	W41-37	L38-40	W79-77
King's Lynn	W44-34	W43-35	W87-69
Oxford	D39-39	L38-40	L77-79
Reading	W46-32	L38-40	W84-72
Sheffield	D39-39	L35-43	L74-82
Wolverhampton	W49-29	L35-43	W84-72

LEAGUE CUP TABLE

Team	Mts	Won	Drn	Lst	For	Agn.	Pts	Bon.	Tot.
Coventry	20	14	1	5	815	743	29	8	37
Oxford	20	13	1	6	810	745	27	9	36
Ipswich	20	12	1	7	801	755	25	5	30
Cradley Heath	20	10	2	8	808	750	22	7	29
Swindon	20	9	3	8	814	746	21	6	27
Sheffield	20	10	2	8	791	762	22	5	27
Bradford	20	9	3	8	798	760	21	5	26
Reading	20	10	0	10	772	778	20	4	24
Belle Vue	20	6	2	12	737	821	14	3	17
Wolverhampton	20	6	1	13	744	816	13	3	16
King's Lynn	20	2	2	16	672	886	6	0	6

Note: Coventry, Oxford, Ipswich and Cradley Heath progressed to the semi-finals.

MIDLAND CUP

Opponents	Home	Away	Aggregate
Wolverhampton (Round one)	D39-39	L27-51	L66-90

CHALLENGE

Opponents	Home	Away
BL Select	L38-40	–
NL Select	D39-39	–

MARTIN HEWLETT MEMORIAL TROPHY FOUR-TEAM TOURNAMENT

(Staged at Exeter)   Oxford 26, Express & Echo Stars 26, Swindon Select 23, Exeter 21.

FOUR-TEAM TOURNAMENT

(Staged at Poole)   Oxford 34, Swindon 23, Reading 22, Poole 17.

EASTER TRIANGLE THREE-TEAM TOURNAMENT

(First leg at Oxford)   Swindon 39, Oxford 37, Reading 32.
(Second leg at Swindon)   Reading 18, Swindon 15, Oxford 13.

(Third leg at Reading)   Oxford 42, Swindon 41, Reading 25.
Aggregate result: Swindon 95, Oxford 92, Reading 75.
Note: The second leg was abandoned after heat seven, with Oxford's total inclusive of 4 points, which they were awarded for being one race behind at the time.

THREE-TEAM TOURNAMENT

(Staged at Ipswich)   Swindon 34, Cradley Heath 23, Ipswich 21.

TNT SAMEDAY BRITISH LEAGUE RIDERS' CHAMPIONSHIP

(Staged at Belle Vue)   Alan Grahame 6 points.

SWINDON FINEBUSH SPROCKETS

BRITISH JUNIOR LEAGUE TABLE

Team	Mts	Won	Drn	Lst	For	Agn.	Pts	Bon.	Tot.
Coventry	20	16	2	2	518	316	34	10	44
Cradley Heath	20	14	1	5	479	356	29	9	38
Wolverhampton	20	11	3	6	442	394	25	7	32
Bradford	19	11	1	7	402	385	23	5	28
King's Lynn	20	10	2	8	423	415	22	4	26
Sheffield	19	9	1	9	390	403	19	5	24
Reading	19	8	2	9	370	410	18	2	20
Ipswich	20	7	2	11	407	429	16	4	20
Oxford	19	4	1	14	349	442	9	2	11
Swindon	18	4	1	13	319	432	9	1	10
Belle Vue	18	4	0	14	311	428	8	2	10

Note: Four matches, Belle Vue v. Swindon, Bradford v. Belle Vue, Oxford v. Reading and Sheffield v. Swindon, were not staged.

1987

Having survived a traumatic 1986 and come back from the brink of extinction, the 1987 season looked potentially difficult, as Swindon kingpin Phil Crump retired and remained in his native Australia after being troubled for some years with a wrist injury. Crumpie would be a hard act to follow, having done so much for the club since signing from Bristol in 1979. In truth, he had been an absolute rock and on many occasions had carried the side when little or no support had been forthcoming from his teammates.

Coming into the Robins' nest was a new signing from Reading: one Mitch Shirra, a Kiwi who had been known to be a tad controversial on occasions. Alun Rossiter, after a very good season with Coventry, came back to race full-time for his hometown team, while Jimmy Nilsen, Richard Hellsen and Brian Karger remained on board from the previous year. Karger in particular was thrilled to return and, as part of the rebirth of the Borough Council, which officially took place on 1 April, his van sported the 'Proud to be Swindon' logo. Swede Erik Stenlund had also been set to link with the club. However, a fortnight before the season the Robins' team-building plans went awry when he broke a leg in a frightening ice racing accident in Holland. The Robins then tried to tempt another Swedish rider, Tommy Nilsson, back to these shores, but the former Coventry man wasn't able to get the necessary time off work. Thankfully, a loan deal was agreed with Arena-Essex for the exciting Andrew Silver as the club's number eight and the services of the Londoner were utilised around his National League commitments for the Purfleet club. Changes weren't restricted solely to those who scored the points and, in the backroom department, Ron Byford became team manager, having gained valuable experience with Exeter.

To the delight of the Swindon supporters, both Jimmy Nilsen and Brian Karger improved, while tireless Swede Richard Hellsen was as steady as ever and didn't miss a match. In mid-season the services of another Swede, Conny Ivarsson, were obtained and he certainly impressed, scoring 117 points from

Swindon Robins, 1987. From left to right, back row: Jimmy Nilsen, Brian Karger, Ron Byford (Team Manager), Conny Ivarsson, Stephen Rose. Front, on bikes: Alun Rossiter, Richard Hellsen, Mitch Shirra.

twenty league matches. His final average was 6.45 and, but for a number of mechanical problems, it would have been significantly higher. Martin Chessell started the season as the compulsory junior and thereby became the third member of his family to represent the Robins, following in the footsteps of older brothers Gary and Mark, although in truth the latter only ever appeared in a solitary challenge match and a four-team tournament. The younger of the Chessell's only held his position for the first six League Cup matches though, and in the main thereafter the junior berth was shared by Matthew Cross and Stephen Rose, the latter trying hard to make a good impression having journeyed over from New Zealand. Both found the going understandably tough, Cross averaging just 1.63, while Rose ended up with a lowly figure, below 1 point per match.

Mitch Shirra proved a delight to have on board and never let the side down. In fact, he and Jimmy Nilsen fought a friendly season-long battle within the club to be the number one Robin. It was a very close-run thing, with Nilsen just nudging ahead to finish with a 9.73 average, while Shirra attained a 9.66 figure. Thanks to the two-pronged attack Swindon, who for a third successive year enjoyed the sponsorship of the *Evening Advertiser*, rose to a very healthy third position in the final league table. The middle-order men gave the side a good balance, with Brian Karger raising his average to 6.88, while Richard Hellsen (6.39) and Alun Rossiter (6.00) also finished with highly satisfactory figures. The Robins became one of the most attractive sides in the country, winning five of their away matches, at Ipswich, King's Lynn, Oxford, Reading and Wolverhampton. At the Abbey, however, it was the same old story, with two defeats and a couple of draws; otherwise the team might have scaled even greater heights. Briefly referring back to Shirra, following a League Cup fixture at Ipswich on 7 May, the diminutive racer defeated Jeremy Doncaster to win the Golden Helmet. Mysteriously, the competition was subsequently discontinued and the Swindon rider never got to defend the title.

In the League Cup, the Robins slipped back to seventh place in the table, but one was left to wonder what might have happened had they turned around some of their slim away defeats. No fewer than five matches were lost 40-38, while a further two resulted in 41-37 reverses. Meanwhile, in the *Speedway Star* Knock-Out Cup, there was a first round victory over Wolverhampton, before the Robins went down 95-84 on aggregate to Reading at the quarter-final stage. Concluding a brief résumé of the quest for team silverware, Swindon did get the better of their M4 rivals in the Midland Cup, only to be knocked out at the semi-final stage by Coventry.

The brilliant duo of Mitch Shirra and Jimmy Nilsen came very close to glory in the Austin Rover British Open Pairs Championship at Reading on 12 July. The twelve competing teams were split into three sections and Swindon found themselves in Group B, along with Bradford, Hackney and local rivals Oxford. In front of a reported 3,000 audience, Oxford totalled 17 points and moved sweetly through to the last four, along with the other two group winners, Cradley Heath and Wolverhampton. However, by virtue of netting 16 points, the Robins pairing also went through as the highest-scoring runners-up. Shirra and Nilsen then repeated their earlier tally to march into the final and, setting up a grand showdown, it was Oxford, represented by Hans Nielsen and Andy Grahame, who accompanied them a couple of points behind. The hopes of a large contingent of travelling Swindon fans were to evaporate in an instant though. With a 4-3-2-0 scoring system, the Robins duo could afford to let Nielsen go, while packing the middle order positions ahead of Grahame. This they did initially, until Nilsen's footrest dramatically snapped on the pits corner, causing him to crash and earn an exclusion from referee Frank Ebdon. That made Shirra's task impossible in the re-run, but worse came when the Kiwi nudged the tapes and was also excluded, leaving the Oxford pair to ride unchallenged to the title in one almighty anti-climax.

On 17 May, Blunsdon again played host to a World Championship qualifying round and this saw Ipswich's Jeremy Doncaster triumph with a superb 15-point maximum. Alun Rossiter and Andrew Silver appeared in the meeting and although neither finished on the rostrum, they both provided much for the Abbey regulars to enthuse over, each netting 9 points. Continuing with the individual theme, in the TNT Sameday British League Riders' Championship at Belle Vue on 11 October,

Swindon Sprockets, 1987. From left to right, back row: Andy Jeffries, Darren Knapman, Martin Chessell, Tony Miller (Team Manager). Front, kneeling: Matthew Cross, Stephen Rose.

Swindon were represented by two riders for the first time, with Mitch Shirra scoring 8 points and Jimmy Nilsen recording 4. Prior to that, the same duo raced in the two-day World Final, held in Amsterdam, Holland on 5-6 September; Nilsen totalling 22 points (9 and 13) to again finish in fourth place overall, while Shirra yielded 12 points (7 and 5).

Stephen Rose and Matthew Cross fared much better for the Finebush Sprockets than they had in the main Swindon team. With 115 points, Rose headed the scoring for the British League Second Division side, while Cross (91), Darren Knapman (75), Kevin Pitts (72) and Martin Chessell (65) all hit acceptable tallies. Meanwhile, others who were limited to but a few outings included Mark White, Andy Jeffries, Andy Witts and Wayne Parker. In a league in which only Reading actually completed their fixtures, Swindon's junior team finished the campaign in seventh place out of twelve. That was a considerable improvement on their early-season League Cup form, which had seen them occupy a lowly eleventh position. Nick Bates was another rider who began the season with the Sprockets, but after making just three League Cup appearances he moved on and saw the season out with Reading's junior side, the 210 Rivets.

SWINDON ADVER ROBINS 1987

(Swindon's score shown first unless otherwise stated)

BRITISH LEAGUE

Opponents	Home	Away	Aggregate
Belle Vue	W41-37	L36-41	L77-78
Bradford	W48-30	L34-44	W82-74
Coventry	L36-42	L36-42	L72-84
Cradley Heath	L36-42	L27-50	L63-92
Hackney	D39-39	L38-40	L77-79
Ipswich	W41-37	W41-37	W82-74
King's Lynn	W48-30	W55-23	W103-53
Oxford	W42-36	W40-38	W82-74
Reading	D39-39	W41.5-36.5	W80.5-75.5
Sheffield	W48-29	L36-42	W84-71
Wolverhampton	W40-38	W42-36	W82-74

BRITISH LEAGUE TABLE

Team	Mts	Won	Drn	Lst	For	Agn.	Pts	Bon.	Tot.
Coventry	22	19	3	0	970	746	41	11	52
Cradley Heath	22	13	1	8	917	796	27	9	36
Swindon	22	12	2	8	884.5	828.5	26	7	33
Sheffield	22	13	0	9	871	840	26	6	32
Bradford	22	10	3	9	882	832	23	7	30
Ipswich	22	10	3	9	874	840	23	6	29
Reading	22	11	2	9	874.5	840.5	24	4	28
Belle Vue	22	10	1	11	843	872	21	5	26
Hackney	22	7	3	12	795	917	17	3	20
Wolverhampton	22	6	2	14	790	923	14	3	17
Oxford	22	6	1	15	825	891	13	3	16
King's Lynn	22	4	1	17	758	958	9	2	11

LEAGUE AVERAGES

Rider	Mts	Rds	Pts	Bon.	Tot.	Avge	Maximums
John Davis	1	4	10	0	10	10.00	–
Jimmy Nilsen	19	83	191	11	202	9.73	1 full; 5 paid
Mitch Shirra	18	77	181	5	186	9.66	2 full; 1 paid
Kelly Moran	1	4	8	1	9	9.00	–
Andrew Silver	4	18	29	4	33	7.33	–
Brian Karger	21	86	123	25	148	6.88	–
Conny Ivarsson	20	80	117	12	129	6.45	–
Richard Hellsen	22	87	119	20	139	6.39	–
Alun Rossiter	18	68	83	19	102	6.00	–
Andy Galvin	1	4	3	2	5	5.00	–

Andy Sell	1	2	1	1	2	4.00	–
Jan Staechmann	1	4	4	0	4	4.00	–
Gary Chessell	1	5	4	0	4	3.20	–
Matthew Cross	12	27	8	3	11	1.63	–
Darren Knapman	2	4	1	0	1	1.00	–
Stephen Rose	9	21	2.5	0	2.5	0.48	–

SPEEDWAY STAR KNOCK-OUT CUP

Opponents	Home	Away	Aggregate
Wolverhampton (Round one)	W47-43	W46-44	W93-87
Reading (Quarter-final)	L43-47	L41-48	L84-95

LEAGUE CUP

Opponents	Home	Away	Aggregate
Belle Vue	W42-36	L33-45	L75-81
Bradford	W45-33	L36-42	W81-75
Coventry	L36-42	L38-40	L74-82
Cradley Heath	W40-38	L38-40	D78-78
Hackney	W44-34	L38-40	W82-74
Ipswich	W44-34	L37-41	W81-75
King's Lynn	W46-32	W45-33	W91-65
Oxford	D39-39	L38-40	L77-79
Reading	D39-39	L37-41	L76-80
Sheffield	W45-33	L35-43	W80-76
Wolverhampton	W45-33	L38-40	W83-73

Note: Following the away match at Cradley Heath, Erik Gundersen defeated Swindon's Jimmy Nilsen in a run-off for the bonus point.

LEAGUE CUP TABLE

Team	Mts	Won	Drn	Lst	For	Agn.	Pts	Bon.	Tot.
Coventry	22	16	1	5	943	772	33	10	43
Oxford	22	14	2	6	884	832	30	9	39
Belle Vue	22	14	1	7	921	792	29	9	38
Cradley Heath	22	14	0	8	888	828	28	8	36
Sheffield	22	13	2	7	889	822	28	5	33
Reading	22	12	1	9	867	847	25	6	31
Swindon	22	9	2	11	878	838	20	6	26
Wolverhampton	22	9	1	12	828	886	19	4	23
Bradford	22	8	2	12	829	885	18	4	22
Hackney	22	6	2	14	801	913	14	3	17
King's Lynn	22	5	1	16	765	947	11	1	12
Ipswich	22	4	1	17	790	921	9	1	10

Note: Coventry, Oxford, Belle Vue and Cradley Heath progressed to the semi-finals.

MIDLAND CUP

Opponents	Home	Away	Aggregate
Reading (Quarter-final)	W41-37	W39-38	W80-75
Coventry (Semi-final)	W42-36	L30-48	L72-84

CHALLENGE

Opponents	Home	Away
Hackney	W51-27	L37-41
Reading	W41-37	L35-43

EASTER TRIANGLE THREE-TEAM TOURNAMENT

(First leg at Oxford)	Oxford 38, Reading 37, Swindon 33.
(Second leg at Swindon)	Swindon 38, Reading 38, Oxford 32.
(Third leg at Reading)	Reading 38, Swindon 38, Oxford 32.
Aggregate result:	Reading 113, Swindon 109, Oxford 102.

AUSTIN ROVER BRITISH OPEN PAIRS CHAMPIONSHIP

(Staged at Reading)   Group B: Oxford 17, Swindon 16, Hackney 14, Bradford 5.
Round two: Swindon 16, Oxford 14, Cradley Heath 13, Wolverhampton 11.
Final: Oxford 7, Swindon 0.

TNT SAMEDAY BRITISH LEAGUE RIDERS' CHAMPIONSHIP

(Staged at Belle Vue)   Mitch Shirra 8 points; Jimmy Nilsen 4 points.

SWINDON FINEBUSH SPROCKETS

BRITISH LEAGUE SECOND DIVISION TABLE

Team	Mts	Won	Drn	Lst	For	Agn.	Pts	Bon.	Tot.
Sheffield	21	18	1	2	553	326	37	10	47
Bradford	20	15	0	5	472	358	30	7	37
Coventry	21	15	1	5	478	397	31	6	37
King's Lynn	21	12	2	7	458	418	26	7	33
Hackney	20	13	1	6	450	382	27	5	32
Oxford	18	9	2	7	393	361	20	4	24
Swindon	21	9	1	11	437	441	19	5	24
Cradley Heath	19	6	3	10	382	408	15	3	18
Reading	22	5	1	16	376	524	11	3	14
Belle Vue	16	4	1	11	293	377	9	1	10
Ipswich	17	3	0	14	293	415	6	1	7
Wolverhampton	20	2	1	17	323	501	5	0	5

1988

It was all change at Blunsdon in 1988, as Mitch Shirra returned to Reading and the spectacular Andrew Silver joined full-time from Arena-Essex, albeit on loan, with the Robins having the option to sign the rider outright at the end of the campaign. Swindon would have loved to track both riders in their side, but the points-limit ruling just wouldn't allow it. With the arrival of Silver, young reserve David Smart went back to Arena-Essex on loan, having previously ridden for the National League side from 1984-1986 inclusive, while also assisting the Robins when required. Conny Ivarsson was another who didn't return from the previous season, but in his place a fellow Swede did finally link with the club, namely World Ice Speedway Champion Erik Stenlund. A new sponsor took over, with local motor company Walker Jackson replacing the *Evening Advertiser*, who had done such a great job for the previous three years.

The Robins hit trouble in the first home meeting of the season against Swedish touring side Getingarna (Stockholm United) on 26 March. In a rerun heat ten, the club's number one Jimmy Nilsen was involved in a nasty track spill with Jan Andersson and Per Jonsson, badly injuring his shoulder and wrist. Nilsen's injuries were to keep him out of the saddle for some weeks and, as if this wasn't enough, Erik Stenlund was hurt in the original running of the same race, aggravating an old shoulder injury. Ron Byford, having taken on the role of co-promoter alongside Bill Chandler, made every effort to fill the gaps in the side, as guests were used in abundance until the return of Nilsen. There was a glimmer of light towards the end of the season, however, when yet another Swede was enlisted, namely Peter Nahlin, who rode in just six league fixtures. In fact, Nahlin arrived as one of the hottest prospects in the sport, having notched 14 points to win the World Under-21 Championship at Slany, Czech Republic in July. Also on the podium with Nahlin were second-placed Henrik Gustafsson and fellow Robin Brian Karger.

Richard Hellsen and Gary Chessell were ever-present in league encounters as the team finished in a disappointing seventh spot. With eleven teams competing, the British League was played out with all the sides facing each other four times (twice at home and twice away). This worked out to be a mammoth forty-match programme, with Swindon suffering from their usual indifferent home form,

Swindon Robins, 1988. From left to right, back row: Brian Karger, Erik Stenlund, Gary Chessell, Richard Hellsen, David Smart, Alun Rossiter. Front, on bike: Jimmy Nilsen.

which saw them lose to Belle Vue (twice), Coventry (twice), Cradley Heath, Ipswich, King's Lynn and Oxford. Thanks to Jimmy Nilsen's early injury there was no real star in the camp, and Peter Nahlin actually topped the averages on a 7.68 figure, slightly ahead of Brian Karger on 7.59 and Nilsen on 7.31. Erik Stenlund showed pretty good form when fit, averaging 6.37, but he appeared in only fourteen league matches due to lengthy spells out through injury. Aside from his knock in the Robins' opening home match of the season, he received a fracture to the fibula in his left leg and severed two ligaments while competing in a long-track meeting at Holzwickeide, Germany in June.

After a bye in the opening round of the *Speedway Star* Knock-Out Cup, the Walker Jackson Robins went down to old rivals Oxford at the next stage. In a two-legged battle of epic proportions, with both teams giving it their all, the Cheetahs came out on top by the narrowest of margins, 91-89 on aggregate. Meanwhile, in the British Open Pairs Championship at Reading on 17 July, Andrew Silver and Brian Karger could only total 8 points as Swindon failed to progress past the opening group phase of the competition.

In celebration of sixty years of British Speedway, a Diamond Jubilee tournament was organised, featuring a series of matches involving England, Denmark, USA and Sweden. As such, on 24 April, Swindon Speedway was proud to host the meeting between Sweden and USA, which was won by the Americans, 47-43. In a thrilling contest, the victors were headed by 10 points from Lance King, while Mike Faria scored 9+1. By comparison, although the Swedes had three men in double figures – Per Jonsson (13), Erik Stenlund (12) and Tony Olsson (10+1) – they lacked the strength in depth of the triumphant American squad.

Something very special happened at Blunsdon on 8 October, when Barry Briggs brought back all the members of the 1967 league title-winning side to race an exhibition match against the Swindon Soft Water All-Stars, a team made up of riders from the same era. It was the All-Stars who won the meeting, 34-32, and the fans flocked to the Abbey Stadium in their hordes, filling the place with its biggest attendance for many years. How they loved to see their former heroes in action, particularly Bob Kilby, who showed that he'd lost none of his lightning speed from the gate.

George White, another Swindon legend of a bygone age, also made a return to the track during the year, riding in Barry Briggs' initial Golden Greats meeting at Coventry on 14 August. Prior to the racing the diminutive White had terrible problems in locating a pair of boots to fit his extremely small feet, but once on track he looked resplendent in a Union Flag race-jacket and was one of the day's star turns. Displaying all his old dash, he swept to victory from Fred Rogers, Jim Lightfoot and Sandor Levai in his first race, prior to losing out to the great Ove Fundin in his other heat. That equated to 5 points and was sufficient for him to reach the Fabulous Fifties final, when he again had to settle for second place behind Fundin. Nonetheless, it was a great event and wee Chalky had spanned the mists of time with a wonderful showing.

On the individual front, Mitch Shirra returned to Blunsdon to win the BCA Classic with a gutsy display on 4 June, defeating Chris Morton, Kelly Moran and Shawn Moran in the six-lap grand final. On 9 October, Brian Karger represented Swindon in the TNT Sameday British League Riders' Championship at Belle Vue, but in a meeting won by fellow Dane Jan O. Pedersen the Robin finished well down the field with just 5 points.

Despite still enjoying sponsorship from Finebush, the Sprockets had a poor campaign in the British League Second Division. The team, managed by Tony Miller, was one of only four to actually complete their fixtures. However, that didn't help them to finish any higher than tenth place out of the eleven sides, with only thirteen wins and four draws gained from their forty matches. Matthew Cross top-scored for the youngsters, netting 147 points from twenty-seven matches, while Stephen Rose was the only other rider to reach the century mark, his tally of 108 points being gleaned from two matches less. Martin Chessell, Darren Knapman, Wayne Parker and Andy Witts were also regulars in the side, while a handful of others made limited appearances, namely Paul Atkins, Derrol Keats, Martin Phillips and John Wainwright. Meanwhile, in the Knock-Out Cup the Finebush Sprockets had a first round bye before, just like their senior counterparts, losing to Oxford, by 33 points to 27 on aggregate.

Coventry, 14 August 1988. George White shows his old dash in the inaugural Golden Greats meeting.

SWINDON WALKER JACKSON ROBINS 1988

(Swindon's score shown first unless otherwise stated)

BRITISH LEAGUE 'A'

Opponents	Home	Away	Aggregate
Belle Vue	L39-51	L37-53	L76-104
Bradford	W57-33	L42-48	W99-81
Coventry	L44-46	L40-50	L84-96
Cradley Heath	L39-50	L39-51	L78-101
Ipswich	L41-49	L38-52	L79-101
King's Lynn	W48-42	D45-45	W93-87
Oxford	L43-47	L41-49	L84-96
Reading	W48-42	L34-56	L82-98
Sheffield	W53-37	L42-48	W95-85
Wolverhampton	W53-37	W48-42	W101-79

BRITISH LEAGUE 'B'

Belle Vue	L44-46	L25-65	L69-111
Bradford	W46-44	W48-42	W94-86
Coventry	L40-49	L25-65	L65-114
Cradley Heath	W46-44	L35-55	L81-99
Ipswich	W51-39	W47-42	W98-81
King's Lynn	L40-49	L39-50	L79-99
Oxford	W47.5-42.5	W49-41	W96.5-83.5
Reading	W46-44	L37-53	L83-97
Sheffield	W46-44	L30-60	L76-104
Wolverhampton	W46-44	W48-42	W94-86

BRITISH LEAGUE TABLE

Team	Mts	Won	Drn	Lst	For	Agn.	Pts	Bon.	Tot.
Coventry	40	31	2	7	1,978.5	1,618.5	64	18	82
Belle Vue	40	26	1	13	1,912	1,686	53	13	66
Cradley Heath	39	22	1	16	1,831	1,675	45	15	60
Oxford	40	20	6	14	1,850	1,743	46	13	59
Reading	40	20	3	17	1,857	1,736	43	12	55
Sheffield	39	19	2	18	1,731.5	1,776.5	40	8	48
Swindon	40	17	1	22	1,706.5	1,888.5	35	8	43
Wolverhampton	40	15	3	22	1,781	1,817	33	8	41
King's Lynn	40	14	3	23	1,718.5	1,878.5	31	7	38
Ipswich	39	13	0	26	1,651	1,854	26	4	30
Bradford	39	10	0	29	1,580	1,924	20	2	22

Note: Two matches were not raced: Bradford v. Ipswich; Sheffield v. Cradley Heath.

LEAGUE AVERAGES

Rider	Mts	Rds	Pts	Bon.	Tot.	Avge	Maximums
Neil Evitts	1	4	9	2	11	11.00	–
Andy Galvin	1	4	8	2	10	10.00	–
Jan O. Pedersen	1	5	12	0	12	9.60	–
Mitch Shirra	3	16	33	2	35	8.75	–
Roland Danno	1	4	5	3	8	8.00	–
Peter Nahlin	6	25	42	6	48	7.68	–
Mark Loram	3	12	20	3	23	7.67	–
Lance King	2	11	21	0	21	7.64	–
Brian Karger	36	166	289	26	315	7.59	–
Jimmy Nilsen	26	121	206	15	221	7.31	–
Kelly Moran	1	5	9	0	9	7.20	–
Andrew Silver	39	193	327	19	346	7.17	1 full
Paul Thorp	1	4	7	0	7	7.00	–
Martin Dugard	2	10	17	0	17	6.80	–
Erik Stenlund	14	59	75	19	94	6.37	1 paid
Richard Hellsen	40	166	217.5	30	247.5	5.96	–
Alun Rossiter	38	165	196	41	237	5.75	–

Martin Goodwin	2	8	9	2	11	5.50	–
Troy Butler	2	6	6	2	8	5.33	–
Gary Chessell	40	156	165	43	208	5.33	–
Kenny McKinna	1	4	4	1	5	5.00	–
Jan Andersson	1	5	5	1	6	4.80	–
Craig Hodgson	2	8	6	1	7	3.50	–
Dean Standing	1	6	4	1	5	3.33	–
David Smart	3	9	5	2	7	3.11	–
Kai Niemi	1	4	3	0	3	3.00	–
Ian Barney	1	3	2	0	2	2.67	–
Glenn Doyle	1	3	1	1	2	2.67	–
Tony Olsson	1	4	2	0	2	2.00	–
Kevin Jolly	1	3	1	0	1	1.33	–
Andy Campbell	1	3	0	0	0	0.00	–
Louis Carr	1	4	0	0	0	0.00	–
Martin Chessell	1	3	0	0	0	0.00	–
Steve Regeling	1	3	0	0	0	0.00	–
Nigel Sparshott	1	2	0	0	0	0.00	–

SPEEDWAY STAR KNOCK-OUT CUP

Opponents	Home	Away	Aggregate
Bye (Round one)	–	–	–
Oxford (Quarter-final)	W47-43	L42-48	L89-91

CHALLENGE

Opponents	Home	Away
Jan Andersson Select	–	W44-40
Getingarna	W47-42	–
Hackney	–	L40-50
Ipswich	W53-43	–

Note: A Swindon and Oxford Select side raced against the Jan Andersson Select, with the meeting staged at Reading.

FOUR-TEAM TOURNAMENT

(Staged at Arena-Essex)	Ipswich 29, Reading 27, Swindon 24, Arena-Essex 15.
(Staged at Exeter)	Exeter 31, Swindon 25, Poole 24, Milton Keynes 16.
(Staged at Swindon)	Swindon 40, Hackney 29, The Anzacs 22, Poole 5.

BRITISH OPEN PAIRS CHAMPIONSHIP

(Staged at Reading)	Group A: Cradley Heath 21, Coventry 14, Ipswich 11, Swindon 8.

TNT SAMEDAY BRITISH LEAGUE RIDERS' CHAMPIONSHIP

(Staged at Belle Vue)	Brian Karger 5 points.

SWINDON FINEBUSH SPROCKETS

BRITISH LEAGUE SECOND DIVISION TABLE

Team	Mts	Won	Drn	Lst	For	Agn.	Pts	Bon.	Tot.
Bradford	39	30	3	6	675	482	63	18	81
Belle Vue	40	24	1	15	630	556	49	13	62
Sheffield	37	19	2	16	559	520	42	12	54
Wolverhampton	40	21	2	17	601	589	44	8	52
Cradley Heath	38	17	4	17	581	545	38	11	49
Oxford	38	18	2	18	548	574	38	10	48
Coventry	39	18	2	19	585	572	38	8	46
Reading	38	17	1	20	557	567	35	7	42
King's Lynn	40	14	4	22	583	598	32	9	41
Swindon	40	13	4	23	528	654	30	6	36
Ipswich	39	9	3	27	474	664	21	2	23

Note: Five 'B' matches were not ridden, namely: Bradford v. Ipswich; Coventry v. Sheffield; Oxford v. Cradley Heath; Reading v. Oxford; Sheffield v. Cradley Heath.

1989

The Sunbrite-sponsored British League lost two teams before the season got underway, with Sheffield closing and Ipswich opting for National League racing, thus leaving just nine tracks. American Bart Bast was welcomed to the Walker Jackson Robins' nest, joining Peter Nahlin and Andrew Silver, who had finally been purchased outright. Also back were Jimmy Nilsen (elected club captain) and Brian Karger, with Gary Chessell and David Smart filling the reserve berths in the side. Meanwhile, Richard Hellsen and Alun Rossiter left for National League racing at Long Eaton and Poole respectively; and Erik Stenlund was ruled out by his continental commitments.

Cruel luck hit the Robins on 6 May in a league match at home to old rivals Oxford, when Peter Nahlin crashed and suffered a fractured vertebra. Danish youngster Tom Knudsen was signed as a replacement, but in the event he didn't stay long, due to a contractual dispute with his parent club back in Denmark. Prior to Knudsen's arrival, co-promoter Ron Byford had actually attempted to lure Per Jonsson to Blunsdon, the speedy Swede having been unable to agree terms with Reading prior to the campaign. When that avenue came to nothing, Byford tried to tempt Conny Ivarsson into a British League return, but that also proved fruitless. There was some light at the end of the tunnel when, having suffered no neurological damage to his back, Peter Nahlin remarkably returned to the side on 27 May in a home league fixture against King's Lynn.

However, with results not going the desired way, more changes were forced upon the Swindon management. Ron Byford again looked around and all-action Czech Roman Matousek was mentioned. However, attention then turned to Polish racer Piotr Swist. Details were actually finalised to sign the Stal Gorzow rider, but due to problems in obtaining the necessary visa the move never materialised. Out of the blue, Byford's prayers were answered when experienced England international John Davis came on board after becoming unsettled at King's Lynn. It was Bart Bast who made way for 'JD', the Californian's contract being cancelled in mid-July after he had gleaned 66 points from sixteen league matches for a 5.15 average.

In the league Swindon were, as usual, vulnerable at home, where they lost six matches – against Coventry (twice), Cradley Heath, Oxford (twice) and Wolverhampton. In a rather mediocre season, they ended the campaign occupying sixth place, with various contributory factors seeing Bart Bast, Peter Nahlin and even Jimmy Nilsen occupying a reserve berth at one time or another. Despite this, Nilsen was the top Robin, averaging 8.33, closely followed by Brian Karger on 8.05. However, the figures for the remaining regulars rather fell away, as follows: Andrew Silver (7.31), John Davis (6.67), Peter Nahlin (6.42), Gary Chessell (5.05) and David Smart (3.70). In fairness to 'Smartie', it was the lack of consistency among some of his teammates that forced him to ride in the main body of the side on many occasions and this was clearly the chief reason for his lowly average.

Looking at other competitions, Wolverhampton saw to it that Swindon didn't progress beyond their opening tie in the *Speedway Star* Knock-Out Cup, while in the new Gold Cup competition, the Robins finished last in the southern group table.

On 30 July, the Abbey Stadium played host to a Sunbrite-sponsored Test match between England and the USA and, somewhat surprisingly, the Lions ran riot to win 75-32. In a powerful performance, England's main men were Kelvin Tatum (15+1), Neil Evitts (15), Jeremy Doncaster (14+1), Martin Dugard (11+4) and Andrew Silver (10+4). The only member of the USA side to offer any real resistance was Lance King, who scored 12 points.

For the first time, a full-blown 1,000cc sidecar meeting was held at Blunsdon on 23 September, when Australia eclipsed England by 50 points to 38 in a Sunbrite Test match. Some of the world's top exponents of the discipline were involved, including Paul Pinfold, Brian Ash, Alan Artus, Darrin Treloar, Gary Moon and Shane Soutar.

The only individual speedway meeting held at Swindon in 1989 was run the day after the sidecar event, and saw John Davis triumph ahead of Jimmy Nilsen, Alan Grahame and Ronnie Correy in the

Swindon Robins, 1989. From left to right, back row: Gary Chessell, Andrew Silver, Peter Nahlin, Ron Byford (Team Manager), Brian Karger, David Smart, Bart Bast. Front, on bike: Jimmy Nilsen.

Swindon Sprockets, 1989. From left to right, back row: Matthew Cross, Tony Miller (Team Manager), Simon Coombs MP, Derrol Keats, Martin Chessell, Andy Witts.

final of the Bike for Life event. The meeting, organised by team sponsor Walker Jackson, was a charity event with the intention of raising sufficient money to pay for Babylog ventilators, to be installed and used in the Paediatric and Special Care Unit at Princess Margaret Hospital in Swindon.

Continuing with the individual theme, Brian Karger rode brilliantly to net 12 points and take third place behind maximum man Shawn Moran (15) and Hans Nielsen (14) in the TNT Sameday British League Riders' Championship. Jimmy Nilsen also represented Swindon in the major event at Belle Vue on 1 October, recording 8 points to finish in sixth position.

The Finebush Sprockets enjoyed a much better season than in 1988. They began by topping the southern section of the British League Second Division Gold Cup, before unfortunately losing heavily in the final, 53-17 to Belle Vue. This was to be expected though, as the Manchester outfit included the likes of Joe Screen, Carl Stonehewer and Scott Smith in their ranks. It was hardly surprising then that the TNT Colts went on to win the League Championship by a huge margin of 22 points from runners-up Oxford. Just three points further behind in third spot, however, were the Sprockets, by virtue of sixteen wins and two draws from the thirty-one matches they completed; the 'B' fixture at Belle Vue not being run. Although Derrol Keats headed the league averages with a figure of 10.77, he actually rode in only four matches. Matthew Cross, meanwhile, remained ever-present, accruing 193 points for an impressive 9.35 average. The other mainstays in Tony Miller's team were Martin Chessell (7.65), Darrin Wilson (5.14) and Steve Camden (4.06), while Andy Witts (3.32) and Wayne Parker (2.22) also had outings.

In the Knock-Out Cup the youngsters had a first round bye, prior to defeating Wolverhampton 40-32 over two legs. Then, in the semi-final, the Sprockets enjoyed a 44-26 success against Bradford, courtesy of home and away victories. They then faced the mighty Belle Vue side in the final, which was run on a full fifteen-heat format, rather than the usual six-race formula. The Sprockets were strengthened by the inclusion of David Smart, David Steen and Darren Grayling for the first leg at Blunsdon on 17 October but, despite this, they went down to a 47-43 defeat. Smart and Grayling again appeared in the second leg at Kirkmanshulme Lane on 27 October, with Gary Chessell and Steve Masters also drafted in. It was to no avail though, as the powerful Manchester side won 52-35 to not only complete a 99-78 aggregate success, but also a clean sweep of all the available trophies.

The Swindon track came in for a lot of criticism during the year, due to the reintroduction of stock car racing after many years' absence. From a business point of view this was regarded a success, with the car events being well attended. However, the damage to the circuit too often proved impossible to correct before the Robins' fixture that followed, regrettably resulting in a number of meetings taking place on a sub-standard surface. This obviously affected the confidence of some team members and doubtless Swindon's home form would have been better on a smoother racing strip.

SWINDON WALKER JACKSON ROBINS 1989

(Swindon's score shown first unless otherwise stated)

SUNBRITE BRITISH LEAGUE 'A'

Opponents	Home	Away	Aggregate
Belle Vue	W52-38	L41-49	W93-87
Bradford	W50-40	L40-50	D90-90
Coventry	L43-47	D45-45	L88-92
Cradley Heath	L33-57	L32-58	L65-115
King's Lynn	W52-38	L42-48	W94-86
Oxford	L39-51	L37-53	L76-104
Reading	W47-43	L41-49	L88-92
Wolverhampton	L43-47	L31-59	L74-106

Note: Following the away match at Bradford, Brian Karger beat Paul Thorp in a bonus point run-off.

SUNBRITE BRITISH LEAGUE 'B'

Belle Vue	W56-33	L35-55	W91-88
Bradford	W55-35	L39-51	W94-86
Coventry	L42-48	L44-46	L86-94

Cradley Heath	W54-36	L31.5-58.5	L85.5-94.5
King's Lynn	W54-36	W46-44	W100-80
Oxford	L44-46	W49-41	W93-87
Reading	W51-39	L39-51	D90-90
Wolverhampton	W47-43	L41-49	L88-92

Note: Following the away match at Reading, Brian Karger beat Jeremy Doncaster in a bonus point run-off.

SUNBRITE BRITISH LEAGUE TABLE

Team	Mts	Won	Drn	Lst	For	Agn.	Pts	Bon.	Tot.
Oxford	32	22	1	9	1,580	1,293	45	13	58
Wolverhampton	32	19	2	11	1,511	1,366	40	12	52
Cradley Heath	32	19	3	10	1,550.5	1,327.5	41	10	51
Belle Vue	32	19	2	11	1,496	1,378	40	10	50
Coventry	32	15	3	14	1,389	1,486	33	8	41
Swindon	32	12	1	19	1,395.5	1,483.5	25	8	33
Reading	32	13	1	18	1,356	1,521	27	5	32
Bradford	32	9	2	21	1,347	1,529	20	3	23
King's Lynn	32	8	1	23	1,319	1,560	17	3	20

LEAGUE AVERAGES

Rider	Mts	Rds	Pts	Bon.	Tot.	Avge	Maximums
Kelly Moran	1	6	13	2	15	10.00	–
Paul Thorp	1	5	11	1	12	9.60	–
Jimmy Nilsen	28	145	281	21	302	8.33	1 full; 3 paid
Brian Karger	32	161	297	27	324	8.05	1 paid
Matthew Cross	1	1	1	1	2	8.00	–
Neil Evitts	1	4	7	1	8	8.00	–
Ronnie Correy	1	6	9	2	11	7.33	–
Andrew Silver	30	139	227	27	254	7.31	–
Tony Olsson	1	5	9	0	9	7.20	–
John Davis	16	63	90	15	105	6.67	–
Gert Handberg	1	3	4	1	5	6.67	–
Peter Nahlin	30	125	167.5	33	200.5	6.42	–
Joe Screen	1	5	7	1	8	6.40	–
Antal Kocso	1	3	4	0	4	5.33	–
Bart Bast	16	66	66	19	85	5.15	–
Gary Chessell	25	88	99	12	111	5.05	–
Robert Pfetzing	1	4	3	2	5	5.00	–
Andy Phillips	1	4	4	1	5	5.00	–
Tom Knudsen	2	6	5	1	6	4.00	–
David Smart	32	121	91	21	112	3.70	–
Martin Chessell	1	2	0	0	0	0.00	–
Derrol Keats	1	1	0	0	0	0.00	–

SPEEDWAY STAR KNOCK-OUT CUP

Opponents	Home	Away	Aggregate
Wolverhampton (Quarter-final)	D45-45	L41-49	L86-94

GOLD CUP

Opponents	Home	Away	Aggregate
Coventry	W46-44	D45-45	W91-89
King's Lynn	W48-42	L39-51	L87-93
Oxford	L41-49	L34-56	L75-105
Reading	L44-46	L43-46	L87-92

GOLD CUP (SOUTHERN GROUP) TABLE

Team	Mts	Won	Drn	Lst	For	Agn.	Pts	Bon.	Tot.
Oxford	8	6	1	1	409	309	13	4	17
Reading	8	5	0	3	351	366	10	2	12
King's Lynn	8	2	2	4	346	374	6	2	8
Coventry	8	2	2	4	350	368	6	1	7
Swindon	8	2	1	5	340	379	5	1	6

Note: Oxford progressed to the final.

CHALLENGE

Opponents	Home	Away
British League All-Stars	W47-43	–
Poole	W48-41	W58-38
Reading	–	L39-51

FOUR-TEAM TOURNAMENT

(Staged at Arena-Essex)	Cradley Heath 34, Swindon 25, Reading 22, Arena-Essex 14.
(Staged at Exeter)	Berwick 39, Exeter 28, Hackney 15, Swindon 13.
(Staged at Newcastle)	Swindon 36, Newcastle 27, Ipswich 19, Middlesbrough 14.
(Staged at Reading)	Hackney & Ipswich Select 29, Reading 27, Swindon 22, Poole 17.
(Staged at Wimbledon)	Oxford 28, Reading 24, Wimbledon 22, Swindon 22.

TNT SAMEDAY BRITISH LEAGUE RIDERS' CHAMPIONSHIP

(Staged at Belle Vue)	Brian Karger 12 points (3rd); Jimmy Nilsen 8 points (6th).

SWINDON FINEBUSH SPROCKETS

BRITISH LEAGUE SECOND DIVISION TABLE

Team	Mts	Won	Drn	Lst	For	Agn.	Pts	Bon.	Tot.
Belle Vue	28	27	0	1	705	295	54	12	66
Oxford	28	16	1	11	534	467	33	11	44
Swindon	31	16	2	13	546	554	34	7	41
Wolverhampton	31	16	0	15	545	559	32	6	38
Bradford	30	15	0	15	546	528	30	7	37
Cradley Heath	31	12	2	17	495	612	26	5	31
King's Lynn	31	11	1	19	508	601	23	6	29
Reading	31	12	0	19	487	624	24	3	27
Coventry	29	7	0	22	455	581	14	5	19

Note: Several 'B' matches were not staged, namely: Belle Vue v. Coventry; Belle Vue v. Cradley Heath; Belle Vue v. Oxford; Belle Vue v. Swindon; Coventry v. Bradford; King's Lynn v. Oxford; Oxford v. Coventry; Oxford v. Reading; Wolverhampton v. Bradford.

1990

It was very much a case of repetition in 1990, with still only nine teams in the Sunbrite British League, and Ron Byford's boys again finished in sixth position. This was in spite of a greatly improved home racing strip, created through a combination of major track work and the absence of any stock car racing. Four defeats and one drawn match at Blunsdon certainly didn't help and indeed, if those results had been more favourable, Swindon would have been challenging for a top-three slot.

After two years, Walker Jackson were replaced as team sponsor by Coastal, a company famous for their high-quality doors and windows. An important signing for Swindon had been that of young Australian sensation Leigh Adams, who had previously ridden for National League Poole. Both Adams, who arrived for a reputed £20,000 transfer fee, and new club captain John Davis received personal sponsorship from Coastal. The side, therefore, became known as the Team Coastal Robins. The spectacular Andrew Silver was back, as were the Swedes, Jimmy Nilsen and Peter Nahlin, plus local lad David Smart and Dane Brian Karger.

Regrettably, Brian Karger's season ended prematurely when he crashed in a Danish Super League match on 22 June, suffering a broken thigh and a fractured jaw. The name of Conny Ivarsson again did the rounds as a possible replacement for the popular Dane but, thanks to sponsorship from a number of enthusiasts, it was old favourite Phil Crump who flew in from Australia to fill the gap. Crumpie, however, was not the rider of old and his final average of 5.64 reflected this. Andrew Silver was an ever-present in league matches, and finished with a useful average of 7.53, while Leigh Adams

Swindon Robins, 1990. From left to right, back row: John Anderson (Sponsor), Brian Karger, Leigh Adams, Peter Nahlin, Andrew Silver, Ron Byford (Team Manager). Front row, kneeling: Jimmy Nilsen, David Smart. On bike: John Davis.

showed he was 'on the pace' with a 6.81 figure. Top Robin was again Jimmy Nilsen, who scored 285 points for an average of 8.61. From the eleven matches in which he rode, Brian Karger recorded a 7.91 average, while Peter Nahlin scored 213 points for a 7.36 average. It must be said that David Smart did very well though, for he only missed a single league match and averaged 5.13. In the *Speedway Star* Knock-Out Cup, Swindon defeated Coventry to reach the semi-final, before losing by a whisker to Bradford, 91-89 on aggregate. Meanwhile, in the Gold Cup, the Robins finished third in the four-team southern section, with local rivals Oxford and Reading occupying first and second places respectively.

The Swindon Soft Water Classic was the only individual event staged at the Abbey in 1990. The meeting, held on 13 May, saw Jan O. Pedersen reveal his class to win the final from Kelvin Tatum, Andrew Silver and Leigh Adams. It was a great night for Pedersen for not only did he win the meeting but, in heat two, he scorched around the Blunsdon bowl in 65.2 seconds, thereby equalling the five-year-old track record held by fellow Dane Erik Gundersen. Unfortunately for Pedersen and Gundersen, 'Main Dane' Hans Nielsen annihilated this time on 8 September when he rounded the track in a time of 64.8 seconds, clipping an amazing four-tenths of a second off the previous best.

Following the success of the sidecar meeting the previous year, two events were staged in 1990, and these saw the World All-Stars defeat England 47-43 on 9 June, while Paul Pinfold and partner John Bowkett won the Homefire Sidecar Masters on 14 July. Interestingly, Pinfold had originally started the meeting with Nathan Murray in the chair, only for Bowkett to take over after two outings. New Zealander Murray, from Hamilton, North Island, was better known as a speedway rider and he would later go on and represent the Robins some years later in 2000.

Barry Briggs attempted to bring the Golden Greats to Blunsdon on 19 August, but rain caused the meeting to be postponed. However, on the rescheduled date of 16 September, the crowds flocked through the turnstiles to see their former favourites in action. Among others, speedway legends Ove Fundin, Gote Nordin, Anders Michanek and Bert Harkins took to the Blunsdon circuit again. Former Swindon favourites Mike Broadbanks, Barry Duke, John Bishop and Briggo himself also took to the track, in what was probably the most successful meeting of an average season. Roy Trigg came out on top of the Fabulous Fifties section, while Terry Betts was triumphant in the Swinging Sixties event.

Andrew Silver was one of two Swindon representatives at Belle Vue for the Groundwork/Dunlop British League Riders' Championship on 14 October, when he impressed with 8 points to finish in seventh position. Meanwhile, the other Robin, Jimmy Nilsen, could only manage 3 points, in what was a disappointing performance by his standards. Prior to that Nilsen did, however, reach the Sunbrite World Final, held at the Odsal Stadium in Bradford on 1 September, when he gave an excellent showing to finish fifth having yielded a 10-point tally.

The Finebush Sprockets ended up one place higher than their senior counterparts, occupying fifth position in the British League Second Division table. Matthew Cross enjoyed another good term with Tony Miller's side, raising his league average to 9.93, having scored 191 points from twenty-eight matches. In fact, only five riders completed over ten meetings for the Swindon juniors and aside from Cross, the other regulars were Martin Chessell (7.82), Wayne Freeman (7.40), Andy Witts (6.00) and Steve Camden (5.95). There were a number of others who appeared though, including Anthony Blake, Darren Boulton, Peter Byrne, Rob Camden, Mike Courage, Dean Scott, Brett Wakeling and Darrin Wilson. One other interesting name was that of Australian Frank Smart, who raced in just one league fixture at home to Wolverhampton on 28 April. Smart was to go on and enjoy a career with the likes of Exeter and Newport but, coincidentally, like the previously mentioned Nathan Murray, he also rode for the senior Robins' team in 2000.

In the Knock-Out Cup, the Sprockets ousted local rivals Oxford in the first round before facing Bradford in the semi-final. Unfortunately, they suffered a hefty 28-8 reverse in the first leg at Odsal Stadium and, despite having senior team member David Smart on board for the return, the best they could do was an 18-18 draw as they headed out on aggregate. Martin Chessell represented the Sprockets in the Second Division Riders' Championship at Belle Vue on 9 September, but despite knocking up a creditable 10 points, he finished outside the podium positions.

SWINDON TEAM COASTAL ROBINS 1990

(Swindon's score shown first unless otherwise stated)

SUNBRITE BRITISH LEAGUE 'A'

Opponents	Home	Away	Aggregate
Belle Vue	W55-35	L42-48	W97-83
Bradford	W50-40	L41-49	W91-89
Coventry	W64-26	D45-45	W109-71
Cradley Heath	W46-44	L37-53	L83-97
King's Lynn	W59-31	W46-44	W105-75
Oxford	W57-31	W46-44	W103-75
Reading	L40-50	L31-59	L71-109
Wolverhampton	W57-33	L41-49	W98-82

SUNBRITE BRITISH LEAGUE 'B'

Belle Vue	L42-48	L36-54	L78-102
Bradford	W46-44	L32-58	L78-102
Coventry	W54-36	W46-44	W100-80
Cradley Heath	L38-52	L42-48	L80-100
King's Lynn	W59-31	W55-35	W114-66
Oxford	L43-47	L41-49	L84-96
Reading	D45-45	L37-53	L82-98
Wolverhampton	W57-33	L32-58	L89-91

SWINDON SPEEDWAY

SUNBRITE BRITISH LEAGUE TABLE

Team	Mts	Won	Drn	Lst	For	Agn.	Pts	Bon.	Tot.
Reading	32	19	3	10	1,513.5	1,360.5	41	13	54
Wolverhampton	32	17	5	10	1,446	1,431	39	10	49
Belle Vue	32	19	2	11	1,454	1,418	40	7	47
Oxford	32	17	2	13	1,467	1,405	36	10	46
Bradford	32	16	1	15	1,470	1,407	33	8	41
Swindon	32	15	2	15	1,462	1,416	32	8	40
Cradley Heath	32	12	1	19	1,425.5	1,454.5	25	7	32
Coventry	32	10	3	19	1,386	1,487	23	7	30
King's Lynn	32	7	5	20	1,315	1,560	19	2	21

LEAGUE AVERAGES

Rider	Mts	Rds	Pts	Bon.	Tot.	Avge	Maximums
Jan Andersson	1	6	13	1	14	9.33	–
Jimmy Nilsen	28	137	285	10	295	8.61	1 full; 1 paid
Billy Hamill	1	4	7	1	8	8.00	–
Per Jonsson	2	8	13	3	16	8.00	–
Brian Karger	11	47	89	4	93	7.91	1 paid
Andrew Silver	32	145	244	29	273	7.53	2 paid
Peter Nahlin	31	143	213	50	263	7.36	–
Neil Collins	1	4	5	2	7	7.00	–
Leigh Adams	29	141	218	22	240	6.81	1 paid
Richard Knight	1	6	10	0	10	6.67	–
John Davis	25	84	124	15	139	6.62	1 full
Stephen Davies	1	4	5	1	6	6.00	–
Joe Screen	1	4	5	1	6	6.00	–
Paul Thorp	2	9	13	0	13	5.78	–
Phil Crump	16	61	63	23	86	5.64	–
Bobby Ott	2	8	11	0	11	5.50	–
David Smart	31	124	123	36	159	5.13	–
Tony Olsson	1	4	5	0	5	5.00	–
Glenn Doyle	2	10	10	0	10	4.00	–
Peter Ravn	1	4	4	0	4	4.00	–
Alastair Stevens	1	3	2	1	3	4.00	–
Neil Evitts	1	2	0	0	0	0.00	–
Chris Morton	1	3	0	0	0	0.00	–

SPEEDWAY STAR KNOCK-OUT CUP

Opponents	Home	Away	Aggregate
Bye (Round one)	–	–	–
Coventry (Quarter-final)	W56-34	W53-37	W109-71
Bradford (Semi-final)	W50-40	L39-51	L89-91

GOLD CUP

Opponents	Home	Away	Aggregate
King's Lynn	W51-39	L43-47	W94-86
Oxford	L38-51	W51-39	L89-90
Reading	W47-42	L39-51	L86-93

GOLD CUP (SOUTHERN SECTION) TABLE

Team	Mts	Won	Drn	Lst	For	Agn.	Pts	Bon.	Tot.
Oxford	6	4	0	2	283	256	8	3	11
Reading	6	4	0	2	269	270	8	2	10
Swindon	6	3	0	3	269	269	6	1	7
King's Lynn	6	1	0	5	257	283	2	0	2

Oxford progressed to the final.

CHALLENGE

Opponents	Home	Away
Poole	W44-40	D48-48

FOUR-TEAM TOURNAMENT

(Staged at King's Lynn)	Swindon 37, King's Lynn 29, British League Select 19, Belle Vue 11.
(Staged at Peterborough)	Swindon 'B' 30.5, Swindon 'A' 28.5, Peterborough 'B' 19, Peterborough 'A' 18.
(Staged at Reading)	Poole 29, Wimbledon 25, Reading 23, Swindon 19.
(Staged at Reading)	Reading 27, Oxford 27, British League Select 25, Swindon 16.
(Staged at Swindon)	Swindon 'A' 35, Swindon Select 34, Exeter 15, Poole 12.
(Staged at Swindon)	Swindon 35, Wolverhampton 28, Oxford 21, Belle Vue 12.

THREE-TEAM TOURNAMENT

(Staged at Exeter)	Exeter 32, Swindon 24, *Express & Echo* Rangers 22.

GROUNDWORK/DUNLOP BRITISH LEAGUE RIDERS' CHAMPIONSHIP

(Staged at Belle Vue)	Andrew Silver 8 points; Jimmy Nilsen 3 points.

SWINDON FINEBUSH SPROCKETS

BRITISH LEAGUE SECOND DIVISION TABLE

Team	Mts	Won	Drn	Lst	For	Agn.	Pts	Bon.	Tot.
Wolverhampton	32	26	4	2	723	417	56	16	72
Reading	32	20	2	10	637	505	42	12	54
King's Lynn	32	19	2	11	620	526	40	11	51
Bradford	32	15	1	16	588	554	31	8	39
Swindon	32	13	2	17	578	562	28	6	34
Belle Vue	32	12	3	17	553	578	27	6	33
Cradley Heath	32	12	1	19	500	635	25	6	31
Oxford	32	10	1	21	481	662	19	4	23
Coventry	32	9	0	23	449	690	18	3	21

Note: Oxford had two points deducted for using an ineligible rider.

1991

In 1991 the domestic set-up was changed to First and Second Divisions, with four teams from the former National League joining the new higher section, namely Berwick, Ipswich, Poole and Wimbledon. Naturally, Swindon were in the top flight, but there were changes on the personnel front. Jimmy Nilsen went to Berwick on loan, David Smart opted for Second Division racing with Exeter and John Davis linked with one of his former clubs, Wimbledon. Aussie Rod Colquhoun moved to Blunsdon from Poole, while Paul Dugard arrived via Eastbourne. A fit-again Brian Karger was made captain and, along with Leigh Adams, Andrew Silver and Peter Nahlin, the Team Coastal Robins had an attractive side. Completing the team, the Swindon management gave another opportunity to Taunton-born Matthew Cross, who had performed so admirably for the Sprockets since 1986.

Behind the scenes, former Robin Malcolm Holloway came back on board to fill the role of team coach and the set-up at Blunsdon looked ideal. It seemed as if it would only be a matter of time before Swindon were perched on top of the league. However, not long had passed before things began to go horribly wrong. Brian Karger suffered a loss of form following a crash at Berwick and then broke his collarbone in a BSPA Cup match at Poole on 28 May. Team manager Ron Byford reacted by signing Andy Smith on loan from Bradford as a replacement for the Dane, who subsequently joined Second Division Arena-Essex in a shock move. At the same time, Dean Standing, formerly of Stoke, was also brought in as a replacement for Matthew Cross, the youngster having found the pace a little too hot. Many supporters were far from happy about Karger's release and, for a time, the atmosphere at Blunsdon meetings wasn't a pleasant one. In late July, another change saw Paul Smith, Andy's younger brother, also join the club after Paul Dugard had left by mutual consent.

The signing of Andy Smith proved a resounding success, as the gritty Yorkshireman battled for every point, but his stint in the side unfortunately didn't last long. Bad luck befell the diminutive racer when he represented England in a Test match against the USA at Bradford on 4 August. He was involved in a frightening first heat crash with Rick Miller, which left him nursing a broken neck. That brought to an abrupt end his short and successful run in the Swindon side, which had yielded 53 points from seven league matches for a 7.75 average. More team changes ensued. Wimbledon had closed down in June, moving their operation to Eastbourne and, as a result, John Davis eventually returned to Blunsdon in September. Danish youngster Morten Andersen also arrived for the last few matches, on loan from Oxford, at the expense of Andrew Silver, who had drastically and inexplicably lost form. Silver's last match was a point-less return from a crucial league fixture at Eastbourne on 27 September, as the Robins went down 50-40.

Still the results didn't come and Swindon were to finish last in the Sunbrite-sponsored league. Worse still, it looked as if the club would become the first in the history of British racing to be automatically relegated. Really, only the fact that Berwick (who had suffered severe financial problems) opted out of the First Division allowed Swindon to stay in the top league. The constitution of the BSPA stated that the Second Division should always have at least an equal number of tracks to the First Division. Berwick's failure and Mildenhall's application for Second Division racing in 1992 undoubtedly saved the Robins, but nonetheless it was a worrying winter, during which keen supporter Rod Leverton organised a 'Save Our Speedway' petition.

Top Robin in 1991 was Leigh Adams, who accrued 249 points and also represented the club in the Dunlop British League First Division Riders' Championship at Belle Vue on 20 October, scoring 3 points. Regrettably, the Aussie received little backing until John Davis returned to average 8.47 from the eight matches he appeared in. Dean Standing could be regarded a success and a 6.30 average clearly emphasised that. However, the remaining riders were a huge disappointment, as reflected in their final averages: Andrew Silver (5.88), Paul Smith (4.49), Rod Colquhoun (4.23), Paul Dugard (4.13) and Morten Andersen (4.00).

Belle Vue removed Swindon from the *Speedway Star* Knock-Out Cup at the first hurdle, while the Robins could only manage fourth position (from seven) in the southern section of the Gold Cup. That was after heading the table at one stage, only to slump following a home defeat against Poole on 4 May, when Leigh Adams fell in the opening heat, dislocating a shoulder in the process. Although Adams missed the rest of that particular match, despite being very sore he amazingly returned for the team's next fixture and was to only be absent from one official meeting all season, a league encounter at Coventry on 24 August. The Robins also fared poorly in the BSPA Cup, a revamped version of the old Inter-League Knock-Out Cup, with a first round exit at Poole on 28 May, albeit by the smallest of margins, 46-44.

Blunsdon played host to another England *v.* USA Test match on 25 August, with the home nation enjoying a 57-51 success. The top scorers for England were the unbeaten Gary Havelock (16+2), along with Kelvin Tatum (9+1) and Chris Louis (also 9+1). Meanwhile, the American scorechart was headed by Greg Hancock (12+1), Ronnie Correy (12) and Billy Hamill (10+3). That was the only big meeting staged at the Abbey all year, since there were no individual meetings for the first time since 1953. There were, however, a couple of 1,000cc sidecar events. The first was a round of the World of Rebels Superprix on 3 August, which resulted in victory for the Australian duo of Darrin Treloar and Phil Hudson, following a run-off against British lads Paul Pinfold and Keith Wall. The Superprix series was run over four rounds in total and either side of the meeting at Blunsdon were rounds at Coventry and Reading respectively. The series then concluded at Blunsdon on 31 August, when Treloar and Hudson again took victory on the night, although it was Pinfold and Wall who came out on top overall, having accumulated a greater number of series points.

Turning to the Sprockets, there was a new sponsor in the shape of Castrol and, with thirteen sides participating instead of the previous year's nine, Swindon slipped one place to sixth in the renamed First Division Reserve League. Only six riders were used during the twenty-four-match campaign, with Paul Smith occupying pole position in the averages on a massive 10.96 figure. Matthew Cross did very well too, remaining ever-present to post a 10.30 average, with the rest of the side finishing thus: Steve Camden (7.04), Darren Boulton (5.94), Andy Witts (2.77) and Kevin Howse (2.42). Still managed by Tony Miller, the youngsters dipped out of the Knock-Out Cup in the opening round, losing narrowly, 36-35, on aggregate to Belle Vue. Meanwhile, in the Gold Cup, the Castrol

Swindon Robins, 1991. From left to right, back row: Peter Nahlin, Matthew Cross, Rod Colquhoun, Ron Byford (Team Manager), Paul Dugard, Andrew Silver, Leigh Adams. Front, on bike: Brian Karger.

Sprockets finished fourth out of the seven competing sides in the southern section. Aside from the riders already mentioned, several others were used in the Gold Cup, including Martin Chessell, Emmerson Fairweather, Derrol Keats, Steve Knott, Andy Mountain, Jason Smith and Brett Wakeling. The Reserve League Riders' Championship took place at Wolverhampton on 8 September and the Swindon representative was Matthew Cross. However, with 9 points he could only manage sixth position in a meeting won by Ben Howe of Ipswich.

SWINDON TEAM COASTAL ROBINS 1991

(Swindon's score shown first unless otherwise stated)

SUNBRITE BRITISH LEAGUE FIRST DIVISION

Opponents	Home	Away	Aggregate
Belle Vue	W55-35	L40-50	W95-85
Berwick	L41-49	L36-54	L77-103
Bradford	W52-38	L30-59	L82-97
Coventry	L44-46	L40-50	L84-96
Cradley Heath	L44-46	L37-52	L81-98
Eastbourne	L43-47	L40-50	L83-97
Ipswich	W52-38	L41-48	W93-86
King's Lynn	L41-49	L44-46	L85-95
Oxford	D45-45	L36-54	L81-99
Poole	W47-43	L41-48	L88-91
Reading	W47-43	L37-53	L84-96
Wolverhampton	L43-47	L42-48	L85-95

SUNBRITE BRITISH LEAGUE FIRST DIVISION TABLE

Team	Mts	Won	Drn	Lst	For	Agn.	Pts	Bon.	Tot.
Wolverhampton	24	19	1	4	1,205.5	952.5	39	10	49
Bradford	24	15	4	5	1,184.5	973.5	34	9	43
Cradley Heath	24	15	1	8	1,118	1,032	31	10	41

Belle Vue	24	12	3	9	1,042	1,082	27	6	33
Berwick	24	13	0	11	1,073	1,053	26	6	32
Ipswich	24	12	1	11	1,065.5	1,089.5	25	7	32
Coventry	24	12	0	12	1,076	1,079	24	6	30
King's Lynn	24	12	1	11	1,013.5	1,139.5	25	5	30
Oxford	24	8	3	13	1,069	1,085	19	6	25
Poole	24	8	2	14	1,053	1,103	18	5	23
Reading	24	9	0	15	1,030	1,123	18	3	21
Eastbourne	24	6	3	15	1,027	1,125	15	3	18
Swindon	24	5	1	18	1,018	1,138	11	2	13

Note: Eastbourne took over the results and remaining fixtures of Wimbledon, who had completed just two league matches prior to closing down.

LEAGUE AVERAGES

Rider	Mts	Rds	Pts	Bon.	Tot.	Avge	Maximums
Leigh Adams	23	126	249	18	267	8.48	–
John Davis	8	34	70	2	72	8.47	1 full
Chris Louis	1	6	12	0	12	8.00	–
Andy Smith	7	32	53	9	62	7.75	–
Peter Nahlin	21	105	181	8	189	7.20	1 full
Dean Barker	1	5	7	1	8	6.40	–
Dean Standing	21	106	144	23	167	6.30	–
Andrew Silver	18	83	102	20	122	5.88	–
Gary Allan	1	5	4	3	7	5.60	–
Brian Karger	3	12	14	2	16	5.33	–
Paul Smith	15	57	52	12	64	4.49	–
Matthew Cross	3	9	8	2	10	4.44	–
Rod Colquhoun	24	86	75	16	91	4.23	–
Paul Dugard	8	30	25	6	31	4.13	–
Morten Andersen	6	24	22	2	24	4.00	–
Steve Camden	1	0	0	0	0	0.00	–

SPEEDWAY STAR KNOCK-OUT CUP

Opponents	Home	Away	Aggregate
Belle Vue (Round one)	W46-44	L35-55	L81-99

GOLD CUP

Opponents	Home	Away	Aggregate
Ipswich	W52-38	W48-42	W100-80
King's Lynn	W49-41	L44-46	W93-87
Oxford	L44-46	L39-51	L83-97
Poole	L43-47	W46-44	L89-91
Reading	L40-50	W46-44	L86-94
Wimbledon	W54-36	L44-46	W98-82

GOLD CUP (SOUTHERN SECTION) TABLE

Team	Mts	Won	Drn	Lst	For	Agn.	Pts	Bon.	Tot.
Oxford	12	10	0	2	580	500	20	6	26
Reading	12	7	0	5	561	518	14	4	18
Wimbledon	12	6	0	6	554	525	12	4	16
Swindon	12	6	0	6	549	531	12	3	15
Poole	12	5	1	6	523	556	11	2	13
King's Lynn	12	4	1	7	519	560	9	2	11
Ipswich	12	3	0	9	491	587	6	0	6

Oxford progressed to the final.

BSPA CUP

Opponents	Home	Away
Poole (Round one)	–	L44-46

THAMES VALLEY TROPHY

Opponents	Home	Away
Oxford	W52-38	L42-48
Reading	W49-41	L29-61

THAMES VALLEY TROPHY TABLE

Team	Mts	Won	Drn	Lst	For	Agn.	Pts
Reading	4	2	0	2	196	164	4
Swindon	4	2	0	2	172	188	4
Oxford	4	2	0	2	172	188	4

Note: Swindon and Oxford finished equal second in the standings.

CHALLENGE

Opponents	Home	Away
Cradley Heath	–	L34-56
Exeter	W56-33	L39-51

HEAT FOUR-TEAM CHAMPIONSHIP

Qualifying group:
(First leg at Reading)	Reading 34, Wimbledon 24, Swindon 19, Poole 19.
(Second leg at Poole)	Reading 32, Poole 25, Wimbledon 22, Swindon 17.
(Third leg at Swindon)	Poole 32, Swindon 31, Reading 19, Eastbourne 14.
(Fourth leg at Eastbourne)	Reading 29, Swindon 26, Eastbourne 22, Poole 19.
Aggregate result:	Reading 114, Poole 95, Swindon 93, Eastbourne 82.

Note: Eastbourne took over the results and fixtures of Wimbledon after the 'Dons' had closed down.

THAMES VALLEY THREE-TEAM TOURNAMENT

(First leg at Oxford)	Oxford 34, Swindon 26, Reading 18.
(Second leg at Reading)	Oxford 30, Reading 26, Swindon 21.
(Third leg at Swindon)	Oxford 32, Swindon 27, Reading 19.
Aggregate result:	Oxford 96, Swindon 74, Reading 63.

TRI-TOWN THREE-TEAM TOURNAMENT

(First leg at Swindon)	Ipswich 29, Poole 28, Swindon 21.
(Second leg at Ipswich)	Ipswich 39, Poole 23, Swindon 16.
Aggregate result:	Ipswich 68, Poole 51, Swindon 37.

Note: Due to fixture congestion, Poole were unable to stage a third leg of the tournament.

DUNLOP BRITISH LEAGUE FIRST DIVISION RIDERS' CHAMPIONSHIP

(Staged at Belle Vue)   Leigh Adams 3 points.

SWINDON CASTROL SPROCKETS

BRITISH LEAGUE FIRST DIVISION RESERVE LEAGUE TABLE

Team	Mts	Won	Drn	Lst	For	Agn.	Pts	Bon.	Tot.
Cradley Heath	24	18	1	5	483	378	37	9	46
Oxford	24	16	1	7	497	361	33	10	43
Ipswich	24	14	3	7	472	389	31	10	41
King's Lynn	24	15	2	7	477	384	32	8	40
Poole	24	14	2	8	459	400	30	7	37
Swindon	24	14	1	9	453	401	29	6	35
Wolverhampton	24	12	0	12	451	404	24	8	32
Bradford	24	12	2	10	421	438	26	6	32
Eastbourne	24	11	1	12	401	420	23	5	28
Coventry	24	7	0	17	379	480	14	2	16
Reading	24	6	1	17	360	498	13	3	16
Belle Vue	24	4	2	18	360	484	10	2	12
Berwick	24	4	2	18	321	497	10	1	11

1992

Having been granted a relegation reprieve, Swindon hoped for better things in 1992. On the team front, Leigh Adams was retained, along with John Davis and Dean Standing. With Berwick dropping to the Second Division, Jimmy Nilsen was welcomed back to the Robins' camp, while Mitch Shirra also returned and delightedly accepted the club captaincy. It was Shirra who recommended that the Robins gave an opportunity to German Peter Schroeck, and this they did, handing him one of the reserve berths, together with promising junior Steve Camden. Although weak in that particular position, Swindon did boast a strong top five, so things should have worked out for the team, now backed by their stadium owners, ADT Auctions. One important change at the Abbey in 1992 saw the regular race day change from Saturday to Thursday, in order to allow greyhound racing to take place on the night that had been traditional for speedway ever since 1949. Needless to say, this move wasn't generally well received by supporters of the shale sport.

The season kicked off with the Gold Cup competition, but Swindon could only manage to win three of their six home matches, while losing all but one away from Blunsdon. This was a disappointing start to the campaign, as the Robins finished a poor sixth in the southern section table. The competition wasn't without incident, for on 24 April at Arena-Essex John Davis broke a leg and this was the start of many problems for the club. Two days later, in the return match against Arena-Essex, the Robins lost 46-43, with former riders Bo Petersen and Brian Karger scoring 12+1 and 10+1 points respectively for the visitors.

Prior to Davis' injury, in an effort to strengthen the reserve position, firstly Darren Boulton was tried and then Justin Elkins, a talented junior, came from Poole but, despite the fact that he had plenty of promise, it was still hard for him. Then, at the end of April, Peter Nahlin travelled to Swindon, expecting to again link with the club in time to ride against Wolverhampton in a *Speedway Star* Knock-Out Cup tie. However, the management instead opted to sign Kelly Moran on loan from Belle Vue, and it was he who rode against Wolverhampton, scoring just 3 points, as the ADT Auctions Robins lost 47-43. Another change saw the release of Peter Schroeck and in came Steve Masters from Eastbourne, who had signed former Robin Andrew Silver during the winter break. Regrettably, the moves didn't prevent Swindon from being dumped out of the *Speedway Star* Knock-Out Cup, Wolverhampton winning the second leg 50-40 at Monmore Green on 11 May.

Things went from bad to worse as the Gold Cup dragged on, with Kelly Moran suffering a broken collarbone in a spectacular heat thirteen spill at Poole on 13 May. To his credit, the diminutive American only missed two matches, a 49-41 Gold Cup victory at Eastbourne and 49-40 league defeat at King's Lynn. However, he clearly wasn't fit when he bravely returned and after struggling through two matches, he was rested for a Gold Cup match against King's Lynn at Blunsdon on 28 May. This was to be a disastrous meeting for the die-hard fans to endure, since Mitch Shirra was delayed at Heathrow Airport following an afternoon meeting in Germany. The Kiwi only arrived in time for his last two outings as the depleted Robins crashed to a hefty 54-36 defeat.

In mid-June, Second Division Mildenhall closed down and this led to David Smart, who had joined the Fen Tigers via Exeter, returning to Swindon the following month, initially at the expense of Steve Masters. Although the fans appreciated Smart's all-out efforts, regrettably they often didn't generate the points he deserved. With the league campaign well underway, the HEAT Four-Team Championship offered a break from the stresses and Swindon did well enough to qualify for the final at Peterborough. Unfortunately, things didn't go the Robins' way in the big meeting on 26 July and, with a 12-point total, they finished a disappointing fourth behind Belle Vue, Ipswich and Oxford respectively. Two days before the Peterborough showdown, the wheels really came off the wagon in a typically charged local derby league match at Oxford. The Cheetahs were minus their number one Hans Nielsen and although Swindon forced a 45-45 draw it came at a cost, as Dean Standing broke his collarbone in a heat one crash.

Swindon Sprockets, 1992. Left to right: Tony Miller (Team Manager), Darren Boulton, Scott Broad, Rob Vincent (on bike), Steve Camden, Dawn Adams (Sponsor).

Swindon Robins, 1992. From left to right, back row: Steve Camden, Peter Schroeck, Ron Byford (Team Manager), John Davis, Dean Standing. Front, on bikes: Leigh Adams, Mitch Shirra, Jimmy Nilsen.

The rot really set in after Standing's injury and between 30 July and 30 September the Robins raced in thirteen matches, losing twelve and drawing one. The draw occurred in the BSPA Cup at home to Poole, with Leigh Adams subsequently winning a run-off against Steve Schofield to put Swindon through to the quarter-finals… or so they thought. The Pirates' management protested to the SCB about this way of deciding the result and their appeal was upheld, with the Dorset side subsequently thumping the Robins 58-32 in the replay. During this time, team manager Ron Byford suffered much unjust criticism from the terraces as the team plunged nearer the foot of the league table.

In the end, it was also Poole who finished Swindon off in the league when, on 15 October, in the last home match, they beat the troubled Robins 47-43. A 50-40 defeat followed at Bradford two days later, again leaving the Wiltshire club at the foot of the Homefire British League First Division standings, and this time relegation couldn't be avoided. The final table revealed that the side had won just five of their twenty-four matches, with a staggering seven defeats witnessed by the Blunsdon regulars.

The one bright spot in a disappointing season was the form of Leigh Adams, who often carried the side and scored 298 points for a 9.55 average as he remained ever-present throughout the league campaign. Adams also represented the Robins at Bradford in the Dunlop British League First Division Riders' Championship on 3 October, scoring 11 points. That the Aussie didn't even get on the rostrum was a travesty of justice, since he was leading heat twelve when his steed was hit by an electrical fault. That cost him the chance of first place, which, with 14 points, went the way of Belle Vue's Joe Screen. Unbelievably, Adams then finished fourth in a five-man run-off to determine the other podium positions, behind Per Jonsson, Gary Havelock and Marvyn Cox, with Simon Wigg at the rear after all had finished on the 11-point mark. There had been glory for Adams a matter of weeks beforehand on 23 August, however, when he enjoyed a great success in the World Under-21 Championship in Pfaffenhofen, Germany, defeating Mark Loram in a title run-off after both had tied on 14 points.

Looking through the rest of the 1992 team, the riders' final averages tell their own story in a season that everyone wanted to forget as quickly as possible. Mitch Shirra was next in line to the immaculate Leigh Adams, scoring 184 points for a 7.32 average, while Jimmy Nilsen's efforts could only yield a 7.28 figure. Despite an indifferent year domestically, Nilsen did make it through to the World Final at Wroclaw, Poland on 29 August, when 7 points gave him seventh position overall.

Going back to the Robins, Kelly Moran averaged 6.25, which was a poor reflection of his undoubted class and ability. The remaining riders all finished below the 6-point mark as follows: Dean Standing (5.28), David Smart (3.67), Steve Masters (2.78) and Justin Elkins (2.65). Swindon staged two individual meetings during the season, with Glenn Cunningham storming to a 15-point maximum to take the honours in the Bee-Line Lubricants Junior Classic on 21 May. Then, on 5 July, track specialist Zdenek Tesar took victory in the Super Pink Pizza Classic, a meeting jointly sponsored by Super Bowl, Pinkerton's café bar restaurant and Pizza Hut, beating Jimmy Nilsen, Kelly Moran and Brian Karger in the grand final. The Blunsdon regulars also had a taste of Test match action once more as England were defeated by the USA on 27 September. In a meeting that was close throughout, the Americans won 58-50, with the spectacular Bobby Ott scorching to 16 points, with excellent support supplied by Greg Hancock (14), Ronnie Correy (12) and Sam Ermolenko (11+4). Meanwhile, for England, Mark Loram led the way with 12+3 points, while Gary Havelock scored 10+2.

Compared to their senior counterparts, the Castrol Sprockets had a much more enjoyable term, winning seventeen of their twenty-four matches to finish as runners-up to Ipswich in the First Division Reserve League. Long-serving team manager Tony Miller utilised the services of just seven riders and his troops maintained a 100 per cent home record, with Justin Elkins the top man having scored 167 points from a full quota of matches for a 10.17 average. Matthew Cross, in his seventh season with the side, was second in the averages (9.73), while Steve Masters (9.42) completed a particularly strong attack. The figures rather fell away after that, thus: Steve Camden (4.09), Rob Vincent (3.64) and Dean Ing (0.80), while Steve Woolley failed to score from just two meetings. The story wasn't so good regarding the other competitions though, with the Sprockets only finishing fourth in the southern section of the Gold Cup and, like the Robins, exiting the Knock-Out Cup at the first hurdle against Wolverhampton. Adding to the previously named seven riders, two others made appearances in the Gold Cup, namely Darren Boulton and Scott Broad. Individually, Justin Elkins was the Swindon representative in the First Division Reserve League Riders' Championship at Poole on 18 October, posting a 9-point tally.

SWINDON ADT AUCTIONS ROBINS 1992

(Swindon's score shown first unless otherwise stated)

HOMEFIRE BRITISH LEAGUE FIRST DIVISION

Opponents	Home	Away	Aggregate
Arena-Essex	W53-37	W47-43	W100-80
Belle Vue	L43-47	L36-54	L79-101
Bradford	L41-49	L40-50	L81-99
Coventry	L43-47	L40-50	L83-97
Cradley Heath	W46-44	L38-51	L84-95
Eastbourne	D45-45	L41-49	L86-94
Ipswich	L42-48	L28-62	L70-110
King's Lynn	W46-44	L40-49	L86-93
Oxford	W46-44	D45-45	W91-89
Poole	L43-47	L33-57	L76-104
Reading	L40-50	L39-51	L79-101
Wolverhampton	L40-50	L41-49	L81-99

HOMEFIRE BRITISH LEAGUE FIRST DIVISION TABLE

Team	Mts	Won	Drn	Lst	For	Agn.	Pts	Bon.	Tot.
Reading	24	19	1	4	1,199	944	39	11	50
Bradford	24	15	0	9	1,132	1,027	30	8	38
Poole	24	15	2	7	1,129	1,028	32	6	38
Cradley Heath	24	14	2	8	1,118.5	1,038.5	30	8	38
Wolverhampton	24	14	1	9	1,106	1,051	29	9	38
Belle Vue	24	14	1	9	1,144	1,011	29	8	37
Ipswich	24	11	2	11	1,090	1,065	24	6	30
Coventry	24	10	1	13	1,057.5	1,097.5	21	5	26
King's Lynn	24	9	0	15	1,005	1,136	18	7	25
Oxford	24	8	4	12	1,053	1,103	20	4	24
Arena-Essex	24	7	0	17	1,008	1,149	14	3	17
Eastbourne	24	6	2	16	965	1,191	14	1	15
Swindon	24	5	2	17	996	1,162	12	2	14

LEAGUE AVERAGES

Rider	Mts	Rds	Pts	Bon.	Tot.	Avge	Maximums
Leigh Adams	24	129	298	10	308	9.55	2 full; 2 paid
Mitch Shirra	22	106	184	10	194	7.32	–
Jimmy Nilsen	24	117	192	21	213	7.28	–
Kelly Moran	23	105	145	19	164	6.25	–
Dean Standing	13	47	51	11	62	5.28	–
David Smart	17	73	56	11	67	3.67	–
Steve Masters	13	46	23	9	32	2.78	–
Justin Elkins	23	80	43	10	53	2.65	–
Matthew Cross	3	6	2	0	2	1.33	–
David Clarke	4	13	2	1	3	0.92	–
Steve Camden	1	2	0	0	0	0.00	–

SPEEDWAY STAR KNOCK-OUT CUP

Opponents	Home	Away	Aggregate
Wolverhampton (Round one)	L43-47	L40-50	L83-97

GOLD CUP

Opponents	Home	Away	Aggregate
Arena-Essex	L43-46	L37-53	L80-99
Eastbourne	W49-41	W49-41	W98-82
Ipswich	W47-43	L39-51	L86-94
King's Lynn	L36-54	L43-47	L79-101
Poole	W48-42	L42-48	D90-90
Reading	L44-46	L42-48	L86-94

Note: Following the home match v. Poole, Leigh Adams defeated Marvyn Cox in a run-off for the bonus point.

GOLD CUP (SOUTHERN SECTION) TABLE

Team	Mts	Won	Drn	Lst	For	Agn.	Pts	Bon.	Tot.
Reading	12	10	0	2	566.5	512.5	20	5	25
King's Lynn	12	9	0	3	554	525	18	4	22
Ipswich	12	7	0	5	582	498	14	5	19
Arena-Essex	12	6	0	6	555	524	12	4	16
Poole	12	5	0	7	527.5	552.5	10	1	11
Swindon	12	4	0	8	519	560	8	2	10
Eastbourne	12	1	0	11	474	606	2	0	2

Note: Reading progressed to the final.

BSPA CUP

Opponents	Home	Away
Exeter (Round one)	–	W53-37
Poole (Round two)	D45-45	–
Poole (Replay)	–	L32-58

Note: Following the home match v. Poole, referee Mick Barnes deemed that a run-off should take place, which saw Leigh Adams defeat Steve Schofield. Although Swindon were declared the winners, Poole subsequently protested to the SCB and their appeal was upheld, with a replay ordered to decide the tie.

EASTER TROPHY

Opponents	Home	Away
Oxford	L42-48	–

CHALLENGE

Opponents	Home	Away
Cradley Heath	L43-47	–
Poole	W47-43	L44-46

HEAT FOUR-TEAM CHAMPIONSHIP

Qualifying group:	
(First leg at Coventry)	Oxford 33, Swindon 27, Coventry 25, Reading 11.
(Second leg at Reading)	Swindon 34, Poole 31, Coventry 16, Reading 15.
(Third leg at Swindon)	Swindon 29, Poole 27, Oxford 27, Coventry 13.
(Fourth leg at Oxford)	Swindon 29, Oxford 27, Poole 24, Reading 16.
(Fifth leg at Poole)	Oxford 30, Poole 28, Reading 28, Coventry 10.
Aggregate result:	Swindon 119, Oxford 117, Poole 110, Reading 70, Coventry 64.
Final:	
(Staged at Peterborough)	Belle Vue 24, Ipswich 18, Oxford 18, Swindon 12.

DUNLOP BRITISH LEAGUE FIRST DIVISION RIDERS' CHAMPIONSHIP

(Staged at Bradford)   Leigh Adams 11 points.

SWINDON CASTROL SPROCKETS

BRITISH LEAGUE FIRST DIVISION RESERVE LEAGUE TABLE

Team	Mts	Won	Drn	Lst	For	Agn.	Pts	Bon.	Tot.
Ipswich	23	22	0	1	536	288	44	11	55
Swindon	24	17	0	7	493	365	34	10	44
Wolverhampton	24	16	1	7	485	375	33	8	41

Bradford	24	13	2	9	465	395	28	7	35
King's Lynn	21	13	0	8	423	332	26	8	34
Cradley Heath	23	13	1	9	424	400	27	7	34
Reading	23	11	1	11	434	391	23	5	28
Belle Vue	24	9	0	15	400	446	18	5	23
Oxford	24	9	0	15	362	484	18	3	21
Arena-Essex	24	7	3	14	391	468	17	3	20
Eastbourne	24	7	1	16	355	502	15	1	16
Poole	24	6	1	17	344	514	13	3	16
Coventry	24	5	0	19	355	507	10	3	13

Note: Three matches were not ridden, namely King's Lynn v. Cradley Heath, King's Lynn v. Ipswich and Reading v. King's Lynn.

1993

A fresh era began for the Robins in 1993. Having been relegated from the First Division, a new promotion – Betterment Properties (Leisure Activities) Ltd, headed by Mervyn Stewkesbury and Peter Ansell, who also ran the sport at Poole – took over at the Abbey Stadium and introduced Second Division racing to the public of Swindon. Although there was no team sponsor for the first time in nine seasons, the traditional Saturday race night did return and a brand new team was put together, with Steve Masters being the only member of the 1992 line-up to claim a place. It had been hoped to also include Dean Standing from the previous season, but the Southampton-born youngster quit the sport to study for university, expressing an interest in either osteopathy or physiotherapy as a career change.

Continuing with the 1993 line-up, Alun Rossiter returned to skipper the side, and Gary Chessell came 'home' from Stoke. Aside from that, there was the son of a famous father in Jason Crump, who had been at Peterborough the previous season. Gary Allan also joined the ranks, along with Glenn Cunningham and Peter Jeffery, while youngster Jason Green was initially introduced to complete the eight-man side, having impressed in a trial. One rider that got away, however, was Australian Mark Lemon; Swindon's application for a work permit was turned down. Meanwhile, to handle the side, former rider Martin Yeates was installed as the new team manager. It was just a pity that David Smart, who moved up the road to Oxford, could not be accommodated in the team plans, as he had been granted a Testimonial year.

Early on in the season Alun Rossiter fractured his left wrist and, as a temporary replacement, the management wasted no time in recalling young Dane Tom Knudsen, who had briefly appeared in 1989. Rosco was missing for over six weeks, his injury having been sustained in a bizarre off-track accident while fixing a trailer. As the season progressed it became obvious that the Swindon supporters were enjoying the Second Division experience, for there was much enthusiasm on the terraces. The explosive Jason Crump was proving to be every bit as good as his father Phil had been in his heyday. Peter Jeffery found form hard to come by though, and left the club to be replaced by Nigel Leaver. For Jason Green too, the going was tough and while both Martin Willis and Andy Mountain had spells at reserve it was Steve Camden who held the position more than most. Camden in fact had one exceptional meeting, when he ripped around the Blunsdon raceway to score a 12-point maximum against Edinburgh in a league encounter on 26 September.

On 31 July, in a Second Division match against Glasgow, Gary Allan burned up the Abbey Stadium circuit to equal the track record (64.8 seconds) set by Hans Nielsen in 1990. Modern technology had seen race times being measured to one one-hundredth of a second since the start of the 1993 season, and although Allan was actually timed at 64.87 seconds, it was still considered to have equalled the time of the Main Dane. Just to make sure there was no doubt, however, the following week (7 August), in a Phonesport Knock-Out Cup match against Edinburgh, Allan established a new record of 64.70 seconds!

Swindon continued to serve up excellent racing and enjoyed a marvellous run in the Knock-Out Cup, beating Exeter and Edinburgh to reach the final. Unfortunately, their opponents were a powerful

Swindon Robins, 1993. From left to right, back row: Steve Masters, Gary Allan, John Jefferies, Martin Yeates (Team Manager), Gary Chessell, Jason Crump. Front, kneeling: Glenn Cunningham, Peter Jeffery. On bike: Alun Rossiter.

Glasgow side, who forced a tremendous 54-54 draw in the first leg at Blunsdon on 16 October before winning 64-44 in the return leg at Shawfield the following night. Although the Robins had lost on aggregate there was no disgrace in defeat, as the result completed a glorious league and cup double for the all-conquering Glasgow boys. The Swindon supporters could be forgiven for thinking that the Scottish clubs had something of a voodoo over their team since, earlier in the season, the Robins had also battled through to the final of the HEAT Four-Team Championship, held at Peterborough on 25 July, when a determined effort saw them finish as runners-up, just two points adrift of a triumphant Edinburgh side.

In the league the Robins ended up in fourth place, having won every one of their twenty home matches. This was only the fourth time that they had enjoyed a 100 per cent home record since opening in 1949, with the other three occasions occurring in 1957, 1966 and 1967. Thrill merchant Jason Crump led the way, storming to an amazing 470 points for a 10.67 average. Crumpie junior also rattled up twelve full and three paid maximums throughout an exciting domestic campaign. Gary Allan proved to be a revelation and gave superb support, scoring 454.5 points for an 8.98 average. Meanwhile, the solid-scoring back-up men returned averages as follows: Alun Rossiter (7.44), Gary Chessell (6.83), Nigel Leaver (6.17), Glenn Cunningham (5.91), Steve Camden (4.93) and Steve Masters (3.71).

David Smart celebrated his Testimonial meeting at Blunsdon on 5 September with a four-team tournament, won by Smartie's Cheetahs (with 31 points) from Gary's Robins (23), Dave's Falcons (22) and Leigh's Hammers (20). Among the riders who turned out to honour Smart were Armando Castagna and David Mullett, as well as former Robins Richard Hellsen and Leigh Adams.

The Dunlop British League First Division Riders' Championship was finally raced at Blunsdon, albeit at the third attempt, on 31 October, having twice fallen victim to the weather, with the brilliant Per Jonsson emerging as the winner. Both Gary Allan and Jason Crump took part in the meeting, scoring 6 and 5 points respectively. One other individual event was staged at Blunsdon in 1993, and this saw Martin Goodwin triumph in a World Championship qualifying round on 10 April.

On 25 September, super-quick Gary Allan represented Swindon in the Barum Division Two Riders' Championship at King's Lynn and, to the delight of the travelling hordes, he won the meeting by beating Mick Poole in a run-off, after both had recorded 13 points. Jason Crump also appeared in the meeting, scoring 9 points.

1993 would also be remembered for rain and plenty of it, with the Swindon management suffering eight rained-off meetings during the course of the season. Previously, the most fixtures lost to the elements was six, something that happened in both 1981 and 1987. Interestingly, as a guide to the changing nature of Britain's weather, a total of forty-seven meetings were washed out at Blunsdon between 1949 and 1979, whereas an amazing total of fifty-five meetings were lost to the wet stuff between 1980 and 1993 inclusive!

There was no league racing for the Sprockets in 1993, with the side instead participating in only a handful of three-heat challenge matches. It wouldn't be until 1996 that the Sprockets reappeared in more meaningful competition, when they joined the Conference League.

SWINDON ROBINS 1993

(Swindon's score shown first unless otherwise stated)

BRITISH LEAGUE SECOND DIVISION 'A'

Opponents	Home	Away	Aggregate
Edinburgh	W59-49	L39-67	L98-116
Exeter	W65-43	W57-51	W122-94
Glasgow	W56-52	L47-61	L103-113
Long Eaton	W55-53	L38-70	L93-123
Middlesbrough	W60-47	L44-64	L104-111
Newcastle	W59.5-48.5	D53-53	W112.5-101.5
Oxford	W58-50	W61-46	W119-96
Peterborough	W59-48	L43-64	L102-112
Rye House	W67-40	L53-55	W120-95
Sheffield	W56-51	L47-61	L103-112

BRITISH LEAGUE SECOND DIVISION 'B'

Edinburgh	W61-47	L49-59	W110-106
Exeter	W77-31	W56-52	W133-83
Glasgow	W55-53	L41-66	L96-119
Long Eaton	W59-49	L52-56	W111-105
Middlesbrough	W73-35	L52-56	W125-91
Newcastle	W62-46	L47-60	W109-106
Oxford	W64-44	L52-55	W116-99
Peterborough	W65-43	L50-58	W115-101
Rye House	W61-47	L52-55	W113-102
Sheffield	W67-41	L46-62	W113-103

BRITISH LEAGUE SECOND DIVISION TABLE

Team	Mts	Won	Drn	Lst	For	Agn.	Pts	Bon.	Tot.
Glasgow	40	27	1	12	2,416	1,900	55	19	74
Long Eaton	40	25	0	15	2,302	1,970	50	13	63
Peterborough	40	24	0	16	2,260	2,012	48	13	61
Swindon	40	23	1	16	2,217.5	2,088.5	47	13	60
Edinburgh	40	20	1	19	2,272	2,041	41	15	56
Newcastle	40	21	2	17	2,138.5	2,133.5	44	8	52
Middlesbrough	40	21	0	19	2,125	2,189	42	8	50
Rye House	40	20	0	20	2,133	2,177	40	9	49
Sheffield	40	15	0	25	1,959	2,320	30	5	35
Exeter	40	12	0	28	1,881	2,429	24	3	27
Oxford	40	9	1	30	1,934	2,378	19	4	23

LEAGUE AVERAGES

Rider	Mts	Rds	Pts	Bon.	Tot.	Avge	Maximums
Tony Langdon	1	5	15	0	15	12.00	1 full
Jason Crump	34	183	470	18	488	10.67	12 full; 3 paid
Robert Nagy	1	5	10	3	13	10.40	–
Matthew Cross	1	3	5	2	7	9.33	–
Gary Allan	39	210	454.5	17	471.5	8.98	2 full; 1 paid
Mark Thorpe	1	5	10	0	10	8.00	–
Alun Rossiter	33	158	263	31	294	7.44	3 paid
Scott Swain	2	7	9	3	12	6.86	–
Gary Chessell	37	185	283	33	316	6.83	–
Nigel Leaver	32	153	197	39	236	6.17	1 paid
Glenn Cunningham	31	132	178	17	195	5.91	–
Tom Knudsen	3	13	16	2	18	5.54	–
Paul Fry	1	6	8	0	8	5.33	–
John Jefferies	1	4	4	1	5	5.00	–
Steve Camden	31	99	107	15	122	4.93	1 full
Peter Jeffery	7	32	29	4	33	4.13	–
Chris Simpson	1	3	2	1	3	4.00	–
Steve Masters	38	177	133	31	164	3.71	–
Andy Mountain	7	21	11	3	14	2.67	–
Martin Willis	6	19	10	2	12	2.53	–
Jason Green	6	16	3	1	4	1.00	–

PHONESPORT KNOCK-OUT CUP

Opponents	Home	Away	Aggregate
Bye (Round one)	–	–	–
Exeter (Quarter-final)	W60-48	L51-57	W111-105
Edinburgh (Semi-final)	W61-47	L48-60	W109-107
Glasgow (Final)	D54-54	L44-64	L98-118

CHALLENGE

Opponents	Home	Away
Exeter	W67-41	W61-47
Poole	L52-56	L35-73

HEAT FOUR-TEAM CHAMPIONSHIP

Qualifying group:	
(First leg at Oxford)	Rye House 30, Swindon 25, Oxford 24, Exeter 17.
(Second leg at Swindon)	Swindon 33, Rye House 32, Oxford 18, Exeter 13.
(Third leg at Rye House)	Rye House 30, Exeter 29, Swindon 21, Oxford 15.
(Fourth leg at Exeter)	Exeter 33, Swindon 31, Rye House 23, Oxford 9.
Aggregate result:	Rye House 115, Swindon 110, Exeter 92, Oxford 66.
Final:	
(Staged at Peterborough)	Edinburgh 22, Swindon 20, Long Eaton 18, Rye House 12.

BARUM BRITISH LEAGUE SECOND DIVISION RIDERS' CHAMPIONSHIP

(Staged at King's Lynn)	Gary Allan 13 points (1st); Jason Crump 9 points.

DUNLOP BRITISH LEAGUE FIRST DIVISION RIDERS' CHAMPIONSHIP

(Staged at Swindon)	Gary Allan 6 points; Jason Crump 5 points; Glenn Cunningham 2 points; Steve Camden 0 points. Note: Cunningham and Camden were track reserves.

1994

In 1994 it came as no surprise when Jason Crump, a revelation the previous year, moved up to the First Division to race for Poole. Surprisingly, Gary Allan decided to retire and returned to New Zealand, while Nigel Leaver was another to depart, meaning there were team places to be filled at Swindon. In came Tony Olsson from near-neighbours Reading, plus Tony Langdon, who had enjoyed a terrific season at Oxford. Man of many tracks David Blackburn added experience to the team, while a brand new Swede, Patrik Olsson (no relation to Tony), was signed following a successful series of pre-season trials. Joining Glenn Cunningham at reserve was local grass-tracker John Jefferies, who had broken into the team in the very last match of the previous term, at Long Eaton on 27 October. The side was completed by Gary Chessell, who was to miss the opening matches with a broken collarbone, sustained after falling in pre-season practice at Reading's training track. This wasn't quite the line-up team manager Martin Yeates had originally envisaged, since work permit applications were turned down for both Australian Mark Lemon and Pole Dariusz Sledz. This was the second year running that Swindon were refused a permit for Lemon, with the reason seeming more a question of politics than the rider's ability. When it appeared that the unlucky Chessell would be out of action for a while, the management moved quickly to sign Finnish rider Mika Pellinen, who had caught the eye at the club's annual Press and Practice Day.

Things were looking good, as Patrik Olsson started the season like a rocket by scorching to a 15-point maximum in his first ever league match in British racing at home to Sheffield on 9 April. Then Gary Chessell returned to action at the end of the month, with Mika Pellinen leaving to join Exeter. However, a series of injuries were to play a big part in Swindon's season, beginning with a broken collarbone and severe concussion for John Jefferies, suffered in the first leg of the Midland Shield final at home to Long Eaton on 30 May. The next injury occurred to Tony Langdon in June, with the Aussie having the misfortune to break his collarbone in a charity cycle-speedway meeting. The Robins then signed Dutchman Henk Bangma, following an abortive return attempt from Jefferies, but he was very badly injured in what was his debut ride for the club at Peterborough on 1 July, fracturing his thigh in six places. Matters simply got worse the following day in a home match against Edinburgh, when Patrik Olsson crashed and suffered a broken forearm. It took time to heal and he was never the same rider again. Amazingly, prior to getting back on a bike Langdon had the sheer bad luck to re-break his collarbone in a road traffic accident. Thankfully, he was able to return at the end of July and, aside from a bout of 'flu near the end of the campaign, he managed to avoid any further misfortune. Main man Tony Olsson also suffered with injuries, but bravely battled on and only missed two league matches. David Blackburn was the only rider to stay ever-present throughout the Second Division programme, but he ended the season in a bad way, fracturing a thigh while riding for the Hans Nielsen Select in a challenge match at Peterborough on 30 September.

Despite all the problems, both Tony's more than flew the flag for the club. Olsson (with 12 points) was second, while Langdon (11) was third in the Barum-Jawa Second Division Riders' Championship at Coventry on 17 September. Much earlier in the year, the dynamic duo also rode brilliantly to take the *Speedway Star* Second Division Pairs Championship at Arena-Essex on 28 May, beating the Glasgow pairing of Nigel Crabtree and David Walsh in the final. Having said that, Patrik Olsson had been due to partner his namesake but missed the meeting through another injury, with 'Lango' doing a wonderful job as his replacement.

The Robins again finished fourth in the league, with Tony Olsson the top man, scoring 435 points for a 10.02 average. When you consider the club lost four home matches and drew another, it was a disappointing fourth-place finish, which could have been so much better. A total of five away victories – at Exeter (twice), Middlesbrough, Oxford and Sheffield – just demonstrates what might have been. Collectively, however, the injuries cost Swindon dearly and valuable league points

Swindon Robins, 1994. From left to right, back row: Martin Yeates (Team Manager), Patrik Olsson, David Blackburn, Tony Olsson, John Jefferies, Gary Chessell, Glenn Cunningham. Front, on bike: Tony Langdon.

Tony Langdon and Tony Olsson with the spoils of victory after the Second Division Pairs Championship at Arena-Essex in 1994.

went astray when they wouldn't have if the team had remained intact. It was indeed frustrating for supporters and management alike.

Tony Langdon was next in the final analysis, averaging 8.30, while David Blackburn plugged away throughout to finish with a 6.86 figure. The remaining four regulars finished thus: Gary Chessell (6.77), Patrik Olsson (6.46), Glenn Cunningham (5.44) and John Jefferies (1.96). Several others had a run-out in the side, including promising teenager Graeme Gordon, who was initially drafted into the side when Jefferies was injured. Scott Swain enjoyed the odd meeting too, while Steve Camden had another spell before Jefferies eventually returned in August, following protracted problems with his collarbone.

After losing to Glasgow in the Phonesport Knock-Out Cup final the previous season, Swindon were unfortunate enough to face the Tigers again at the quarter-final stage, with the powerhouse Scottish side taking a comfortable aggregate victory by 106 points to 86. In a repeat of 1993, Glasgow went on to complete a back-to-back league and cup double and, in fact, the Tigers produced the outstanding performance of the season when they arrived at Blunsdon with just five riders for a league match on 3 September, yet somehow still managed to conjure up a 49-47 win. The Robins did triumph in the Midland Shield though, defeating Oxford in the semi-final before beating Long Eaton by 100 points to 91 on aggregate in the final. In the Four-Team Championship, Oxford easily qualified for the final, but Swindon and Peterborough tied for the second qualifying position. It was decided to stage a run-off to settle the outcome, and it was no surprise when track specialist Zdenek Tesar defeated Tony Olsson 2-0 in a match race series at the Abbey Stadium to take Peterborough through.

The Dunlop First Division Riders' Championship was again allocated to Swindon and staged on 9 October. It proved to be a well-organised event, won with a peerless 15-point full-house by Sam Ermolenko of Wolverhampton from Coventry's Hans Nielsen (13) and Eastbourne's Martin Dugard (11). Aside from that, two further individual meetings were held at Blunsdon and these saw David Blackburn defeat Paul Hurry in a run-off to win a qualifying round of the World Championship on 2 April, after both had totalled 14 points. Meanwhile, on 10 September, Zdenek Tesar again revelled on the Blunsdon circuit to emerge from a classy field and take victory in the grand final of the Swindon Classic, ahead of Roman Matousek, Jan Staechmann and Mick Poole respectively.

SWINDON ROBINS 1994

(Swindon's score shown first unless otherwise stated)

BRITISH LEAGUE SECOND DIVISION 'A'

Opponents	Home	Away	Aggregate
Edinburgh	L47-49	L33-63	L80-112
Exeter	W55-41	W55-41	W110-82
Glasgow	L47-49	L39-57	L86-106
Long Eaton	W56-40	L38-58	L94-98
Middlesbrough	L40-55	L46-50	L86-105
Newcastle	W53-43	L45-48	W98-91
Oxford	W56-40	L41-55	W97-95
Peterborough	W49-47	L41-55	L90-102
Sheffield	W58-38	W50-46	W108-84

BRITISH LEAGUE SECOND DIVISION 'B'

Opponents	Home	Away	Aggregate
Edinburgh	W55-41	L45-51	W100-92
Exeter	W67-29	W50-46	W117-75
Glasgow	W57-39	L45-51	W102-90
Long Eaton	L45-51	L37-59	L82-110
Middlesbrough	W57-39	W49-47	W106-86
Newcastle	W56-40	L42-54	W98-94
Oxford	D48-48	W52-44	W100-92
Peterborough	W49-47	L47-48	W96-95
Sheffield	W56-40	L46-49	W102-89

BRITISH LEAGUE SECOND DIVISION TABLE

Team	Mts	Won	Drn	Lst	For	Agn.	Pts	Bon.	Tot.
Glasgow	36	26	1	9	1,955	1,494	53	14	67
Long Eaton	36	24	2	10	1,835	1,614	50	15	65
Edinburgh	36	20	1	15	1,760	1,690	41	10	51
Swindon	36	18	1	17	1,752	1,698	37	12	49
Peterborough	36	18	2	16	1,752	1,681	38	10	48
Middlesbrough	36	19	1	16	1,744.5	1,706.5	39	9	48
Newcastle	36	15	1	20	1,729.5	1,714.5	31	9	40
Oxford	36	15	1	20	1,691	1,743	31	7	38
Sheffield	36	10	1	25	1,537	1,914	21	3	24
Exeter	36	9	1	26	1,474	1,975	19	1	20

LEAGUE AVERAGES

Rider	Mts	Rds	Pts	Bon.	Tot.	Avge	Maximums
Tony Olsson	34	186	435	31	466	10.02	2 full; 5 paid
Alan Mogridge	1	6	13	1	14	9.33	–
Tony Langdon	28	148	286	21	307	8.30	1 full; 1 paid
Rene Madsen	1	6	9	3	12	8.00	–
Paul Bentley	1	6	10	1	11	7.33	–
Robert Nagy	1	6	11	0	11	7.33	–
David Blackburn	36	196	299	37	336	6.86	–
Gary Chessell	29	153	228	31	259	6.77	1 paid
Jan Andersen	1	6	10	0	10	6.67	–
Patrik Olsson	24	112	166	15	181	6.46	1 full
Toni Svab	1	7	9	1	10	5.71	–
Glenn Cunningham	33	169	203	27	230	5.44	–
Mika Pellinen	3	14	16	3	19	5.43	–
Scott Swain	5	20	12	2	14	2.80	–
Steve Camden	3	10	4	1	5	2.00	–
John Jefferies	28	100	41	8	49	1.96	–
Henk Bangma	1	1	0	0	0	0.00	–
Graeme Gordon	1	3	0	0	0	0.00	–
Danny O'Brien	1	5	0	0	0	0.00	–

PHONESPORT KNOCK-OUT CUP

Opponents	Home	Away	Aggregate
Bye (Round one)	–	–	–
Glasgow (Quarter-final)	W56-40	L30-66	L86-106

MIDLAND SHIELD

Opponents	Home	Away	Aggregate
Oxford (Semi-final)	W56-40	W54-42	W110-82
Long Eaton (Final)	W56-39	L44-52	W100-91

CHALLENGE

Opponents	Home	Away
Reading	W50-46	L40-56

BRITISH LEAGUE SECOND DIVISION FOUR-TEAM CHAMPIONSHIP

Qualifying group:
(First leg at Sheffield) Oxford 28, Sheffield 25, Peterborough 24, Swindon 19.
(Second leg at Oxford) Oxford 38, Swindon 29, Exeter 15, Sheffield 14.
(Third leg at Swindon) Swindon 31, Oxford 30, Peterborough 22, Exeter 13.
(Fourth leg at Peterborough) Peterborough 29, Sheffield 26, Exeter 22, Swindon 19.
(Fifth leg at Exeter) Sheffield 28, Oxford 25, Peterborough 23, Exeter 20.
Aggregate result Oxford 121, Peterborough 98, Swindon 98, Sheffield 93, Exeter 70.
Note: Zdenek Tesar of Peterborough subsequently beat Swindon's Tony Olsson 2-0 in a match race series at Blunsdon to decide the runner-up qualifying place.

SPEEDWAY STAR BRITISH LEAGUE SECOND DIVISION PAIRS CHAMPIONSHIP

(Staged at Arena-Essex)   Qualifying round: Swindon 20, Glasgow 17, Edinburgh 16, Peterborough 16,
                          Long Eaton 14, Middlesbrough 13, Newcastle 13, Exeter 9, Oxford 9, Sheffield 8.
                          Semi-final: Swindon 5 Peterborough 4.
                          Final: Swindon 6 Glasgow 3.

BARUM-JAWA BRITISH LEAGUE SECOND DIVISION RIDERS' CHAMPIONSHIP

(Staged at Coventry)   Tony Olsson 12 points (2nd), Tony Langdon 11 points (3rd).

1995

The year 1995 saw all the teams in the First and Second Divisions come together to form a twenty-one-team Premier League, and there were the usual comings and goings on the team front at Swindon. Tony Langdon decided to stay put in Australia and Tony Olsson went back to parent club Reading. On the plus side, world number three rider Craig Boyce, who was unable to agree terms with Poole, came to Blunsdon and was made captain. Messrs Ansell and Stewkesbury then dipped into the coffers to purchase New Zealander Mark Thorpe from Newcastle, the rider having long expressed the view that Swindon was his favourite track, so it was a dream move for him. Finally, a work permit was granted for Polish star Dariusz Sledz but, in the event, he never turned a wheel for the Robins, the feeling being that an assessed 7.50 average was a tad too high. The name of Mark Lemon was also mooted again but, for a third year running, the Aussie was refused the necessary permit to work in this country. Therefore, two newcomers came into the reckoning for a place in the team – Swede Frank Richt and Finn Jarno Kosonen – so with Gary Chessell, Glenn Cunningham and Patrik Olsson, Swindon looked to have the right blend of youth and experience. Happily, a new sponsor was unveiled for the first time in three seasons, namely Poole-based businessman John Tarr, meaning the team rode under the banner of the JT Commercials Robins.

Frank Richt missed the opening match due to a dispute over transport and, in fact, only rode in a single league match, at home to Eastbourne – a meeting that was significant for being the first to have Martin Yeates and his partner Peter Toogood in charge. In the first instance, Peter Ansell stayed on to give welcome help and advice, but it was the new twosome of Yeates and Toogood who were the promotional duo. Having lost two of their first three away fixtures, the management quickly realised that extra strengthening was required and crowd favourite Peter Nahlin was subsequently brought back. This then gave Swindon three very good heat-leaders, since Mark Thorpe's form was proving to be a revelation. To accommodate Nahlin, however, it meant releasing Jarno Kosonen, with the rider relocating to Long Eaton on loan.

By early May, Yeates was finding the combination of his promotional duties and looking after the team too much, so back came Malcolm Holloway to manage the side. On track things were going well for the Robins, despite several changes at reserve, which saw John Jefferies, Lance Sealey and Justin Walker all have a stint as the right mix was sought. The month of June was significant, as Peter Nahlin was hurt while riding in his native Sweden, so in came another former favourite in Brian Karger, who arrived on a short-term contract. Somehow, in spite of all the chopping and changing, between 29 April and 15 July inclusive Swindon managed to string together a brilliant run of fifteen wins and a draw from nineteen league matches.

On 10 August, after a match at Middlesbrough, Gary Chessell stunned everyone by deciding to quit racing there and then. It was a great pity, as Peter Nahlin had just returned and the side looked capable of challenging for honours. Swindon battled on and the signing of Poole junior Martin Willis (following a spell from Spencer Timmo) looked to be filling the troublesome reserve berth in the side. However, the side then slumped to nine defeats out of their last eleven league matches, during which Nahlin was injured again, breaking a wrist in a home match against Long Eaton on 23 September. The dismal run-in saw them end the season in eleventh spot, leaving everyone connected with the club to

Swindon Robins, 1995. From left to right, back row: John Tarr (Sponsor), Glenn Cunningham, Patrik Olsson, Mark Thorpe, Jarno Kosonen, Gary Chessell, Martin Yeates (Team Manager). Front, on bike: Craig Boyce.

ponder on what might have been, especially considering the fact that no less than seven of their away matches had ended in victory – at Coventry, Cradley Heath, Exeter, Ipswich, Long Eaton, Poole and Sheffield. The Robins also gained two draws on their travels, thanks to solid performances at King's Lynn and Middlesbrough. However, if the away form was exceptionally good then the home results were the exact opposite, with six defeats and a draw being a lot for the Blunsdon regulars to bear.

Top Robin was Craig Boyce, who enjoyed a tremendous year to end the campaign with 388 points in league racing and with it a tremendous 10.05 average. The Aussie did well on the world stage too, accumulating 60 points in the inaugural Grand Prix series to finish in eleventh place. Meanwhile, Kiwi Mark Thorpe actually outscored Boyce for Swindon, plundering 417 points in all for a splendid 8.35 average. Peter Nahlin achieved a 7.79 figure from the nineteen matches he appeared in, while Gary Chessell was averaging 6.01 at the time of his shock retirement. In a season when the Robins used a staggering total of thirty-seven riders, only two others made more than eight appearances: Glenn Cunningham, who averaged 5.60, and the hugely disappointing Patrik Olsson, who could only muster a 4.69 figure.

In the *Speedway Star* Knock-Out Cup Swindon had a bye at the first hurdle, before defeating Exeter in round two. They then faced Belle Vue at the quarter-final stage, but a heavy defeat at the Manchester venue in the first leg proved too much to overcome and the Robins eventually went out on the wrong end of a 118-95 aggregate defeat. The Four-Team Championship didn't offer much in the way of comfort either, although there was some amusement created by the fact that there were actually five sides in Swindon's qualifying group! With a total of 99 points from the four legs in which they participated, the Robins finished in third place, some way behind Black Country rivals Wolverhampton (143) and Cradley Heath (127), both of whom progressed to the semi-finals.

On 5 August, American racer Sam Ermolenko again showed his liking for the Blunsdon circuit by recording a 15-point maximum to win the Swindon Classic ahead of Leigh Adams (13). Continuing with the individual theme, the Jawa-Dunlop Premier League Riders' Championship was held at Swindon and saw a huge field of twenty-four riders compete for the title on 14 October. The eventual winner was Gary Havelock, who put on a terrific display of riding before beating Billy Hamill, Jason Crump and Leigh Adams in the grand final. The Robins were represented by Craig Boyce in the prestigious event, but the Aussie could only muster 7 points on the night.

SWINDON JT COMMERCIALS ROBINS 1995

(Swindon's score shown first unless otherwise stated)

PREMIER LEAGUE

Opponents	Home	Away	Aggregate
Arena-Essex	W56-40	L42-54	W98-94
Belle Vue	W49-46	L36-59	L85-105
Bradford	L45-51	L41-55	L86-106
Coventry	W53-43	W53-43	W106-86
Cradley Heath	W53-43	W49-47	W102-90
Eastbourne	L47-48	L36-60	L83-108
Edinburgh	D48-48	L42-54	L90-102
Exeter	W53-43	W50-46	W103-89
Glasgow	W50-46	L40-56	L90-102
Hull	W53-43	L41-55	L94-98
Ipswich	W51-45	W50-46	W101-91
King's Lynn	L46-50	D48-48	L94-98
Long Eaton	L43-51	W56-40	W99-91
Middlesbrough	W63-33	D48-48	W111-81
Oxford	W53-43	L40-56	L93-99
Peterborough	W53-43	L42-54	L95-97
Poole	W51-45	W49-47	W100-92
Reading	L45-51	L40-56	L85-107
Sheffield	W58-38	W49-47	W107-85
Wolverhampton	L44-51	L42-53	L86-104

PREMIER LEAGUE TABLE

Team	Mts	Won	Drn	Lst	For	Agn.	Pts	Bon.	Tot.
Eastbourne	40	28	3	9	2,041	1,785	59	18	77
Bradford	40	25	2	13	2,072.5	1,761.5	52	17	69
Cradley Heath	40	25	1	14	2,058	1,771	51	17	68
Peterborough	40	25	0	15	1,982.5	1,848.5	50	12	62
Wolverhampton	40	23	0	17	1,981	1,831	46	14	60
Ipswich	40	23	0	17	2,000	1,835	46	13	59
Glasgow	40	21	1	18	1,957.5	1,876.5	43	14	57
Belle Vue	40	20	1	19	1,968	1,841	41	14	55
Edinburgh	40	20	4	16	1,904.5	1,923.5	44	10	54
Arena-Essex	40	21	0	19	1,935	1,903	42	10	52
Swindon	40	20	3	17	1,908	1,925	43	9	52
Poole	40	18	2	20	1,920	1,911	38	9	47
Reading	40	17	4	19	1,876	1,959	38	9	47
Sheffield	40	19	0	21	1,858	1,977	38	9	47
Coventry	40	17	1	22	1,929	1,905	35	8	43
Hull	40	17	2	21	1,822	2,014	36	4	40
Oxford	40	16	1	23	1,858	1,976	33	6	39
Long Eaton	40	14	4	22	1,848	1,984	32	7	39
King's Lynn	40	14	4	22	1,867	1,966	32	6	38
Middlesbrough	40	10	2	28	1,728	2,094	22	2	24
Exeter	40	8	3	29	1,705	2,132	19	2	21

LEAGUE AVERAGES

Rider	Mts	Rds	Pts	Bon.	Tot.	Avge	Maximums
Jason Crump	5	27	70	1	71	10.52	1 full; 1 paid
Jason Lyons	1	5	13	0	13	10.40	–
Craig Boyce	29	158	388	9	397	10.05	4 full; 1 paid
Zdenek Tesar	1	6	13	2	15	10.00	–
Brian Karger	9	48	100	6	106	8.83	1 full
Leigh Adams	1	5	11	0	11	8.80	–
Mark Thorpe	39	215	417	32	449	8.35	1 paid
Ronnie Correy	1	6	12	0	12	8.00	–
Peter Nahlin	19	94	172	11	183	7.79	–
Alan Mogridge	2	11	19	2	21	7.64	–
Steve Masters	4	26	39	6	45	6.92	–

Brian Andersen	1	6	10	0	10	6.67	–
Gary Chessell	26	135	173	30	203	6.01	–
Martin Goodwin	1	6	6	3	9	6.00	–
Glenn Cunningham	35	177	210	38	248	5.60	–
Patrik Olsson	39	179	185	25	210	4.69	–
Richard Green	2	7	7	1	8	4.57	–
David Mason	1	3	2	1	3	4.00	–
Toni Svab	2	10	9	1	10	4.00	–
Lance Sealey	3	10	5	4	9	3.60	–
Will Beveridge	1	3	1	1	2	2.67	–
Chris Cobby	1	3	1	1	2	2.67	–
Frank Richt	1	3	1	1	2	2.67	–
Martin Willis	8	38	21	4	25	2.63	–
Chris Readshaw	1	4	1	1	2	2.00	–
Spencer Timmo	4	12	4	2	6	2.00	–
Justin Walker	5	16	5	2	7	1.75	–
Jarno Kosonen	4	14	3	2	5	1.43	–
John Jefferies	8	26	6	3	9	1.38	–
Barry Campbell	1	3	1	0	1	1.33	–
Anthony Reason	1	3	1	0	1	1.33	–
Brent Werner	1	3	1	0	1	1.33	–
Paul Fudge	1	4	1	0	1	1.00	–
Peter Boast	1	4	0	0	0	0.00	–
Greg Daniels	1	3	0	0	0	0.00	–
Mark Harrison	1	3	0	0	0	0.00	–
Andy Howe	1	4	0	0	0	0.00	–

SPEEDWAY STAR KNOCK-OUT CUP

Opponents	Home	Away	Aggregate
Bye (Round one)	–	–	–
Exeter (Round two)	W55-50	W57-47	W112-97
Belle Vue (Quarter-final)	W57-50	L38-68	L95-118

CHALLENGE

Opponents	Home	Away
Exeter	W51-45	–
Peterborough	W49-47	L46-50
Poole	L45-51	L46-50
Wolverhampton	W51-44	–

PREMIER LEAGUE FOUR-TEAM CHAMPIONSHIP

Qualifying group:
(First leg at Wolverhampton)	Wolverhampton 37, Cradley Heath 30, Swindon 16, Oxford 13.
(Second leg at Oxford)	Wolverhampton 36, Cradley Heath 31, Oxford 24, Exeter 5.
(Third leg at Cradley Heath)	Cradley Heath 32, Wolverhampton 32, Swindon 20, Exeter 12.
(Fourth leg at Swindon)	Wolverhampton 38, Swindon 33, Oxford 19, Exeter 6.
(Fifth leg at Exeter)	Cradley Heath 34, Swindon 30, Exeter 26, Oxford 6.
Aggregate result	Wolverhampton 143, Cradley Heath 127, Swindon 99, Oxford 62, Exeter 49.

JAWA-DUNLOP PREMIER LEAGUE RIDERS' CHAMPIONSHIP

(Staged at Swindon)	Craig Boyce 7 points.

1996

The 1996 season saw former Robins Jimmy Nilsen and Brian Karger return to the club, having been purchased outright from Bradford and Arena-Essex respectively. Meanwhile Craig Boyce rejoined Poole and, to replace his scoring power, Swindon signed Dane John Jorgensen from Coventry. Also in the team was Glenn Cunningham, as well as Mark Thorpe, who had been such a success the previous year, plus Jarno Kosonen and Steve Masters, who returned after loan stints with Long Eaton and Poole respectively. There was new team sponsorship in the shape of the local Westmead Nissan motor vehicle company, and things looked very promising as the tapes went up on the Robins' forty-eighth successive season of racing. They began well too and, although Mark Thorpe seemed to be hampered by machine troubles, both Nilsen and Karger were showing their best form while Jorgensen, in backing their efforts, was excellent.

Team manager Malcolm Holloway guided his troops to a draw at Oxford and early away wins at Middlesbrough, Long Eaton and Coventry, the victories showing that Swindon were a team to be reckoned with. Mark Thorpe sorted out his machine problems and began to show his old form, thus giving the Westmead Nissan Robins four riders capable of filling heat-leader slots and briefly they sat nicely on top of the league standings. Unfortunately, bad luck was to dog Thorpe, beginning at Belle Vue on 31 May when Swindon recorded a marvellous 49-47 victory. The Kiwi was involved in a track spill through no fault of his own and was left nursing a broken wrist. He returned to action in mid-July, only to be injured again at Hull. Bravely, Thorpe was soon back again, but his return didn't last long. On 17 August, in a home match against Exeter, he was injured in a freak accident when he turned around from the starting gate to de-mist his goggles and inadvertently hit the tractor as it graded the track. This time it was more serious, and he was out for the rest of the season, meaning the unwanted but necessary call on numerous guests. Prior to that, Jarno Kosonen was injured in a match at Poole on 17 July when he and Pirates rider Lars Gunnestad crashed, demolishing part of the safety barrier. The fence took too long to repair and, with Swindon leading 44-34, the match was abandoned with the league points coming to Blunsdon. The Finn received serious damage to thigh muscles in the smash and was eventually replaced by Scott Pegler.

The Robins subsequently finished fourth in the league, although they would surely have fared even better but for the problems encountered by Mark Thorpe. Home form was the key to what was nonetheless a healthy rise up the league ladder, with the Robins winning all but one of their Blunsdon encounters, the odd one out being a 48-48 draw against Hull on 14 September, while away from home the team couldn't improve on the five successes previously detailed. Averaging 9.35, Jimmy Nilsen led the scoring stakes, ahead of Brian Karger (8.96) and John Jorgensen (8.49). The unfortunate Thorpe only completed eighteen league matches to average 6.88, while Steve Masters battled away in his own inimitable style for a 5.37 figure. Meanwhile Jarno Kosonen, although very quick from the gate, could only achieve a 4.62 average from his twenty matches. Disappointingly Glenn Cunningham's form failed to show the expected improvement, and this was reflected in his final average of 4.60, while Scott Pegler found the pace a little hot and only yielded a 1.50 average from his eight meetings in the side.

Swindon fared reasonably well in the *Speedway Star* Knock-Out Cup, disposing of Oxford in the opening round before accounting for Eastbourne at the next stage. Somewhat surprisingly though, Exeter came to Blunsdon in the first leg of the quarter-final tie and stole away with a 48-48 draw on 17 August. The Falcons then dumped the Robins out of the competition by virtue of an 8-point victory at their super-fast County Ground venue in the second leg on 9 September. Turning to the Four-Team Championship, Swindon totalled 91 points and could only manage third position in their qualifying group, behind Oxford (121) and Poole (101), with Exeter (70) bringing up the rear.

The Abbey played host to the British Under-21 Championship on 27 April, when Savalas Clouting beat Scott Nicholls in a run-off for the coveted title, both riders having tied on 13 points. The line-up also included many of the sport's other up-and-coming youngsters, including Andre Compton, Leigh Lanham, Phil Morris and Stuart Robson. Much later, on 19 October, the Dunlop Premier League Riders' Championship was staged at Bradford, with Jimmy Nilsen carrying the Westmead Nissan Robins' flag and scoring 8 points in the qualifying heats, before being eliminated at the semi-final stage. This was after Swindon's original representative, Brian Karger, was forced to miss the event due to a nasty 'flu bout.

With the promotion keen to encourage young talent, Swindon also entered a team in the Conference League, with six such matches and a challenge fixture being held at Blunsdon during the season. The Sprockets side, sponsored by Thamesdown Forklift Services, duly finished fifth out of the thirteen competing teams, winning all of their home matches, plus one on their travels, at Sittingbourne. The league was actually run on a percentages basis, worked out on the number of points gained from the maximum total available, with a great disparity between the number of meetings completed by each side – ranging from the eleven of Devon to the twenty-seven of Arena-Essex! Scott Pegler topped the Sprockets' averages on 10.32, receiving solid support from Krister Marsh, who finished on a 9.26 figure. Other regulars in team manager David Broome's side included Scott Donovan, Keith Lansley, Simon Paget, Gary Phelps and Martin Williams, while Malcolm Holloway also donned his leathers again on four occasions, his appearances restricted by rib injuries and a dislocated shoulder, sustained in a bizarre first heat accident at the Exeter home of Devon on 13 May. Keeping it in the family, cousins Richard and Wayne Holloway also rode for the side, the former being the son of Malcolm. In the Conference League Riders' Championship at Long Eaton on 7 September, Krister Marsh participated on behalf of the Sprockets, but failed to win a race and also suffered a tapes exclusion on his way to a 7-point tally.

Overall, Swindon did very well with the weather in 1996, holding thirty-three consecutive meetings at the Abbey without the intervention of rain, right up until the very last scheduled International Ace of Aces individual meeting on 27 October when, with the track underwater, the event was cancelled and never restaged!

Swindon Robins, 1996. From left to right, back row: Glenn Cunningham, Mark Thorpe, Martin Yeates (Promoter), Jarno Kosonen, Jimmy Nilsen, Malcolm Holloway (Team Manager). Front, kneeling: John Jorgensen, Steve Masters. On bike: Brian Karger.

Swindon Sprockets, 1996. From left to right, back row: Martin Yeates (Promoter), Keith Lansley, Krister Marsh, Simon Paget, Scott Donovan, Gary Phelps. Front, kneeling: Martin Williams. On bike: Malcolm Holloway.

Co-promoter Martin Yeates decided to quit at the end of the campaign, due to the pressures of his business interests, but it was also known that he had become frustrated with many aspects of the sport. Peter Toogood pledged that he would carry on by himself, and that the Robins would operate in the highest possible league, a pledge that meant if the proposed Elite League were formed, he would want Swindon to be part of it.

Finally, there was great sadness at the end of 1996, when the death of Bob Jones was announced in December. Aged seventy-seven, Joner was affectionately known as Mr Swindon Speedway, and proudly claimed to have never missed a meeting at Blunsdon since the track had opened in 1949!

SWINDON WESTMEAD NISSAN ROBINS 1996

(Swindon's score shown first unless otherwise stated)

PREMIER LEAGUE

Opponents	Home	Away	Aggregate
Belle Vue	W60-36	W49-47	W109-83
Bradford	W49-46	L39-57	L88-103
Coventry	W52-43	W52-44	W106-87
Cradley Heath & Stoke	W51-45	L43-53	L94-98
Eastbourne	W59-37	L44-52	W103-89
Exeter	W53-43	L45-51	W98-94
Hull	D48-48	L41-54	L89-102
Ipswich	W56-39	L37-59	L93-98
London	W53-43	L32-64	L85-107
Long Eaton	W55-41	W51-45	W106-86
Middlesbrough	W68-28	W49-47	W117-75
Oxford	W53-43	D48-48	W101-91
Peterborough	W56-40	L46-50	W102-90
Poole	W52-44	W44-34	W96-78

Reading	W56-40	L43-53	W99-93
Scottish Monarchs	W56-40	L43-53	W99-93
Sheffield	W61-35	L44-52	W105-87
Wolverhampton	W52-44	L37-59	L89-103

Note: The league match at Poole was abandoned after heat thirteen, with the score at the time being allowed to stand as the result. The reason for the abandonment was a heat fourteen crash involving Jarno Kosonen and Poole rider Lars Gunnestad, which partially demolished the safety fence.

PREMIER LEAGUE TABLE

Team	Mts	Won	Drn	Lst	For	Agn.	Pts	Bon.	Tot.
Wolverhampton	36	29	0	7	1,941	1,504	58	18	76
Peterborough	36	23	0	13	1,834	1,615	46	15	61
Eastbourne	36	23	1	12	1,808	1,634	47	12	59
Swindon	36	22	2	12	1,777	1,657	46	12	58
Cradley Heath & Stoke	36	21	1	14	1,819	1,633	43	13	56
Belle Vue	36	21	1	14	1,775	1,651	43	12	55
Hull	36	20	3	13	1,774	1,675	43	11	54
Ipswich	36	20	0	16	1,799	1,654	40	12	52
London	36	20	0	16	1,732.5	1,693.5	40	11	51
Coventry	36	16	2	18	1,770	1,679	34	10	44
Bradford	36	16	0	20	1,692	1,717	32	9	41
Scottish Monarchs	36	16	0	20	1,673	1,780	32	5	37
Oxford	36	12	4	20	1,676	1,748	28	8	36
Poole	36	13	2	21	1,633	1,801	28	5	33
Exeter	36	13	2	21	1,614	1,841	28	4	32
Middlesbrough	36	11	1	24	1,607	1,843	23	6	29
Long Eaton	36	12	0	24	1,615	1,807	24	4	28
Sheffield	36	13	0	23	1,533	1,871	26	2	28
Reading	36	11	1	24	1,590.5	1,859.5	23	2	25

LEAGUE AVERAGES

Rider	Mts	Rds	Pts	Bon.	Tot.	Avge	Maximums
Ronnie Correy	1	7	18	1	19	10.86	–
Tony Olsson	3	17	43	1	44	10.35	1 full
Zdenek Tesar	2	10	21	3	24	9.60	–
Jimmy Nilsen	33	175	377	32	409	9.35	2 full; 2 paid
Brian Karger	32	163	350	15	365	8.96	3 full; 1 paid
John Jorgensen	33	171	334	29	363	8.49	1 full
Alun Rossiter	2	10	17	2	19	7.60	–
Alan Mogridge	2	11	15	4	19	6.91	–
Mark Thorpe	18	82	116	25	141	6.88	–
Savalas Clouting	7	34	45	6	51	6.00	–
Toni Svab	2	10	14	0	14	5.60	–
Steve Masters	35	152	172	32	204	5.37	–
Josh Larsen	2	5	5	1	6	4.80	–
Jarno Kosonen	20	78	77	13	90	4.62	–
Glenn Cunningham	32	146	146	22	168	4.60	–
Neville Tatum	2	8	8	1	9	4.50	–
Paul Fry	1	5	4	1	5	4.00	–
Dalle Andersson	1	4	3	0	3	3.00	–
Paul Pickering	1	5	3	0	3	2.40	–
Scott Pegler	8	24	7	2	9	1.50	–
Martin Willis	1	3	1	0	1	1.33	–
Krister Marsh	5	15	1	0	1	0.27	–
Rene Aas	2	6	0	0	0	0.00	–
Roman Matousek	1	3	0	0	0	0.00	–

SPEEDWAY STAR KNOCK-OUT CUP

Opponents	Home	Away	Aggregate
Oxford (Round one)	W51-45	L46-50	W97-95
Eastbourne (Round two)	W59-37	L39-56	W98-93
Exeter (Quarter-final)	D48-48	L44-52	L92-100

£1,000 CHALLENGE

Opponents	Home	Away	Aggregate
Oxford	W54-42	L45-51	W99-93

CHALLENGE

Opponents	Home	Away
Coventry	W54-42	–
Poole	–	L46-50
Reading	W57-39	13-11 (aban.)
Reading Select	–	15-27 (aban.)

Notes: The challenge match at Reading was abandoned after heat four. The 'Robins' side that rode against the Reading Select was a Swindon Select, with the meeting being abandoned after heat seven.

FOUR-TEAM CHAMPIONSHIP

Qualifying group:	
(First leg at Oxford)	Oxford 38, Poole 21, Swindon 18, Exeter 18.
(Second leg at Swindon)	Swindon 32, Poole 32, Oxford 25, Exeter 7.
(Third leg at Exeter)	Exeter 28, Oxford 28, Poole 24, Swindon 16.
(Fourth leg at Poole)	Oxford 30, Swindon 25, Poole 24, Exeter 17.
Aggregate result	Oxford 121, Poole 101, Swindon 91, Exeter 70.

DUNLOP PREMIER LEAGUE RIDERS' CHAMPIONSHIP

(Staged at Bradford)   Jimmy Nilsen was fourth in qualifying heats with 8 points and subsequently finished third in the semi-final.

SWINDON THAMESDOWN FORKLIFT SPROCKETS

CONFERENCE LEAGUE TABLE

Team	Mts	Won	Drn	Lst	For	Agn.	Pts	%
Linlithgow	23	18	0	5	1,033	747	36	78.26
Devon	11	7	1	3	436	417	15	68.18
Berwick	12	8	0	4	523	412	16	66.67
Ryde (Isle of Wight)	19	12	1	6	735	742	25	65.79
Swindon	12	7	0	5	469.5	462.5	14	58.33
Arena-Essex	27	14	1	12	1,027	1,061	29	53.70
Mildenhall	19	10	0	9	776	700	20	52.63
Buxton	21	10	2	9	867	761	22	52.38
Peterborough	13	5	1	7	491	510	11	42.31
Owlerton	12	5	0	7	423	506	10	41.67
Reading	13	5	0	8	477	508	10	38.46
Eastbourne	16	1	2	13	512.5	700.5	4	12.50
Sittingbourne	18	1	2	15	577	820	4	11.11

1997

This was a very important year for speedway, as it saw the formation of the Elite League, which comprised ten tracks. A number of rider allocations took place to ensure a higher standard of racing, with nearly all of the best speedsters from home and abroad competing in the new league. The fresh set-up also saw teams of just six riders, in an attempt to ensure it was literally the highest-quality league in the world. With Peter Toogood now in sole charge of the Westmead Nissan Robins, he set about putting a team together that would give a good account of itself. His first signing was Mick Bell, as team manager, and this was an inspired piece of business by the Swindon promoter. Jimmy Nilsen, Brian Karger and Steve Masters were retained from the 1996 line-up, and to these three were added former Robin Leigh Adams, who was available on loan due to the unfortunate closure of

London following just one season of league racing at their Hackney base. Two other riders arrived on loan, both of whom had also previously ridden for the club, namely Tony Olsson from Reading and Alun Rossiter from Poole. Going the other way, Glenn Cunningham joined Reading on loan in the restructured Premier League, while John Jorgensen returned to his parent track Coventry. Meanwhile, the unlucky Mark Thorpe stayed at home in New Zealand, with Jarno Kosonen moving to Premier League Edinburgh.

The season began with three defeats in the revamped *Speedway Star* Knock-Out Cup, which saw the ten Elite League teams split into two groups of five, with the top two in each progressing to the semi-final stage. The poor results led to some of the fans questioning Mr Toogood's judgement on his team selection. However, on 23 March Swindon narrowly won a Knock-Out Cup thriller against Bradford, 47-42, and from that moment they were not to taste defeat at home until Coventry won a league fixture at the Abbey on 27 September. Away from Blunsdon the Robins also enjoyed some memorable nights and, as they headed the Elite League table for a number of weeks, promoter Toogood had silenced the critics. Only towards the end of the season did Swindon let it slip, their problems beginning in August when Tony Olsson broke his left foot while riding in a home match for Bysarna against Rospiggarna in the Swedish Elite League. Later that same month there was a further injury to contend with, since Alun Rossiter hurt his right knee in an awkward-looking crash in the Robins' league fixture at Bradford. Regrettably, these two occurrences were to prove decisive. Rossiter was very difficult to replace, as suitable guests were not always available, and the rider-replacement rules put far too much strain on Steve Masters.

Swindon, therefore, finished third in the new league. This was a very fine effort indeed, there being just that single home defeat against Coventry, while the Robins collected three well-earned away successes, at Coventry, King's Lynn and Peterborough, plus a hard-fought draw at Poole. In fact, they could well have finished as runners-up in the final standings, but lost no less than three bonus-point run-offs during the course of the season! Leigh Adams had a tremendous year, scorching to 444 points and topping the averages with a tremendous 9.96 figure. Jimmy Nilsen backed the consistent Aussie with a solid 8.88 return, while Brian Karger did well to average 8.09. Tony Olsson proved to be very reliable and finished with a creditable 6.84 average, while Alun Rossiter yielded a 4.49 figure from his season's work. Steve Masters battled away throughout the campaign, but it wasn't easy against the world's best riders and this was clearly evident from his final average of 2.57.

Reflecting on the Knock-Out Cup, Swindon found themselves in the northern section and their eight group matches yielded just three wins, so it was hardly surprising that they ended up at the foot of the table. In the inaugural end-of-season Craven Shield, the Robins reached the semi-finals but were well beaten by Coventry, who took victory in both legs to triumph 99-81 on aggregate. Swindon did partake in one final in 1997, however, when they rode in the Four-Team Championship at Peterborough on 3 August. It wasn't their day though as they finished joint third with Belle Vue, behind victorious hosts Peterborough and runners-up Bradford. On the individual front, Leigh Adams appeared in the NPI-sponsored Elite League Riders' Championship at Bradford on 11 October, but on a night when simply nothing went right for Swindon's main man he only managed to glean a single point. Turning to the Grand Prix, two of the Robins appeared throughout the series, Jimmy Nilsen finishing in eighth position with 71 points, while Leigh Adams was two places behind after totalling 42.

Having run a second team in the Conference League the previous season, Swindon joined forces with Reading and competed in the renamed Amateur League in 1997. The side was known as the M4 Raven Sprockets and were sponsored by Swindon Forklift Services, with the fixtures equally split between the two circuits. With the team-managing duties shared by David Broome and Mick Hester, the composite side completed twenty-four league fixtures, winning ten and drawing three, to finish seventh in the thirteen-team league. One meeting worth recalling occurred at the Abbey on 17 May, when the junior side faced Belle Vue Colts in atrociously wet conditions. In the nominated heat the home duo of Gary Phelps and Martin Williams came down and remounted, while both visiting riders, James Birkinshaw and Scott Donovan, retired. Phelps went on to win ahead of his teammate, thus sealing a 41-32 success, with the winning time being a sluggish 93.85 seconds! It wasn't the slowest ever recorded at the Swindon raceway, however. That dubious honour is long held by Mike Broadbanks, who clocked 139.2 seconds way back on 12 April 1958.

Swindon Robins, 1997. From left to right, back row: Mick Bell (Team Manager), Alun Rossiter, Jimmy Nilsen, Steve Masters, Peter Toogood (Promoter). Front row: Leigh Adams, Brian Karger, Tony Olsson.

Getting back to the Amateur League boys of 1997, John Jefferies led the scoring with 207 points for an impressive 9.62 average, while other regulars included Gary Phelps (8.21), Ian Clarke (7.24), Karl Bainbridge (6.98), Keith Lansley (6.71), Martin Williams (5.16), Shane Colvin (5.14), Simon Moon (4.43), Steve Targett (4.37) and Wayne Holloway (3.57). Clarke it was who represented the M4 Raven Sprockets in the Amateur League Riders' Championship at Long Eaton on 7 September, but he could only muster 3 points in the prestigious event.

With Swindon running Amateur League fixtures on top of the Elite League racing it was another bumper year for the Blunsdon regulars, with a remarkable thirty-four home meetings being staged. One of those was the Bob Jones Memorial on 25 May, held in honour of the Swindon great who had died the previous December. Future Robin Steve Johnston won the special meeting, defeating Brian Karger, Tomas Topinka and Zdenek Tesar in the grand final. The Abbey also hosted a Test match between England and Australia on 14 September, with victory going to the Antipodeans by 54 points to 42. Steve Johnston again excelled, leading the scoring for the Roos with 14 points, while Leigh Adams (13+1) and Jason Crump (13) provided solid backing. Meanwhile, on a disappointing evening for the home nation, Chris Louis (14) and Mark Loram (12) did all they could to keep the Lions in contention.

At the end of the season, Peter Toogood shocked supporters by announcing that he had sold out to the new stadium owners, the Bristol Stadia Group. However, Toogood would be staying on to head a promotion team, which included former Robins' rider Richard Evans, who was now an employee of the BS Group.

SWINDON WESTMEAD NISSAN ROBINS 1997
(Swindon's score shown first unless otherwise stated)

ELITE LEAGUE 'A'

Opponents	Home	Away	Aggregate
Belle Vue	W51-39	L37-53	L88-92
Bradford	W47-43	L44-46	W91-89
Coventry	W50-40	W49-41	W99-81
Eastbourne	W54-36	L42-48	W96-84
Ipswich	W52-38	L37-53	L89-91
King's Lynn	W46-44	L39-51	L85-95
Peterborough	W47-43	W49-41	W96-84
Poole	W55-35	D45-45	W100-80
Wolverhampton	W56-34	L42-48	W98-82

ELITE LEAGUE 'B'

Opponents	Home	Away	Aggregate
Belle Vue	W54-36	L36-54	D90-90
Bradford	W49-41	L38-52	L87-93
Coventry	L43-47	L36-54	L79-101
Eastbourne	W47-43	L35-55	L82-98
Ipswich	W59-31	L43-47	W102-78
King's Lynn	W53-37	W48-42	W101-79
Peterborough	W49-41	L41-49	D90-90
Poole	W57-33	L42-48	W99-81
Wolverhampton	W54-36	L36-54	D90-90

Notes: Leigh Adams lost to Mikael Karlsson in a run-off for the bonus point following the home 'B' match v. Wolverhampton. Leigh Adams lost to Billy Hamill in a run-off for the bonus point following the away 'B' match at Belle Vue. Swindon guest John Jorgensen lost to Jason Crump in a run-off for the bonus point following the away 'B' match at Peterborough.

ELITE LEAGUE TABLE

Team	Mts	Won	Drn	Lst	For	Agn.	Pts	Bon.	Tot.
Bradford	36	23	1	12	1,733	1,506	47	14	61
Eastbourne	36	20	0	16	1,665	1,570	40	11	51
Swindon	36	20	1	15	1,662	1,578	41	9	50
Ipswich	36	16	2	18	1,617	1,616	34	13	47
King's Lynn	36	18	3	15	1,592	1,645	39	8	47
Belle Vue	36	18	0	18	1,646	1,587	36	9	45
Wolverhampton	36	18	0	18	1,572	1,658	36	7	43
Coventry	36	15	1	20	1,582	1,653	31	7	38
Peterborough	36	14	0	22	1,556	1,679	28	6	34
Poole	36	13	2	21	1,551	1,684	28	6	34

LEAGUE AVERAGES

Rider	Mts	Rds	Pts	Bon.	Tot.	Avge	Maximums
Leigh Adams	35	182	444	9	453	9.96	5 full; 3 paid
Jimmy Nilsen	35	181	377	25	402	8.88	1 full; 1 paid
John Jorgensen	2	10	20	1	21	8.40	–
Brian Karger	35	177	333	25	358	8.09	–
Mark Lemon	1	6	10	2	12	8.00	–
Tomas Topinka	2	11	18	3	21	7.64	–
Scott Nicholls	1	5	7	2	9	7.20	–
David Norris	1	5	7	2	9	7.20	–
Zdenek Tesar	1	5	8	1	9	7.20	–
Tony Olsson	30	152	213	47	260	6.84	1 paid
Paul Thorp	3	15	19	5	24	6.40	–
Alun Rossiter	27	123	111	27	138	4.49	–
Shane Bowes	1	3	1	1	2	2.67	–
Steve Masters	35	188	90	31	121	2.57	–
Jesper B. Jensen	1	5	2	1	3	2.40	–
Jon Armstrong	1	5	2	0	2	1.60	–
Gary Phelps	3	6	0	0	0	0.00	–

CRAVEN SHIELD

Opponents	Home	Away	Aggregate
Belle Vue (Quarter-final)	W60-30	Walkover	W60-30
Coventry (Semi-final)	L41-49	L40-50	L81-99

Note: The second leg of the quarter-final at Belle Vue was abandoned after heat five, with Swindon holding a 19-11 lead at the time. As the Manchester outfit was unable to find a restaging date, the Robins were given a walkover into the semi-final.

SPEEDWAY STAR KNOCK-OUT CUP

Opponents	Home	Away
Belle Vue	W56-34	L40-52
Bradford	W47-42	L34-56
Coventry	L41-49	L40-51
Wolverhampton	W65-25	L38-52

KNOCK-OUT CUP (NORTHERN SECTION) TABLE

Team	Mts	Won	Drn	Lst	For	Agn.	Pts
Bradford	8	5	0	3	396	323	10
Coventry	8	4	1	3	365	358	9
Belle Vue	8	4	0	4	348	375	8
Wolverhampton	8	3	1	4	333	386	7
Swindon	8	3	0	5	361	361	6

Bradford and Coventry progressed to the semi-finals.

CHAMPAGNE CHALLENGE

Opponents	Home	Away	Aggregate
Poole	W47-43	W48-43	W95-86

FOUR-TEAM CHAMPIONSHIP

Final (Staged at Peterborough)   Peterborough 27, Bradford 21, Swindon 15, Belle Vue 15.

NPI ELITE LEAGUE RIDERS' CHAMPIONSHIP

(Staged at Bradford)   Leigh Adams 1 point

SWINDON M4 RAVEN SPROCKETS

AMATEUR LEAGUE TABLE

Team	Mts	Won	Drn	Lst	For	Agn.	Pts
Peterborough	24	22	1	1	1,064	729	45
Berwick	24	17	2	5	999	767	36
Ryde (Isle of Wight)	24	15	1	8	987	857	31
Buxton	24	15	0	9	948	901	30
Mildenhall	24	13	2	9	961	874	28
St Austell	24	13	0	11	963	871	26
M4 Raven Sprockets	24	10	3	11	820	848	23
Western Warriors	24	10	0	14	909	946	20
Oxford	24	9	0	15	901	909	18
Shuttle Cubs	24	9	0	15	799	969	18
Belle Vue	24	7	0	17	798	967	14
Lathallan	24	7	0	17	819	1,024	14
Anglian Angels	24	4	1	19	725	1,031	9

1998

Swindon Speedway reached the landmark of fifty years in 1998; however, Saturday night would no longer be speedway night, as this would now be reserved for greyhound racing, while the super shale sport had to move back to Thursday evenings. On the team front, Leigh Adams (re-signed on a full transfer), Jimmy Nilsen and Brian Karger all returned, having enjoyed a good deal of success the previous year. Alun Rossiter and Steve Masters were also back, while the final piece of the jigsaw was completed by young Danish prospect Charlie Gjedde, although regrettably there was no place for the extremely popular Tony Olsson. The Robins again started badly in the *Speedway Star* Knock-Out Cup, winning only two matches and finishing bottom of their group. Charlie Gjedde looked impressive, but Alun Rossiter, in his Testimonial year, appeared off the pace. A combination of loss of form and the fact that his knee, injured at Bradford the previous year, was still troubling him, saw Rosco temporarily retire from racing to become presenter of meetings at Blunsdon instead.

It soon became obvious to the promotional frontmen of Richard Evans and Peter Toogood, as well as team manager Mick Bell, that the side badly needed strengthening. Tony Olsson was the initial choice but, when the Swede declined the invitation to return, John Jorgensen, who had been such a hit in 1996, came back to notch 8+1 points in a 47-43 victory over Belle Vue at the Abbey on 4 June. Meanwhile Steve Masters, who was enduring a tough time, made up his mind that he would do better in the Premier League and, with the blessing of the management, he went on loan to the Isle of Wight. Travelling in the opposite direction, Philippe Berge arrived on loan from the Islanders but, unfortunately, found the pace too hot to handle. At King's Lynn on 15 July the Robins lost Jimmy Nilsen with a shoulder injury and the skipper was out of action for a month, with his absence being covered by guest riders. However, luck smiled on the Robins when they learned that Andy Smith had finished with Belle Vue, and promoter Richard Evans moved quickly to acquire his services on loan. This proved to be the signing of the year, as 'Smudger' served up some spectacular stuff, much to the delight of the Blunsdon faithful who actually voted him their Rider of the Year, despite the fact he only rode in a dozen Elite League matches!

Thankfully, Jimmy Nilsen returned to action in a home league match against Eastbourne on 9 August, storming to 12+2 points. The Swede was having a marvellous season, both home and abroad, and his performances in the Grand Prix were sensational. Swindon, with John Jorgensen and Andy Smith, by this time looked very competent, but they were to lose Brian Karger under a suspension by the BSPA. The Dane had missed a home match against Wolverhampton on 13 August, claiming injury, but with no supporting medical certificate the Robins were forced to use John Jefferies in his place. The following week, Karger didn't return to Britain for a league fixture at Eastbourne and was duly suspended. Efforts were made to bring in highly rated Norwegian Rune Holta, but the move didn't come off and the team saw out the season using guests in place of the banned Dane. Despite all the rider comings and goings, with Swindon actually using a staggering total of thirty-four riders in their 32 league matches, they did well to finish the season in a creditable fourth position. The usual susceptibility at home undoubtedly cost them a higher finish, with five defeats in front of their own fans, against Coventry (twice), Ipswich (twice) and Oxford.

Once again, Leigh Adams was top of the scoring charts with a haul of 418 points, well ahead of the next man, Jimmy Nilsen, on 241. Running through the finishing averages of the seven riders whose appearances reached double figures reveals a lack of real firepower at the top end, coupled with some inconsistencies: Leigh Adams (8.95), Jimmy Nilsen (8.09), Andy Smith (7.70), John Jorgensen (7.15), Brian Karger (6.32), Charlie Gjedde (4.49) and Steve Masters (3.12). After thrashing Eastbourne, the Robins reached the semi-final of the Craven Shield for the second year running, only to lose to all-conquering Ipswich, who won both legs with relative ease. In a glorious campaign for the Witches, they went on to take victory in the final against Coventry, thereby adding to their Elite League and

*Swindon Robins, 1998. From left to right, back row: John Jorgensen, Leigh Adams, Mick Bell (Team Manager),
Charlie Gjedde, Peter Toogood (Promoter), Andy Smith. Front, on bike: Jimmy Nilsen.*

Knock-Out Cup successes to complete a marvellous treble. The Elite League Riders' Championship
was held at Swindon on 11 October, with Leigh Adams battling his way through to the grand final,
only to retire and have to settle for fourth position behind Tony Rickardsson, Jason Crump and Joe
Screen. The Robins actually had two representatives on the big night and, although Jimmy Nilsen
performed well, he was eliminated at the semi-final stage.

One other individual event, staged at Blunsdon on 3 September, was the Stars of Tomorrow Junior
Trophy, which was won in impressive fashion by Marc Norris. The line-up featured several up-and-
coming talented riders, including Matt Read, Glen Phillips, Chris Neath, Shane Colvin and Seemond
Stephens.

Dreadful weather wrecked Alun Rossiter's Testimonial plans by twice causing his special meeting
to be postponed. This was cruel luck on the chirpy Rosco, who had to be patient for an awfully
long time before finally managing to stage his benefit meeting many months later at Poole, in March
2000. On the international front, Jimmy Nilsen, who had ridden brilliantly throughout the Grand
Prix series, became world number two, totalling 99 points to finish behind fellow Swede Tony
Rickardsson, who tallied 111. Both Leigh Adams and Andy Smith also graced the GP series, recording
totals of 51 and 43 points respectively.

A winter of worry ensued as the BS Group counted the cost of staging Elite League racing and
a new pay structure for the riders was to be introduced. Jimmy Nilsen and Leigh Adams were
understandably unable to accept the terms on offer, and for several weeks the future looked bleak as
rumours circulated. It was finally announced that Swindon would be applying to race in the Premier
League in 1999. The application to run in the lower league was eventually accepted by speedway's
hierarchy and, shortly afterwards, Peter Toogood stepped back in as sole promoter, having reached an
acceptable agreement with the BS Group.

Looking at the younger element, the Sprockets spent the year in the Dunlop-sponsored Youth
Development League. This was run in the same fashion as that employed by the Conference League
two years beforehand, when the competing sides were marked in percentages, based on the ratio of

Leigh Adams.

points gained from the number of matches completed. Swindon raced in a total of sixteen meetings and, with eight wins plus a draw, their percentage was 53.13, giving them a final position of eighth in the seventeen-team league. Malcolm Smart (father of future Sprocket Lee) performed the team-managing duties and just three of his charges reached double figures in terms of the number of meetings ridden, namely John Jefferies, Simon Paget and Andy Carfield, meaning the final averages were a little misleading. For instance, James Birkinshaw had a perfect 12.00 figure, but only completed two matches, whereas Seemond Stephens finished on 11.56 from five meetings. Running through the rest of the side's representatives who averaged in excess of 6 points per match, the list featured Jefferies (10.12), Matt Fearn (7.20), Paget (6.59) and Carfield (6.47). No less than ten other lads appeared for the side and, in alphabetical order, these were Aaron Bellerby, Neil Cochrane, Graig Gough, Rob Hayward, Bradley Kite, Keith Lansley, Chris Naylor, Glen Phillips, Tony Starke and Martin Williams.

SWINDON ROBINS 1998

(Swindon's score shown first unless otherwise stated)

ELITE LEAGUE 'A'

Opponents	Home	Away	Aggregate
Belle Vue	W47-43	L31-59	L78-102
Coventry	L42-47	L37-53	L79-100
Eastbourne	W49-41	L38-52	L87-93
Ipswich	L31-59	L29-61	L60-120
King's Lynn	W55-35	L38-52	W93-87
Oxford	W51-39	L44-46	W95-85
Poole	W53-37	W52-38	W105-75
Wolverhampton	W52-38	L35-55	L87-93

ELITE LEAGUE 'B'

Opponents	Home	Away	Aggregate
Belle Vue	W55-35	L33-57	L88-92

Coventry	L42-48	L42-48	L84-96
Eastbourne	W64-26	L35-55	W99-81
Ipswich	L44-46	L32-58	L76-104
King's Lynn	W56-34	W48-42	W104-76
Oxford	L38-52	D45-45	L83-97
Poole	W59-31	W48-42	W107-73
Wolverhampton	W56-34	W48-42	W104-76

ELITE LEAGUE TABLE

Team	Mts	Won	Drn	Lst	For	Agn.	Pts	Bon.	Tot.
Ipswich	32	26	1	5	1,653.5	1,211.5	53	16	69
Belle Vue	32	20	0	12	1,524.5	1,353.5	40	12	52
Coventry	32	18	1	13	1,474	1,401	37	11	48
Swindon	32	15	1	16	1,429	1,450	31	7	38
Eastbourne	32	15	0	17	1,430	1,449	30	7	37
Wolverhampton	32	14	1	17	1,421	1,444	29	8	37
Oxford	32	13	2	17	1,388	1,490	28	5	33
Poole	32	11	1	20	1,348	1,529	23	5	28
King's Lynn	32	8	1	23	1,270	1,610	17	1	18

LEAGUE AVERAGES

Rider	Mts	Rds	Pts	Bon.	Tot.	Avge	Maximums
Jason Lyons	1	6	16	2	18	12.00	1 paid
Chris Louis	1	6	14	0	14	9.33	–
Leigh Adams	32	198	418	25	443	8.95	3 full; 1 paid
Jimmy Nilsen	24	131	241	24	265	8.09	1 full; 1 paid
Craig Boyce	1	7	14	0	14	8.00	–
Jan Staechmann	1	5	7	3	10	8.00	–
Andy Smith	12	66	105	22	127	7.70	–
John Jorgensen	17	94	155	13	168	7.15	–
George Stancl	4	20	32	3	35	7.00	–
Mark Loram	1	6	10	0	10	6.67	–
Scott Nicholls	1	5	5	3	8	6.40	–
Brian Karger	20	112	165	12	177	6.32	–
Shane Parker	7	38	47	10	57	6.00	–
Lee Richardson	1	4	5	1	6	6.00	–
Glenn Cunningham	1	5	4	2	6	4.80	–
Steve Johnston	1	5	5	1	6	4.80	–
Charlie Gjedde	26	115	112	17	129	4.49	–
Todd Wiltshire	2	9	10	0	10	4.44	–
James Grieves	1	4	4	0	4	4.00	–
Petri Kokko	2	7	7	0	7	4.00	–
David Walsh	1	5	4	1	5	4.00	–
Frank Smart	2	7	5	1	6	3.43	–
Steve Masters	13	50	32	7	39	3.12	–
Philippe Berge	6	19	7	4	11	2.32	–
Richard Juul	1	3	1	0	1	1.33	–
Jan Pedersen	1	3	1	0	1	1.33	–
Shaun Tacey	1	3	1	0	1	1.33	–
Alun Rossiter	2	4	1	0	1	1.00	–
Magnus Zetterstrom	2	6	1	0	1	0.67	–
John Jefferies	1	3	0	0	0	0.00	–
Jarno Kosonen	1	1	0	0	0	0.00	–
Paul Lee	1	3	0	0	0	0.00	–
Seemond Stephens	1	3	0	0	0	0.00	–
Tomas Topinka	1	3	0	0	0	0.00	–

CRAVEN SHIELD

Opponents	Home	Away	Aggregate
Eastbourne (Quarter-final)	W68-22	L41-49	W109-71
Ipswich (Semi-final)	L40-50	L41-49	L81-99

SPEEDWAY STAR KNOCK-OUT CUP

Opponents	Home	Away
Belle Vue	L40-50	W48-41
Coventry	L41-49	L43-47
Oxford	W46-44	L32-58
Wolverhampton	L41-49	L40-50

KNOCK-OUT CUP (NORTHERN SECTION) TABLE

Team	Mts	Won	Drn	Lst	For	Agn.	Pts
Coventry	8	5	2	1	379	341	12
Wolverhampton	8	5	2	1	370	349	12
Belle Vue	8	3	1	4	356	362	7
Oxford	8	2	1	5	361	357	5
Swindon	8	2	0	6	331	388	4

Coventry and Wolverhampton progressed to the semi-finals.

CHAMPAGNE CHALLENGE

Opponents	Home	Away	Aggregate
Poole	L44-46	W50-40	W94-86

CHALLENGE

Opponents	Home	Away
Oxford	L41-49	–

ELITE LEAGUE RIDERS' CHAMPIONSHIP

(Staged at Swindon)   Leigh Adams was third in the qualifying heats with 11 points and subsequently finished first in the semi-final, prior to occupying fourth spot in the final. Jimmy Nilsen was fifth in the qualifying heats with 11 points and subsequently finished third in the semi-final.

SWINDON SPROCKETS

YOUTH DEVELOPMENT LEAGUE TABLE

Team	Mts	Won	Drn	Lst	For	Agn.	Pts	%
Berwick	14	12	1	1	288	204	25	89.29
Oxford	14	10	1	3	298	192	21	75.00
Peterborough	18	13	1	4	360	264	27	75.00
St Austell	15	11	0	4	329	211	22	73.33
Wolverhampton	17	11	1	5	323	261	23	67.65
Owlerton	14	8	0	6	267	226	16	57.14
Devon	14	8	0	6	251	246	16	57.14
Swindon	16	8	1	7	310	262	17	53.13
Arena-Essex	15	7	1	7	271	259	15	50.00
King's Lynn	16	8	0	8	277	295	16	50.00
Armadale	14	7	0	7	231	256	14	50.00
Belle Vue	19	6	3	10	342	341	15	39.47
Mildenhall	15	4	1	10	205	327	9	30.00
Coventry	15	4	0	11	226	312	8	26.67
Buxton	15	3	0	12	210	328	6	20.00
Glasgow	14	2	1	11	195	299	5	17.86
Eastbourne	15	2	1	12	219	319	5	16.67

1999

The drop down a league necessitated the Swindon side's complete rebuilding, with Glenn Cunningham returning to his parent club to fill the number one berth, having enjoyed two terrific seasons on loan at Reading and Peterborough in 1997 and 1998 respectively. Somewhat surprisingly, former England international Neil Collins became available, and Peter Toogood wasted no time in snapping him up from Stoke. Steve Masters also returned to the fold following his stint with the Isle of Wight, and it was hoped that he would fill the third heat-leader berth in the new-look Robins' septet. Completing the side was Krister Marsh, along with promising youngsters Oliver Allen, David Mason and local lad Gary Phelps. Off track there was good news commercially, since Westmead Nissan came back on board as team sponsors after a year's absence.

The season opened at Blunsdon on 18 March, with the Thames Valley Trophy against local rivals Reading, during which Gary Phelps broke a bone in his left hand. Martin Williams initially replaced him before Swindon drafted in a former Sprocket from the early 1980s, Steve Bishop, who by this time was something of an experienced speedster, having ridden for the likes of Exeter, Stoke, Arena-Essex, Long Eaton and, latterly, St Austell in the Conference League. Although only signed on a short-term contract, 'Bish' brought the house down with an outstanding 17+1 points in his first match against Sheffield in the Premier National Trophy at the Abbey on 1 April. Following that wonder display, strenuous efforts were made to ensure that he would remain with the Robins for the remainder of the season. Bishop had actually made his debut for the senior team way back on 17 June 1981 in a British League match at Poole, but had only enjoyed fleeting outings for the side. Some eighteen years later, this was to be his longest stint for the club!

By the end of April, Swindon had dispensed with the services of David Mason, who just hadn't been able to string the points together in the early encounters, despite having good equipment and a tidy riding style. Cornishman Seemond Stephens, who had starred in a handful of Youth Development League fixtures for the Sprockets in 1998, was introduced into the Robins' line-up to replace Mason, and opened with a brilliant 11+2 points in a Premier League fixture at Exeter on 3 May.

Swindon fared quite well at home, winning most meetings comfortably, although Sheffield forced a sensational 45-45 draw in a league encounter on 9 May. Away from Blunsdon, however, it was a different story, with a 62-28 mauling at Edinburgh on 14 May being followed by a poor display at Berwick the following evening. As if that wasn't enough, the day after that the Robins went down 46-44 in a last-heat decider at Glasgow. A team that proved a real thorn in Swindon's side during the season was Newport, as they became the only visitors to triumph in the league at Blunsdon after using a 'golden double' tactical substitute to overcome a 6-point deficit before winning 50-43 on 27 May. Not only that, but with the Robins winning the central section of the Premier National Trophy it was the Welsh outfit who subsequently won both legs to dispatch them at the semi-final stage of the competition. In the Knock-Out Cup, a poor team performance saw Swindon lose 55-35 at Arena-Essex in their quarter-final encounter and, although they rallied to win the second leg, it was the Purfleet side that progressed to the semi-final with a 4-point aggregate victory.

On their travels, no less than six matches frustratingly slipped away on last-heat deciders, as Mick Bell's troops finished the league campaign in fourth place. Having ended the two previous seasons with averages of 10.06 and 9.68 at Reading and Peterborough respectively, Glenn Cunningham's 1999 figure of 8.54 was not quite the expected or hoped-for return. Steve Masters always tried hard and was probably steadier than ever before, ending up with an 8.41 average. Meanwhile, Neil Collins was a revelation and finished the year with an 8.32 average and the Rider of the Year award, which wasn't bad for a rider at the veteran stage of his career. 'Olly' Allen got better and better throughout the season, undoubtedly learning fast from being paired with the wily Collins, and a final average of 5.87 was a tremendous achievement for the youngster. Seemond Stephens proved to be an excellent signing and a very likeable lad, whose term ended with a highly creditable 5.22 figure from his

Swindon Robins, 1999. From left to right, back row: Peter Toogood (Promoter), David Mason, Neil Collins, Gary Phelps, Steve Masters, Krister Marsh, Olly Allen, Mick Bell (Team Manager). Front row, kneeling: Lee Smart (Club Mascot). On bike: Glenn Cunningham.

twenty-three league matches. Meanwhile, Krister Marsh (5.68) and Steve Bishop (4.83) disappointed somewhat as the season wore on, the latter in particular after his wonderful start.

In the Young Shield Swindon won both legs of their quarter-final tie with Newcastle but were sent packing by a powerful Sheffield side at the semi-final stage. The Westmead Nissan Robins also reached the semi-final of the Four-Team Championship but, at the Peterborough-staged event on 29 August, they failed to progress any further after finishing behind the Isle of Wight and Newport. Glenn Cunningham represented Swindon in the Premier League Riders' Championship at Sheffield on 12 September, but the Bristol-born rider could only muster 9 points in defence of the title he had so brilliantly won the previous year. Perhaps the most memorable night of the season occurred on 9 September when Swindon staged their Golden Jubilee meeting, an event that also incorporated the Bob Jones Memorial. Watched by over sixty former Robins and racing friends of Joner, it was Carl Stonehewer who went on to win an absorbing final from Glenn Cunningham, Frank Smart and Craig Watson. It was a marvellous night of nostalgia and a special celebration was held in the stadium restaurant, which was enjoyed by everyone lucky enough to be present.

Regrettably, there was little sign of the Sprockets in 1999 and they were to stay on the back burner until being revived with a couple of full-blown challenge matches at the end of 2001, which were a prelude to them competing in the Conference Trophy the following season.

It is impossible to end a review of 1999 without making mention of Glynn Shailes. The Purton-based speedway historian was a captivated spectator at Blunsdon's first meeting in 1949 and later worked for the club in various capacities, including those of a programme contributor from 1983-1992, during which time he beautifully crafted many tales about the early days of the Robins; stories that otherwise would have been lost in the mists of time. Latterly, he took on the dual role of press officer and programme editor in 1996, but the 1999 season was to be his last in the position.

SWINDON WESTMEAD NISSAN ROBINS 1999
(Swindon's score shown first unless otherwise stated)

PREMIER LEAGUE

Opponents	Home	Away	Aggregate
Arena-Essex	W53-37	L39-51	W92-88
Berwick	W53-37	L41-49	W94-86
Edinburgh	W49-41	L28-62	L77-103
Exeter	W52-38	L44-45	W96-83
Glasgow	W53-37	L44-46	W97-83
Isle of Wight	W58-32	L43-46	W101-78
Newcastle	W52-38	L44-46	W96-84
Newport	L43-50	L39-51	L82-101
Reading	W56-36	W47-45	W103-81
Sheffield	D45-45	L29-61	L74-106
Stoke	W57-34	L43-47	W100-81
Workington	W54-39	L44-48	W98-87

PREMIER LEAGUE TABLE

Team	Mts	Won	Drn	Lst	For	Agn.	Pts	Bon.	Tot.
Sheffield	24	18	2	4	1,223	936	38	12	50
Newport	24	16	1	7	1,147	1,023	33	9	42
Edinburgh	24	14	0	10	1,157	1,013	28	9	37
Swindon	24	11	1	12	1,110	1,061	23	9	32
Newcastle	24	11	1	12	1,104	1,066	23	8	31
Exeter	24	13	0	11	1,071	1,087	26	5	31
Berwick	24	13	1	10	1,009	1,140	27	4	31
Isle of Wight	24	11	1	12	1,085	1,078	23	7	30
Arena-Essex	24	12	1	11	1,081	1,081	25	5	30
Stoke	24	10	0	14	1,026	1,138	20	4	24
Workington	24	8	1	15	1,039	1,132	17	3	20
Glasgow	24	9	0	15	999	1,160	18	1	19
Reading	24	5	1	18	1,004	1,140	11	2	13

LEAGUE AVERAGES

Rider	Mts	Rds	Pts	Bon.	Tot.	Avge	Maximums
Glenn Cunningham	24	118	243	9	252	8.54	4 full; 1 paid
Steve Masters	24	117	231	15	246	8.41	2 paid
Neil Collins	24	113	219	16	235	8.32	–
Olly Allen	24	94	117	21	138	5.87	–
Krister Marsh	24	93	108	24	132	5.68	–
Seemond Stephens	23	92	104	16	120	5.22	–
Steve Bishop	23	87	84	21	105	4.83	–
David Mason	1	3	2	1	3	4.00	–
Mark McIlkenny	1	3	0	0	0	0.00	–

YOUNG SHIELD

Opponents	Home	Away	Aggregate
Newcastle (Quarter-final)	W55-35	W46-44	W101-79
Sheffield (Semi-final)	W51-39	L36-54	L87-93

KNOCK-OUT CUP

Opponents	Home	Away	Aggregate
Bye (Round one)	–	–	–
Arena-Essex (Quarter-final)	W53-37	L35-55	L88-92

PREMIER NATIONAL TROPHY

Opponents	Home	Away	Aggregate
Sheffield	W48-43	L39-54	L87-97
Stoke	W51-40	W49-40	W100-80
Workington	W49-40	W46-44	W95-84

PREMIER NATIONAL TROPHY (CENTRAL SECTION) TABLE

Team	Mts	Won	Drn	Lst	For	Agn.	Pts	Bon.	Tot.
Swindon	6	5	0	1	282	261	10	2	12
Sheffield	6	3	0	3	300	255	6	3	9
Workington	6	3	0	3	263	284	6	1	7
Stoke	6	1	0	5	251	296	2	0	2

Note: As a result of topping the group, Swindon progressed to the semi-finals.

Opponents	Home	Away	Aggregate
Newport (Semi-final)	L43-47	L30-59	L73-106

FOUR-TEAM CHAMPIONSHIP

Qualifying group:	
(First leg at Swindon)	Swindon 34, Sheffield 26, Stoke 26, Workington 10.
(Second leg at Sheffield)	Sheffield 38, Swindon 24, Stoke 20, Workington 14.
(Third leg at Stoke)	Sheffield 27, Workington 26, Stoke 22, Swindon 21.
(Fourth leg at Workington)	Sheffield 26, Workington 24, Stoke 23, Swindon 22.
Aggregate result	Sheffield 117, Swindon 101, Stoke 91, Workington 74.
Semi-final:	
(Staged at Peterborough)	Isle of Wight 17, Newport 13, Swindon 12, Edinburgh 6.

THAMES VALLEY TROPHY

Opponents	Home	Away	Aggregate
Reading	W50-43	L41-52	L91-95

M4 TROPHY

Opponents	Home	Away	Aggregate
Newport	W50-40	W48-45	W98-85

CHALLENGE TROPHY

Opponents	Home	Away	Aggregate
Exeter	W64-26	L36-54	W100-80

CHALLENGE

Opponents	Home	Away
Sweden Under-23	L43-46	–

PREMIER LEAGUE RIDERS' CHAMPIONSHIP

(Staged at Sheffield)	Glenn Cunningham 9 points.

2000

Going into the 2000 season Swindon made several changes both on and off the track. Peter Toogood remained as promoter with Mick Bell becoming promoting manager, while Jed Stone was installed as the new team boss. Commercially, a new team sponsor was unveiled in the shape of the Swindon Soft Water Centre, whose owner, Brian Cox, had long been a fan of the shale sport at Blunsdon. Team changes saw Glenn Cunningham and Steve Masters move into the Elite League, with Peterborough and King's Lynn respectively, while Seemond Stephens joined Exeter and Krister Marsh went to Reading. Meanwhile, Steve Bishop opted for further Conference League racing and linked with the new operation at Somerset. That left just Neil Collins and Olly Allen from the previous season's septet, and they were joined by the all-action Australian Frank Smart from Newport, and Dane Claus Kristensen from Berwick. It would be fair to say that the Robins' management showed great courage with their other three signings, bringing in the vastly experienced duo of Martin Dixon and Paul Fry, while the final team spot went to teenager and former Coventry mascot Mark Steel.

Things started well, with an away win at Stoke in the Premier Trophy, but this was quickly offset by a home loss against the same opponents five nights later. Thankfully, that was to be the Robins' only home defeat in a season that saw a remarkable change of fortune to the club's years in the silverware wilderness. The Soft Water Robins won their remaining five home matches in the Premier Trophy, while collecting a further away success at Reading and draws at Newport and Arena-Essex. That was sufficient for them to finish on top of the southern section, but despite losing by only 4 points in the first leg of the semi-final tie at Hull on 5 July, the Vikings journeyed down to Blunsdon and forced a 45-45 draw on 10 August, sending Swindon tumbling out of the competition.

In between the Premier Trophy group matches and the semi-final with Hull, the Robins' season had been rocked by the events of 22 June, when a Premier League fixture against Exeter was rained off at Blunsdon. More significantly, as it turned out, six riders, including Frank Smart, were selected at random for a drugs test. Rumours began to do the rounds, until it was revealed on 16 July that two riders had failed the test. Unfortunately Smart was one of them but, to his eternal credit, he was quick to admit his guilt and apologised to everyone at Swindon for the embarrassment he had caused. It was subsequently announced that he had been handed a twelve-month ban from racing, and the Robins ended up using guest replacements for the remainder of the season.

Prior to Smart's ban, the Aussie had joined forces with Paul Fry to represent Swindon in the Harper & Hebson Audi-sponsored Premier League Pairs Championship at Workington on 8 July. Unluckily, in a curtailed meeting run in continuous rain, the duo only just failed to reach the semi-final stage in an event that was dominated by the home pairing of Carl Stonehewer and Mick Powell.

Despite the home draw with Hull in the Premier Trophy, Swindon went on to win every one of their league fixtures at Blunsdon, while also serving up some marvellous racing for the public on their wonderful raceway, which was so well prepared by Colin Meredith. Remarkably, this was only the fifth time in fifty-two seasons that the Robins had achieved a 100 per cent home record from their league programme. Any reservations that people might have had about the make-up of the side had been dispelled, as Swindon proved to be a very solid outfit, even after the departure of Frank Smart.

Swindon Robins, 2000. From left to right, back row: Paul Fry, Neil Collins, Frank Smart, Olly Allen, Jed Stone (Team Manager), Martin Dixon, Claus Kristensen, Mark Steel.

The battle for the League Championship saw one of the greatest ever finishes to a speedway season, as five teams fought for supremacy right up to the last match. Swindon were one of those five teams and, on 28 September, it all came to a head as the Robins entertained Newcastle at the Abbey. The equation was simple – Swindon, having lost 49-41 at Newcastle four days previously, needed to win the match and collect the aggregate bonus point, so basically a 50-40 victory would suffice. Things were going along relatively smoothly, as the Robins led 45-33 with just two heats to go. The cruel hand of fate then intervened to scupper Swindon's hopes, as the riders came to the line for heat fourteen. Suddenly, Olly Allen's clutch disintegrated and he was excluded for exceeding the two-minute time allowance. When the race got underway Claus Kristensen held second place, only to suffer a puncture on the last lap and hand the visitors a 5-1. Therefore, with one race to go, Swindon held a 46-38 advantage, but more significantly, the scores were level on aggregate. Newcastle's Danish sensation Bjarne Pedersen duly took the flag in the final heat, but Paul Fry and Kristensen shared the race to force a run-off for the much sought-after bonus point. It was Pedersen who roared away to take the run-off from Fry and break Swindon's hearts, as Exeter subsequently gained the bonus point at Workington two evenings later which gave them the Championship by the narrowest of margins on race points difference. In fact, in an incredible finish, the top five teams all finished within two points of each other, as follows: 1st Exeter, 44 points; 2nd Swindon, 44 points; 3rd Hull, 43 points; 4th Sheffield, 42 points; 5th Workington, 42 points.

Paul Fry enjoyed an amazing year, remaining ever-present throughout Swindon's twenty-six league fixtures and accumulating 272 points for an 8.96 average in what was his best-ever season since starting way back in 1984. A deserving winner of the Rider of the Year award, Fry was an unquestionable success, for he had arrived after an injury-ravaged year at Stoke and had actually started the season with a lowly green-sheet average of 6.44. The flying 'Fryer' also represented the Soft Water Robins in the Premier League Riders' Championship at Sheffield on 10 September, when he mustered 8 points with a typical never-say-die effort. Looking further into the Robins of 2000, the swashbuckling Frank Smart had provided some excellent entertainment while he was around, and this was mirrored in his 8.37 average. Due to a severe dose of glandular fever fast-gating Claus Kristensen took a long time to settle down, but he was very popular with the fans and a final average of 7.18 showed great promise of much more to come.

Following his great season in 1999, Neil Collins' average dropped from 8.32 to 7.08, but he still produced plenty of his trademark surges from the back for the supporters to enthuse over. 'Mad Dog' Martin Dixon averaged 6.57 and proved to be the engine room of the side, with solid scoring both at home and away. Meanwhile, Olly Allen continued to progress steadily and finished with an identical figure to that of Dixon. Young Mark Steel was simply outstanding; having joined the ranks with limited experience in the Conference League at Buxton, he rode with great maturity throughout the year and finished with a superb 5.40 average. This was in spite of an alarming crash at Stoke on 27 May, when he lost part of a thumb and then missed nearly two months of action while he recuperated. Lee Herne, Martin Williams, Simon Paget and Jamie Holmes were all used to plug the gap before Nathan Murray stepped in as a temporary replacement for Steel and the Kiwi never let the side down, netting 22 points from seven league matches for a 4.31 average.

In the Knock-Out Cup Swindon enjoyed a marvellous run, beginning with a hard-fought first round aggregate victory over rivals of old, Reading. Further success came with an even tougher 2-point quarter-final success over Berwick while, in the semi-final, the Robins easily saw off the challenge of Exeter. On 12 October, Swindon proudly hosted the first leg of the final against the self-same Hull side that had disposed of them in the Premier Trophy. But the Robins were in no mood for complacency, as they rattled up an outstanding 59-31 victory. Six nights later, they journeyed to Humberside for the second leg and, although going down to a 6-point defeat, much to the delight of a large travelling contingent, they had won their first piece of major silverware in thirty-three years!

Within a fortnight, Swindon made it a glorious double by also scooping the Young Shield. They initially faced Edinburgh at the quarter-final stage and the encounter with the Monarchs could have gone either way, since the two sides were deadlocked at 90 points apiece following the second leg at Armadale on 6 October. In a run-off to determine who went through, home man Peter

The Knock-Out Cup winners proudly show off the silverware after defeating Hull in the 2000 final. From left to right, back row: Mick Bell (Promoting Manager), Claus Kristensen, Martin Dixon, Peter Toogood (Promoter), Olly Allen, Jed Stone (Team Manager), Mark Steel. Front, on bike: Paul Fry.

Carr's engine dramatically blew up while he held the lead, leaving Martin Dixon to complete the race unchallenged. In the semi-final, the Robins put up a fabulous performance at Sheffield on 19 October, narrowly losing by 4 points before winning the second leg 49-40 to triumph 92-87 on aggregate. Having reached the final the Robins faced League Champions Exeter but, after losing out on one trophy to the Falcons, they determinedly gained revenge, winning both legs for an overall victory by 112 points to 67.

The season was plagued by rain throughout, with seven home meetings being postponed, just one short of the record set in 1993, which, co-incidentally, was the last time that the Robins had maintained a 100 per cent home record in the league. However, with two trophies in the cabinet, the year 2000 was definitely one to savour for Swindon Speedway.

SWINDON SOFT WATER ROBINS 2000

(Swindon's score shown first unless otherwise stated)

PREMIER LEAGUE

Opponents	Home	Away	Aggregate
Arena-Essex	W57-33	L41-50	W98-83
Berwick	W46-44	W48-42	W94-86
Edinburgh	W54-36	L43-46	W97-82
Exeter	W48-42	L33-57	L81-99
Glasgow	W66-24	W46-44	W112-68
Hull	W50-42	L39-51	L89-93
Isle of Wight	W50-40	W46-44	W96-84
Newcastle	W49-41	L41-49	D90-90
Newport	W60-30	W50-40	W110-70
Reading	W62-28	W58-32	W120-60
Sheffield	W49-41	L34-56	L83-97

Stoke	W52-38	L42-48	W94-86
Workington	W46-44	L39-52	L85-96

Note: Swindon's Paul Fry lost to Bjarne Pedersen in a run-off for the bonus point following the home match v. Newcastle.

PREMIER LEAGUE TABLE

Team	Mts	Won	Drn	Lst	For	Agn.	Pts	Bon.	Tot.
Exeter	26	15	1	10	1,335	1,003	31	13	44
Swindon	26	18	0	8	1,249	1,094	36	8	44
Hull	26	16	2	8	1,201	1,142	34	9	43
Sheffield	26	16	1	9	1,192	1,069	33	9	42
Workington	26	15	2	9	1,216	1,114	32	10	42
Edinburgh	26	15	1	10	1,213	1,140	31	8	39
Stoke	26	12	2	12	1,166	1,178	26	5	31
Newcastle	26	11	1	14	1,178.5	1,157.5	23	7	30
Glasgow	26	10	2	14	1,063	1,198	22	5	27
Newport	26	10	1	15	1,089	1,245	21	5	26
Isle of Wight	26	8	2	16	1,128.5	1,208.5	18	6	24
Berwick	26	10	0	16	1,133	1,210	20	3	23
Arena-Essex	26	11	0	15	1,054	1,272	22	1	23
Reading	26	7	1	18	1,075	1,262	15	2	17

LEAGUE AVERAGES

Rider	Mts	Rds	Pts	Bon.	Tot.	Avge	Maximums
Robbie Kessler	1	5	12	2	14	11.20	–
Brent Werner	1	5	12	0	12	9.60	–
David Walsh	3	13	27	3	30	9.23	–
Paul Thorp	2	8	18	0	18	9.00	–
Paul Fry	26	129	272	17	289	8.96	1 full; 3 paid
Frank Smart	11	54	105	8	113	8.37	–
Alan Mogridge	2	11	21	1	22	8.00	–
Paul Bentley	4	18	27	6	33	7.33	–
Claus Kristensen	26	112	186	15	201	7.18	1 paid
Neil Collins	26	113	173	27	200	7.08	1 paid
Paul Pickering	1	4	6	1	7	7.00	–
Martin Dixon	24	101	140	26	166	6.57	–
Olly Allen	26	112	158	26	184	6.57	1 full
Andre Compton	1	5	8	0	8	6.40	–
Mark Steel	17	57	60	17	77	5.40	1 paid
Nathan Murray	7	26	22	6	28	4.31	–
Jamie Holmes	1	3	0	0	0	0.00	–
Martin Williams	1	3	0	0	0	0.00	–

YOUNG SHIELD

Opponents	Home	Away	Aggregate
Edinburgh (Quarter-final)	W49-41	L41-49	D90-90
Sheffield (Semi-final)	W49-40	L43-47	W92-87
Exeter (Final)	W65-25	W47-42	W112-67

Note: Following the quarter-final at Edinburgh, a run-off saw Swindon's Martin Dixon defeat Peter Carr to take the Robins through to the semi-final.

KNOCK-OUT CUP

Opponents	Home	Away	Aggregate
Reading (Round one)	W46-44	W47-43	W93-87
Berwick (Quarter-final)	W49-41	L42-48	W91-89
Exeter (Semi-final)	W48-23	L44-46	W92-69
Hull (Final)	W59-31	L42-48	W101-79

PREMIER TROPHY

Opponents	Home	Away	Aggregate
Arena-Essex	W61-29	D45-45	W106-74
Exeter	W61-29	L26-64	L87-93
Isle of Wight	W55-35	L37-53	W92-88

Newport	W47-43	D45-45	W92-88
Reading	W52-39	W47-43	W99-82
Stoke	L43-47	W47-43	D90-90

Note: Following the home match against Stoke, a restarted bonus point run-off saw Swindon's Frank Smart defeat the Potters' reserve Martin Williams after Paul Pickering had been excluded for a tapes offence.

PREMIER TROPHY (SOUTHERN SECTION) TABLE

Team	Mts	Won	Drn	Lst	For	Agn.	Pts	Bon.	Tot.
Swindon	12	7	2	3	566	515	16	5	21
Exeter	12	6	0	6	600	480	12	6	18
Stoke	12	6	0	6	553	528	12	3	15
Newport	12	5	2	5	540	539	12	3	15
Isle of Wight	12	5	1	6	526	553	11	2	13
Reading	12	5	0	7	525	554	10	2	12
Arena-Essex	12	5	1	6	469	610	11	0	11

Note: As a result of topping the group, Swindon progressed to the semi-final.

Opponents	Home	Away	Aggregate
Hull (Semi-final)	D45-45	L43-47	L88-92

CHALLENGE

Opponents	Home	Away
Young Sweden	W54-36	–

GWENT TRIANGULAR CUP

(Staged at Newport)	Newport 28, Swindon 24, Exeter 20.

PREMIER LEAGUE FOUR-TEAM CHAMPIONSHIP

(Staged at Peterborough)	Semi-final: Swindon 14, Sheffield 13, Newcastle 12, Workington 9.
	Final: Sheffield 30, Isle of Wight 16, Swindon 14, Berwick 12.

HARPER & HEBSON AUDI PREMIER LEAGUE PAIRS CHAMPIONSHIP

(Staged at Workington)	Group A: Workington 14, Isle of Wight 8, Swindon 8, Newcastle 8, Newport 7.

PREMIER LEAGUE RIDERS' CHAMPIONSHIP

(Staged at Sheffield)	Paul Fry 8 points.

2001

The highs of the previous season were always going to be hard to surpass, but promoter Peter Toogood certainly did his utmost to ensure that the Swindon Soft Water Robins remained one of the leading forces in the Premier League. From the successful 2000 side Paul Fry, Olly Allen, Martin Dixon, Mark Steel and Claus Kristensen were retained, while Alan Mogridge, a man of many tracks, was brought in to add some strength at the top end. Rookie Ritchie Hawkins, the son of former Peterborough, Nottingham and Coventry rider Kevin, was the final piece of the jigsaw, having previously only had a handful of outings with Sheffield Prowlers in the Conference League. Unfortunately, due to averages and the points limit, Swindon were unable to retain popular stalwart Neil Collins but, even so, everything looked to be in place for the side to go one better in 2001 and, hopefully, lift the League Championship.

On track, things certainly started brightly as the Robins began with home and away victories against Newport to win the M4 Trophy. Everyone rode well, including young Ritchie Hawkins, who certainly impressed the supporters with his all-action style and bubbly enthusiasm. Off track, however, there was a major shock when it became clear that team manager Jed Stone had quit, even before the first week of the season was over. This meant a quick return to running the side for Mick Bell, who had only moved upstairs at the start of the 2000 campaign when acquiring the role of promoting manager.

On 22 March, a joint memorial meeting was staged at Blunsdon, honouring Bob Jones and Ray Morse – two men who had played an important part in the long history of Swindon Speedway. Jones, of course, had been a rider, manager and mechanic during his long association with the Robins, while Morse, although lesser known outside the town, had been a diligent clerk of the course for many years, as well as being instrumental in launching the successful Swindon Speedway Junior Club in 1982. Oxford's super Czech Ales Dryml sped to victory in the Bob Jones Memorial, and it was fitting that Ritchie Hawkins produced a breathtaking performance to win the event staged in respect of Ray Morse.

The Premier Trophy began with Swindon taking part in the Southern section, along with six other sides. At the Abbey the Robins were dominant, notching successive victories against all comers, including huge 68-22 and 60-29 wins against Trelawny and the Isle of Wight respectively. On their travels Swindon also looked good, winning at Newport and Arena-Essex, while going close in their other four matches. The Robins deservedly topped the group and progressed forward to face Workington in the semi-final. The first leg was staged at the well-appointed Derwent Park Stadium in deepest Cumbria on 19 May, when Swindon rode superbly to secure a 45-45 draw. Guarding against complacency, the Robins completed the job with a comfortable 54-36 victory at Blunsdon twelve days later, and confidently marched into the final to meet Sheffield. On 24 June the Abbey Stadium played host to the first leg of the showdown on what was a gloriously sunny evening, only for the Robins to completely capitulate against their South Yorkshire opponents, suffering an embarrassing 53-37 defeat. What exactly went wrong nobody knows, but the Swindon side seemed overawed by the occasion, and simply nothing went right on the day. Needless to say, the return leg was a foregone conclusion on 1 July, when the rampant Tigers raced to a 65-25 success to take the silverware with a crushing 118-62 aggregate victory.

The first leg of the Premier Trophy final had seen Mark Steel lose control and fall while leading heat two, and this was to be the start of a twenty-four-hour roller-coaster ride that would lead to the youngster quitting the sport. Although he eventually managed to glean 5+2 points from the match, the lad was clearly troubled. The following night Swindon were in league action at Exeter, but Steel suffered more problems, beginning with another fall in the reserves' race. Later he was to suffer two exclusions for exceeding the time allowance, before eventually making an emotional speech over the public address system, citing the difficulties of trying to maintain competitive equipment and hold down a full-time job at the same time. Effectively, Steel's promising career in the saddle was over, although he was to briefly flirt with the Sprockets in 2002, when he appeared in four Conference Trophy matches.

Swindon's defence of the Knock-Out Cup had begun against Glasgow in May, but despite comfortably moving through to the next stage the away match at the brilliant Ashfield home of the Tigers was marred by a serious injury to Olly Allen. A twice-started heat ten had seen the youngster take a couple of nasty-looking falls, the second of which had seen him suffer three broken bones in the right hand. With the adrenalin pumping, he bravely rode in the third attempt to complete the heat and, although barely able to hold on to his machine, he followed Glasgow's Les Collins across the line in what had become a two-man race following a couple of exclusions. In spite of the obvious discomfort, he sensationally found himself excluded by referee Jim McGregor for not making a bona fide attempt to race. Allen was to miss out on over two months of racing while he slowly recovered and, in his absence, the rider-replacement facility proved to be an unsatisfactory way of covering his brilliant point-plundering ability. Continuing on in the Knock-Out Cup, Swindon saw off Workington at the quarter-final stage, securing a tense 6-point aggregate victory. The second leg of the tie against the Comets at Blunsdon on 5 July marked the return to the Robins' side of Alun Rossiter, who had been released by Elite League Wolverhampton, and he jumped at the chance of rejoining his local team as the replacement for Mark Steel.

Having seen off the challenge of Workington, the Robins moved through to a semi-final encounter against Exeter, with the first leg being staged at the Abbey on 12 August. Time and again, the Falcons

Swindon Robins, 2001. From left to right, back row: Mick Bell (Team Manager), Ritchie Hawkins, Alun Rossiter, Paul Fry, Alan Mogridge, Claus Kristensen, Olly Allen, Peter Toogood (Promoter). Front, on bike: Martin Dixon.

riders jumped ahead from the tapes and generally made life difficult for a Swindon side which eventually managed to eke out a 51-39 win. However, it was generally felt that this wouldn't be a sufficient enough lead to take down to the daunting County Ground circuit the following night. And so it proved when, with one heat remaining, the sides were tied on aggregate at 87 points apiece. There appeared to be contact going into the first bend of the last race, with Alan Mogridge tumbling down as a result. Amid high drama, 'Moggo' was excluded and despite protestations, referee Craig Ackroyd was adamant that he had seen nothing amiss. The home side gained a 4-2 in the subsequent rerun and the Robins' reign as cup holders was over.

Prior to injury, Olly Allen made his fourth successive appearance in the British Under-21 Final at Wolverhampton on 21 April. He rode well too, netting 12 points to force a run-off for second place, having matched the tallies of David Howe and Paul Lee. Regrettably, a fall on the first lap of the extra race meant fourth place overall, but at least that represented a big improvement on his previous best of thirteenth spot in 1998.

The evening of 19 July was an historic one for Swindon Speedway, since the cameras of Sky Sports were in place to beam the league match against Workington live from the Abbey Stadium. With a large audience packing the terraces, there was a real air of excitement as both sides fought out a scintillating 45-45 draw in what proved to be the Robins' only dropped home point of the league campaign. Away from Blunsdon, wins were gained at Glasgow, Newport and Berwick, while draws were forced at Reading and Exeter. Meanwhile, narrow defeats at Stoke, Edinburgh, Workington and Arena-Essex undoubtedly cost Mick Bell's boys very dearly. In the final analysis Swindon had to settle for fifth position in the standings, just eight points adrift of Champions Newcastle.

Briefly running through the riders and how they fared, Olly Allen returned to the saddle late in the season and showed just what had been missing from the side, rattling up 105 points from fourteen matches to top the league averages with an 8.30 figure. A niggling mid-season knuckle injury caused Paul Fry to miss several meetings, and he was obviously affected by it upon his return, but even so he still managed to total 220 league points for an 8.17 average. For the second year running, Fryer also represented the club in the Jawa Premier League Riders' Championship at Coventry on 9 September and, in an excellent performance, he accrued 11 points to finish fourth in the qualifying heats. That gave him a spot in the semi-final, but he unfortunately ran a last and failed to progress further. Claus Kristensen revealed flashes of brilliance during the season, but a final average of 7.90 showed only a slight improvement on the previous year. Alan Mogridge came into the Robins' line-up with a green-sheet average of 8.74, but an end-of-term return of 7.58 reflected something of an inconsistent season for the often-spectacular racer. Alun Rossiter certainly pepped up the side upon his arrival and rode extremely well to notch 136 points for a 7.24 average. Veteran Martin Dixon captained the team and remained ever-present throughout the year, increasing his average to 6.98, and also celebrated twenty-five years in the saddle with a Testimonial meeting at Blunsdon on 27 September. Prior to his premature retirement, Mark Steel had again shown glimpses of his terrific riding of the previous year, scoring 38 points for a 5.87 average. Steel's starting partner at reserve, Ritchie Hawkins, certainly took all the plaudits as the season wore on though, riding with great determination to score 110 points for a wonderful 4.54 average in his first full season of racing.

As the season drew to a close Swindon also lost their grip on the Young Shield, which they had so brilliantly won in 2000, suffering defeat at the hands of Sheffield in the quarter-final. The Robins put up a much better show than they had in the Premier Trophy final against the Tigers, winning their home leg 49-41 on 4 October before going down to a 58-32 defeat at Owlerton Stadium a week later. Swindon asset Steve Masters became the second rider to stage a Testimonial meeting at Blunsdon in 2001 with a well-organised event won in scintillating fashion by Aussie ace Ryan Sullivan on 14 October. Indeed, 'Flyin' Ryan' opened the meeting in breathtaking fashion by clocking a super-fast 64.65 seconds to eclipse the track record that had been set by Gary Allan in August 1993.

After two years in the speedway wilderness, Swindon Sprockets returned to the track with a couple of late-season fifteen-heat challenge matches against Somerset and Eastbourne. Jointly managed by Peter Oakes (who had previously helped at Swindon in a consultancy capacity in 1979) and Kevin Hawkins, the side tasted victory in both meetings and, more importantly, the level of support paved the way for the Sprockets to enter the Conference Trophy in 2002.

SWINDON SOFT WATER ROBINS 2001

(Swindon's score shown first unless otherwise stated)

PREMIER LEAGUE

Opponents	Home	Away	Aggregate
Arena-Essex	W43-29	L43-47	W86-76
Berwick	W54-36	W50-40	W104-76
Edinburgh	W55-35	L43-47	W98-82
Exeter	W49-41	D45-45	W94-86
Glasgow	W55-35	W53-37	W108-72
Hull	W50-40	L38-52	L88-92
Isle of Wight	W59-31	L39-51	W98-82
Newcastle	W49-41	L33-57	L82-98
Newport	W52-38	W55-34	W107-72
Reading	W46-44	D45-45	W91-89
Sheffield	W53-37	L33-57	L86-94
Stoke	W65-25	L44-46	W109-71
Trelawny	W51-39	L40-50	W91-89
Workington	D45-45	L44-46	L89-91

PREMIER LEAGUE TABLE

Team	Mts	Won	Drn	Lst	For	Agn.	Pts	Bon.	Tot.
Newcastle	28	20	1	7	1,327.5	1,166.5	41	12	53
Hull	28	17	3	8	1,377	1,124	37	13	50
Sheffield	28	18	0	10	1,378	1,125	36	11	47
Isle of Wight	28	18	0	10	1,374	1,145	36	11	47
Swindon	28	16	3	9	1,331	1,170	35	10	45
Workington	28	16	2	10	1,263	1,256	34	8	42

Exeter	28	13	2	13	1,290	1,239	28	8	36
Edinburgh	28	13	1	14	1,257	1,242	27	8	35
Reading	28	12	3	13	1,272	1,250	27	6	33
Arena-Essex	28	12	1	15	1,230	1,269	25	5	30
Stoke	28	13	1	14	1,196	1,316	27	3	30
Berwick	28	10	1	17	1,204.5	1,317.5	21	4	25
Glasgow	28	10	0	18	1,131	1,369	20	3	23
Trelawny	28	6	1	21	1,075	1,447	13	2	15
Newport	28	6	1	21	1,115	1,385	13	1	14

LEAGUE AVERAGES

Rider	Mts	Rds	Pts	Bon.	Tot.	Avge	Maximums
Charlie Gjedde	1	5	15	0	15	12.00	1 full
Paul Thorp	1	4	12	0	12	12.00	1 full
Glenn Cunningham	3	14	29	2	31	8.86	–
Lawrence Hare	1	5	10	1	11	8.80	–
Olly Allen	14	54	105	7	112	8.30	–
Paul Fry	23	116	220	17	237	8.17	–
Claus Kristensen	26	119	219	16	235	7.90	1 full
Alan Mogridge	27	133	223	29	252	7.58	–
Neil Collins	3	14	24	2	26	7.43	–
Alun Rossiter	20	90	136	27	163	7.24	1 paid
Martin Dixon	28	129	185	40	225	6.98	1 paid
Mark Steel	7	30	38	6	44	5.87	–
Ritchie Hawkins	27	118	110	24	134	4.54	–
Krister Marsh	1	5	4	0	4	3.20	–
Lee Hodgson	1	3	1	0	1	1.33	–

YOUNG SHIELD

Opponents	Home	Away	Aggregate
Sheffield (Quarter-final)	W49-41	L32-58	L81-99

KNOCK-OUT CUP

Opponents	Home	Away	Aggregate
Glasgow (Round one)	W70-20	L42-45	W112-65
Workington (Quarter-final)	W50-40	L43-47	W93-87
Exeter (Semi-final)	W51-39	L38-52	L89-91

PREMIER TROPHY

Opponents	Home	Away	Aggregate
Arena-Essex	W58-32	W46-42	W104-74
Exeter	W48-41	L40-49	L88-90
Isle of Wight	W60-29	L42-48	W102-77
Newport	W52-38	W48-41	W100-79
Reading	W49-40	L42-48	W91-88
Trelawny	W68-22	L44-46	W112-68

PREMIER TROPHY (SOUTHERN SECTION) TABLE

Team	Mts	Won	Drn	Lst	For	Agn.	Pts	Bon.	Tot.
Swindon	12	8	0	4	597	476	16	5	21
Isle of Wight	12	7	1	4	548	522	15	4	19
Reading	12	7	0	5	592	486	14	4	18
Exeter	12	5	1	6	522	542	11	4	15
Arena-Essex	12	6	0	6	511	555	12	3	15
Trelawny	12	4	0	8	471	607	8	1	9
Newport	12	4	0	8	511	564	8	0	8

Note: Swindon progressed to the semi-final and subsequently also to the final.

Opponents	Home	Away	Aggregate
Workington (Semi-final)	W54-36	D45-45	W99-81
Sheffield (Final)	L37-53	L25-65	L62-118

CHALLENGE

Opponents	Home	Away
Swindon Past	W53-37	–

M4 TROPHY

Opponents	Home	Away	Aggregate
Newport	W43-29	W47-43	W90-72

ALFRED McALPINE HOMES PREMIER LEAGUE PAIRS CHAMPIONSHIP

(Staged at Workington)   Group A: Reading 25, Exeter 19, Sheffield 18, Swindon 18, Newport 10.

JAWA PREMIER LEAGUE RIDERS' CHAMPIONSHIP

(Staged at Coventry)   Paul Fry was fourth in the qualifying heats with 11 points and
subsequently finished fourth in semi-final.

2002

In 2002, Swindon unveiled a new club sponsor in Impact Exhibitions and Signs, while Peter Oakes was named as team manager, having done much to help budding youngsters on Blunsdon's centre-green training track the year before. As such, there was an accent on youth in the make-up of the side and only three riders were retained from 2001, namely Olly Allen, Ritchie Hawkins and Paul Fry, who took over as skipper. Joining the trio was Charlie Gjedde, a rider who had previously represented the club in 1998, while newcomers were Chris Neath and Paul Lee. The final place then went to sixteen-year-old Jason King, who had greatly impressed in the two Conference-level challenge matches held at the back end of 2001. This left Fry, at the age of thirty-seven, as the oldest team member by a long chalk, with Gjedde the next oldest – and he was only twenty-two!

Cheery Charlie Gjedde was to miss the start of the campaign, having injured his left Achilles' tendon while playing football in his native country in January. Thankfully, he only missed the opening home and away Premier Trophy matches against Newport, being adequately replaced by Alun Rossiter, who had been such a hit during the second half of 2001. Aside from Gjedde, there was also cause for concern over Ritchie Hawkins, who had toured Australia with Young Great Britain. The Peterborough-born youngster had performed reasonably well Down Under, but things went wrong in the sixth Test against Young Australia at Shepparton, Victoria on 26 January when, in heat fourteen, he dislocated a shoulder in a first-bend fall. Unfortunately, the repercussions of this were to affect both rider and club for almost the entire season.

While the Impact Robins picked up home wins in the Premier Trophy, they enjoyed just one success on their travels, winning 48-42 at Exeter on 1 April. Despite this, they still had a chance of qualifying for the semi-finals when they journeyed down to the Clay Country Moto Parc for their final group match against Trelawny on 23 April. However, after being in contention in the early stages, the boys in red and white slipped to a 49-41 defeat and it was therefore the Cornish side that topped the table, finishing a single point ahead of the Robins. The match marked the Swindon debut of Adam Allott, who came in as a temporary replacement at reserve for the below-par Ritchie Hawkins.

The good form at Blunsdon continued when the league schedule got underway, while away from home the Robins forced a 45-45 draw at Arena-Essex and also secured a 47-43 victory at Stoke. The Premier League programme was briefly interrupted by Knock-Out Cup activity and inopportune timing was to play a big part in Swindon losing narrowly on aggregate to Rye House. The first leg took place at the Abbey on 30 May and, significantly, Chris Neath was ruled out of action, having sustained a broken bone to his left hand while appearing in the Elite League for Wolverhampton the

Swindon Robins, 2002. From left to right, back row: Peter Toogood (Promoter), Olly Allen, Jason King, Ritchie Hawkins, Tommy Allen, Paul Lee, Peter Oakes (Team Manager). Front, kneeling: Chris Neath, Charlie Gjedde. On bike: Paul Fry.

Swindon Sprockets, 2002. From left to right, back row: Tom Brown, Mark Steel, Jack Gledhill, Tommy Allen. Front, kneeling: Simon Dyminski, Simon Walker. On bike: Jason King.

previous evening. Utilising rider replacement in his absence, the match ended all-square at 45-45, with the Rockets completing the job two evenings later, courtesy of a hard-fought 46-44 success.

Ritchie Hawkins returned to the side for a home encounter with Workington on 13 June as Swindon tracked their proposed starting septet for what turned out to be the one and only time in the league. Adam Allott had been inconsistent during his spell in the side, his scores ranging anywhere from 0 to 12 points and this was reflected in an average of 5.55. Just forty-eight hours after Hawkins' comeback, the club was dealt a huge body-blow at Berwick, when a freak heat three accident left Paul Fry nursing broken fibula and tibia bones in his right leg. Olly Allen was subsequently handed the club captaincy and the inspirational Fry was to sit out the remainder of the season, with a succession of guests brought in to cover his place. Showing his importance to the side, from the twelve league matches he had completed Fry had scored 119 points for a 9.67 average. Regrettably, more problems were just around the corner for Hawkins. On 20 June, the unlucky youngster sprained an ankle in an awkward fall against Arena-Essex at Blunsdon, and six days later at Hull he looped the loop in a meeting that was eventually abandoned, suffering knee ligament damage in the process. That meant another spell on the sidelines, although he bravely returned for a home match against Glasgow on 1 August and was to see out the rest of the term in determined fashion, finally averaging 3.62 from the sixteen league matches he appeared in.

Prior to the loss of Paul Fry, the Impact Robins had actually climbed to the head of the league standings by mid-May and although they remained in contention for some time, home losses to Newport and Newcastle effectively put them out of the title race. Given the injury to Fry and the problems endured by Ritchie Hawkins, a final league position of sixth wasn't too bad at all. Aside from the productive performances at Arena-Essex and Stoke as already mentioned, Swindon were victorious at Somerset and also gained revenge for their Knock-Out Cup exit by winning at Rye House, while the fixture at Trelawny was drawn. Their league position gave them a place in the Young Shield against Berwick, but the Robins' participation didn't last long, as the Bandits gained a quick-fire double, winning 49-41 at Blunsdon on 3 October before easing to a 52-38 success at Shielfield Park two nights later.

Paul Fry.

In the statistical run-down, Charlie Gjedde enjoyed a good year back in the Robins' colours, with 320 points yielding a league average of 8.94 as he thrilled the fans with his attacking style of racing. The Dane was the club's representative in the Premier League Riders' Championship at Belle Vue on 8 September, but he could only manage a solitary race win on his way to a 5-point tally. Olly Allen was the next in line and having battled back from injury in 2001 he had to overcome another broken bone to his right hand. This was sustained at the Sheffield-staged British Under-21 Final on 18 April when, in spite of considerable discomfort, he finished third, bettering his performance of the previous year by one position. Thankfully, Allen only missed a few of Swindon's meetings through the injury and also went on to reach the World Under-21 Final at Slany, Czech Republic on 7 September, when he scored 5 points. For the Robins, he completed twenty-nine league matches, totalling 277 points for an increased 8.47 average. Delving deeper into the side, Chris Neath had a penchant for being something of a heat fourteen specialist when sporting the number four race-jacket, yet Swindon supporters unfortunately never really saw the best of him at Blunsdon. As such, his final average was 6.39 and to his credit he vowed to come back and do better in 2003. Paul Lee, meanwhile, was a well-liked team member and although he served up the odd moment of brilliance along the way, an average of 5.05 could be regarded as a little disappointing from a lad with so much untapped potential. It was clearly a sharp learning curve for Jason King, but he plugged away and some useful performances gave him a creditable final average of exactly 4.00. There were also two appearances apiece for Simon Dyminski and Olly Allen's younger sibling, Tommy, who enjoyed a memorable debut at Glasgow on 3 June, when, in his first outing (heat two), he popped away from the gate and went on to record a fine win.

The Abbey hosted just one individual meeting during the season, with the staging of the Championship of Great Britain semi-final on 26 September. The Isle of Wight's Danny Bird showed his liking of the circuit to triumph with 12 points, while also progressing through were Olly Allen, Chris Harris and Leigh Lanham, each of whom tallied 11. Allen subsequently made his debut appearance in the final at Coventry on 12 October, notching a 4-point return.

Peter Oakes, as well as managing the senior team, was also in charge of the Sprockets as they embarked on a regular return to action in the Conference Trophy. Sponsored by Pro-Fit Flooring Specialists, the side won only three of their ten matches to occupy fifth place in the final table. The results weren't all that important, however, since it was all about the development of youth, a fact that was appreciated by the public, who responded with encouraging levels of support at Blunsdon. Jason King posted a 9.65 figure to sit on top of the averages, while 'old hand' Malcolm Holloway, such a positive influence on the youngsters, finished on 9.10. Other regulars included Tom Brown (7.57), Tommy Allen (6.15), Daniel King (6.06), Simon Dyminski (5.96), Simon Walker (5.33) and Jack Gledhill (2.06). Meanwhile, Mark Steel briefly made a comeback to the sport to average 9.20 from four matches and there were also limited outings for Ritchie Hawkins, Nick Lee, Nick Mallett and Matt Tutton, together with cousins Ashley and Wayne Holloway.

SWINDON IMPACT ROBINS 2002

(Swindon's score shown first unless otherwise stated)

PREMIER LEAGUE

Opponents	Home	Away	Aggregate
Arena-Essex	W49-41	D45-45	W94-86
Berwick	W47-43	L33-57	L80-100
Edinburgh	W54-36	L42-48	W96-84
Exeter	W51-39	L36-54	L87-93
Glasgow	W52-38	L44-45	W96-83
Hull	W47-43	L40-50	L87-93
Isle of Wight	W53-36	L37-53	W90-89
Newcastle	L44-46	L35-55	L79-101
Newport	L43-47	L41-49	L84-96
Reading	W50-40	L43-47	W93-87
Rye House	W55-35	W51-41	W106-76

Sheffield	W54-36	L43-48	W97-84
Somerset	W47-43	W49-43	W96-86
Stoke	W49-41	W47-43	W96-84
Trelawny	W59-31	D45-45	W104-76
Workington	W49-40	L40-50	L89-90

PREMIER LEAGUE TABLE

Team	Mts	Won	Drn	Lst	For	Agn.	Pts	Bon.	Tot.
Sheffield	32	20	1	11	1,612	1,268	41	15	56
Newcastle	32	21	1	10	1,501	1,364	43	13	56
Isle of Wight	32	21	1	10	1,542	1,328	43	12	55
Berwick	32	17	3	12	1,520	1,360	37	12	49
Hull	32	19	0	13	1,444	1,419	38	11	49
Swindon	32	17	2	13	1,474	1,408	36	10	46
Stoke	32	17	1	14	1,453	1,423	35	8	43
Reading	32	17	0	15	1,427	1,448	34	7	41
Edinburgh	32	14	4	14	1,425	1,450	32	8	40
Exeter	32	14	0	18	1,463	1,415	28	10	38
Arena-Essex	32	13	3	16	1,417	1,456	29	6	35
Newport	32	13	2	17	1,394	1,472	28	6	34
Rye House	32	13	2	17	1,373	1,496	28	5	33
Trelawny	32	13	1	18	1,342	1,540	27	4	31
Workington	32	12	3	17	1,368	1,518	27	3	30
Somerset	32	9	2	21	1,344	1,536	20	4	24
Glasgow	32	9	0	23	1,335	1,533	18	2	20

LEAGUE AVERAGES

Rider	Mts	Rds	Pts	Bon.	Tot.	Avge	Maximums
Paul Fry	12	55	119	14	133	9.67	2 paid
Andre Compton	2	10	22	2	24	9.60	–
Claus Kristensen	6	26	57	2	59	9.08	–
Charlie Gjedde	30	149	320	13	333	8.94	3 full; 2 paid
Olly Allen	29	135	277	9	286	8.47	1 full; 1 paid
Glenn Cunningham	4	19	37	3	40	8.42	–
Garry Stead	6	31	60	3	63	8.13	–
Adam Shields	1	6	11	1	12	8.00	–
Leigh Lanham	1	4	7	0	7	7.00	–
Davey Watt	1	4	6	1	7	7.00	–
Chris Neath	32	137	187	32	219	6.39	–
Paul Bentley	1	5	8	0	8	6.40	–
Ross Brady	1	6	9	0	9	6.00	–
Chris Harris	2	8	11	1	12	6.00	–
Adam Allott	10	44	51	10	61	5.55	–
Paul Lee	31	118	130	19	149	5.05	–
Aidan Collins	1	4	3	1	4	4.00	–
Jason King	31	116	99	17	116	4.00	–
Ritchie Hawkins	16	63	48	9	57	3.62	–
Chris Schramm	1	5	4	0	4	3.20	–
Tom Brown	1	3	1	1	2	2.67	–
Tommy Allen	2	8	4	0	4	2.00	–
Simon Dyminski	2	7	2	1	3	1.71	–

Note: Olly Allen's figures include one golden double ride (2 points), modified to normal score (i.e. 1 point).

YOUNG SHIELD

Opponents	Home	Away	Aggregate
Berwick (Quarter-final)	L41-49	L38-52	L79-101

KNOCK-OUT CUP

Opponents	Home	Away	Aggregate
Rye House (Round one)	D45-45	L44-46	L89-91

PREMIER TROPHY

Opponents	Home	Away	Aggregate
Exeter	W50-40	W48-42	W98-82
Newport	W48-42	L33-57	L81-99
Somerset	W48-43	L43-47	W91-90
Trelawny	W55-35	L41-49	W96-84

PREMIER TROPHY (WESTERN GROUP) TABLE

Team	Mts	Won	Drn	Lst	For	Agn.	Pts	Bon.	Tot.
Trelawny	8	5	1	2	383	336	11	3	14
Swindon	8	5	0	3	366	355	10	3	13
Newport	8	5	0	3	369	350	10	2	12
Somerset	8	3	1	4	347	374	7	1	8
Exeter	8	1	0	7	334	384	2	1	3

Note: Trelawny progressed to the semi-final.

CHALLENGE

Opponents	Home	Away
Rye House	–	L37-51

FOUR-TEAM TOURNAMENT

(Staged at Somerset)   Somerset 31, Swindon 26, Neil Collins' All-Stars 20, Exeter 19.

THREE COUNTIES TOURNAMENT

(First leg at Swindon)	Newport 32, Swindon 31, Somerset 26.
(Second leg at Newport)	Swindon 39, Newport 25, Somerset 25.
(Third leg at Somerset)	Somerset 37, Swindon 27, Newport 26.
Aggregate result	Swindon 97, Somerset 88, Newport 83.

PREMIER LEAGUE RIDERS' CHAMPIONSHIP

(Staged at Belle Vue)   Charlie Gjedde 5 points.

SWINDON PRO-FIT SPROCKETS

CONFERENCE TROPHY TABLE

Team	Mts	Won	Drn	Lst	For	Agn.	Pts	Bon.	Tot.
Mildenhall	10	8	0	2	525	375	16	4	20
Carmarthen	10	7	0	3	476	424	14	4	18
Buxton	10	6	0	4	498	398	12	4	16
Wimbledon	10	4	0	6	410	483	8	2	10
Swindon	10	3	0	7	438	464	6	1	7
Wolverhampton	10	2	0	8	345	548	4	0	4

2003

The commercial side of the sport reached a new high at Swindon in 2003 as Dave Prowse concluded a deal that brought Pebley Beach Suzuki on board as the team sponsor. For the first time in their fifty-five-year history, there was no red-breasted bird on the front of the race-jacket, the traditional club emblem being exchanged for the incoming sponsor's logo as the side became known as the Pebley Beach Swindon Robins. With the escalating costs of running the sport, the supporters recognised this as being the way forward and Pebley Beach dealer principal Dominic Threlfall was to become a regular and popular figure at the Abbey on race nights.

Going into the season, Peter Toogood and team manager Peter Oakes opted to retain the services

Swindon Robins, 2003. From left to right, back row: Peter Oakes (Team Manager), Charlie Gjedde, Ritchie Hawkins, Jamie Smith, Simon Dyminski, Olly Allen, Peter Toogood (Promoter). Front, kneeling: Chris Neath, Tommy Allen. On bike: Paul Fry.

of Olly Allen, Paul Fry, Charlie Gjedde, Ritchie Hawkins and Chris Neath. That meant just two changes to the 2002 line-up, with Jamie Smith and Tommy Allen coming into the side to replace Paul Lee and Jason King. Skipper Fry understandably made a tentative return following the leg injuries that curtailed his campaign the previous year, as Swindon began their fixtures in the ill-fated British League Cup. This was a new competition which brought together the Elite and Premier League sides and, although a good idea in essence, the rules regarding the make-up of teams appeared to be somewhat 'flexible', making it difficult to take seriously. The Robins participated in the 'D' group and, although further progression had long since been ruled out, they didn't actually complete their fixtures until entertaining Eastbourne on 7 September.

Swindon's interest in the Knock-Out Cup ended in round one, as they went down in both legs to the competition's eventual winners, the Isle of Wight. The Robins lost 54-38 in the away tie on 13 May, having gone into the match without the high-scoring Charlie Gjedde, who had sustained a hand injury in a pits accident while representing his 'doubling-up' side Oxford. Although the Dane roared back to plunder 18+1 points in the second leg at Blunsdon two days later, his superhuman efforts couldn't prevent a 51-49 defeat on the night.

Prior to their Knock-Out Cup exit, Swindon began the league programme on fire, posting away successes at Somerset and King's Lynn as they won four out of their first five meetings to get among the early pacesetters. At Rye House on 31 May, a thrilling 45.5-44.5 victory kept them in contention, but with no further wins on the road until much later on they were reliant on good home form to keep them in the hunt. This it did and the Pebley Beach Robins were to occupy pole position in early July, albeit briefly, until injuries, as so often in the past, again took their toll on the club. The unlucky Ritchie Hawkins had been the first to suffer when he took a knock to the ankle in a home encounter with Newcastle on 19 June and subsequently spent a couple of weeks on the sidelines. In the match he returned, at home to Somerset on 3 July, it was Jamie Smith's turn to sustain an injury, when a fall saw the lanky racer receive torn muscles and ligament damage to the left leg. Swindon were to use the rider-replacement facility while he recovered, but in the meantime there was more anguish for Hawkins when Exeter visited the Abbey on 17 July. Brought into the opening heat for

The Four-Team Champions of 2003. From left to right, back row: Paul Fry, Charlie Gjedde. Front, kneeling: Chris Neath, Olly Allen, Jamie Smith.

one of Smith's rider-replacement outings, the teenager came down heavily in the run to the first corner, suffering head and neck injuries.

Olly Allen was to have more than his fair share of injury problems too, and these began at the tight Wimbledon circuit on 9 July when he took a number of bangs while representing Great Britain Under-21s against their Swedish counterparts. Although he turned out for the Robins the following evening in the British League Cup against Reading, he clearly looked uncomfortable and after bravely posting race victories in his first two programmed outings he was signed off by the track doctor. The elder of the Allen brothers was subsequently ruled out of Swindon's three-day tour of Scotland/Northumberland and, with Jamie Smith also missing through his aforementioned leg injury, the club was far from being in an ideal situation. Matters got even worse when Tommy Allen's sojourn ended, virtually as soon as it had begun, when he injured an elbow on the first corner of his initial ride at Edinburgh. The Robins were to lose 48-42 to the eventual League Champions and were left to rue what might have been, as narrow 47-43 and 46-44 defeats followed at Berwick and Glasgow respectively. Even those who made guest appearances for Swindon didn't escape injury, as Edinburgh's Frede Schott found when he broke a collarbone in a dramatic finish to the latterly mentioned match at Glasgow on 13 July.

Unfortunately, Olly Allen was in the wars again at the Abbey on 21 August, when he broke a scaphoid in heat one against bogey side the Isle of Wight. This was most certainly a contributory factor in the Islanders becoming the only side to triumph in the league at Blunsdon (47-43), following their Knock-Out Cup victory and an earlier draw in the British League Cup. Despite the enforced absence of the senior Allen, the Pebley Beach Robins bounced back with away wins

Swindon Sprockets, 2003. From left to right, back row: Kevin Hawkins (Reserve Team Manager), Tommy Allen, Simon Dyminski, Malcolm Holloway, Jack Gledhill, Peter Oakes (Team Manager). Front row, kneeling: Lee Smart, Darren Smith, Ritchie Hawkins.

at Newport and Reading on successive nights, as respective guests Mark Lemon and Chris Harris ably filled the vacancy. Allen Mk 1 returned on 18 September and almost scored a maximum against King's Lynn, dropping a single point from four starts. Regrettably, it was to be his last meeting of the term in Swindon colours, since he suffered a recurrence of his wrist injury, ironically while riding at King's Lynn in the Pride of the East meeting just six days later. Coincidentally, Jamie Smith's season also ended in the big individual meeting at the Norfolk Arena when, in a first heat fall, he aggravated the injury to his left leg and also took a hefty knock to the right ankle.

Following the injuries that left the side without Olly Allen and Jamie Smith, Newport came to Blunsdon on 25 September and forced a 45-45 draw as the Robins dropped their only other home point of the year. Given their luck, or lack of it, Swindon did well to finish fourth in the standings, representing an improvement of two places on 2002. Leading the side from the front throughout was Charlie Gjedde, whose tally of 329 points yielded a 9.79 average and gave him seventh position in the entire Premier League figures. During the year, he furthered his career when recording 4 points as a wildcard entrant in his debut Grand Prix at Parken, Denmark on 28 June. There was much to be learned from the experience and also that of the World Cup Final at Vojens, Denmark on 9 August, when he scored 12 points and helped his country finish in third place. Pushing Gjedde for top spot in the Swindon statistics was Olly Allen and, despite being hampered by injury, he did well to finish just behind on a 9.52 average. Meanwhile Chris Neath enjoyed a much better time of it, mastering the Abbey raceway and raising his final figure to 7.82. Paul Fry had an up-and-down year and although this was to be expected, he still remained ever present and posted a solid 7.55 average. Key team member Jamie Smith suffered through injury and, as a result, never really got the chance to shine, as reflected in a 5.68 average. Delving down to the bottom end of the side, there was the most unfortunate Ritchie Hawkins, who boldly returned seven weeks after the knock to his head against Exeter, only to quickly end his comeback and temporarily quit the sport in protest at being refused permission to ride for the Sprockets in a Conference-level challenge match at Weymouth on 12 September. He went out with a 4.41 average and, although an improvement on the previous year, the continued bangs had clearly sapped the confidence and enthusiasm of his initial year with the club in 2001. Tommy Allen might only have averaged 2.72, but he rode with a lot of fire and undoubtedly possessed the right attributes to go a long way in the sport. Mention must also be made of forty-six-year-old warhorse Malcolm Holloway, who had joined Trelawny in June, yet still made eleven guest appearances at reserve for the Robins, attaining a more-than-satisfactory 4.74 average.

For a second time, Blunsdon hosted the Championship of Great Britain semi-final on 1 May, and this saw the Isle of Wight's Danny Bird repeat his success of the previous year. Although both Paul Fry and Chris Neath finished level with Bird on 12 points, the podium positions were decided on the count-back system, with Swindon's captain placed in second spot, ahead of his teammate. The Robins were to have three riders in the final at Eastbourne on 5 July, with Olly Allen gaining a reprieve (having notched only 7 points in the semi-final) after several riders had pulled out through injury. All three were outclassed in the big event though, Allen doing the best in scoring 7 points, just one more than Neath, while Fry totalled 3. One other individual event to take place at the Abbey was Leigh Adams' Testimonial meeting on 31 July, when a large crowd paid tribute to a giant of the modern era, with a quality line-up assembled in his honour. Fittingly, it was Adams himself who eventually won the grand final, defeating Jason Lyons, Joe Screen and Travis McGowan. Staying with individual events, both Jamie Smith and Olly Allen made it through to the World Under-21 Championship Final at Kumla, Sweden on 13 September. Neither enjoyed much luck on the big day, however, Smith scoring 5 points and Allen notching just 2. Finally, Paul Fry was Swindon's representative in the Premier League Riders' Championship at Sheffield on 28 September, but a tally of 5 points left him well down the field.

Fortune didn't quite shine on Swindon in the Cumbrian Seafoods-sponsored Premier League Pairs Championship at Workington on 19 July. Charlie Gjedde was partnered by Olly Allen for the event and between them the duo netted 20 points in their group, falling just a single point short of the totals achieved by King's Lynn and host club Workington as both progressed to the semi-final stage. Shortly afterwards, a big day out occurred at Blunsdon on 27 July with the staging of the Premier League Four-Team Championship, jointly sponsored by Suzuki dealers Pebley Beach and Artdeans. Run on a balmy Sunday afternoon, a large audience saw the Robins use home-track advantage to good effect as they stormed to victory in the semi-final ahead of Glasgow, Edinburgh and the Isle of Wight, led by a brace of wins from Gjedde. The final subsequently proved a tense affair but, spurred on by their supporters, Swindon accumulated 25 points to come out on top and land the silverware from Trelawny (22), Newport (21) and Glasgow (4), with Gjedde brilliantly taking his personal total of wins on the day to five out of five.

Having enjoyed good support for the Sprockets in 2002, Swindon entered their junior team in the Conference League, with Peter Oakes' side again sponsored by Pro-Fit. This meant more speedway fixtures at Blunsdon, with the stock cars making way for the increased level of two-wheeled activity. Malcolm Holloway was a natural leader for the youngsters, but when he linked with Premier League Trelawny he was precluded from continuing with the Sprockets. Prior to that the side had also lost the services of Ritchie Hawkins, due to his rolling average being above 4 points per match for Swindon's senior team. Upon Holloway's departure, Glaswegian Barry Campbell took over the captaincy and did an admirable job as the young side eventually finished in fifth place. Hawkins sat on top of the averages with a 10.25 figure from the three matches he appeared in, while a further half-dozen riders finished in excess of 6 points per match: Tommy Allen (9.42), Holloway (9.16), Simon Walker (7.41), Campbell (7.41), Simon Dyminski (7.14) and Adam Roynon (6.52). Others to represent the Pro-Fit Sprockets were Jack Gledhill, Nick Lee, Simon Paget, Lee Smart and Darren Smith, while several riders made but a solitary appearance apiece, namely Mark Baseby, Jamie Holmes, Andrew Jackson, Billy Legg, Scott Nettleship and Tim Warnes. In the Elmside & Bates-sponsored Conference League Riders' Championship, staged at Rye House on 30 August, it was the younger Allen who represented Swindon, scoring 3 points. It transpired that an historic event coincided with the Sprockets' fixture on 11 September, when they faced Newport and Mildenhall in a double-header; the meeting being the 1,500th held at Blunsdon.

The season provided much in way of entertainment for the regular patrons at the Abbey, with a total of thirty-five meetings staged. This was the third highest figure in fifty-five successive seasons of racing, being bettered only by totals of thirty-seven in 1979 and thirty-six in 1982.

For promoter Peter Toogood, it was to be his last year in the Blunsdon hot seat and although the odd whisper had done the rounds, no-one was really expecting his departure when it came. Indeed, the dust had only just settled on the season when a deal was concluded in early November that saw the club taken over by Terry Russell – a man who first got involved in the promoting side of the sport at National League level with Crayford in 1981 and had latterly been a major player in bringing live Elite League action into millions of homes on Sky TV, beginning in 1999.

PEBLEY BEACH SWINDON ROBINS 2003

(Swindon's score shown first unless otherwise stated)

PREMIER LEAGUE

Opponents	Home	Away	Aggregate
Arena-Essex	W49-41	L42-51	L91-92
Berwick	W57-26	L43-47	W100-73
Edinburgh	W51-39	L42-48	W93-87
Exeter	W48-36	L41-49	W89-85
Glasgow	W49-41	L44-46	W93-87
Hull	W56-34	L42-48	W98-82
Isle of Wight	L43-47	L40-50	L83-97
King's Lynn	W52-37	W46-44	W98-81
Newcastle	W50-42	L37-53	L87-95
Newport	D45-45	W50-40	W95-85
Reading	W51-39	W48-42	W99-81
Rye House	W49-41	W45.5-44.5	W94.5-85.5
Sheffield	W50-40	L36-54	L86-94
Somerset	W60-30	W48-42	W108-72
Stoke	W55-35	L44-46	W99-81
Trelawny	W48-42	L42-48	D90-90
Workington	W52-37	L43-47	W95-84

Notes: The home match v. Berwick originally ended 57-33, but the result was subsequently amended as guest Lee Smethills' appearance in the visiting side was deemed ineligible. Following the match at Trelawny, a restarted bonus point run-off saw Chris Harris defeat Swindon reserve Ritchie Hawkins after Olly Allen had crashed out at the first attempt. The home match v. Exeter was abandoned after heat fourteen, with the result permitted to stand.

PREMIER LEAGUE TABLE

Team	Mts	Won	Drn	Lst	For	Agn.	Pts	Bon.	Tot.
Edinburgh	34	26	0	8	1,653	1,393	52	14	66
Sheffield	34	22	0	12	1,655	1,397	44	13	57
Isle of Wight	34	22	0	12	1,603	1,463	44	12	56
Swindon	34	20	1	13	1,598.5	1,451.5	41	12	53
Berwick	34	20	1	13	1,563	1,465	41	12	53
King's Lynn	34	19	1	14	1,598	1,448	39	13	52
Arena-Essex	34	19	0	15	1,609	1,421	38	13	51
Trelawny	34	19	0	15	1,599.5	1,470.5	38	12	50
Workington	34	19	2	13	1,551	1,489	40	9	49
Newport	34	17	2	15	1,504	1,546	36	8	44
Newcastle	34	17	0	17	1,525	1,518	34	9	43
Glasgow	34	17	2	15	1,479	1,529	36	7	43
Exeter	34	13	0	21	1,435	1,592	26	5	31
Rye House	34	12	1	21	1,441	1,612	25	5	30
Stoke	34	10	1	23	1,443	1,597	21	3	24
Reading	34	9	2	23	1,404	1,653	20	2	22
Somerset	34	9	2	23	1,357	1,705	20	2	22
Hull	34	8	1	25	1,395	1,663	17	2	19

LEAGUE AVERAGES

Rider	Mts	Rds	Pts	Bon.	Tot.	Avge	Maximums
Brent Werner	1	5	12	1	13	10.40	–
Simon Stead	2	7	18	0	18	10.29	1 full
Frede Schott	2	12	28	2	30	10.00	–
Charlie Gjedde	28	143	329	21	350	9.79	1 full; 2 paid

Olly Allen	23	105	242	8	250	9.52	1 full; 1 paid
Chris Harris	6	29	63	6	69	9.52	1 full; 1 paid
Mark Lemon	1	5	11	0	11	8.80	–
Kevin Little	1	5	9	1	10	8.00	–
Chris Neath	33	146	261.5	24	285.5	7.82	1 full
Paul Fry	34	160	272	30	302	7.55	1 paid
Leigh Lanham	1	5	9	0	9	7.20	–
Garry Stead	1	5	9	0	9	7.20	–
Antonio Lindback	1	4	6	0	6	6.00	–
Jamie Smith	24	93	116	16	132	5.68	–
Benji Compton	1	3	2	2	4	5.33	–
Malcolm Holloway	11	54	47	17	64	4.74	–
Ritchie Hawkins	19	79	77	10	87	4.41	–
Craig Branney	1	3	2	1	3	4.00	–
Daniel King	1	4	4	0	4	4.00	–
Tommy Allen	32	128	70	17	87	2.72	–
Adam Allott	1	5	3	0	3	2.40	–
Simon Cartwright	1	6	3	0	3	2.00	–
Carl Wilkinson	1	6	2	1	3	2.00	–
Danny Norton	1	3	0	0	0	0.00	–
Simon Paget	1	2	0	0	0	0.00	–

Note: Charlie Gjedde's figures include one golden double ride (6 points), modified to the normal score (i.e. 3 points).

KNOCK-OUT CUP

Opponents	Home	Away	Aggregate
Isle of Wight (Round one)	L49-51	L38-54	L87-105

BRITISH LEAGUE CUP

Opponents	Home	Away	Aggregate
Eastbourne	W51-39	L37-52	L88-91
Isle of Wight	D45-45	L41-49	L86-94
Oxford	W48-37	L40-50	W88-87
Reading	W52-38	D45-45	W97-83

Note: The home match against Oxford originally ended 48-41 but the result was subsequently amended as Lukasz Jankowski's appearance in the visiting side was deemed ineligible.

BRITISH LEAGUE CUP (GROUP D) TABLE

Team	Mts	Won	Drn	Lst	For	Agn.	Pts	Bon.	Tot.
Eastbourne	8	5	2	1	393	322	12	4	16
Isle of Wight	8	4	2	2	366	353	10	2	12
Oxford	8	4	1	3	366	343	9	2	11
Swindon	8	3	2	3	359	355	8	2	10
Reading	8	0	1	7	306	417	1	0	1

Note: Eastbourne progressed to the quarter-finals.

M4 TROPHY

Opponents	Home	Away	Aggregate
Newport	D45-45	L40-50	L85-95
Reading	W55-35	D45-45	W100-80

M4 TROPHY TABLE

Team	Mts	Won	Drn	Lst	For	Agn.	Pts	Bon.	Tot.
Swindon	4	1	2	1	185	175	4	1	5
Newport	4	1	2	1	184	176	4	1	5
Reading	4	1	2	1	171	189	4	1	5

Note: With all three sides finishing level on 5 points apiece it was decided to replay the competition, although in the event this never took place.

SUZUKI PREMIER LEAGUE FOUR-TEAM CHAMPIONSHIP

(Staged at Swindon)　　First semi-final: Swindon 15, Glasgow 12, Edinburgh 10, Isle of Wight 10.
Final: Swindon 25, Trelawny 22, Newport 21, Glasgow 4.

THREE-TEAM TOURNAMENT

(Staged at King's Lynn)　　King's Lynn 48, Swindon 32, Hull 28.

CUMBRIAN SEAFOODS PREMIER LEAGUE PAIRS CHAMPIONSHIP

(Staged at Workington)　　Group B: King's Lynn 21, Workington 21, Swindon 20, Trelawny 19, Arena-Essex 9.

PREMIER LEAGUE RIDERS' CHAMPIONSHIP

(Staged at Sheffield)　　Paul Fry 5 points.

SWINDON PRO-FIT SPROCKETS

CONFERENCE LEAGUE TABLE

Team	Mts	Won	Drn	Lst	For	Agn.	Pts	Bon.	Tot.
Mildenhall	24	18	1	5	1,236	917	37	10	47
Rye House	24	18	0	6	1,178	936	36	9	45
Oxford	24	14	0	10	1,179	959	28	11	39
Boston	24	15	0	9	1,103	1,017	30	8	38
Swindon	24	14	0	10	1,042	1,036	28	5	33
Buxton	24	12	1	11	1,095	1,054	25	7	32
Newcastle	24	13	0	11	1,072	1,070	26	5	31
Sheffield	24	10	2	12	1,115	1,016	22	8	30
Wimbledon	24	9	1	14	1,028	1,126	19	5	24
Wolverhampton	24	10	1	13	1,005	1,116	21	2	23
Carmarthen	24	8	0	16	956	1,177	16	4	20
Peterborough	24	6	1	17	950	1,187	13	3	16
Newport	24	5	1	18	895	1,243	11	1	12

2004

Terry Russell's arrival as club owner, under the banner of Go Speed Ltd, meant a return to the Elite League for the Pebley Beach Robins. The incoming head man's first appointment was to install Alun Rossiter as co-promoter and team manager. To say Rosco accepted the position with relish would be an understatement, since it completed an amazing journey that had seen him assume nearly every possible role with Swindon, having first been involved as the club's mascot at just four years of age. He had subsequently been a rider, captain, announcer, presenter, mechanic and training instructor, prior to his new dual role… and all this before the age of forty! Rossiter immediately set about a programme of revamping the track surface and sprucing up the pits area. This was to pay dividends handsomely, particularly the work on the racing strip, which was to serve up some terrific action for the Blunsdon faithful.

Part of Terry Russell's deal was to acquire three top-notch riding assets in Leigh Adams, Charlie Gjedde and Olly Allen from previous promoter Peter Toogood. All three were to represent the Robins in their elevation back to the top flight, although in terms of being the first to sign a contract they were beaten to the punch by extrovert Australian Steve Johnston. A new grading system had been introduced to help both Swindon and Arena-Essex move smoothly up from the Premier League and 'Johno' was seen by Alun Rossiter as an ideal team man, capable of increasing his incoming 6.17 green-sheet average. Adams, having enjoyed two previous spells with the club, was the next to agree terms. He returned to the fold after a glorious 2003 campaign with Poole, which had seen the Dorset side scoop every available trophy – winning the League Championship, the Knock-Out Cup and the British League Cup. Allen and Gjedde quickly followed before Rosco made a double swoop on Poole, signing highly rated Swede David Ruud and fast-trapping Pole Krzysztof Kasprzak on loan. With one space to fill at reserve, Rosco made the most of the 'doubling-up' rules, firstly bringing in Claus Kristensen of Berwick, closely followed by Sheffield's Andy Moore, to share the role. Kristensen was very popular with the fans, having previously represented the club in 2000 and 2001. Meanwhile, completing the squad at numbers eight and nine respectively were Glenn Cunningham and Steve Masters. The side had a very competitive look about it and was hotly tipped to do well, with only Poole rated higher; the Pirates being 5/2 favourites for the league title with bookmakers William Hill, while the Robins looked a good bet at 5/1.

The season began early, with the Robins suffering a 51-39 reverse at a very chilly Poole in the first leg of the Champagne Stakes on 10 March. However, it was positively warm in Dorset compared with the Arctic conditions that prevailed for the return match at Blunsdon the following evening. With heavy snow falling, the track quickly resembled a picturesque Christmas card scene and the meeting was abandoned after just two heats. The weather was to play a major part in Swindon's season, leading to Alun Rossiter being dubbed with a new nickname, that of 'Rain Man', a title he sportingly accepted in the humorous manner it was intended. Aside from the match against Poole, two further home meetings were abandoned without a conclusive result, while, inclusive of the Sprockets fixtures, eleven were postponed. This gave an unprecedented total of fourteen wasted race days, easily surpassing the previous highest total of eight in 1993.

Changes to the management didn't automatically signal an end to the injury jinx that had dogged Swindon over the years. The club hadn't even embarked on their official fixtures when news came through from Poland that Krzysztof Kasprzak had suffered concussion, facial injuries and a fractured right wrist in a dreadful accident during the Criterion of Aces individual event at Bydgoszcz on 21 March. It was clear that the rider was going to be out of action for quite a while, so Alun Rossiter acted fast to engage the services of Andy Smith, for what was his third stint in the Robins' colours.

As touched on previously, the Abbey raceway, looking resplendent with its new air safety barrier in place, was to provide racing to drool over – a case in point occurring on 11 April, with the staging of the inaugural Elite League Pairs Championship, sponsored by Suzuki and supported by Pebley Beach. In front of a packed audience and screened live by Sky Sports, the circuit stood up brilliantly to twenty-four heats, culminating in home duo Leigh Adams and Charlie Gjedde taking victory from the Belle Vue pairing of Jason Crump and Joe Screen in the final.

History was made on 27 April when, for the first time in their fifty-six years of activity, the Robins made the journey to Norkopping, Sweden in order to face Vargarna in what was their debut match outside the British Isles. With Andreas Bergstrom making up the side at number seven, Swindon acquitted themselves well to the 279-metre raceway and ran out comfortable 55-41 victors. Changing sides, Charlie Gjedde returned to race for Vargarna exactly one week later in a Swedish Elite League fixture *v.* Indianerna, but unfortunately a heat ten fall left him with a broken right ankle. Several riders were mooted as possible stopgap replacements for the Dane, including Bohumil Brhel, Jaroslaw Hampel and Niklas Klingberg, but nothing came to fruition and the Robins were to soldier on, by and large unsatisfactorily, using the rider-replacement facility.

Swindon's league form had already been indifferent in the early stages of the campaign and a narrow 47-46 loss at home to Belle Vue came as a big blow on 22 April. Claus Kristensen had found points hard to come by at the higher grade of racing and although Andy Moore had stormed to a brilliant 8+2 return from the home match against Oxford on 8 April, he was rarely available for Blunsdon meetings due to the same Thursday race night of his parent club, Sheffield. As such, Alun Rossiter decided to dispense with the 'doubling-up' reserve and in came Pole Rafal Kurmanski, a much-sought rider who had finished seventh in previous season's World Under-21 Final. A look at the vital statistics showed Rosco to be correct with his decision, Moore having averaged 4.44 from four matches, while Kristensen's three appearances had yielded a disappointing 2.00 figure. Kurmanski duly arrived on these shores to make his club debut in an Elite League match at Poole on 12 May and, although only able to speak limited English, he was evidently happy to be part of the Robins' set-up. Following the return fixture against the Pirates, during which the knowledgeable Abbey regulars

really took to him, the lad who hailed from Zielona Gora made what was to be his third and final appearance for Swindon in a home match against Eastbourne on 27 May. After starting with a third-bend fall in heat two, he recovered brilliantly to take victory five races later, when shepherded home by Leigh Adams. The youngster was then on the receiving end of a 5-1 in heat eleven, but finished in style by leading partner Andy Smith across the line for a match-winning 5-1 in the penultimate race. The joy was there for all to see as he punched the air and, when he returned to the pits, there was an infectious grin from ear-to-ear. The next morning, Alun Rossiter helped to bandage a grazed leg that Kurmanski had sustained in his heat two tumble, before the rider left for his homeland. Tragically, in the early afternoon of Sunday 30 May came the news that he had taken his own life. It was a terrible shock to everyone connected with the club and certainly put any unfavourable on-track results into perspective. Although deeply saddened, Swindon rode with great passion to triumph 47-43 at Coventry the evening following the dreadful news; the win was fittingly dedicated to the memory of the likeable Pole, who had totalled 13 points from his three matches for a 4.67 average.

In what had become a managerial baptism of fire, Alun Rossiter again had to seek out a rider and he initially sought permission to reintroduce the fit-again Krzysztof Kasprzak. This would have meant regrading Kasprzak, who had a slightly higher average than that of the late Rafal Kurmanski, but although sympathetic to Swindon's plight the BSPA Management Committee vetoed the idea. Rosco also considered the option of dropping either Andy Smith, who had initially come into the side as temporary cover for Kasprzak, or the inconsistent David Ruud. However, he decided to stick with Smith and 'Rodney', as Ruud had become known, with Kasprzak subsequently recalled by Poole. There was a breakthrough at the end of June though, when Peter Ljung came on board via Eastbourne, initially as a guest and then as a full club asset. The Swede was to begin well and played a starring role in a 46-30 victory in a rain-affected league match at Peterborough on 7 July, scoring 14+3 points.

Charlie Gjedde returned in mid-July and, for a short time, the Pebley Beach Robins tracked a full-strength team secured some notable away results, winning 48-45 at Arena-Essex and drawing 45-45 at Eastbourne in league encounters, not to mention an amazing 47-46 challenge match victory at

Opposite: *Winners of the inaugural Elite League Pairs Championship. From left to right: Charlie Gjedde, Alun Rossiter (Team Manager), Leigh Adams.*

Right: *Likeable Pole Rafal Kurmanski, who tragically took his own life in May 2004, having made just three league appearances for the Robins.*

Poole. The drawn meeting at Eastbourne took place on 6 September and spelt the end of the season for Olly Allen, after he sustained a back injury in a frightening heat fourteen smash. The long-serving youngster, in his sixth year with the club, had endured a nightmare term, suffering several bad knocks, which began in the home match against Oxford on 8 April, when he awkwardly hit the air safety barrier at full tilt.

Given their problems, Swindon did well to finish the league campaign in sixth position, only just missing out on a place in the Play-Offs to local rivals Oxford. The Robins at least had some late-season interest in the Knock-Out Cup since, having dismissed Wolverhampton from round one on 6 May, they didn't tackle Belle Vue in the quarter-final until 23 September. A 48-42 first leg success at Blunsdon wasn't generally considered a sufficient advantage for the return match but, like Swindon, the Manchester outfit had struggled against the elements, with many meetings postponed at their Kirkmanshulme Lane venue. Unfortunately for the Aces the second leg was twice called off due to inclement weather and with time running out on the season, the BSPA decreed that the Robins should progress through by virtue of their 6-point lead from the first leg of the tie. That put the Wiltshire side into the semi-final against Poole and a quick exit followed as they were trounced 61-30 at Wimborne Road on 6 October, prior to claiming a consolation 53-40 success in the second leg at the Abbey the following evening.

Running through the regular riders, it is impossible to start with anyone else but Leigh Adams, who was absolutely magnificent. The Aussie began the season on fire, reeling off successive full maximums in each of the first five league matches. The sheer speed he generated at Blunsdon was awesome, as he made an all-out assault on the track record, eventually lowering it to 64.46 seconds in another powerhouse performance against Poole on 13 May. He went on to total fifteen maximums (12 full and 3 paid), while accumulating 461 points from thirty-four matches for a fabulous 10.94 average – a figure that put him head and shoulders above everyone else in the entire Elite League. Naturally, Adams was the Swindon

Swindon Robins, 2004. From left to right, back row: Alun Rossiter (Team Manager), Glenn Cunningham, Steve Johnston, Krzysztof Kasprzak, Claus Kristensen, Olly Allen, Charlie Gjedde. Front, kneeling: Andrew Moore, David Ruud. On bike: Leigh Adams.

representative at the Poole-staged Elite League Riders' Championship on 17 October, when 9 points unfortunately wasn't enough for him to progress beyond the qualifying round. On the World stage, he began what was his ninth Grand Prix series in style, winning the first round at Stockholm, Sweden on 1 May. Regrettably, although he reached at least the semi-final stage in the other eight rounds, he was unable to post another victory and a total of 131 points gave him fourth place overall, equalling the highest finish he had achieved in each of the two previous seasons. Looking down the line, Charlie Gjedde came back well from his injury to finish second in the Swindon averages (7.21) while, with the inclusion of a 12+2 return from his initial match as a guest against Peterborough at Blunsdon on 28 June, Peter Ljung nipped into third spot (7.00). Steve Johnston increased his starting average to 6.94 and made many friends with his exuberant personality and on-track battling. However, during Gjedde's absence, the extra responsibility created too much strain and prevented him attaining a higher figure. Meanwhile, pleasant though he was, David Ruud proved a real frustration, possessing much in the way of ability, yet lacking almost completely in confidence. His scores fluctuated from 0 to 16+1, as he averaged 6.05 and aside from the immaculate Adams he was the only other rider to net an unbeaten tally, when scoring 13+2 points from five starts at home to Ipswich on 1 July. Veteran racer Andy Smith, in what was remarkably his twenty-third season in the saddle, served up plenty of thrills on his way to a 5.77 average. Not renowned for his gating ability, the popular Smudger picked up many points from the back and although his form tailed off in the latter half of the season, a major contributory factor was an alarming third-bend spill in the away success at Peterborough on 7 July, when he received severe lacerations to the left leg. Turning attentions to Olly Allen, despite the knocks he received the youngster somehow managed to complete thirty-one league matches for a lowly 3.68 average in what can only be described as a confidence-draining year for one with so much talent. Finally, squad members Glenn Cunningham and Steve Masters found the demands of Elite League racing too much when called into service, averaging 3.10 and 2.35 respectively.

For a second successive year Swindon operated a junior side in the Conference League, with the Sprockets receiving backing from Artdeans Motorcycle & Scooter Centre. Martin Satchell, a

Swindon Sprockets, 2004. From left to right, back row: Simon Walker, Marc Andrews, James Purchase, Jamie Courtney, Danny Warwick, Nathan Irwin, Martin Satchell (Team Manager). Front, kneeling: Daniel Harding, Chris Johnson. On bike: Malcolm Holloway.

former Sprocket himself, who also made six league appearances for the senior Swindon side in 1981, enthusiastically took on the role of team manager. However, having gained experience in the pits by working alongside Bob Webb as machine examiner at Blunsdon since 2002, 'Satch' faced a daunting task, virtually having to build a new team from scratch. With Trelawny having unfortunately closed down and no other Premier League takers, Malcolm Holloway returned to captain the side, while Simon Walker was the only other link with the previous year's line-up... and he was on the injured list when the fixtures kicked off. As Satchell juggled his troops, the Team Artdeans Sprockets, as they were called, lost their first eight league matches on the bounce. The breakthrough was a surprise when it finally came, at second-in-the-table Boston on 11 July, with Swindon winning 47-43. They were to hold their own for the rest of the season, being victorious on another seven occasions to finish tenth in the standings. Although this might not have been anything to write home about, Satchell was to be applauded for sticking with the youngsters in the true spirit of the Conference League.

Australian Trevor Harding topped the averages on 11.00, albeit from just four matches, with Simon Walker next in line on 8.96, having overcome bone damage to his left ankle. The evergreen Malcolm Holloway posted an 8.82 figure, but ended the term prematurely, having suffered several fractures to the vertebrae, two broken ribs and a broken thumb in a nasty smash at Newport on 26 September. Lanky Chris Johnson showed real potential in reaching a 7.95 average and it was a shame that his season was also cut short, when he dislocated his right hip in a spill during the home match against Stoke on 12 September. Mark Thompson was one of three riders that Martin Satchell snapped up from Weymouth and he was both professionally set-up and an excellent team man. Tommo averaged 7.47, but his season was ruined by a broken wrist, suffered while riding at Ashfield in a Premier League match for Glasgow against Reading on 25 July. Although the Essex boy bravely returned late on, he was far from fit and his comeback ended during the same match that halted Holloway's campaign. The other two lads to arrive from Weymouth were Danny Warwick and Nathan Irwin, who finished with figures of 6.58 and 5.69 respectively. Both were extremely well liked, with Warwick being the only team member to remain ever-present, while Irwin, although profoundly deaf, had a penchant for stalking his prey before successfully passing in the latter stages of many a race, as he became a firm favourite at Blunsdon and deservedly scooped the Rider of the Year award. Several youngsters played a part in the season: Jamie Courtney (5.71), who relocated to Oxford after four matches; James Purchase (3.72), the son of former Oxford promoters Steve and Vanessa; Steve Braidford (3.56), whose season was blighted by injury; Daniel Harding (2.60), the younger brother of Trevor; plus the Poole-born duo of Marc Andrews (2.00) and Jordan Frampton (1.88). Meanwhile, with all the injuries, others who stepped in to appear for the side were Danny Betson, Wayne Carter, Martin Elliott, Cal McDade, John Morrison and Jason Prynne.

Unfortunately, support for the junior side was thin on the ground and, with great regret it was later announced that the Sprockets would not be running in 2005, due to the loss of a significant sum of money. Irrespective of exciting on-track action, the poor attendances could be partially attributed to the widening differential between the Conference League and the Elite League; compared to what it was with Premier League racing, when fans were able to see the reserve riders from the PL team in action at Conference League level. Still, it's not the first time the Sprockets have taken a sabbatical, so who knows? They may yet rise from the ashes again in the future.

One last thing worth mentioning that occurred during a busy year in the life of Swindon Speedway was an SCB track inspection, carried out by Colin Meredith on 6 May. This found everything to be in good order at the Abbey and the racing strip was remeasured at 363-metres in length.

PEBLEY BEACH SWINDON ROBINS 2004

(Swindon's score shown first unless otherwise stated)

SKY BET ELITE LEAGUE 'A'

Opponents	Home	Away	Aggregate
Arena-Essex	W47-42	L43-49	L90-91
Belle Vue	L46-47	L42-48	L88-95
Coventry	W47-46	W47-43	W94-89
Eastbourne	W48-42	L32-60	L80-102
Ipswich	W52-40	L40-56	L92-96
Oxford	W54-42	L44-49	W98-91
Peterborough	W63-31	L46-47	W109-78
Poole	W53-39	L38-56	L91-95
Wolverhampton	W48-45	L44-51	L92-96

SKY BET ELITE LEAGUE 'B'

Opponents	Home	Away	Aggregate
Arena-Essex	W51-43	W48-45	W99-88
Belle Vue	W47-42	L30-60	L77-102
Coventry	W50-44	L38-52	L88-96
Eastbourne	D45-45	D45-45	D90-90
Ipswich	W56-37	L46-49	W102-86
Oxford	W52-44	L41-53	L93-97
Peterborough	W52-44	W46-30	W98-74
Poole	D45-45	L38-57	L83-102
Wolverhampton	W49-47	L44-52	L93-99

Notes: The away match at Peterborough was abandoned after heat twelve, with the result permitted to stand. Swindon's Leigh Adams lost to Nicki Pedersen in a run-off for the bonus point following the away 'B' fixture at Eastbourne.

SKY BET ELITE LEAGUE TABLE

Team	Mts	Won	Drn	Lst	For	Agn.	Pts	Bon.	Tot.
Poole	36	23	2	11	1,721	1,603	48	13	61
Wolverhampton	36	21	0	15	1,729	1,586	42	16	58
Ipswich	36	21	0	15	1,701	1,626	42	11	53
Eastbourne	36	18	3	15	1,699	1,632	39	11	50
Oxford	36	19	0	17	1,679	1,672	38	10	48
Swindon	36	18	3	15	1,657	1,667	39	6	45
Belle Vue	35	17	0	18	1,630	1,597	34	9	43
Arena-Essex	36	16	0	20	1,651	1,679	32	8	40

Peterborough	35	12	2	21	1,514	1,722	26	2	28
Coventry	36	9	0	27	1,565	1,762	18	3	21

Note: One match was not ridden: Belle Vue v. Peterborough.

LEAGUE AVERAGES

Rider	Mts	Rds	Pts	Bon.	Tot.	Avge	Maximums
Leigh Adams	34	173	461	12	473	10.94	12 Full; 3 Paid
David Norris	1	5	10	0	10	8.00	–
Simon Stead	1	5	10	0	10	8.00	–
Charlie Gjedde	23	107	183	10	193	7.21	–
Peter Ljung	13	56	84	14	98	7.00	–
Steve Johnston	36	177	288	19	307	6.94	–
David Ruud	29	131	173	25	198	6.05	1 Paid
Andy Smith	35	154	186	36	222	5.77	–
Billy Janniro	1	5	5	1	6	4.80	–
Tomas Topinka	1	5	6	0	6	4.80	–
Rafal Kurmanski	3	12	13	1	14	4.67	–
Andy Moore	4	18	17	3	20	4.44	–
Michael Coles	2	11	8	4	12	4.36	–
Eric Carrillo	1	6	6	0	6	4.00	–
Olly Allen	31	139	112	16	128	3.68	
Glenn Cunningham	8	31	19	5	24	3.10	–
Ross Brady	1	4	3	0	3	3.00	–
Leigh Lanham	1	4	3	0	3	3.00	–
Steve Masters	4	17	7	3	10	2.35	–
Claus Kristensen	3	10	4	1	5	2.00	–

Note: Leigh Adams' figures include 10 tactical rides (58 points), modified to normal score, i.e. 29 points; Steve Johnston's figures include 7 tactical rides (28 points), modified to normal score, i.e. 14 points; Charlie Gjedde's figures include 5 tactical rides (20 points), modified to normal score, i.e. 10 points; David Norris' figures include 1 tactical ride (6 points), modified to normal score, i.e. 3 points; David Ruud's figures include 1 tactical ride (6 points), modified to normal score, i.e. 3 points; Billy Janniro's figures include 1 tactical ride (0 points).

KNOCK-OUT CUP

Opponents	Home	Away	Aggregate
Wolverhampton (Round one)	W56-38	L43-50	W99-88
Belle Vue (Quarter-final)	W48-42	–	W48-42
Poole (Semi-final)	W53-40	L30-61	L83-101

Note: Due to inclement weather, Belle Vue were unable to stage the second leg of the quarter-final tie. However, with Swindon holding a 6-point lead from the first leg at Blunsdon, the BSPA decreed that the Robins should progress through.

CHAMPAGNE STAKES

Opponents	Home	Away
Poole	8-4 (aban.)	L39-51

Note: The home match v. Poole was abandoned after heat two.

AIR-TEK CHALLENGE

Opponents	Home	Away	Aggregate
Belle Vue	W54-40	L47-48	W101-88

INTER-LEAGUE CHALLENGE

Opponents	Home	Away
Isle of Wight	–	L42-48

INTERNATIONAL CLUB CHALLENGE

Opponents	Home	Away
Vargarna	–	W55-41

CHALLENGE

Opponents	Home	Away
Poole	–	W47-46

SUZUKI ELITE LEAGUE PAIRS CHAMPIONSHIP

(Staged at Swindon) Group A: Belle Vue 25, Swindon 25, Oxford 15, Poole 14, Coventry 11.
Semi-final: Swindon 7 Eastbourne 2.
Final: Swindon 5 Belle Vue 4.

ELITE LEAGUE RIDERS' CHAMPIONSHIP

(Staged at Poole) Leigh Adams 9 points.

TEAM ARTDEANS SWINDON SPROCKETS

CONFERENCE LEAGUE TABLE

Team	Mts	Won	Drn	Lst	For	Agn.	Pts	Bon.	Tot.
Mildenhall	24	21	0	3	1,254	952	42	10	52
Rye House	24	19	0	5	1,206	991	38	9	47
Oxford	24	17	0	7	1,199	979	34	10	44
Armadale	24	15	0	9	1,185	990	30	8	38
Boston	24	14	1	9	1,171	1,034	29	8	37
Buxton	24	13	1	10	1,093	1,100	27	7	34
Wimbledon	24	11	0	13	1,138	1,080	22	6	28
Weymouth	24	10	1	13	1,047	1,143	21	5	26
Stoke	24	9	1	14	1,054	1,139	19	4	23
Swindon	24	8	0	16	1,063	1,158	16	5	21
Newcastle	24	7	0	17	998	1,203	14	2	16
Carmarthen	24	5	1	18	998	1,187	11	4	15
Newport	24	4	1	19	883	1,333	9	0	9

SWINDON ROBINS A-Z RIDER INDEX 1949-2004

Rider	Date and place of birth	League Apps	League Pts	NT/KOC Apps	NT/KOC Pts	Others Apps	Others Pts	Total Apps	Total Pts
AAS, Rene	13 August 1969, Tallinn, Estonia	2	0	0	0	0	0	2	0
ADAMS, Leigh	28 April 1971, Mildura, Victoria, Australia	178	2,099	27	305	82	876	287	3,280
ALDRIDGE, Berne	20 March 1921, Tottenham, London	1	1	0	0	0	0	1	1
ALLAN, Gary	21 June 1967, Manchester, Greater Manchester	40	458.5	6	71	9	97	55	626.5
ALLEN, Dave	4 July 1957, Norwich, Norfolk	0	0	0	0	1	5	1	5
ALLEN, Olly	27 May 1982, Norwich, Norfolk	147	1,011	20	127	91	592	258	1,730
ALLEN, Tommy	4 September 1984, Norwich, Norfolk	34	74	2	2	13	37	49	113
ALLOTT, Adam	19 March 1983, Stockport, Cheshire	11	54	2	10	1	0	14	64
ALLOTT, Nicky	15 December 1954, Buxton, Derbyshire	1	4	0	0	0	0	1	4
ANDERSEN, Brian	13 March 1971, Sonderborg, Denmark	1	10	0	0	0	0	1	10
ANDERSEN, Jan	1 August 1969, Sonderborg, Denmark	1	10	0	0	0	0	1	10
ANDERSEN, Morten	11 April 1970, Middelfart, Denmark	6	22	0	0	3	6	9	28
ANDERSON, Cliff	18 July 1951, Twickenham, Middlesex	9	8	2	4	1	0	12	12
ANDERSSON, Bjorn	3 November 1962, Alingsas, Sweden	51	276	7	32	54	317	112	625
ANDERSSON, Dalle	27 September 1974, Stockholm, Sweden	1	3	0	0	0	0	1	3
ANDERSSON, Jan	7 May 1955, Alingsas, Sweden	89	643	9	42	21	142	119	827
ANDREW, Bill	18 June 1982, Reading, Berkshire	1	10	0	0	1	12	2	22
APPLETON, Andrew	3 December 1940, Palmerston North, New Zealand	0	0	0	0	1	5	1	5
ARMSTRONG, Jon	1 August 1974, Manchester, Greater Manchester	1	2	0	0	0	0	1	2
ASHBY, David	11 November 1949, Marlborough, Wiltshire	143	379	14	25	40	100	197	504
ASHBY, Martin	5 February 1944, Marlborough, Wiltshire	452	3,980.5	50	437	139	1,059	641	5,476.5
ATKINSON, Ivor	13 March 1926, Bewdley, Worcestershire	0	0	0	0	2	6	2	6
AUTREY, Scott	9 July 1953, Maywood, California, USA	30	329	6	77.5	20	202	56	608.5
BAILEY, Dick	1 August 1928, Greenwich, London	0	0	0	0	1	1	1	1
BANGMA, Henk	11 January 1971, Joure, Netherlands	1	0	0	0	0	0	1	0
BARCLAY, George	1 April 1937, Elephant and Castle, London	1	3	0	0	0	0	1	3
BARKER, Dean	2 August 1970, Isleworth, Middlesex	1	7	0	0	0	0	1	7
BARKER, John	7 October 1960, Eastbourne, East Sussex	7	11	2	4	7	19	16	34
BARNEY, Ian	15 February 1961, Stamford, Lincolnshire	1	2	0	0	0	0	1	2
BARRETT, Ron	24 January 1932, Edmonton, London	0	0	0	0	1	3	1	3
BASON, George	1 October 1913, Farnham, Surrey	1	1	0	0	0	0	1	1
BASS, Phil	5 July 1952, Banbury, Oxfordshire	1	0	0	0	0	0	1	0
BAST, Bart	4 June 1964, Enano, California, USA	16	66	2	9	9	25	27	100
BASTABLE, Steve	16 September 1956, Birmingham, West Midlands	54	431	5	46	45	376	104	853
BATES, Nick	11 July 1968, Tidworth, Wiltshire	0	0	0	0	1	1	1	1
BEATON, George	4 January 1951, Blantyre, Scotland	1	0	0	0	0	0	1	0
BEDDOE, Mike	23 May 1923, Bolton, Greater Manchester	9	32	0	0	1	2	10	34

Rider	Born	1	2	3	4	5	6	7	8
BELL, Mick	14 October 1945, Oxford, Oxfordshire	2	21	0	0	1	4	3	25
BENGTSSON, Lennart	30 September 1957, Eskilstuna, Sweden	5	9	1	2	3	1	9	12
BENTLEY, Paul	18 January 1968, Newcastle-upon-Tyne, Tyne & Wear	6	45	0	0	0	0	6	45
BERGE, Philippe	20 June 1971, Brive, France	6	7	0	0	0	0	6	7
BERGSTROM, Andreas	27 August 1978, Avesta, Sweden	0	0	0	0	1	6	1	6
BEST, Paul	1928, Bristol (Full details unknown)	2	2	0	0	3	4	5	6
BETTS, Terry	15 September 1943, Harlow, Essex	2	25	0	0	0	0	2	25
BEVAN, Chris	2 June 1958, Leeds, West Yorkshire	1	1	0	0	0	0	1	1
BEVERIDGE, Will	9 September 1975, Hexham, Northumberland	1	1	0	0	1	4	1	1
BIGGS, Jack	21 March 1922, Melbourne, Victoria, Australia	1	11	3	13	6	13	2	15
BISHOP, John	15 January 1945, Amersham, Buckinghamshire	31	66	4	7	32	134	40	86
BISHOP, Steve	28 November 1963, Bristol, Avon	28	88	0	7	0	0	64	229
BLACK, Brian	24 October 1944, Meiklenour, Scotland	1	6	2	0	0	0	1	6
BLACKBIRD, Carl	26 March 1965, Peterborough, Cambridgeshire	36	299	2	13	10	57	48	369
BLACKBURN, David	7 January 1962, Coventry, Warwickshire	1	3	0	0	0	0	1	3
BLOKDYK, Trevor	30 November 1935, Krugersdrop, South Africa	19	48	0	13	19	39	44	100
BOARD, Johnny	7 May 1931, Melbourne, Victoria, Australia	1	0	0	0	0	0	1	0
BOAST, Peter	11 April 1964, Louth, Lincolnshire	1	0	0	0	0	0	1	0
BODIE, Kid	29 December 1943, Cardiff, South Glamorgan	29	57	2	0	3	9	32	60
BOND, James	5 July 1938, Coventry, Warwickshire	8	7	1	6	3	0	13	22
BOOCOCK, Nigel	17 September 1937, Wakefield, Yorkshire	1	5	0	9	0	0	2	14
BOOTHROYD, Eric	26 April 1927, Halifax, West Yorkshire	3	2	0	0	0	0	3	2
BOSLEY, Paul	21 February 1962, London	182	891	19	103	64	346	265	1,340
BOUCHARD, Geoff	5 September 1948, Leicester, Leicestershire	1	8	1	11	0	0	2	19
BOULGER, John	18 June 1945, Adelaide, South Australia	0	0	0	0	0	0	3	3
BOULTON, Darren	9 October 1970, Dorchester, Dorset	18	48	4	13	15	37	37	98
BOWERS, Roy	23 August 1930, High Wycombe, Buckinghamshire	1	1	0	0	0	0	1	1
BOWES, Shane	4 March 1969, Adelaide, South Australia	30	402	4	48	13	112	45	562
BOYCE, Craig	2 August 1967, Sydney, New South Wales, Australia	6	62	0	0	4	33	10	95
BRADLEY, Dick	28 November 1924, Netheravon, Wiltshire	1	3	0	0	0	0	1	3
BRADSHAW, Pete	1947, Melbourne, Victoria, Australia (Full details unknown)	2	12	1	0	0	0	2	12
BRADY, Ross	17 February 1981, Winchburgh, Broxburn, Scotland	1	1	0	0	0	0	1	2
BRAND, Fred	3 February 1925, Spalding, Lincolnshire	1	2	0	0	0	0	1	2
BRANNEY, Craig	31 July 1982, Whitehaven, Cumbria	0	0	0	0	0	0	1	2
BRENNAN, Steve	5 May 1964, Exeter, Devon	0	0	1	0	0	0	2	2
BRETT, Brian	3 April 1938, Stanstead Abbots, Essex	85	374	23	102	48	255	156	731
BRIGGS, Allen	25 January 1925, Peckham, London	2	2	0	0	2	8	4	10
BRIGGS MBE, Barry	30 December 1934, Christchurch, New Zealand	246	2,876	17	221	58	584	321	3,681
BRINE, Cyril	6 February 1919, Boreham Wood, London	1	9	0	0	5	5	1	9
BROADBANK, Terry	10 May 1960, Hoddesdon, Hertfordshire	1	0	0	0	0	5	6	5
BROADBANKS, Mike	25 September 1934, Hoddesdon, Hertfordshire	374	2,819	46	423	140	997	560	4,239
BROADBELT, Eric	8 December 1947, Blackpool, Lancashire	4	9	0	0	1	2	5	11
BROWN, Buster	21 April 1931, Greenford, London	73	447	9	47	19	130	101	624
BROWN, Ivor	30 May 1927, Wymeswold, Leicestershire	0	0	0	0	1	2	1	2

Player	Details								
BROWN, Tom	19 June 1984, Panteg, Pontypool, Wales	1	1	0	0	0	0	1	1
BROWNING, Arthur	22 September 1944, Birmingham, West Midlands	1	3	0	0	0	0	1	3
BURROWS, Mark	6 June 1964, Sheffield, South Yorkshire	0	0	1	10	1	2	1	2
BUSK, Alf	16 April 1958, Silkeborg, Denmark	55	206.5	4	7	63	224	122	440.5
BUTLER, Troy	22 September 1967, Melbourne, Victoria, Australia	2	6	1	0	1	4	4	17
BUTTERFIELD, Brian	22 October 1959, Islington, London	0	0	0	0	0	3	1	3
CAMDEN, Steve	19 June 1973, Oxford, Oxfordshire	36	111	7	15	9	8	52	134
CAMPBELL, Andy	3 October 1959, Guildford, Surrey	1	0	0	0	1	2	2	2
CAMPBELL, Barry	26 August 1979, Glasgow, Scotland	1	1	0	0	0	0	2	1
CANN, Francis	25 June 1929, Exeter, Devon	0	0	2	5	0	0	2	5
CARLSSON, Arne	1939, Motala, Sweden (Full details unknown)	24	130	6	40	4	18	34	188
CARR, Louis	28 January 1960, Preston, Lancashire	3	0	0	0	1	0	3	0
CARR, Peter	22 January 1963, Preston, Lancashire	2	13	0	0	0	5	3	18
CARRILLO, Eric	25 June 1984, Haywood, California	1	6	0	0	0	0	1	6
CARTWRIGHT, Ian	25 July 1954, Crayke, North Yorkshire	1	11	0	0	0	0	1	11
CARTWRIGHT, Simon	2 November 1978, Northallerton, North Yorkshire	1	3	0	0	0	0	1	3
CASTAGNA, Armando	22 September 1963, Arzignano, Italy	0	0	0	0	0	10	1	10
CHAMBERLAIN, Trevor	Details unknown	1	0	0	0	0	0	1	0
CHANDLER, Glyn	8 March 1937, Swindon, Wiltshire	16	33	2	1	14	32	32	66
CHESSELL, Gary	20 January 1965, Ludlow, Shropshire	158	952	16	86	38	183	212	1,221
CHESSELL, Mark	26 July 1966, Ludlow, Shropshire	0	0	0	0	0	0	2	1
CHESSELL, Martin	30 January 1970, Ludlow, Shropshire	2	0	0	0	9	5.5	2	5.5
CLARK, Ian	23 December 1958, Sandon, Chelmsford, Essex	1	3	0	0	0	0	11	3
CLARK, Ron	29 February 1920, Harringay, London	29	135	3	12	12	53	44	200
CLARKE, David	25 March 1969, Rugby, Warwickshire	4	2	0	0	1	1	5	3
CLARKE, Phil	30 June 1922, Norwich, Norfolk	1	5	0	0	0	0	1	5
CLARKE, Tony	6 July 1940, Kensall Rise, London	2	16	0	0	0	0	2	16
CLOSE, Derek	11 May 1927, Barnard Castle, County Durham	0	0	0	10	0	9	2	9
CLOUTING, Savalas	8 September 1975, Ipswich, Suffolk	7	45	2	10	0	17	11	72
COBBY, Chris	18 August 1969, Stoke-on-Trent, Staffordshire	1	1	0	0	1	0	1	0
COLES, Bob	12 February 1944, Exeter, Devon	1	0	0	0	0	0	1	8
COLES, Michael	11 August 1965, Exeter, Devon	2	8	0	0	0	0	2	2
COLLETT, Dave	7 April 1933, Portsmouth, Hampshire	0	0	2	0	0	0	2	2
COLLETT, Mick	Details unknown	0	0	2	0	2	0	2	1
COLLINS, Aidan	21 April 1982, Stockport, Cheshire	1	3	0	0	0	0	2	3
COLLINS, Les	24 May 1958, Partington, Greater Manchester	0	0	1	9	1	10	2	19
COLLINS, Neil	15 October 1961 Partington, Greater Manchester	54	421	12	82	43	348	109	851
COLLINS, Peter	24 March 1954, Urmston, Greater Manchester	1	10	0	0	2	18	3	28
COLLINS, Phil	2 June 1960, Partington, Greater Manchester	3	23	2	0	3	20	6	43
COLQUHOUN, Rod	28 February 1967, Mount Warrigal, NSW, Australia	24	75	2	1	23	93	49	169
COMPTON, Andre	15 May 1977, Dewsbury, West Yorkshire	3	30	0	0	0	0	3	30
COMPTON, Benji	17 September 1986, Tenerife, Spain	1	2	0	0	0	0	1	2
CONWAY, Maurice	1 July 1933, Preston, Victoria, Australia	16	29	4	11	9	13	29	53
CONWAY, Noel	11 December 1929, Preston, Victoria, Australia	0	0	2	6	0	0	2	6

Name	Born								
COOK, Colin	29 August 1954, Southwold, Suffolk	2	6	0	0	1	0	3	6
COOK, John	18 December 1958, Van Nuys, California, USA	1	8	0	0	1	7	2	15
CORREY, Ronnie	8 November 1966, Bellflower, California, USA	3	39	0	0	3	28	6	67
COX, Marvyn	11 July 1964, Whitstable, Kent	3	33	1	13	3	27	7	73
CRAIG, George	6 June 1915, Deptford, South-East London	48	286	3	28	18	85	69	399
CRANE, David	15 July 1946, Taverham, Norfolk	0	0	0	0	1	2	1	2
CRIBB, Bruce	27 June 1946, Palmerston North, New Zealand	1	9	0	0	1	9	2	18
CROOK, Graham	6 May 1954, Burnt Oak, London	1	0	0	0	0	0	1	0
CROSS, Matthew	26 August 1968, Taunton, Somerset	20	24	5	4	34	54	59	82
CROSS, Simon	31 May 1965, Hereford, Hereford & Worcester	0	0	1	3	1	0	1	3
CRUMP, Jason	6 August 1975, Bristol Avon	39	540	6	79	7	69	52	688
CRUMP, Phil	9 February 1952, Red Cliffs, nr. Mildura, Australia	202	2,048	28	332	181	1,874	411	4,254
CUNNINGHAM, Glenn	10 June 1975, Bristol, Avon	171	1,069	20	119	52	393	243	1,581
DANIELS, Greg	23 April 1964, Bridgwater, Somerset	1	0	0	0	0	0	1	0
DANNO, Roland	13 February 1966, Ostersund, Sweden	1	5	0	0	0	0	2	5
DAVEY, Tony	15 August 1951, Framsden, Suffolk	2	17	0	0	0	0	1	17
DAVIES, Stephen	31 January 1964, Newcastle, New South Wales, Australia	1	5	0	0	0	0		5
DAVIS, John	10 November 1954, Oxford, Oxfordshire	52	310	4	39	27	169	83	518
DEARDEN, Doug	21 November 1943, Southampton, Hampshire	1	4	0	0	0	0		4
DEBBAGE, John	17 December 1934, Norwich, Norfolk	9	17	2	5	0	0	11	22
DIXON, Martin	30 May 1961, Hartlepool, Durham	52	325	14	81	44	291	110	697
DOOLAN, Kevin	30 November 1980, Mildura, Victoria, Australia	0	0	0	0	0	4	1	4
DORE, John	30 May 1931, Yarmouth, Norfolk	0	0	0	0	1	0		0
DOWNTON, Bill	1917, Bristol, Avon (Full details unknown)	21	99	2	13	11	60	34	172
DOYLE, Glenn	4 March 1965, Sydney, New South Wales, Australia	3	11	0	0	0	0	3	11
DREWETT, Chris	Details unknown	0	0	0	0	1	0	1	0
DRYML, Ales	10 June 1953, Kolina, Czech Republic	0	0	1	7	1	6	2	6
DUCKWORTH, Bob	25 May 1929, Mossburn, New Zealand	0	0	0	0	0	2	2	9
DUGARD, Martin	18 May, 1969, Worthing, West Sussex	2	17	0	0	1	0		17
DUGARD, Paul	17 October 1972, Shoreham, West Sussex	8	25	2	14	20	73	30	112
DUKE, Barry	28 August 1948, Hampstead, London	77	265	5	22	13	43.5	95	330.5
DUNTON, Danny	13 May 1926, Cholesbury, Buckinghamshire	1	1	0	0	1	1	2	2
DYMINSKI, Simon	18 October 1983, Swindon, Wiltshire	2	2	0	0	0	0	2	2
EADON, Tony	30 July 1932, Coventry, Warwickshire	1	2	0	0	1	0	1	2
EDWARDS, Harry	30 August 1918, Kenton, London	0	0	0	0	0	8	1	8
EDWARDS, John	7 July 1936, Aldershot, Hampshire	1	8	0	0	1	1	2	9
EIDE, Reidar	6 November 1940, Hoyland, Norway	6	39	1	7	15	24	7	46
ELKINS, Justin	27 August 1974, Salisbury, Wiltshire	23	43	2	6	0	0	40	73
ELLIS, John	1941, Southampton, Hampshire (Full details unknown)								
ELLIS, Ray	13 August 1927, Tooting, London	58	266	6	37	16	92.5	80	395.5
ERIKSEN, Preben	9 August 1958, Odense, Denmark	3	8	0	0	1	10	4	18
ERSKINE, Jon	9 February 1942, Salisbury, Wiltshire	1	0	0	0	0	0	1	0
EVANS, Dai	4 March 1938, Bridgenorth, Shropshire	1	4	0	0	0	0	1	4
EVANS, Frank	9 April 1915, Bristol, Avon	119	695	10	50	37	216	166	961

Rider	Born								
EVANS, Miles	2 May 1965, Middlesbrough, Cleveland	0	0	1	0	0	0	1	0
EVANS, Richard	11 February 1954, Bristol, Avon	12	13	1	1	1	0	14	14
EVITTS, Neil	25 September 1964, Birmingham, West Midlands	5	26	0	0	1	5	6	31
FACEY, Clark	8 March 1952, Taunton, Somerset	5	5	0	0	0	0	5	5
FAIRWEATHER, Emmerson	18 August 1973, Ipswich, Suffolk	0	0	0	0	1	1	1	1
FERREIRA, Mike	21 November 1955, Harare, Zimbabwe	41	197	6	34	36	210	83	441
FIALA, Karl	30 January 1956, Harlow, Essex	1	0	0	0	0	0	1	0
FINCH, Steve	8 January 1958, Middlesbrough, Cleveland	0	0	0	0	1	2	1	2
FLANAGAN, Pat	13 September 1925, London	0	0	0	0	1	1	1	1
FLATMAN, Nigel	30 March 1960, Felixstowe, Suffolk	3	9	0	0	0	0	3	9
FLOOD, Garry	1952, Australia (Full details unknown)	2	1	0	0	0	0	2	1
FORTUNE, Rob	24 March 1963, Kidderminster, Worcestershire	19	39	4	5	25	43	48	87
FREEMAN, Wayne	1 April 1969, Townsville, Queensland, Australia	0	0	0	0	3	8.5	3	8.5
FRENCH, Eric	4 August 1913, Cork, Ireland	1	14	0	0	0	0	1	14
FRY, Paul	25 October 1964, Ledbury, Worcestershire	97	895	16	164	71	647	184	1,706
FUDGE, Paul	16 February 1967, Bristol, Avon	1	3	0	0	0	0	1	3
GACHET, Paul	23 April 1955, London	16	49	2	4	4	9	22	62
GALLACHER, Jimmy	24 May 1949, Airdrie, Scotland	0	0	0	0	1	4	1	4
GALLOWS, Tyburn	7 September 1934, Willesden, London	2	11	0	0	1	6	3	17
GALVIN, Andy	13 November 1965, Whitstable, Kent	50	337	6	77	16	98	72	512
GEDDES, Hugh	16 April 1919, Sydney, New South Wales, Australia	0	0	1	8	1	2	2	10
GEER, Trevor	24 June 1953, Eastbourne, East Sussex	2	11	0	0	3	15	5	26
GENZ, Ronnie	17 March 1930, Forest Gate, London	2	11	2	5	3	32	7	48
GERAN, Jack	10 December 1929, Melbourne, Victoria, Australia	0	0	0	0	2	5	2	5
GIBBS, Mark	23 September 1963, Bath, Avon	0	0	1	0	1	0	2	0
GILLIAS, Tony	15 October 1953, Rugby, Warwickshire	0	0	0	0	1	0	1	0
GJEDDE, Charlie	28 December 1979, Holstebro, Denmark	108	959	14	122	37	332	159	1,413
GLANZ, Peter	3 May 1962, Fredericia, Denmark	2	5	0	0	1	7	3	12
GLOVER, Carl	11 October 1952, Sheffield, South Yorkshire	1	6	0	0	0	0	1	6
GLOVER, Derek	2 February 1930, Wigan, Greater Manchester	7	25	0	0	1	0	8	25
GOOCH, Jimmy	16 November 1928, Dagenham, Essex	21	162	2	13	5	36	28	211
GOOD, Bonny	3 October 1918, Upper Weare, Somerset	1	0	0	0	5	10	6	10
GOODWIN, Martin	15 January 1960, Pembury, Kent	3	15	0	0	0	0	3	15
GOODWIN, Steve	11 August 1965, Swindon, Wiltshire	0	0	0	0	4	4	4	4
GORDON, Graeme	16 June 1976, Wallington, Surrey	1	0	0	0	1	2	2	2
GOULD, Jon	16 March 1967, Exeter, Devon	0	0	0	0	1	1	1	1
GRAHAME, Alan	5 February 1954, Birmingham, West Midlands	25	106	1	9	23	153	49	268
GRAHAME, Andy	10 September 1957, Birmingham, West Midlands	4	30	0	0	2	21	6	51
GRAMSTAD, Rolf	5 January 1957, Sandnes, Norway	44	156	5	16	16	51	65	223
GRAY, Alex	29 August 1916, Hackney, London	42	305	6	34	23	155	71	494
GREEN, Jason	28 July 1972, Maidstone, Kent	6	3	0	0	3	6	9	9
GREEN, Richard	16 August 1965, Wreningham, Norfolk	2	7	0	0	0	0	2	7
GREER, Richard	29 November 1946, Peterborough, Cambridgeshire	1	0	0	0	0	0	1	0
GRESHAM, Steve	18 August 1954, Santa Monica, California, USA	89	555	16	123	69	454.5	174	1,132.5

GRIEVES, James	28 September 1974, Paisley, Renfrewshire	1	4	0	0	0	0	1	4
GRIMES, Bill	25 November 1920, Marylebone, London	9	29	2	0	2	13	11	42
GUGLIELMI, Gary	14 February 1958, Sydney, NSW, Australia	1	9	2	0	2	18	3	27
GUNDERSEN, Erik	8 October 1959, Esbjerg, Denmark	0	0	1	0	1	10	1	10
HACKETT, Andy	6 March 1970, Halesowen, West Midlands	0	0	1	0	1	4	2	4
HADEK, Bo	28 April 1968, Plzen, Czech Republic	0	0	1	0	0	2	1	2
HALEY, Arnold	15 September 1942, Leeds, West Yorkshire	1	12	0	0	0	0	1	12
HAMILL, Billy	23 May 1970, Arcadia, California, USA	1	7	0	0	0	0	1	7
HANDBERG, Gert	30 May 1969, Brastrup, Denmark	1	4	0	0	0	0	1	4
HANDLEY, Mick	29 December 1946, Dudley, West Midlands	34	103	5	13	9	26	48	142
HANHAM, Brian	20 April 1932, Southampton, Hampshire	2	18	0	0	0	0	2	18
HARD, Mick	5 April 1930, Bromham, Wiltshire	10	33	4	20	9	26	23	79
HARE, Lawrence	23 December 1969, Elsmett, Suffolk	1	10	0	0	0	0	1	10
HARRIS, Chris	28 November 1982, Truro, Cornwall	8	74	1	12	2	19	11	105
HARRIS, Phil	28 June 1960, Cirencester, Gloucestershire	0	0	0	0	2	4	1	4
HARRIS, Ray	20 January 1920, Allensmore, Hereford, Worcestershire	73	295	13	70	36	158	122	523
HARRISON, Mark	5 February 1963, Hull, East Yorkshire	1	0	0	0	0	0		0
HAWKINS, Kevin	21 July 1954, Buckingham, Buckinghamshire	0	0	0	0	1	3	1	3
HAWKINS, Ritchie	9 November 1983, Peterborough, Cambridgeshire	62	235	8	21	43	135	113	391
HEDGE, Trevor	3 August 1943, Diss, Norfolk	1	7	0	0	0	0	1	7
HELLSEN, Richard	1 June 1951, Stockholm, Sweden	82	445.5	10	56	65	381	157	882.5
HENDERSON, Ron	27 February 1957, Brisbane, Queensland, Australia	1	3	1	3	0	0	2	3
HENDRIKSEN, Arne	14 August 1931, New Malden, Surrey	1	1	0	0	0	0	1	1
HENRY, Robert	28 June 1954, Exeter, Devon	14	36	3	2	0	0	17	38
HERNE, Lee	27 March 1980, Ipswich, Suffolk	0	0	1	0	1	0	2	0
HERNE, Phil	27 March 1955, Ballina, New South Wales, Australia	24	100	2	17	9	53	35	170
HEWLETT, Martin	6 February 1962, Swindon, Wiltshire	29	82	2	6	33	80.5	64	168.5
HITCH, Clive	9 April 1933, Stanstead Abbots, Hertfordshire	226	953	18	78	38	187	282	1,218
HITCH, Martin	11 March 1955, Bishop's Stortford, Hertfordshire	0	0	1	1	0	0	1	1
HODGSON, Craig	8 July 1968, Adelaide, South Australia	2	6	0	0	0	0	2	6
HODGSON, Lee	19 February 1985, Preston, Lancashire	1	1	1	0	1	2	2	3
HOLLAND, Mick	29 November 1918, Christchurch, New Zealand	28	187	5	20	17	118	50	325
HOLLOWAY, Malcolm	22 December 1956, Stratton St. Margaret, Wiltshire	145	594	18	116	107	515	270	1,225
HOLMES, Jamie	19 November 1979, Exeter, Devon	1	0	0	0	0	0		0
HOOK, John	23 September 1927, Wooburn, Buckinghamshire	0	0	1	0	1	4	1	4
HOW, Ron	23 December 1929, Little Missenden, Buckinghamshire	0	0	0	13	0	0	1	13
HOWARD, Dick	24 March 1922, Islington, London	0	0	0	0	1	10	1	10
HOWE, Andy	15 August 1969, Northallerton, North Yorkshire	1	0	0	0	0	0		0
HOWE, Ben	6 December 1974, Crawley, Sussex	0	0	1	0	1	5		5
HUBBARD, Ted	20 June 1949, Lydden, Kent	1	0	0	0	0	0		0
HUGHES, Bob	23 February 1937, Anglesey, North Wales	0	0	0	0	1	4	1	4
HUGHES, Harry	1911, Holyhead, North Wales (Full details unknown)	0	0	0	0	9	42	27	69
HUGHES, Wayne	28 March 1954, Partington, Greater Manchester	18	27	1	0	0	0	1	0
HUMPHREYS, Bob	7 January 1946, Liverpool, New South Wales, Australia	12	49	3	19	10	28	25	96

HUNT, Alan	25 July 1924, Birmingham, West Midlands	2	22	0	0	0	0	2	22
HUNT, Chris	15 February 1964, Wallingford, Oxfordshire	0	0	1	0	0	0	1	0
HUNT, Tim	23 May 1960, Ipswich, Suffolk	6	25	3	13	0	0	9	38
HUNTER, Norman	21 February 1940, Willesden, London	128	687	15	102	48	267	191	1,056
HUSSEY, Gerry	12 March 1932, Hampstead, London	2	15	0	0	0	0	2	15
IVARSSON, Conny	15 April 1965, Vetlanda, Sweden	20	117	2	17	11	36	33	170
JACKSON, Alan	11 March 1945, Hoddesdon, Hertfordshire	17	19	1	1	2	1	20	21
JACKSON, Gerald	14 October 1926, Teddington, Middlesex	0	0	0	0	2	11	2	11
JACKSON, Peter	15 October 1937, Hoddesdon, Hertfordshire	20	31	5	8	7	13	32	52
JAMES, Ticker	23 November 1924, Bournemouth, Hampshire	0	0	0	0	1	10	1	10
JANNIRO, Billy	3 July 1980, Vallejo, California, USA	1	5	0	0	0	0	1	5
JANSSON, Bengt	9 January 1943, Stockholm, Sweden	1	4	0	0	0	0	1	4
JEFFERIES, John	25 June 1977, Swindon, Wiltshire	38	51	0	0	4	6	42	57
JEFFERY, Peter	3 November 1966, Bideford, North Devon	7	29	2	16	0	0	9	45
JENSEN, Finn	9 January 1957, Haderslev, Denmark	0	0	1	6	0	0	1	6
JENSEN, Jesper B.	14 October 1977, Esbjerg, Denmark	1	2	0	0	0	0	1	2
JESSUP, Dave	7 March 1953, Ipswich, Suffolk	4	34	1	4	0	0	5	38
JOHNS, Roger	1 March 1954, Epsom, Surrey	1	1	1	3	0	0	2	4
JOHNSON, Pat	25 February 1948, Cricklade, Wiltshire	1	1	0	0	0	0	1	1
JOHNSTON, Ron	1930, Dunedin, New Zealand (Full details unknown)	1	11	0	0	0	0	1	11
JOHNSTON, Steve	12 October 1971, Kalgoorlie, Western Australia	37	293	5	39	5	37	47	369
JOLLY, Kevin	29 January 1958, Eye, Suffolk	3	13	0	0	1	9	4	22
JONES, Bob	11 June 1919, Swindon, Wiltshire	177	902	22	153	72	298	271	1,353
JONES, Graham	5 May 1963, Oswestry, Shropshire	0	0	1	5	0	0	1	5
JONSSON, Per	21 March 1966, Stockholm, Sweden	4	39	0	0	1	11	5	50
JORGENSEN, John	18 July 1962, Middelfart, Denmark	52	509	5	49	13	94	70	652
JUUL, Richard	30 October 1970, Copenhagen, Denmark	1	1	0	0	0	0	1	1
KARGER, Brian	9 February 1967, Horsans, Denmark	213	1,811	33	285	87	652	333	2,748
KARLSSON, Soren	23 October 1946, Orebro, Sweden	53	225	4	5	20	79	77	309
KASPER, Toni	5 December 1962, Prague, Czech Republic	0	0	0	0	1	6	1	6
KASPRZAK, Krzysztof	18 July 1984, Leszno, Poland	0	0	0	0	3	15	3	15
KEATS, Derrol	26 June 1963, Sheffield, South Yorkshire	1	4	0	0	4	1	5	5
KEATS, Terry	2 August 1942, Hoddesdon, Hertfordshire	0	0	0	0	1	1	1	1
KEEN, Mike	12 December 1937, Minety, Wiltshire	313	1,221	24	118	75	303	412	1,642
KENNEDY, Danny	18 June 1958, Ballarat, Victoria, Australia	1	1	0	0	0	0	1	1
KENNETT, Gordon	2 September 1953, Bromley, Kent	5	24	3	14	10	43	18	81
KENT, Denzil	26 October 1961, Bulawayo, Zimbabwe	3	6	0	0	2	4	5	10
KESSLER, Robbie	5 April 1973, Neuwied, Germany	1	12	0	0	1	4	2	16
KILBY, Bob	23 September 1944, Swindon, Wiltshire	398	2,953	36	310	122	929	556	4,192
KING, Daniel	14 August 1986, Maidstone, Kent	1	4	0	0	0	0	1	4
KING, Gerry	20 July 1938, Broxbourne, Hertfordshire	0	0	0	0	2	8	2	8
KING, Jason	13 April 1985, Maidstone, Kent	31	99	2	3	14	27	47	129
KING, Lance	13 August 1963, Carson City, Nevada, USA	4	31	0	0	0	0	4	31
KNAPMAN, Darren	3 January 1970, Swindon, Wiltshire	2	1	0	0	0	0	2	1

Rider	Born	Matches	Points	Matches	Points	Matches	Points	Total Matches	Total Points
KNIGHT, Richard	26 May 1959, Cambridge, Cambridgeshire	2	19	0	0	0	0	2	19
KNUDSEN, Tom	14 September 1968, Gording, Denmark	5	21	0	0	0	0	5	21
KNUDSEN, Tommy	9 November 1961, Roager, Denmark	0	0	0	0	1	11	1	11
KOCSO, Antal	22 December 1962, Szeged, Hungary	1	4	0	0	0	0	1	4
KOKKO, Petri	14 December 1969, Tampere, Finland	2	7	0	0	0	0	2	7
KOPONEN, Ari	20 July 1959, Lahti, Finland	47	261	4	11	48	223	99	495
KOPPE, Steve	16 April 1953, Bowen, Queensland, Australia	2	5	0	0	8	29	10	34
KOSONEN, Jarno	25 May 1972, Tampere, Finland	25	80	3	6	1	5	29	91
KRISTENSEN, Claus	11 June 1977, Holstebro, Denmark	61	466	14	103	45	289	120	858
KURMANSKI, Rafal	22 August 1982, Zielona Gora, Poland	3	13	0	0	0	0	3	13
LAMBOURNE, Reg	1 July 1911, Worcester, Worcestershire	116	458.5	6	32	34	148	156	638.5
LANGDON, Tony	20 June 1969, Brisbane, Queensland, Australia	29	301	2	12	9	63	40	376
LANHAM, Leigh	15 August 1977, Ipswich, Suffolk	3	19	1	10	0	0	4	29
LARSEN, Josh	12 May 1972, Anaheim, California, USA	2	5	0	0	0	0	2	5
LAWSON, Steve	11 December 1957, Workington, Cumbria	1	4	0	0	2	3	3	7
LEAVER, Nigel	28 September 1965, Walsall, West Midlands	32	197	6	42	7	27	45	266
LEE, John	New Zealand (Full details unknown)	0	0	0	0	1	0	1	0
LEE, Paul	21 March 1981, Nottingham, Nottinghamshire	32	130	2	6	16	62	50	198
LEIGH, Bernie	8 November 1944, Southampton, Hampshire	33	134	2	4	16	72	51	210
LEIGH, Gordon	1932, Australia (Full details unknown)	19	54	0	0	9	30	28	84
LEMON, Mark	12 February 1973, Bairnsdale, Victoria, Australia	2	21	0	0	3	10	5	31
LEONARD, Brian	19 February 1946, Newbury, Berkshire	92	288	9	27	24	80	125	395
LESSITER, Ernie	12 August 1929, Paddington, London	58	209	8	25	46	203	112	437
LEVAI, Sandor	16 July 1935, Debrecen, Hungary	0	0	0	0	1	6	1	6
LIGHTFOOT, Jim	11 November 1933, Binley Woods, Coventry, Warwickshire	0	0	0	0	1	7	1	7
LINDBACK, Antonio	5 May 1985, Rio De Janeiro, Brazil	1	6	0	0	0	0	1	6
LITTLE, Kevin	24 September 1972, Edinburgh, Scotland	1	9	0	0	0	0	1	9
LJUNG, Peter	30 October 1982, Aseda, Sweden	13	84	3	15	1	7	17	106
LOMAS, Steve	24 April 1949, Manchester, Greater Manchester	0	0	0	0	0	0	0	0
LORAM, Mark	12 January 1971, Mtarfa, Malta	4	30	1	0	0	0	5	30
LOUIS, Chris	9 July 1969, Ipswich, Suffolk	2	26	0	0	0	0	2	26
LOVAAS, Dag	25 February 1951, Holmestrand, Norway	1	12	0	0	0	0	1	12
LUCKHURST, Jamie	26 January 1965, Ashford, Kent	0	0	0	0	1	3	1	3
LUCKHURST, Reg	11 November 1935, Ashford, Kent	1	2	0	0	6	27	7	29
LUKEHURST, Des	3 October 1937, Romney Marsh, Kent	1	6	0	0	27	0	28	6
LYONS, Jason	15 June 1970, Mildura, Victoria, Australia	2	29	0	0	0	0	2	29
McAULIFFE, Leo	16 December 1933, Clydach, West Glamorgan	6	9	0	0	8	36	14	45
McCONNELL, Shawn	26 April 1959, Anaheim, California, USA	27	125	2	6	13	46	42	177
McCOY, Bluey	10 August 1929, Melbourne, Victoria, Australia	6	6	0	0	1	1	7	7
McDERMOTT, Maurice	1 May 1928, Battersea, London	1	4	0	0	0	0	1	4
McGREGOR, Gordon	28 November 1921, Linlithgow, West Lothian, Scotland	1	3	0	0	0	0	1	3
McILKENNY, Mark	15 June 1978, Paisley, Renfrewshire, Scotland	1	0	0	0	0	0	1	0
McKEE, Colin	7 May 1941, Napier, New Zealand	0	0	0	0	5	15	5	15
McKEOWN, Brian	12 June 1927, Christchurch, New Zealand	0	0	0	0	2	17	2	17

Name	Birth details								
McKINLAY, Ken	7 June 1928, Blantyre, Scotland	2	18	0	0	0	0	2	18
McKINNA, Kenny	21 October 1962, Glasgow, Scotland	1	4	0	0	1	3	2	7
McKNIGHT, Sumner	9 September 1946, USA (Full details unknown)	7	4	0	1	2	3	10	7
McMILLAN, Jim	3 December 1945, Glasgow, Scotland	0	0	1	1	1	5	1	5
McNEIL, Bobby	27 February 1955, Canterbury, Kent	88	414	8	48	31	141	127	603
McNEILL, John	4 August 1955, Footscray, Melbourne, Australia	0	0	0	0	4	10	4	10
MADSEN, Rene	1 December 1972, Silkeborg, Denmark	1	9	0	0	1	8	2	17
MAIDMENT, Cyril	31 January 1929, Wandsworth, London	0	0	0	0	1	1	1	1
MALONE, Danny	31 October 1921, Bristol, Avon	179	1,013	26	190	59	328	264	1,531
MANCHESTER, Chris	28 June 1973, St. Louis, Missouri, USA	0	0	1	11	0	0	1	11
MARSH, Krister	23 March 1976, Hereford, Hereford & Worcester	30	113	4	10	21	76	55	199
MASON, David	20 December 1976, Crawley, West Sussex	2	4	0	0	10	31	12	35
MASTERS, Steve	6 December 1970, Eastbourne, East Sussex	166	727	32	95	56	289	254	1,111
MASTRUP, Steen	2 June 1958, Naestved, Denmark	114	420	15	83	92	358	221	861
MATOUSEK, Roman	23 May 1964, Slany, Czech Republic	1	0	0	0	0	0	1	0
MATTHEWS, Ken	21 May 1952, Buckingham, Buckinghamshire	0	0	0	0	0	0	1	0
MAUGER, Ivan	4 October 1939, Christchurch, New Zealand	2	13	0	0	0	0	2	13
MAXTED, Brian	26 June 1941, Beckingham, Lincolnshire	0	0	0	0	1	0	1	0
MAY, Eddie	Details unknown	0	0	0	0	0	0	0	0
MEEK, Norman	Details unknown	8	10	0	0	7	14	15	24
MEREDITH, Brian	3 August 1939, Coventry, Warwickshire	38	99	9	35	30	113	77	247
MEREDITH, Colin	24 January 1953, Hereford, Hereford & Worcester	0	0	0	0	1	1	1	1
MIDDLEDITCH, Ken	5 October 1925, Camberley, Surrey	19	148	0	0	26	212.5	45	360.5
MIDDLETON, Garry	19 July 1948, Corowa, New South Wales, Australia	1	7	0	0	0	0	5	7
MILLARD, Keith	18 November 1964, Newent, Gloucestershire	2	6	0	5	3	10	5	16
MILLER, Rick	12 January 1961, Reseda, California, USA	0	0	1	5	0	0	1	5
MITCHELL, Mick	19 December 1914, London	29	199	2	3	5	38	36	240
MOGRIDGE, Alan	6 November 1963, Westminster, London	34	291	7	63	24	196	65	550
MOLYNEUX, Alan	12 August 1950, Derby, Derbyshire	0	0	0	0	1	7	6	7
MOORE, Andrew	6 October 1982, Lincoln, Lincolnshire	4	17	1	4	1	3	6	24
MOORE, Peter	28 April 1929, Melbourne, Victoria, Australia	31	283	9	81	8	55	48	419
MOORE, Ronnie	8 March 1933, Hobart, Tasmania	2	29	0	0	1	12	3	41
MORAN, Kelly	21 September 1960, Lakewood, California, USA	26	175	2	7	11	64	39	246
MORAN, Shawn	19 November 1961, Lakewood, California, USA	0	0	0	0	2	19	2	19
MORETON, Roy	1 March 1928, Birmingham, West Midlands	5	11	1	3	14	26	20	40
MORTON, Chris	22 July 1956, Davyhulme, Greater Manchester	2	9	0	0	0	0	2	9
MORTON, Dave	24 September 1953, Eccles, Greater Manchester	1	10	0	0	0	0	2	10
MOUNTAIN, Andy	3 March 1973, King's Lynn, Norfolk	7	11	0	0	0	6	7	11
MOUNTFORD, Ron	31 May 1927, Birmingham, West Midlands	1	5	0	0	0	7	2	11
MUDGE, Geoff	30 September 1935, Adelaide, South Australia	1	5	0	0	1	0	2	12
MULLARKEY, Kelvin	29 March 1951, Chelmsford, Essex	1	0	0	0	0	0	1	0
MUNDAY, Pete	11 March 1939, Totton, Hampshire	194	654	14	44	38	148	246	846
MURRAY, Brian	2 April 1947, Liberton, Scotland	1	0	0	0	0	0	1	0
MURRAY, Nathan	8 December 1966, Hamilton, North Island, New Zealand	7	22	2	7	1	3	10	32

Rider	Born								
MURRAY, Peter	18 March 1948, Wimbledon, South London	1	0	0	0	0	0	1	0
MUSSON, Richie	14 July 1973, Leeds, West Yorkshire	0	0	1	4	0	0	1	4
NAGY, Robert	20 September 1967, Szeged, Hungary	2	21	0	0	0	0	2	21
NAHLIN, Peter	1 May 1968, Eskilstuna, Sweden	107	775.5	10	67	53	406	170	1,248.5
NEATH, Chris	29 January 1982, Worcester, Worcestershire	65	448.5	2	10	28	195	95	653.5
NEVITT, Norman	22 October 1936, Sandbach, Cheshire	1	0	0	0	0	0	1	0
NEWTON, Dennis	2 March 1929, London	0	3	7	27	6	25	14	55
NICHOLLS, Ginger	1 September 1927, Edmonton, London	0	0	0	0	6	25	6	25
NICHOLLS, Reg	1939, London (Full details unknown)	2	12	0	0	4	6	4	6
NICHOLLS, Scott	16 May 1978, Ipswich, Suffolk	1	4	0	0	1	3	3	15
NIELSEN, Hans	26 December 1959, Arrentsminde, Brovst, Denmark	5	9	0	0	1	11	2	15
NIELSEN, Henry	17 May 1956, Brovst, Denmark	4	25	2	0	1	0	6	9
NIEMI, Kai	15 September 1955, Pori, Finland	1	9	0	11	25	228	31	264
NIKOLAISEN, Sam	28 February 1961, Lokken, Denmark	2	9	0	0	1	13	2	22
NILSEN, Jimmy	19 November 1966, Varmdo, Stockholm, Sweden	243	2,316	35	379	130	1,120	408	3,815
NORDIN, Gote	2 July 1935, Falun, Sweden	1	15	0	0	0	0	1	15
NORRIS, David	20 August 1972, Eastbourne, East Sussex	2	17	0	1	1	11	3	28
NORTON, Danny	27 August 1986, Hull, East Yorkshire	1	0	0	0	0	0	1	0
NUNAN, Tim	20 April 1953, Wentworth, New South Wales, Australia	1	1	0	0	0	0	1	1
NYGREN, Olle	11 November 1929, Stockholm, Sweden	3	28	0	0	0	0	3	28
O'BRIEN, Danny	30 March 1973, Kingston-upon-Thames, Surrey	2	0	1	0	0	0	2	0
ODEGAARD, Jon	25 May 1937, Revagen, Norway	9	9	0	0	2	1	4	10
OLSEN, Jesper	10 February 1967, Valby, Copenhagen, Denmark	0	0	1	10	1	4	2	14
OLSSON, Patrik	13 December 1967, Vastervik, Sweden	63	351	5	17	18	104	86	472
OLSSON, Tony	13 March 1965, Visby, Sweden	70	707	10	81	15	130	95	918
OSBORNE, Russell	15 July 1945, Norwich, Norfolk	1	1	0	0	0	0	1	1
OTT, Bobby	17 November 1962, Inglewood, California, USA	2	11	0	0	0	7	3	18
PAGET, Simon	24 March 1975, Swindon, Wiltshire	1	1	1	1	0	0	2	1
PANDER, Arne	12 July 1931, Herning, Denmark	1	4	0	0	0	0	1	4
PARKER, Shane	29 April 1970, Adelaide, South Australia	7	47	1	8	5	43	13	98
PATTEN, Dave	12 November 1947, Guernsey, Channel Islands	1	0	0	0	1	2	2	2
PEDERSEN, Jan	27 July 1967, Brandekilde, Denmark	1	1	0	0	0	0	1	2
PEDERSEN, Jan O.	9 November 1962, Middelfart, Denmark	12	12	0	0	0	0	1	12
PEGLER, Scott	3 August 1973, Exeter, Devon	8	7	2	4	5	8	15	19
PELLINEN, Mika	23 March 1968, Helsinki, Finland	3	16	0	0	0	0	3	16
PENDLEBURY, Craig	30 January 1951, Manchester, Greater Manchester	1	7	0	0	0	0	1	7
PERKS, Dave	16 December 1951, Halesowen, West Midlands	0	0	0	0	1	4	1	4
PERSSON, Bernt	24 June 1946, Eskilstuna, Sweden	0	0	0	0	0	12	1	12
PETERSEN, Bo	21 February 1958, Bolbro, Denmark	45	416	3	24	55	521	103	961
PFETZING, Robert	4 October 1959, Santa Ana, California, USA	3	3	0	0	1	0	1	3
PHELPS, Gary	30 March 1977, Swindon, Wiltshire	0	0	0	0	0	2	4	2
PHILLIPS, Andy	10 October 1968, Worcester, Hereford & Worcester	1	4	0	0	0	0	1	4
PICKERING, Paul	15 February 1966, Hartlepool, Durham	2	9	1	8	0	0	3	17
PLANT, Wilf	28 August 1915, Melton Mowbray, Leicestershire	0	0	0	0	1	3	1	3

Player	Born									
POOLE, Mick	27 November 1966, Sydney, New South Wales, Australia	0	0	0	0	0	1	0	1	9
POPE, Kevin	16 August 1953, Reading, Berkshire	7	4	0	0	3	3	0	10	7
PRATT, Colin	10 October 1938, Hoddesdon, Hertfordshire	0	0	10	0	0	3	21	10	21
PRESTON, Ron	15 July 1958, Newport Beach, California, USA	1	3	1	0	0	1	4	2	7
PUGH, Lionel	24 December 1931, Coventry, Warwickshire	3	3	0	0	0	0	0	3	3
PULLEN, Ashley	18 February 1956, Oxford, Oxfordshire	3	0	1	0	0	1	0	1	3
PULLEYN, Scott	22 December 1967, Reading, Berkshire	0	0	0	0	0	1	0	0	0
PUSEY, Geoff	1 June 1953, Maghull, Merseyside	0	1	1	0	0	1	0	1	0
QUICK, Cyril	19 January 1919, Taunton, Somerset	0	0	0	0	0	1	11	1	11
RABA, Leonard	8 December 1954, Kolejarz, Poland	5	0	1	0	0	3	11	8	11
RAMM, Leo	23 April 1927, Mannum, South Australia	1	0	3	0	0	1	3	2	3
RASMUSSEN, Jens	26 May 1959, Odense, Denmark	0	0	1	0	0	1	0	1	0
RAVN, Peter	16 March 1962, Bogense, Denmark	0	4	0	0	0	6	6	3	6
RAWLINS, Ernie	20 April 1922, Southampton, Hampshire	1	0	1	10	0	3	12	3	26
READING, Pete	10 April 1948, Retford, Nottinghamshire	0	0	3	0	0	3	22	3	22
READSHAW, Chris	14 January 1974, Middlesbrough, North Yorkshire	1	2	0	0	0	1	0	1	2
REASON, Anthony	Details unknown	1	1	0	0	0	0	0	1	1
REDMOND, Trevor	16 June 1927, Christchurch, New Zealand	13	48	0	0	0	5	13	18	61
REEVES, Eddie	8 April 1946, Highgate, London	0	0	5	0	0	1	4	1	4
REGELING, Steve	2 October 1959, Mount Isa, Australia	1	0	1	0	0	0	0	1	0
RICHARDSON, Colin	24 November 1958, London	3	6	0	0	0	5	5	4	11
RICHARDSON, Derek	22 July 1958, Earlsheaton, West Yorkshire	1	0	5	0	0	0	0	1	0
RICHARDSON, Lee	25 April 1979, Hastings, East Sussex	1	5	0	0	0	0	0	1	5
RICHT, Frank	20 September 1974, Sandviken, Sweden	1	1	0	0	0	0	0	1	1
RIVETT, Alan	21 March 1956, Whangerei, New Zealand	0	0	0	0	0	0	0	1	5
ROBINS, Chris	2 January 1954, Newton Abbot, Devon	1	2	1	0	0	1	5	1	5
ROBSON, Scott	15 August 1971, Sunderland, Tyne and Wear	0	0	0	0	0	1	2	1	2
ROGER, Bert	5 January 1924, Ashford, Kent	0	14	1	0	0	1	4	1	4
ROGER, Bob	14 June 1928, Ashford, Kent	1	14	0	0	0	0	0	1	14
ROGER, Cyril	27 December 1922, Ashford, Kent	97	1,016	14	15	142	66	551	178	1,709
ROSE, Stephen	6 December 1963, Hamilton, North Island, New Zealand	3	28	0	0	0	0	0	3	28
ROSSITER, Alun	23 July 1965, Swindon, Wiltshire	9	2.5	12	0	2	9	9	23	11.5
RUMSEY, Les	27 July 1955, Canterbury, Kent	183	890	2.5	26	137	93	402	302	1,429
RUUD, David	21 January 1980, Gislaved, Sweden	0	0	1	27	5	1	3	1	3
SADLER, Nigel	17 September 1978, Blackwood, Adelaide, South Australia	29	173	5	0	0	5	25	39	225
SAMPSON, Peter	24 September 1939, Hoddesdon, Hertfordshire	0	0	2	8	2	2	18	2	18
SATCHELL, Martin	14 October 1962, Swindon, Wiltshire	30	73	5	1	2	5	15	37	96
SAVILLE, Les	3 October 1931, Subiaco, Western Australia	6	5	1	3	1	1	0	8	6
SCHOFIELD, Steve	27 February 1958, Carshalton, Surrey	1	1	0	0	2	3	0	3	4
SCHOTT, Frede	28 December 1970, Kolding, Denmark	1	1	0	0	0	1	0	1	1
SCHRAMM, Chris	30 May 1984, Maldon, Essex	2	28	0	0	0	2	0	2	28
SCHROECK, Peter	18 September 1966, Aschaffenburg, Germany	1	4	0	0	0	1	0	1	4
SCREEN, Joe	27 November 1972, Chesterfield, Derbyshire	2	12	10	0	0	10	18	10	18
SEALEY, Lance	8 March 1970, Swindon, Wiltshire	3	5	1	0	0	1	2	4	7

Name	Born								
SELL, Andy	26 March 1964, Bristol, Avon	1	1	0	0	1	4	2	5
SHIELDS, Adam	8 February 1977, Kurri Kurri, New South Wales, Australia	44	11	0	0	1	11	2	22
SHIRRA, Mitch	27 September 1958, Auckland, New Zealand	120	412	6	47	56	489	106	948
SHUTER, Frank	17 June 1945, Rotorua, New Zealand	123	362	8	24	25	82	153	468
SILVER, Andrew	13 January 1967, Hampstead, North London	21	929	11	88	67	511	201	1,528
SIMMONS, Malcolm	20 March 1946, Tonbridge, Kent	0	130	2	15	29	258	52	403
SIMPSON, Chris	9 August 1974, Congleton, Cheshire	0	2	0	0	0	0	1	2
SIMPSON, Darryl	24 January 1961, Mildura, Victoria, Australia	0	0	0	0	2	0	0	0
SIZMORE, Roy	17 November 1950, Hillingdon, Middlesex	0	0	0	0	1	0	0	0
SMART, David	28 December 1965, Swindon, Wiltshire	87	276	4	10	45	149	136	435
SMART, Frank	27 October 1969, Perth, Western Australia	13	110	6	43	14	158	33	311
SMART, Kevin	3 September 1963, Inglesham, Wiltshire	3	2	2	0	6	9	11	11
SMITH, Alan	15 June 1930, London	1	12	0	0	1	0	2	12
SMITH, Andy	25 May 1966, York, North Yorkshire	54	344	4	23	13	80	71	447
SMITH, Dudley	1932 (Full details unknown)	12	20	0	0	4	7	16	27
SMITH, Jamie	20 July 1983, Peterborough, Cambridgeshire	24	116	2	8	10	53	36	177
SMITH, Kevin	29 July 1961, Canterbury, Kent	5	19	1	2	3	12	9	33
SMITH, Paul	17 July 1970, York, North Yorkshire	15	52	0	0	2	11	17	63
SMITH, Pete	11 July 1942, Hanworth, Feltham, Middlesex	1	1	0	0	0	0	1	1
SOFFE, Melvin	13 July 1957, Southampton, Hampshire	0	0	2	2	2	4	4	4
SORENSEN, Alan	1954, Australia (Full details unknown)	1	1	0	0	0	0	1	1
SORENSEN, Per	20 June 1962, Sundbylille, Denmark	66	247	6	15	77	280	149	542
SOVA, Emil	30 October 1954, Mlade Boleslaw, Czech Republic	1	4	2	0	0	0	1	4
SPARREY, Al	26 February 1928, Edmonton, London	17	50	2	6	15	25	34	81
SPARSHOTT, Nigel	2 September 1961, Swanley, Kent	1	0	0	0	0	0	0	0
SPELTA, Bob	27 July 1953, Ayr, Queensland, Australia	1	8	0	2	0	0	1	8
SPENCER, Gary	4 February 1955, Frome, Somerset	0	3	0	0	1	1	1	1
SPINK, Mike	25 February 1958, Peterborough, Cambridgeshire	1	0	0	0	0	0	1	3
SPINKA, Milan	5 May 1951, Pardubice, Czech Republic	31	103	4	29	17	76	52	208
STAECHMANN, Jan	5 June 1966, Kolding, Denmark	2	11	1	1	3	5	4	17
STANCL, George	19 August 1975, Prague, Czech Republic	4	32	2	6	26	9	8	47
STANDING, Dean	20 June 1969, Southampton, Hampshire	35	199	8	14	21	142	63	355
STANGELAND, Edgar	22 July 1945, Sandnes, Norway	66	498	8	50	0	153	95	701
STAPLETON, Alan	Adelaide, South Australia (Full details unknown)	7	9	0	0	1	0	8	9
STEAD, Garry	5 January 1972, Holmfirth, Yorkshire	7	69	0	0	2	3	8	72
STEAD, Paul	25 December 1962, Mirfield, Yorkshire	0	0	0	0	1	3	2	3
STEAD, Simon	25 April 1982, Sheffield, South Yorkshire	3	28	6	28	37	15	4	43
STEEL, Mark	26 July 1983, Northampton, Northamptonshire	24	98	0	0	2	155	67	281
STEEN, David	12 March 1966, Harare, Zimbabwe	0	0	1	0	2	5	2	5
STENLUND, Erik	26 May, 1962, Uppsala, Sweden	14	75	2	10	9	14	17	99
STEPHENS, Seemond	9 August 1967, St Austell, Cornwall	24	104	2	12	0	44	35	160
STEVENS, Alastair	15 October 1968, Aylesbury, Buckinghamshire	1	2	0	0	0	0	0	2
STREET, Neil	15 January 1931, Melbourne, Victoria, Australia	136	919.5	29	214	81	669	246	1,802.5
SUMMERS, George	10 June 1939, Aberdeen, Scotland	0	0	0	0	7	6	7	6

Name	Details								
SVAB, Toni	9 June 1974, Vlasim, Czech Republic	5	32	0	0	2	7	7	39
SWAIN, Scott	29 October 1971, Eastbourne, East Sussex	7	21	0	0	0	0	7	21
SWAINE, Ron	19 April 1929, Croydon, London	102	496	16	85	38	207	156	788
SWEETMAN, Tommy	21 July 1930, London	2	2	2	1	2	4	6	7
TABET, Bob	December 1948, Sydney, NSW, Australia (Full details unknown)	0	0	0	0	0	0	0	0
TACEY, Shaun	27 November 1974, Norwich, Norfolk	2	1	0	0	0	0	2	1
TATUM MBE, Kelvin	8 February 1964, Epsom, Surrey	1	8	0	0	0	0	1	8
TATUM, Neville	21 July 1965, Epsom, Surrey	2	8	0	0	2	14	2	8
TAYLOR, Chum	4 April 1927, Perth, Western Australia	1	1	0	0	1	11	3	15
TAYLOR, Mel	26 April 1961, West Row, Suffolk	0	0	0	0	0	0	1	11
TAYLOR, Ron	19 November 1938, Hereford, Hereford & Worcester	17	29	6	13	16	29	39	71
TAYLOR, Roy	1929, Bristol (Full details unknown)	7	14	6	21	4	6	17	41
TEODOROWICZ, Tadeusz	17 June 1931, Wilno, Poland	87	541	23	160	58	434	168	1,135
TESAR, Zdenek	31 July 1964, Ostrava, Czech Republic	4	42	1	1	1	7	5	49
THOMAS, Barry	29 October 1951, Harrow, Middlesex	3	19	0	0	0	0	3	19
THOMAS, Bob	23 November 1934, Muswell Hill, London	1	1	0	0	3	3	4	4
THOMSEN, Finn	16 February 1955, Arhus, Denmark	21	101	5	32	17	91	43	224
THORP, Paul	9 September 1964, Macclesfield, Cheshire	10	80	1	15	0	0	11	95
THORPE, Mark	26 March 1969, Christchurch, New Zealand	58	543	8	68	12	99	78	710
TIMMO, Rick	27 July 1947, Napier, New Zealand	0	0	0	1	1	8	1	8
TIMMO, Spencer	3 January 1966, Oxford, Oxfordshire	4	4	2	0	0	0	6	5
TITMAN, John	26 January 1951, Brisbane, Queensland, Australia	2	4	0	1	0	0	2	4
TOPINKA, Tomas	5 June 1974, Prague, Czech Republic	4	24	2	0	0	0	6	30
TRIGG, Roy	29 April 1943, Morden, London	1	7	0	6	2	7	3	14
TROTT, Reg	2 January 1930, Mitcham, Surrey	0	0	1	0	0	0	1	13
TRZESZKOWSKI, Jerzy	10 January 1945, Sparta, Poland	11	17	0	13	5	6	16	23
TUCK, Ron	1931, Bethnal Green, London (Full details unknown)	0	0	0	0	1	0	3	5
TULLOCH, Terry	27 October 1958, Mildura, Victoria, Australia	0	0	2	5	1	0	1	0
TUORINIEMI, Veijo	7 April 1958, Lahti, Finland	2	0	0	5	1	2	7	2
TYRER, Paul	5 December 1952, Manchester, Greater Manchester	1	11	0	5	5	0	3	0
UNDERWOOD, Doug	28 May 1949, Perth, Western Australia	3	1	0	0	0	0	2	11
VALENTINE, Bobo	18 June 1949, Auckland, New Zealand	2	1	0	0	0	0	1	1
VERNER, Jan	9 March 1951, Mlade Boleslav, Czech Republic	8	29	2	4	13	43	23	76
VERNER, Vaclav	6 May 1949, Prague, Czech Republic	1	8	0	0	1	9	2	17
WALKER, Justin	16 February 1971, Wordsley, West Midlands	5	5	2	1	1	1	8	7
WALKER, Simon	19 February 1980, Bristol, Avon	0	5	0	2	1	1	1	3
WALL, Billy	Details unknown	8	3	3	0	0	3	10	3
WALLACE, Stuart	February 1944, Southampton, Hampshire (Full details unknown)	1	1	0	0	1	1	1	1
WALLER, Ralph	1 October 1949, London	1	1	0	0	0	1	8	1
WALSH, David	29 August 1963, Sowerby Bridge, West Yorkshire	4	31	2	26	2	20	8	77
WARNER, Bob	12 June 1932, Camberwell, London	0	0	0	0	2	1	2	1
WATERMAN, Split	27 July 1921, New Malden, Surrey	1	12	2	0	0	0	1	12
WATSON, Craig	6 August 1976, St George, Sydney, NSW, Australia	0	0	1	2	1	0	2	2

Name	Born								
WATT, Davey	6 January 1978, Townsville, Queensland, Australia	1	6	0	0	0	0	1	6
WEATHERLEY, Steve	26 November 1957, Dartford, Kent	1	6	0	0	0	0	1	6
WEBSTER, Alf	29 August 1925, Manchester, Greater Manchester	11	52	0	0	1	5	12	57
WELLS, Bob	26 December 1915, Bushey Heath, Watford, Hertfordshire	63	372	5	50	12	90	80	512
WERNER, Brent	15 April 1974, Los Angeles, California, USA	3	25	0	0	1	6	4	31
WHITE, George	24 May 1931, Dalston, London	133	1,147.5	27	250	105	838	265	2,235.5
WHITE, Keith	27 August 1956, Hackney, London	1	10	1	6	1	5	3	21
WHITE, Phil	25 February 1956, Sheffield, South Yorkshire	2	11	0	0	0	0	2	11
WIGG, Bob	1928, Palmerston North, New Zealand (Full details unknown)								
WIGG, Simon	15 October 1960, Aylesbury, Buckinghamshire	0	0	0	0	3	6	3	6
WIGGINS, Ken	16 November 1926, Blunsdon, Swindon, Wiltshire	1	12	1	3	0	0	2	15
WIGLEY, Pete	11 June 1951, Emsworth, Hampshire	54	112.5	7	24	18	46	79	182.5
WILCOCK, Steve	24 January 1954, Dewsbury, West Yorkshire	1	4	0	0	0	0	1	4
WILKINSON, Carl	16 May 1981, Boston, Lincolnshire	1	2	0	0	0	0	1	2
WILLIAMS, Eric	17 November 1927, Port Talbot, West Glamorgan	1	12	1	11	0	0	2	23
WILLIAMS, Ian	4 August 1931, Port Talbot, West Glamorgan	264	1,980	47	334	136	1,138.5	447	3,452.5
WILLIAMS, John	29 December 1957, Gloucester, Gloucestershire	0	0	0	0	0	0	1	0
WILLIAMS, Martin	25 October 1979, Gloucester, Gloucestershire	1	0	0	0	1	3	2	3
WILLIS, Martin	23 August 1972, Bournemouth, Hampshire	15	32	2	2	4	15	21	49
WILLMOTT, Sean	23 May 1961, Bristol, Avon	3	11	0	0	1	5	4	16
WILSON, Brian	5 February 1929, Sheffield, South Yorkshire	0	0	0	0	1	7	1	7
WILSON, Ray	12 March 1947, Merton, Surrey	2	23	0	0	9	0	2	23
WILSON, Tom	Tewkesbury, Gloucestershire (Full details unknown)	12	11	0	0	0	22	21	33
WILTSHIRE, Todd	26 September 1968, Bankstown, Sydney, NSW, Australia	2	10	0	0	0	0	2	10
WOLSTENHOLME, Simon	25 January 1971, Sheffield, South Yorkshire	0	0	0	0	1	1	1	1
WOODIFIELD, Brett	15 March 1976, Gawler, South Australia	0	0	0	0	2	14	2	14
WOODS, Paul	17 January 1959, Canterbury, Kent	0	0	0	0	1	9	1	9
WOODWARD, Brian	9 May 1952, Monmouth, Gwent	0	0	0	0	1	0	1	0
WOOLFORD, Mac	1 August 1945, Purton, Swindon, Wiltshire	23	29	3	1	3	4	29	34
YEATES, Martin	24 November 1953, Salisbury, Wiltshire	36	138	3	11	48	127	87	276
YOUNG, Kevin	12 October 1957, Gloucester, Gloucestershire	10	17	0	0	6	13	16	30
ZETTERSTROM, Magnus	9 December 1971, Eskilstuna, Sweden	2	1	1	3	0	0	3	4